LEGAL RESEARCH

A Guide for Hong Kong Students

LEGAL RESEARCH

A Guide for Hong Kong Students

JILL COTTRELL

香港大學出版社

HONG KONG UNIVERSITY PRESS

Hong Kong University Press
14/F Hing Wai Centre
7 Tin Wan Praya Road
Aberdeen
Hong Kong

© Hong Kong University Press, 1997
First published 1997
Reprinted 1999, 2002, 2003, 2005, 2007, 2008

ISBN-13   978-962-209-430-7
ISBN-10   962-209-430-9

Printed in Hong Kong by Caritas Printing Training Centre, in Hong Kong, China

Contents

PREFACE *xi*

UNIT 1   WELCOME TO THE STUDY OF LAW   *1*
■ *Supplementary material* • *Windows* *4*

UNIT 2   THIS BOOK: ITS ORGANIZATION, PURPOSES AND ASSUMPTIONS   *5*
Objectives *5*
The philosophy of the book *5*
Organization of the book *6*
Treatment of electronic sources *7*
1997 *8*
The law libraries in Hong Kong *9*
Symbols and conventions *9*

UNIT 3   LEGAL RESEARCH: PRELIMINARY THOUGHTS   *11*
Objectives *11*
Essays and problems *12*
Research *14*
Self-test questions *20*
■ *Supplementary material* • *A good legal researcher* *19*

UNIT 4   CASES: AN INTRODUCTION   *21*
Objectives *21*
The idea of a 'case' *21*
Reading a case *24* • Further reading *24* • Why? *24*
Anatomy of an unreported case *26* • Explanatory notes *27*
Anatomy of a reported case *28*
A note on headnotes *34*
Case names *34* • Criminal cases *34* • Hong Kong before 1997 *35* •
Hong Kong after 1997 *35* • Other cases with 'R' in the name *35* • Maiden
names *35* • Which name comes first? *36* • Other oddities *36* •
References *37*

How to read a case *37* • Should you read the headnote? *37* • Making a casenote *38*
Contents of a casenote *38* • A possible note on Check Chor-ching *41*
Self-test questions *42*
■ *Supplementary material* • *Abbreviations for Judges* *28* • *Ratios and dicta* *40*

UNIT 5   **LAW REPORTS**   *43*
Objectives *43*
Law reports: the development of an institution *43* • Why should you bother about yearbooks? *44* • Nominate reports *45* • Beginning of the modern era *46* • The Incorporated Council *46* • The All England Law Reports *46* • Reporting *46*
Law reports: what you are likely to find in a law library *48* • Finding the nominate reports *48* • The Incorporated Council of Law Reporting reports *50* • Other major series *52* • Modern specialist reports *53*
Hong Kong reported cases *54* • General reports *54* • Specialist reports *55* • Other reports in which Hong Kong cases may appear *58* • Short reports of Hong Kong cases *58* • Cases in Mainland China *59*
Self-test questions *60*
■ *Supplementary material* • *The doctrine of precedent* *47* • *Parts of a volume of law reports* *54*

UNIT 6   **FINDING CASES (I)**   *61*
Objectives *61*
Finding reported cases when you have a complete reference *61* • Some tips *64* • Finding the reprinted nominate reports *65*
Unreported judgments *73*
Electronic access to unreported judgments *74*
Self-study questions *75*
■ *Supplementary material* • *Shapes of brackets* *62* • *Organizing the unreported judgments* *73*

UNIT 7   **FINDING CASES (II)**   *77*
Objectives *77*
Finding a reference to a case when you know the name *77* • For Hong Kong cases *78* • For English cases *78* • Using electronic sources *81*
Tracing the history of a case after it is first decided *82*
Finding a case on a particular topic *84* • Finding Hong Kong unreported judgments by subject *84* • Hong Kong cases on CD-ROM *85* • Hong Kong Law Reports and Digest *86*
English law reports *87* • The Electronic law reports *87* • The Weekly Law Reports *88* • All England Law Reports *88* • The English Reports *89*
Self-study questions *89*

■ *Supplementary material* • *In summary: finding a case knowing only its name (paper resources only) 81*

UNIT 8   INTRODUCTION TO LEGISLATION   *91*
Objectives *91*
Legislation *91* • Who makes legislation? *92* • What do you read a statute for? *93* • What do you do with legislation? *93*
The anatomy of an ordinance *97*
Bills *98*
Delegated legislation *99*
Self-study questions *101*
■ *Supplementary material* • *Life cycle of an ordinance 95* • *Amending UK and Hong Kong statutes 98*

UNIT 9   READING A STATUTE   *103*
Objectives *103*
Control of Exemption Clauses Ordinance *105*
Ways of dealing with statutes *117* • Breaking up sections *117* • Algorithms *118*
Interpretation and General Clauses Ordinance Cap 1 *119*
Other help in understanding the words in a statute *121* • Dictionaries of legal definitions *121*
Legislative history *122* • Background to Hong Kong legislation *123* • Background to UK legislation *123*
Self-study questions *124*
■ *Supplementary material* • *Interpretation of statutes 122*

UNIT 10   FINDING LEGISLATION AND RELATED MATTERS   *125*
Objectives *125*
Hong Kong legislation *125* • Gazette *125* • The Loose-leaf Edition *126* • The Revised Edition *129* • The Annotated Ordinances of Hong Kong *130* • Using the Annotated Ordinances *131*
How to update Hong Kong legislation *132* • Step by step for updating using paper material *133* • Is it in force? *136*
The relationship between Hong Kong and foreign law *137* • Statutes judicially considered *138*
BLIS *139*
United Kingdom legislation *140* • Form of reference to UK legislation *141* • Finding an English statute *142* • Is it in force? *143* • Judicial consideration *143* • Other useful things *144* • Delegated legislation *145* • Transitional issues *146* • National laws applying in Hong Kong *146*
Self-study questions *147*

■ *Supplementary material* • *Finding the statutory position at a point in the past 135* • *UK legislation applying in Hong Kong 147*

UNIT 11 **APPROACHING RESEARCH** *149*
Objectives *149*
Unpacking your subject *149* • What branch of the law? *150* • Which jurisdiction? *151* • Words, words, words! *152*
Different types of books *154* • Student texts *154* • Specialist books *155* • Monographs *155* • Books on comparative law *155* • Practitioners' books *156* • Loose-leaf texts *156* • Encyclopaedias *156* • Updating *156*
Types of electronic resources *157* • Content *157* • Relationship with print media *157* • Electronic format *158* • Updating *158* • Who maintains them? *158* • Cost of use *159*
Framing searches *159* • Undigested or pre-digested? *159* • Search tools *160*
Summary *161*
■ *Supplementary material* • *A word on indexes 153*

UNIT 12 **GENERAL WORKS OF REFERENCE** *163*
Objectives *163*
Hong Kong *164* • Hong Kong Law Digest *164* • Current Law Hong Kong *170* • Halsbury's Laws of Hong Kong *172*
England *175* • Current Law *175* • Halsbury's Laws of England *177* • The Digest *182*
Self-study questions *186*

UNIT 13 **JOURNALS** *189*
Objectives *189*
Varieties of journals *189* • Hong Kong based journals *191* • Other countries *192* • Regional journals *192*
Why would a law student read journals? *193*
The structure of journals *194*
How to find out what articles exist — indexes *194* • Legal journals index *196* • Index to legal periodicals *198* • Index to legal periodicals and books: the CD-ROM version *199* • Index to foreign legal periodicals *201* • Index to periodical articles related to law *203*
Self-study questions *205*
■ *Supplementary material* • *Brackets for journals 194* • *Journals and articles 194* • *Electronic journals 204*

UNIT 14   **GOVERNMENT PUBLICATIONS**   *207*
Objectives *207*
Publications of the Hong Kong Government *207* • Hong Kong Government Gazette *207* • Codes of Practice *208* • Hansard *208* • Proceedings of the Urban and Regional Councils *210* • Committees of Legco *210* • White Papers *210* • Consultative documents *210* • Law Reform Commission *211* • Commissions of Inquiry *211* • Departmental reports *211* • Other publications *211*
Publications of other governments *212*
Self-study questions *213*

UNIT 15   **OTHER LAW-RELATED MATERIALS**   *215*
Objectives *215*
Other legal reference materials *215* • Tariffs *215* • Precedents *216* • Practitioner's texts *217* • Annotated codes of procedure *220*
The legal profession *221* • Other publications *221* • Law Society circulars *221*
Bibliographies *222*
Self-study questions *223*

UNIT 16   **OTHER SYSTEMS**   *225*
Objectives *225*
Why look at other countries? *225*
Systems of law *226* • Common law systems *227* • Civil law systems *228*
Singapore, Malaysia and Brunei *228* • Malaysia *229* • Singapore *231* • Brunei *231* • The legal literature of Malaysia, Singapore and Brunei *232*
Australia *235* • Introduction *235* • Why would you want to look at Australian law *236* • Australian law reports *236* • Research material on Australian law *237* • How to find cases in Australian law reports *238* • Electronic sources for Australian law *241* • Laws of Australia: CD-ROM version — a guide to making simple searches *243* • Journals *245* • Law reform *247* • Further reading *247*
New Zealand *247* • Law reports *247* • Statutes *248* • Journals *248* • Reference material *248*
India *248* • Law reports *248* • Journals *249* • Reference material *249*
Canada *250* • Why would you want to look at Canadian law? *250* • Law reports *251* • Research tools *251* • Keeping up-to-date *256* • Canadian cases on the Internet *257* • Legislation *257* • Canadian periodicals *258* • Index to Canadian legal literature *259* • Further reading *260*
The United States of America *260* • Introduction *260* • Law reports *261* • Statutes *262* • Reference works *263* • Restatement of law *265* • US law on the Internet *266*
Self-test questions *267*

UNIT 17   **'NON-LAW' MATERIALS**   *269*
Objectives *269*
Books *270*
Bibliographies *270*
Historical documents *271*
Journals *271*
Indexes and abstracts *273*
Self-study questions *274*

UNIT 18   **ELECTRONIC SOURCES**   *275*
Objectives *275*
An introduction to BLIS (Bilingual Laws Information Service)   *276*   •
Version dates *279* • Printing *279*
Law on the web *280* • Getting started *280* • What will you find on the
web? *280* • Searching the Net *281* • Moving around *281* • Keeping what
you find *281* • How useful is the Internet? *281*
LEXIS *282* • The steps for an elementary LEXIS search and a few more
sophisticated ideas *282* • Further reading *284*
■ ***Supplementary material*** • *A few terms: Internet, World Wide Web,*
Netscape, url *281*

UNIT 19   **HOW TO CITE, QUOTE AND PRESENT YOUR MATERIAL**   *285*
Objectives *285*
Footnote reference *288* • Referring to pages *289* • Referring to cases *290*
• Legislation *291* • Official publications *291* • Legislative proceedings
291 • Abbreviations *293* • For records from the Internet *293* • Further
reading *294*
Quoting *294*
Self-test questions *294*
■ ***Supplementary material*** • *Plagiarism* *286* • *Italics or underlining?*
289

APPENDIX I   LAW LIBRARIES IN HONG KONG *295*
APPENDIX II   A DICTIONARY *299*
APPENDIX III   ABBREVIATIONS *305*
APPENDIX IV   CASE REFERENCE NUMBERS IN HONG KONG *307*

Preface

There is great emphasis these days on 'skills' education. This book, based on the teaching materials prepared for an introductory course on Legal Research and Writing at The University of Hong Kong, is intended to be a modest contribution to this aspect of legal education. It is designed to help students explore some of the sorts of resources which they will use in the course of their legal education, and, indeed, thereafter in the practice of law, if that is the way their careers take them.

Common sense and experience show that this sort of topic can hardly be 'taught' — but not that it cannot be learned. However, lectures and abstract discussion of materials and techniques are even less likely to 'stick' in the student's mind than any other sort of lecture. Students will learn, if at all, by doing. The hope is therefore that students will make use of this book while sitting in a library; will get up and look at, touch and open the materials, rather than just read about them. To this end there are in most chapters examples and exercises.

This book is written with first year students in mind, but I hope it does not talk down to the students so much that others will find the style too much to stomach. It may, in the absence of much literature on Hong Kong legal materials, be of use to those who have left their first year studies some way behind.

This book inevitably reflects my own views on legal education, which include the hope that students will consider it not just a passport to practice, but as an enterprise of value in its own right, in which they have the opportunity to reflect on the nature of law, and to pursue issues about the law, as well as learning legal rules and techniques. There is here, for this reason, coverage on non-law material which may illuminate the study of law. There is also some introductory material on finding the law of countries other than Hong Kong and the United Kingdom, which tend to be the main focus of the common law side of a Hong Kong law student's studies.

This is the age of the digital library, and this book also covers electronic databases, both On-line and CD-ROM based.

My debts are numerous. First of all to the students at The University of Hong Kong whose experiences I have to some extent drawn on, and who have been the impetus to my preparing these materials. Several colleagues have helped me with aspects of the Hong Kong system or other systems which they are more familiar with; I have acknowledged their assistance where appropriate. Finally, I would like to express my gratitude to publishers who have permitted me to use excerpts from their various publications:

- Butterworths Australia for *Australian Current Law*
- Butterworths Asia for *The Annotated Statutes of Hong Kong, Halsbury's Laws of Hong Kong, Hong Kong Cases*
- Butterworths Law Publishers for *Halsbury's Laws of England* and the *Digest*
- Carswell: a division of Thomson Canada Ltd for *Index to Canadian Legal Literature*, the *Canadian Encyclopedic Digest* (Ont, 3rd), *The Canadian Abridgment Second Edition, Canadian Current Law — Case Law Digest, Canadian Current Law — Case Digest, Canadian Statute Citations*
- FT Law and Tax for the *Hong Kong Law Digest*
- Glanville Publishers Inc for *Index to Periodical Articles Related to Law*
- Hong Kong Government for the *Hong Kong Government Gazette* and the *Laws of Hong Kong Loose-Leaf Edition*
- The International Political Science Association for *International Political Science Abstracts*
- Law Book Company for the *Australian Digest* and *Australian Legal Monthly Digest*
- Lawyers' Cooperative Publishing, a Division of Thomson Information Services Inc for *American Jurisprudence* (AmJur) and *American Law Reports* (ALR)
- Legal Information Resources Ltd for *Legal Journals Index*
- Her Majesty's Stationery Office for the *Consolidated Table of the Statutes* and the *Index to the Statutes*
- Sweet & Maxwell for various parts of *Current Law* and *Current Law: Hong Kong*
- West Publishing Company for an extract from the *United States Code Annotated*

Jill Cottrell
The University of Hong Kong
October 1996

The second impression of this book has been somewhat revised, though not so completely as to merit the description 'Second Edition'. Most of the revisions relate to Hong Kong materials, for it was impossible to ignore the substantial changes that have taken place in the law publishing scene here in the last few years. Most of the other changes relate to electronic resources, where also changes are constant and rapid. Any future editions will have to give more detailed information on the use of the Internet, however, than has been possible here.

January 1999

Unit 1 Welcome to the Study of Law

(Readers other than new law students should perhaps go directly to Unit 2.)

There is a risk that the formal study of any subject can make it sterile and boring — people who love reading novels may decide they don't want to be university students of literature because they do not want to lose the beauty in the process of analysing the techniques and dissecting the language. Rather the same thing can happen with the study of law.

But the chances are that you do not think of law as having beauty. There are certain legal devices which have a certain elegance. There are some judges who have expressed themselves with wit and style. But I would not dream of suggesting to you that you are likely to become fascinated with law as an aesthetic matter — especially not the common law which is the system which applies in Hong Kong. This has developed in so haphazard a fashion, so dependent upon history, and sometimes even accident, that it often seems to lack coherence. It is very different from systems of law which use codes — formal statements of the law which are prepared often by scholars and may achieve elegance of concepts and organization, or even of language, which can be satisfying in a way the common law rarely is.

As I say, I don't imagine that 'beauty' is a word you would associate with law. What do you associate with law?

❖ Try it now. Jot down the words which come to your mind when you think of law. It might be interesting to keep the piece of paper and do the exercise again at the end of your first year of studies and see whether the word associations have changed.

I wonder whether one of your words was 'justice' or 'fairness'. This is one of the ideas that I fear may be driven out of your head by the study of law. The process will begin as soon as you begin classes. Even, I am afraid, as soon as you move further in this book! Law as a subject of study is necessarily divided into categories. And within each category, or 'subject', it is again divided. You will break it down into little pieces; it will be dissected and desiccated for you and by you. You may well be seduced by the pleasures of learning new techniques, and new words (or old words in odd new meanings). You will be a little like the blind men (let us say blind people) in the old story, who encountered an elephant. One felt its tail and said 'It's a bell-rope'; one felt a leg and said 'It's a tree'; one felt the trunk and said 'It's a snake'. But, I am not telling you that somewhere there is some large and majestic creature which is **THE LAW**. I am afraid there is no elephant!

But there is a bigger picture. Some people will tell you that you have to learn to 'think like a lawyer'. To the extent that this means thinking logically, learning to sort out the relevant from the irrelevant, this is a good thing. But the question — or one question — must be: what **is** relevant?

This is a book not about studying law generally, but about how to find materials relevant to your studies (and ultimately relevant to the practice of law) and how to use them. But before you allow yourselves to be swallowed up by the machine of legal education, while you are still thinking like people and not like lawyers, I suggest you might try to get a glimpse of the larger picture, and to do it in ways which reflect legitimate concerns of this book — that is, through looking at materials which might prove later to be useful in your studies.

❖ First, get hold of a copy of today's newspaper. You might do this with a friend or two. Go right through the paper, beginning from page 1 and proceeding right through the rest including the sports pages and the cinema announcements and the weather forecast. (If there is a big classified section of jobs, I don't seriously expect you to look at every one, but do look at a few.) Think about the possible connection between all the items and the law. Notice how many items actually mention law. You may be surprised; these days it is not uncommon to find legal items on the sports pages. But go further: how many news items, or advertisements (including those for jobs) might have legal aspects to them. Imagine how someone might complain about the events recounted in the news, or even about the report in the paper.

I am not going to suggest that law is some sort of intrusive monster that invades all our lives. Most people go through life having very little contact with law, and, a good thing too! But you can get a sense of the potential of law for affecting almost every aspect of life. It is a tendency which is sometimes to be resisted. But maybe sometimes you can see the good that law could do.

❖ Second, go for an exploratory stroll through your Law Library. I hesitate to suggest you do this with a friend as I fear that may lead to gossiping! Take your time — don't rush. You have the time now to begin to get to know it. This will pay off in the future when you need to find books quickly.

Wander all the way round. ☺ Take at least an hour looking at books of various kinds. Don't say to yourself, 'I don't think I shall ever need to use that!'. What sorts of books are in the library? Some of them are in serried ranks of identical volumes. Maybe they say 'Law Reports' or 'Law Review' on the spine. Pick up one or two of each type. See what is in them. Look at the sorts of stories that may lie behind the law, what range of issues the law touches on. In fact the best place to look at law journals (or law reviews) may be on the display shelves where you will find current, unbound issues. You can easily see from the covers of many what sorts of articles they contain. Look at the variety of things people are writing about. Some you probably won't understand, but don't worry about this. Look for things you do understand and which sound interesting.

You will also see shelves of books which are not uniform. These are probably textbooks and books of essays or book length studies of different aspects of law. Wander right through these. You will be asked to look at a very small proportion of these as a student. But that does not mean you should not read them! Can you get a sense of different styles of law book? Can you see books that look at law in a theoretical way? (Many of them ask, 'What is law?') Or books which marry law and another discipline such as economics or sociology? Or empirical studies (what actually happens)? Books on comparative law — comparing the legal systems of different countries, for example. Or international law?

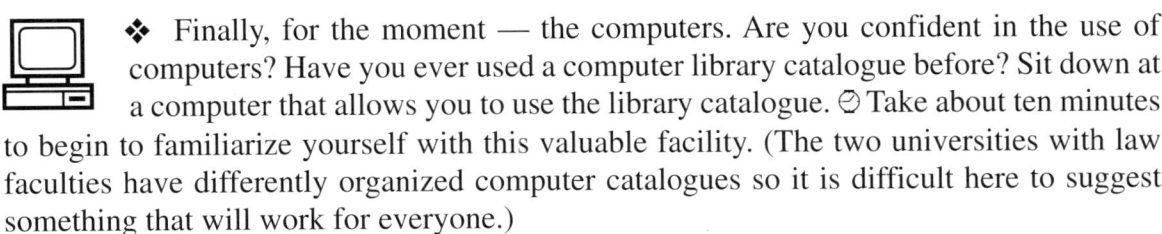

❖   Finally, for the moment — the computers. Are you confident in the use of computers? Have you ever used a computer library catalogue before? Sit down at a computer that allows you to use the library catalogue. ☺ Take about ten minutes to begin to familiarize yourself with this valuable facility. (The two universities with law faculties have differently organized computer catalogues so it is difficult here to suggest something that will work for everyone.)

Can you find out how to search for an author? If you are at the City University of Hong Kong, type in Tyler, E. You will undoubtedly see a few books which Professor Tyler has written or edited. If you are at the University of Hong Kong, type in Wesley-Smith. You will see what Professor Wesley-Smith has written. Of course you can try any name; I just chose one for each place whom I think you would be interested to see and because I know they would have several books listed.) Can you get back to the Main Menu? If so you will see that you can actually get through to the catalogue of the other university (and of all the universities in Hong Kong!).

While you are at the computer, can you find one which allows you to use the World Wide Web? This will require you to use Windows (see box on p. 4).

☺   Give yourself at least 15 minutes to look at what is available on the Web. Some of you may be familiar with this from your home computer, but you may not have realized how much law there is on the Internet. Follow the instructions for your particular institution. At the time of writing the best strategy for getting access to legal materials is to find your way either to the University of Hong Kong Law Library 'Home Page' or to that of the Faculty of Law at the University of Hong Kong.

➤   There is a tendency for the addresses of web sites (known as the url address) to change. At the time of writing, the address for the HKU Law Library list of web sites by subject is: **<http://www.hku.hk/lib/in/law.html>.**

That for the Law Faculty list of 'Other law related web sites' is: **<http://www.hku.hk/ law/other.html>.**

City University has a similar set of links at **<http://www.cityu.edu.hk/lib/subject/law/ general.htm>.**

If you have reached a Law Faculty or Law Library list site you will find a long list of different sites. There are other law schools in several countries, legal periodicals, entries from law firms, collections of laws and cases from various countries including the US, Australia, Canada, as well as a site for the laws of Hong Kong (**<http:// www.justice.gov.hk/>**). There are several pages of information from various agencies in Hong Kong. Try for example the Legislative Council page: you will find it under 'Hong Kong Information Network' on the HKU home page; its url address is: **<http://legco.gov.hk/>**).

Windows

This is the computer software which is supposed to be easier to use. You move a little pointer around the screen by means of moving a mouse or a tracker ball with your hand, and then clicking a button to carry out an operation.

It is this I refer to when I say 'click on ... '. Sometimes you need to click twice — once to identify what you want, and the second time to activate it. Sometimes also this needs to be done twice very quickly, a knack which you will develop quickly unless you are very clumsy!

You should be able to find a short tutorial on using Windows on your institution's computer network.

That is probably enough for a very elementary welcome to the study of law and some of the materials you may use.

Unit 2　This Book: Its Organization, Purposes and Assumptions

OBJECTIVES

At the end of this Unit you will:

- understand the purposes for which this book is written
- know what elements the book contains and how to find the bits of it you need
- understand the symbols used in the book

☺ How long will it take you? It should not take you more than about 30 minutes to read through this short Unit, even if you do try to answer the self-test questions at the end.

The style adopted is intended for students beginning their study of law. I hope other users will not find this too irritating (for I think other users will find this book useful too). There is currently no other publication describing the use of Hong Kong legal materials.[1] Practitioners, especially those in the early stages of their careers, or those unfamiliar with Hong Kong materials because they have come from another jurisdiction, or even the older members of the profession for whom CD-ROM and On-line databases are new, and possibly intimidating, things may also find it valuable. I hope so!

THE PHILOSOPHY OF THE BOOK

Perhaps that is a bit grandiose for a book on such elementary issues! However, I want to make it clear that this book is not intended only to introduce law students to the 'nuts and bolts' skills of the lawyer. A lawyer is not a mere technician who should have no care for the social implications of the law, and a law student is not someone who is being trained to be such a technician. A student is going through a process of education, and will be expected to (and, I hope, would be interested to) think about the origins of law, the social, economic and

---

1　Since I wrote this sentence, there has appeared Dobinson and Roebuck *Introduction to Law in the Hong Kong SAR* (Hong Kong: Sweet and Maxwell, 1996) which does have a chapter (5) on this topic.

political implications of law. Students will write essays on topics for which legal materials alone will not be enough. This book therefore gives some elementary introduction to ways of finding material on subjects such as history and the social sciences.

It is also the assumption of this book that the sorts of skills involved in research cannot be learned by reading about them. Legal research is the sort of thing which ultimately is learned by doing. In the past it was learned by a process of trial and error, and what this book can perhaps best achieve is to reduce the amount of error involved in the trial! The chances are very strong that if you simply read a Unit you will have forgotten all the information by the following morning if not sooner. I would strongly urge you to do three things designed to make the information 'stick'.

- If possible read this in the library and go to look at the materials mentioned. Pick them up. Become familiar with their appearance. Learn where they are on the shelves. Look inside so you can see what they contain.
- Do the small exercises which are suggested at various points in most chapters.
- Try to answer the questions at the end. The purpose of these is to make you go back straight away to the material in the Unit.

What you have read three times and have tried to put into practice will stay in your head more than three times as long as something you simply read once!

ORGANIZATION OF THE BOOK

This book begins with some of the skills law students are likely to need at the earliest stage of their study, and then moves on to the more demanding ones. Thus Units 3 to 9 are concerned with the most basic matters which a beginning law student needs to know about the use of legal materials. Unit 3 simply tries to explain and illustrate what legal research for law students is about, and the rest of these early Units assume that the student is trying to find material which someone else has suggested that he or she find — because a class teacher or a textbook has suggested that a particular case or a piece of legislation should be looked at.

At the end of these Units a student should also be able to discover for himself or herself how later courts have treated a case (specifically a Hong Kong student might wish to know how, if at all, an English case has been treated in the courts of Hong Kong). He or she should also be able, with some imagination, to find out whether there is in Hong Kong the equivalent of a particular piece of English legislation. Finally he or she should be able to ensure that he or she has absolutely the most up-to-date version of the law.

Early Units (specifically 4 and 9) are designed to help students to begin learning how to read a case or a statute. Please understand that it is not basic literacy that I am talking about — but to know what it is one should be getting out of a case or statute.

I hesitate to call these 'research' skills. They really are the most elementary techniques. There is nothing difficult about them. It is, however, impossible to exaggerate their importance. It is often said that a lawyer does not need to know the law, just to be able to find it. This is a serious over-simplification: you must have some knowledge in order to get started. But the law you learn will be out-of-date by the time you graduate (even perhaps by the time you take your examinations!). In future you will need to know how to find the law for yourselves. This is even more important in Hong Kong where the literature of the law is rather underdeveloped. For now you need to know these things in order to be a good law student.

Although I say they are basic and not difficult, all too many lawyers, not to mention law students, have difficulty with these things. What you should do is to gain such familiarity with the library and the most important materials in it that you can go straight to the cases and statutes you need.

While these techniques are not difficult, they do require some of the characteristics of a good researcher: most importantly persistence and meticulousness. Good habits developed now will save you enormous amounts of time and frustration, not to mention avoid risking accusation of professional incompetence in the future!

These materials are designed to be an adjunct to the tasks of learning the law. You should use them when you need to. When you are first asked to read cases, read Unit 4. When you are first asked to read a provision of a statute, whether it is just a short section or a whole Ordinance, read Unit 9. Do not delay in reading Unit 9 just because you have not yet read Unit 8.

Subsequent Units look at secondary sources, works of reference which will give you a discussion on the topic, will help you find which cases and legislation are relevant to your work, will offer criticism of the cases, legislation or general state of the law. One could say that we are now beginning to look at something which could genuinely be called 'research'. These are the tools you will need to find something out, as opposed to finding what someone else has suggested you find. We look first at the works of reference which are the research tools of the practising lawyer. But before that we look briefly at the intellectual tasks you must undertake when faced with any new question: what is it you are looking for? How do you formulate your question in a way which will extract the material you need from the literature? (These are addressed in Unit 11.) These Units also deal briefly with the research material of some other important jurisdictions, with non-legal materials, and finally with how to cite material you have found out, and how to present written work.

TREATMENT OF ELECTRONIC SOURCES

It has not been easy to decide how best to deal with these. Clearly the age of the CD-ROM and On-line database is upon us. Future generations of lawyers will never see some publications in any other form even though they originated as paper publications. Students like to use these things and given a chance will not use the paper version! I sympathize — the electronic version are often more effective. I still believe that where possible students should become familiar with the paper version before going on to the electronic versions. When you can hold a book in your hands and turn its pages you can get a much better idea of what it contains than from the manual, or the help screen, of a database. Searching techniques (not only those of law students) are often unsophisticated, and much relevant material is not found because the searcher does not think carefully or imaginatively enough about what to look up. There will be times when you will **have** to use paper sources — the library in which you are working may not have the electronic version, or 'the computer may be down', or someone else is using the only terminal. And sometimes it is quicker to go straight to a book, rather than loading a CD.

However, having read (in the *Sunday South China Morning Post* for 2 June 1996) of the plans to put the Hong Kong statutes onto the Internet, I decided that it no longer made sense to try to postpone students' use of electronic sources. I have tried therefore to integrate consideration of the paper and non-paper version of material. In each case, however, I have put the paper versions first, and ➤ I strongly urge students to become familiar with these first before trying the electronic versions.

1997

This is a book for Hong Kong users. But much of the law of Hong Kong is derived from that of the United Kingdom, or more specifically from that of England. Therefore the assumption is made that the reader will need to find material from the UK as well as from Hong Kong.

Under the Basic Law which came into operation on 1 July 1997,

> **Article 8**
> The laws previously in force in Hong Kong, that is, the common law, rues of equity, ordinances, subordinate legislation and customary law shall be maintained ...

Though English statutes do not apply as such after the handover, applying the 'common law' still involves using the reports of decision in English courts. And lawyers may still wish to refer to English statutes because Hong Kong Ordinances have very often been based on them. However,

> **Article 84**
> The courts of the Hong Kong Special Administrative Region ... may refer to precedents from other common law jurisdictions ...

This may mean that courts are more willing to make use of reported decisions from countries like Canada, Australia, New Zealand, Malaysia, Singapore and India which are common law jurisdictions. Indeed, in some areas they already do so.

There is no material in this book on the law of China. This is mainly because I am not competent to deal with it. It is to be hoped that guides will appear in the next few years to the material on Chinese law.

THE LAW LIBRARIES IN HONG KONG

This book originated as materials for a course at the University of Hong Kong on 'Legal Research and Writing'. But in its published form it will, I hope, be used by other people as well. I have sometimes included information about the holdings of the four 'public' law libraries in Hong Kong: those of the two Universities with Law Faculties — the City University of Hong Kong and the University of Hong Kong, and those of the Supreme Court and the Attorney-General's Chambers. Some of the big law firms and chambers have good libraries of their own, but law students and many practitioners will be reliant upon these four libraries. You will find Appendix I on the Law Libraries of Hong Kong indicating in general terms the way in which their collections are organized and what their strengths and weaknesses are.

SYMBOLS AND CONVENTIONS

Throughout the book I have used certain symbols or formatting styles to draw your attention to particular features, or to point out to you where else in the book you may find information. Here is a list of them.

◷ This little watch will always be used when I am suggesting how long a task might take.

➤ This indicates something I think you should note especially: something important, or a hint or tip for successful research.

❖ This indicates a task I suggest you perform to put into practice the information.

📖 You will sometimes find in a note information about the arrangement in, or contents of, one or more of the law libraries in Hong Kong. This will be represented by this symbol.

> **I**
>
> Is it not rather casual, not to say self-centred, to use the first person pronoun like this? Traditionally it was much more common to use 'we', or to use formulations such as 'It is suggested ... '. Nowadays it is acceptable, and much more straight-forward, to say 'I'. But there may be formal contexts in which this would not be appropriate. In my view it is entirely appropriate for a book of the style of this one.

 I use this to indicate materials available on computer.

Words in **CAPITAL LETTERS** like this will be found in the Dictionary of Useful Words which is Appendix II.

REVERSE TYPE   Words in type like this mean that you should find further information in this book on this topic. Look in the Contents page.

> Material in a grey box is supplementary material that is important, though it may not fit easily into the flow of what I am saying.

> Material in double bordered box is usually something interesting I want to draw to your attention, or possibly some opinionated comment of my own!

Unit 3 | Legal Research: Preliminary Thoughts

OBJECTIVES

At the end of this Unit you will:

- have an elementary idea of some of the sorts of writing you will be likely to do as a law student
- understand something about the sorts of things you might specifically be expected to write as a first year student
- have a clearer idea of what is meant by 'Research' in the context of law study

☺ Something over one hour if you do everything you are asked to.

A t this point (assuming this point is an early stage in your undergraduate career), you may be unclear about what is meant by 'Research', and this may seem an intimidating and even pretentious term for the sorts of activities you expect to be involved in as a student. So let us think for a few minutes about the tasks which law students, and ultimately practitioners of law, will carry out which involve 'research'.

A **law student** will be required to write:

- essays
- answers to problem questions
- exams

You will also participate in 'moots' (see box on p. 12), even perhaps an international mooting competition, such as the Jessup Moot.

(Maybe you will also want to write an article for the *Hong Kong Student Law Review*, edited by students at the University of Hong Kong.)

Moot

Probably '**moot**' is another mysterious term to you. A moot is an exercise in which students argue a case as though they were in court. You will probably be required to participate in at least one competition in your law school and there are outside competitions including the Deacons Cup competition between the two Hong Kong law schools, and the Jessup Moot — an international competition organized from the United States. Participating teams in the latter are expected to set out their argument in written form, known as a 'brief'.

A **lawyer** will:

- advise clients as to their legal position
- draft documents
- negotiate
- prepare arguments for a court case
- argue a case in court

to mention only the tasks which may involve research.

ESSAYS AND PROBLEMS

Essays may be quite short things of 1500 words, or as long as 10 000. However, before you get terrified at the idea, let us look at some of the writing enterprises you may be engaged in as a first year student. Here are a few examples of the sorts of things which you might be expected to write about:

(A)   Consider the case of *Wilkinson v Downton*. Academics have written that its significance goes far beyond the facts of the case itself. Does it play a significant role in the modern law of tort, and what are the implications for the law of tort today?

(B)   Discuss the views of Weber concerning the importance of law in the development of capitalism.

(C)   Why does Hong Kong have two legal professions (barristers and solicitors), and should that situation continue?

(D)   *A* works in a factory. Because the factory is rather remote, *A*'s employer provides a bus which takes the employees to the nearest MTR station. One day *A* had left the factory premises and was in the process of boarding the bus (in fact she had one hand on the handle at the door of the bus, though both her feet were still on the ground) when a car came by at great speed. *A* was knocked over, but the car did not stop. No one knew who was driving the car. *A* was seriously injured. Advise *A* whether she has any chance of claiming compensation for the injuries. (Assume there was no negligence on the part of the employer or the bus driver.) Is the state of the law as you describe it satisfactory? (This is what we would call a **problem question**. It is also a simplified version of a task which a lawyer might have to do in practice.)

What would you be expected to do in answering these questions? In the left hand column of the following table are some of the research and writing tasks which you may find you need to do as a student.

❖ In each of the right hand boxes, put the letter or letters of the questions which you think would involve the task in the corresponding left hand box. This would be best done in collaboration with others. ☺ This could well take over 30 minutes if done thoroughly.

Task	Required by
To find out what the law is on a particular practical question	
To find out and understand the views of a particular writer	
To find out what criticisms have been made of a particular writer's views	
To find out what comments or criticisms have been made about a certain rule of law or institution	
To think about whether a particular rule or set of rules is suitable for Hong Kong	
To think about whether a particular rule seems to you to be fair	
To apply some rules to a particular set of facts	
To find out how it is that a particular rule or institution came to be part of Hong Kong law	
To suggest whether going to law is the best solution for problems	
To evaluate the evidence in support of a particular statement or viewpoint	

RESEARCH

So what do we mean by 'Research'? We do not mean experiments which scientists tend to mean by 'research'. The word 'research' means 'to find things out'; according to one of my dictionaries, it comes from the Medieval French word meaning 'to investigate'. If you think about it, the answers to most of the questions above involve finding things out. You will find most of them out in the library, or from the teaching materials distributed to you, or from a textbook.

Let us think a little more about some of the sorts of questions you will be asking when you are doing research. If we take question D, which I reprint here for convenience:

> *A* works in a factory. Because the factory is rather remote, *A*'s employer provides a bus which takes the employees to the nearest MTR station. One day *A* had left the factory premises and was in the process of boarding the bus (in fact she had one hand on the handle at the door of the bus, though both her feet were still on the ground) when a car came by at great speed. *A* was knocked over, but the car did not stop. No one knew who was driving the car. *A* was seriously injured. Advise *A* whether she has any chance of claiming compensation for the injuries. (Assume there was no negligence on the part of the employer or the bus driver.) Is the state of the law as you describe it satisfactory?

A has been injured. You are told that she has no idea who the driver of the car was or who it belonged to. Do not waste time discussing what would be the position if she did know this. One of the things which must be learned by a lawyer (and indeed anyone else involved in intellectual activity) is how to be relevant — to discuss only what is required by the enterprise in hand.

Before going any further to think about who might be under a legal duty to pay *A* compensation, think about the word 'compensation' for a moment: what would *A* be looking for? 'Money' is the crude answer. The law cannot give *A* another job, or a new leg, which might be the only way to compensate *A* for the loss. The law can only give *A* money which will support her if she has no job, or pay for her doctor's bills, an artificial leg or a wheel chair, or which will buy her a holiday, or nourishing food (or comforting bottles of whisky if that is her tendency) to make her feel less unhappy. So *A* wants to find someone who will pay her money because *A* has had expenses, or has lost a job or some income, or has suffered physically and emotionally from the accident.

So what other possibilities are there if the driver who was actually responsible cannot be found? I can think of five:

- Can she claim any compensation from her **employer**, since she was just leaving work?
- Is there any system sponsored or operated by the government which provides compensation for people injured in **accidents of any type**?

- Is there any system which provides compensation for people who are injured by **hit-and-run drivers**?
- Is there any system which provides compensation for people who are injured by **criminal** activities of other people, even if the other people are not identified?
- Is there any system of government operated or sponsored payments to people who are **out of work**, whether for injuries or other reasons?

Look back at the other questions as well. Ask what sorts of things you would be looking for. Take question C:

> Why does Hong Kong have two legal professions (barristers and solicitors), and should that situation continue?

The first part of this question invites you to look at history. The second does not ask simply just for your opinion (though you are entitled to give your **informed** view, which means a view taking account of the evidence and of the views of previous writers). It should lead you to find out what interested parties have said on the subject in Hong Kong in the past and currently (views of the two legal professions and academic writers, even of newspapers), and also what is the practice in other countries which operate a legal system, like Hong Kong's, based on the common law of England.

So, to answer all these questions, what sorts of material would you need for your research? Much of it would be in books, using that word in a wide sense — by which I mean anything which looks like a book, in that it consists of paper, between covers or in a file, which includes journals and loose-leaf publications. There may be electronic publications too, in the form of databases whether in the form of a CD-ROM or on a computer, locally or far away. We need a word which includes books as well as these non-paper sources. ➤ In future I shall use the word 'resources' if these may be in paper or electronic format, and 'book' if I mean a paper resource. Materials you would need for your research include:

- resources which describe the rules
- resources which tell you where to find the rules
- resources which give you the **actual rules** (i.e. resources **of** rules, not resources **about** rules)
- cases which may make the rules or apply them
- resources which evaluate the rules and institutions
- resources which may give you the history of the rules or institutions
- resources which answer certain questions about Hong Kong society or economy (so you can make informed observations about how appropriate certain rules and institutions might be for Hong Kong)
- books which are written by Weber
- resources which tell you what Weber wrote (especially helpful as an introduction or if Weber's views are very difficult)
- dictionaries

You might also need materials in written form but not books, such as newspapers. And if you are doing a major research project (thought not for a first year essay of 1500 words), you might even want to interview some people about their views, for example, about the legal professions.

Let me take you through the process in question D:

—   You are going to need to find some resources, probably some **Legislation**, and possibly in the end some cases which deal with compensation for personal injuries. You are not quite sure what field of law this is (tort, criminal law, contract, etc.).

❖   So make a note of your ideas about possible topics to look up.

☺   This might take you about five minutes.

My suggestions would be:
*   compensation
*   personal injury
*   damages
*   road accident
*   hit-and-run-driver
*   accident at work
*   employer
*   compensation for crime
*   insurance
*   unemployment pay

➤   Note that the first thing you do before looking for the law is to think carefully about the facts. This is a very important part of the skill of being a lawyer — or a law student. All the legal research skills in the world will not get you far if you are not asking the right questions because you have not thought fully about the facts.

—   You may think that compensation for a personal injury looks a bit like tort. So perhaps you look for a book on the law of tort in Hong Kong (in terms of my suggestions above 'a book **about** the law'. There are now three: Martin, *Law of Tort in Hong Kong,* recently superseded by Bachner, *Hong Kong Tort Law,* and Srivastava and Tennekone, *The Law of Tort in Hong Kong.*

—   Having found a relevant book you need to find the right place in it. If you have found Martin you would find that rather irritatingly it has no index. Bachner has an index which does not include any of the words listed above. Srivastava and Tennekone has an index which is rather more helpful, and does, for example, have entries under 'Compensation' and 'Employees'. If you look at the contents pages of the first book, you will find a chapter on personal injury damages. That turns out to be not much help because it deals only with compensation for torts, and really no-one against whom *A* can claim has committed a tort (the hit-and-run-driver has but he is nowhere to be found!). **Don't give up (that is one of the most important things to remember in legal research!).** Look at the contents page again, and you will find a chapter on Employers Liability, a topic which also appears in Bachner. Under that you will find a section about the Employees Compensation Ordinance. Turn to that page, and you will find that it says that an employee can claim compensation from his employer, even if the employer was not negligent (which he was not in *A*'s case) provided that the injury arose 'out of and in the course of his employment'.

– Maybe you ought to go and read the Ordinance. (You will find this in **The Laws of Hong Kong** — a book **of** rules.)

When you do that you find that in s. 5 it says this:

---

(4) For the purposes of this Ordinance—

(*d*) an accident to an employee shall be deemed to arise out of and in the course of his employment if it happens to the employee while he is, with the express or implied permission of his employer, travelling as a passenger by any means of transport to or from his place of work and at the time of the accident, the means of transport is being operated—
  (i) by or on behalf of his employer or by some other person pursuant to arrangements made with his employer; and
  (ii) other than as part of a public transport service;

– How do you make sure you have the latest version of the Ordinance?

– Now you need to think about this provision: Was *A* covered by this provision? How do you decide?

– Partly you use your common sense. Was *A* a passenger at the time of the accident? What do you think?

– You could try a **dictionary**.

– Maybe there is a **case** which decides whether someone crossing the road to get onto his employer's bus is a passenger for the purposes of this section. How do you find such a case? Maybe such a case is decided in Hong Kong. (In fact one such case is *Check Chor-ching v Wik Far East Ltd.* [1991] 2 HKLR 224. (See next Unit.)

–   But the same language may be used in laws in other countries, especially England, so maybe there is an English case which discusses the same question. How do you make sure you have the most recent cases? Clearly you need some types of **reference resources** or other materials which list cases by topic.

–   How about my other suggestions — about compensation for victims of crime or compensation for the victims of hit-and-run drivers or schemes for compensating unemployed people? The tort books are no help on this.

–   How about a book on criminal law? The only ones on Hong Kong law — Findlay and Howarth, *Criminal Law in Hong Kong: Cases and Commentary* or the *Digest of Hong Kong Criminal Law* — are no help on this topic.

–   So try an English book. You might find something there.

–   But if there is, how do you find out whether there is similar law in Hong Kong?

There is in fact a book called Atiyah, *Accidents, Compensation and the Law* which would give you some useful ideas. It is an English book. How would you know it exists unless I tell you?

–   Could you go straight to the *Laws of Hong Kong* — the Ordinances — and hope to find something relevant? Is there an index to the Ordinances?

The lawyer and the law student would have been pursuing the same route so far. The lawyer will probably stop here — at least for the purpose of advising a client. The law student still has more to do: the question still asks you to **discuss** the law.

–   So you might want to read something which is critical of the law on personal injuries (again, Atiyah would help).

–   But has anyone written anything which discusses the law in Hong Kong in a critical way? You know there is nothing in the books, but how about periodicals? There is in fact some material in *The Hong Kong Law Journal*, and it may be worth your while to look in *Law Lectures for Practitioners*. But how will you know there is something useful without sitting down and looking at the contents pages of all the volumes of these two series? And suppose someone has written about the law of Hong Kong, but not in something published in Hong Kong? How do you find this?

–   When you are asked to discuss whether the law is satisfactory, it can quite often be useful to look at the law of other countries and see whether they have any valuable experience. Atiyah's book will in fact give you some idea for this particular topic, although his book was written and published in England. But for a topic where there is no such thoughtful book, how would you find out about the law of Canada, Australia and New

Zealand, for example? Can you get hold of resources about or resources of the law of those countries? How about cases from those countries? (Another question, which we shall return to and which might be puzzling you at this stage, is why do I suggest those three countries?)

— Finally, when you have read what people have suggested for other countries, or what the law is in other countries, you might want to consider the economic and social conditions of Hong Kong and ask whether other countries' ideas and solutions are appropriate for Hong Kong.

— Where can you get **resources about Hong Kong society, politics and economy**?

— Or up-to-date **statistics** (like how many road accidents there are in Hong Kong or how many people claim for compensation for injuries at work)?

A Good Legal Researcher

- Plans the research before starting.

- Is imaginative.

- Is thorough.

- Is flexible.

- Keeps her 'eye on the ball' — does not lose sight of the objective; the amount of work done for a 1500 word essay should not be the same as for a 10 000 word dissertation.

- Is curious — that is **wants** to find things out.

- Is meticulous in being up-to-date.

- Is meticulous in recording references, always making a full note of the source of any material, and putting direct quotations into inverted commas (so as to avoid risks of plagiarism later).

- Having looked in several places for materials, makes a note of the ones looked at, even if they yielded nothing. This saves looking in the same place more than once.

- Has a good system for keeping notes; doesn't let them get dog-eared, dirty and ultimately lost.

SELF-TEST QUESTIONS

⊘ Five minutes.

1. What sorts of activities which may involve research would a law student do which a practising lawyer would be unlikely to do?

2. What sorts of activities which may involve research would a practising lawyer do which a law student would be unlikely to do?

3. What (according to this Unit) is a brief?

4. What is the origin of the word 'research'?

Unit 4　Cases: An Introduction

OBJECTIVES

By the end of this Unit you will:

* understand several related meanings of the word 'Case'
* have given a little thought to the question of how 'cases' originate
* know why you might want to read a case
* know what to expect to be able to find in an unreported case
* know what you might find in the reported version of a case
* be alerted to the different ways in which cases may be named and referred to
* know what might go into a simple 'Casenote' for your own purposes

☺ If you read the material carefully, and think about the self-study questions, it will probably take you something like three hours.

THE IDEA OF A 'CASE'

Someone will give you a case, or more probably a lot of cases, very early in your career as a law student (there is the beginning of a case on p. 26 and a whole one on pp. 29–33). What this word means in this context is a particular sort of document, which has been defined in these terms:

> A case is the written memorandum of a dispute or controversy between persons, telling with varying degrees of completeness and of accuracy, what happened, what each of the parties did about it, what some supposedly impartial judge or other tribunal did in the way of bringing the dispute or controversy to an end, and the avowed reason of the judge or tribunal for doing what was done.[1]

1　Twining and Miers, *How To Do Things With Rules* (3rd ed., London: Weidenfeld & Nicolson, 1991) 280, itself adapted from Dowling et al., *Materials for Legal Method* (2nd ed., 1952) 34–5.

Since this is the first of several meanings of the word 'case' we shall meet in this Unit, let us call it **Case 1**.

The bulk of what you will receive, or find for yourself, as a Case 1 will consist of the account of the things mentioned in the quotation above things by the **judge** (or judges) — not a memorandum by other parties or observers. If you are presented with an 'unreported case', **all** you will get will be the judge's judgment, or part of it.

Reflect for a moment about how a case get to court. (Stop here — haven't I used the word 'case' in a different sense here? I have used it to mean the whole dispute as presented to the court, and not in the sense of 'document' only? Let us call this **Case 2**.)

Let us assume that the Case 2 is about a disagreement between two neighbours: one person complains that his or her neighbour constantly plays very loud music and prevents the first person from sleeping or watching television. This would be the tort of nuisance, if anything. Why does such a Case 2 end up in court? Very probably there is a history of bad relationships between the parties, otherwise why didn't the person complained against behave more reasonably? Or maybe the noise is not unreasonable but the first person is looking for a reason to complain about the second. Even if one party goes to a lawyer to ask about suing there is a good chance that the advice will be: don't bother; you may not win; it will be expensive; why don't you reconcile with your neighbour?

Reading the Case 1, especially if it is just the judge's judgment, will never tell us much about the real nature of the dispute. In some instances we would have to know much more about social and economic conditions, or even politics, in order to be able to understand the Case 2 properly.

And when we read a judge's judgment, we learn something about what legal arguments each party made, but very often there was a great deal more argument and evidence which the judge does not find it necessary to discuss. A case may have gone on for weeks, with many witnesses being called (here I am using it in a slightly different sense again, meaning the actual process of hearing witnesses and arguing in court — let's call this **Case 3**), but the case which you read will be a few pages long. How little you really know about all the efforts made by the lawyers, and whether the witnesses were telling the truth, and so on! (As we shall see, in some good series of law reports there will be a summary of argument, though not of evidence).

Some disputes lead to several hearings in court at different stages, and several different outcomes, and judgments — each of which is a Case 1. There may be applications at an early stage (for example to prevent one party from leaving Hong Kong or from destroying the property in dispute, or arguing that the person bringing the case to court has 'No Case to Answer' (a slightly different sense — it means a body of evidence and argument that stands some chance of winning — the plaintiff's case against the defendant. One can also speak of the defendant's case in the same sense. We might call this sense **Case 4**.)) Each of these may lead to a separate response from the judge. Then even after the judge has given the decision the party who loses may appeal: to the Court of Appeal or even in the end to the Judicial Committee of the Privy Council (or Court of Final Appeal), and there will be a new decision, or another Case 1, at each stage.

➤ In order to make sure you are reading different stages of the same case* you should check the reference number. Sometimes one person may bring more than one action against the same other person, with the result that confusion is possible. The reference number will be found at the top right-hand corner of a Hong Kong unreported case, and under the title if the case is reported. But, if the case goes on appeal it will get a new number. Each court administration gives its own numbers. You then have to hope that the judgment makes it possible to link the appeal to the earlier Case 1; the best way of doing this is by referring to the previous reference number, but this does not always happen.

(*Here I think we are using the word in a sense somewhat like Case 2 — the whole dispute — but the law might sometimes define it more narrowly than the parties would. For example, in the nuisance example, one neighbour might bring a **CIVIL ACTION** against the other, and also complain to the police or the Environmental Protection Department who might bring a **CRIMINAL CHARGE**. These would be treated as two cases by the law — Case 2's.)

Reverting to the 'Case 1', in the sense of document: most of those you read will probably be 'reported cases' — that is those which have been published. You will virtually never be given a case from England which has not been published in this way. In the US they publish (or report) most cases. In Hong Kong it has until now been very common to read unreported cases (just the photocopied, or in the past stencilled, judgments of the judges); the new series of law reports, *Hong Kong Cases,* has made this necessary less often.

When you read Unit 5 on law reports, you will learn — as you may do by opening some law reports — that sometimes there is a summary of the arguments made by the lawyers in the case, and sometimes there is not. There is also, traditionally, a **headnote** or summary of the case at the beginning.

Suppose you want to learn more about the background of the case. As you may imagine, in most instances this is difficult. Most people who take cases to court are not famous. We know very little or nothing about them which is not in the Case 1 itself. One or two historians have written about a few cases, explaining all the context which, as I observed earlier, you are unlikely to find in what the judges say. For example you might see articles by AWB Simpson on cases you are likely to encounter — on the case of *Carlill v Carbolic Smoke Ball Company* see (1985) 14 *Legal Studies* 345, and on *Rylands v Fletcher* see (1984) 13 *Legal Studies* 209.[2]

---

2   You will also find these and other articles in his book, *Leading Cases in the Common Law* (Oxford: Clarendon Press, 1995). For references to a few other examples, see *How to Do Things With Rules*, p. 455.

READING A CASE

Further Reading

How to Do Things With Rules, Chap. 8.1; Bradney et al. *How to Study Law* (3rd. ed., London: Sweet and Maxwell, 1995) 58–69 and 135–167; Krever, *Mastering Law Studies and Law Exam Techniques*, (3rd ed., Sydney: Butterworths, 1995), Chap. 3.

Why?

OK, you read cases because a teacher asks you to do so. I hope you are not so unenterprising that this is the only reason. You will need to read cases to prepare for class, to write essays and so on, and you may sometimes have to decide for yourself which cases to read. But even teachers will not necessarily always want you to get the same thing out of cases. They might want you to read a case for a point of law, or of procedure, or to see how the doctrine of precedent works. In the future, in practice or even in preparing a moot argument, you will have to choose for yourself what the case might be good for. The following are some suggestions:

- In order to know the outcome in the particular dispute.

- In order to know what the law is according to the judges in this case:
  (i) because the case actually **decides** what the law is,
  (ii) because the case **explains** what the law already is.*

- Because it illustrates well the operation of the law.

- In order to use it to support the argument in another case.

- Because you know it will be relied upon by your opponent in another case.

- To predict the outcome in a later case.

*How much of a difference is there between (i) and (ii)? Traditionally the judges said they always did the latter — this was known as the 'declaratory theory of the common law'. They denied that they made law. Now judges are much more prepared to admit that they make law. If the law was unclear, and a court explains what it is in a way which other courts will follow, they have in effect made law. Similarly if there is a new situation which the law did not have to tackle before, and the judges derive from the previous cases a solution for the new situation. You are quite likely to come across the case of *Rylands v Fletcher* (1868) L.R. 3 H.L. 330 at some point, and there you will find Lord Justice Blackburn in effect making new law, while talking as though he is simply applying existing law. In *Donoghue v Stevenson* [1932] A.C. 562, 40 years or so later, Lord Atkin knew and admitted he was making new law (at least he admitted it to his children!).

For a discussion of the 'declaratory theory' see Wesley-Smith, *Souces of Hong Kong Law* (Hong Kong: Hong Kong University Press, 1994) p. 21ff.

The last three involve one of the most interesting and challenging aspects of the common law system. It is how the law moves on, progresses (or sometimes moves backwards). I suggested in Unit 3 that the case of *Check Chor-ching* could be used to decide the problem of *A*. (The full case is reproduced on pp. 29–33.) If you were the lawyer for the employer you would have relied on *Check*. If you were the lawyer for *A* you would have needed to know about *Check* either to try to defeat the argument, or to advise *A* that it was not worth suing the employer. If a new case is different from the earlier case, it may still be possible to build an argument on the earlier case, by showing that the earlier case is really quite similar, or that it makes no sense to have a different rule in the new case. The other party will be arguing that the earlier case is so different that the rule should be different. To predict the outcome of the new case you must engage in the same intellectual exercise.

- As part of a series of cases to study the development of the law or to build up a picture of an area of the law.

More unusual purposes might include:

- To study judicial technique:
  (i) of a single judge, or
  (ii) of judges generally.

(Imagine, for example, a research project on 'Whether Hong Kong judges take English cases more seriously than Canadian ones'.[3])

- To study the political role, or the biases of judges.[4]

One might research whether judges are influenced in their decisions by their social backgrounds or political views.

- Sociological or historical study through litigated disputes.

This is something which should be done with caution, because cases which go to court indicate that something has gone wrong in society, and hardly show society working as usual. On the other hand, there have been many interesting studies in the past based upon court records.

➤ Always have a clear idea of why you are reading a case. Know what you are looking for.

---

3   I found, for example, that someone wrote an article on 'The Use of Authority in Statutory Interpretation: An Empirical Analysis' (Zeppos in (1992) 70 *Texas Law Review* 1073–1144).

4   See, for example, Griffith, *The Politics of the Judiciary* (Fontana).

ANATOMY OF AN UNREPORTED CASE

Below is the beginning of an unreported Hong Kong case (Case 1). This is the way the editors of law reports in Hong Kong receive the case. At several points on the page is an asterisk and a number. Following are some explanatory notes corresponding to these numbers.

IN THE COURT OF APPEAL ***1**

1994, No. 29 ***2**
(Civil)

BETWEEN

CITY WEST INVESTMENT LTD
DAILY SHINE DEVELOPMENT LTD
FORTUNE MATE DEVELOPMENT LTD
SUPER GEAR INVESTMENT LTD ***3**
SURF WIDE INVESTMENT LTD   Plaintiffs
(Respondents)

and

THE HONG KONG BAR ASSOCIATION   Defendant ***4**
(Appellant)

*5 Coram: Hon Litton, Bokhary, JJ.A. and Mayo J.
Date of hearing : 14 April 1994
*6 Date of delivery of decision : 20 April 1994

DECISION ***7**

Litton, J.A.:

By a judgment dated 11 March 1994 we allowed an appeal by the

Hong Kong Bar Association against an Order of Barnett J. whereby he made

(i) a declaration and (ii) an order for costs against the Hong Kong Bar

Association. The developers who brought those proceedings against the Hong

Kong Bar Association now seek leave to appeal to Her Majesty in Council, ***8**

pursuant to rule 2(b) of the Order-in-Council regulating appeals from Hong

Kong to the Privy Council. Rule 2(b) reads:

"2.   Subject to the provisions of these Rules, an Appeal shall lie-

(b)   at the discretion of the Court, from any.....judgment of
the Court..... if in the opinion of the Court, the question

Explanatory Notes

1. This obviously indicates which court the case was heard in. As explained earlier, this may be only one stage of the case. A case in the Court of Appeal, like this one, must have been to another court — against the decision of which there is this appeal. This particular case has an interesting history. City West Investment Ltd and the rest appealed under the Building Ordinance against a decision of the Building Authority. Such an appeal goes to the Buildings Appeal Tribunal, a special body set up under s. 43 of the Building Ordinance. City West etc. wanted to employ a barrister from England; the Bar Association argued that the barrister had to be admitted as a barrister in Hong Kong before he could be allowed to appear before the Tribunal. A decision on this required an interpretation of the Building Ordinance. To get an authoritative ruling, City West etc. applied to the High Court for a declaration — a sort of legal remedy with which you will become familiar later. The declaration (which was in favour of City West etc.) was made by Mr Justice Barnett, sitting in Chambers (not in open court) on 17 February 1994 (note that I came across this by accident; the Court of Appeal here gives neither the reference number nor the date of Barnett J's Order). The Bar Association opposed the declaration (which is why the case has the name it does here). The Bar Association appealed to the Court of Appeal and won, on 11 March 1994. You will see from the first paragraph of what you have here why the case came back to the Court of Appeal for a second time on 14 April 1994.

2. The reference number. When the case has not been reported, this is the most precise way of referring to the case. Sometimes you will see a case referred to by its number alone — in this case this would be Civ App. No. 29 of 1994. (This method, though simple, is not recommended.) The number would be given at the time the appeal was filed.

3. The 'plaintiffs' (City West etc.) brought the case in the High Court. Here, however, they did not bring the case to the Court of Appeal; the Bar Association did, as I have said in Note (**1**). So the plaintiffs are now the respondents — they are responding to the appeal.

4. Conversely, the Bar Association who defended in the court below, were the ones who appealed and are therefore described as 'appellants'.

5. *Coram* is Latin for 'in the presence of' or 'before'. In this case the court consisted of three judges, as is usual in the Court of Appeal. Two of them are regular members of the Court of Appeal and are known as 'Justices of Appeal'. There is an abbreviation for this: JA, or in the plural, as here, JJA. The third member of the court was a High Court Judge, Mr Justice Mayo, and for him the abbreviation is J.

6. Note that the court took a few days to make its decision — they 'reserved' judgment. This is very common. However, Barnett J in the High Court delivered his decision on the same day as the hearing.

Note: the High Court is now (since 1997) called the Court of First Instance.

7. This is called ' a decision', rather than a judgment. The latter term is used for the ruling on the substantive issue rather than a procedural one like this. Interestingly, the decision of Barnett J in the High Court is called a 'decision'. The reversal on the same issue in the Court of Appeal is called a judgment! (Don't get too bothered about all this!)

8. Here you can see what was at stake in this hearing: whether the Court of Appeal would approve a further appeal going to the Privy Council. The Queen does not actually hear these cases, despite the reference to 'Her Majesty in Council'! They are heard by the Judicial Committee of the Privy Council, the final appeal court for Hong Kong until 1997, superseded by the Court of Final Appeal in 1997.

Abbreviations for Judges

It is customary in law reports and in secondary literature to abbreviate the titles of Judges, as you see in this case. The common abbreviations are:

J	Mr/Mrs Justice (Plural JJ)
LJ#	Lord/Lady Justice (Plural LJJ) (Note in Hong Kong there are no women judges at a higher level than the High Court!)
JA*	Justice of Appeal (Plural JJA)
CJ	Chief Justice
LCJ#	Lord Chief Justice
MR#	Master of the Rolls
LC#	Lord Chancellor
VC#	Vice Chancellor
P#	President
V-P*	Vice-President (of CA)
PJ*	Permanent Judges of the Court of Final Appeal[1]

CJHC* is used for Chief Judge of the High Court (comprising the Court of First Instance and the Court of Appeal) while CJ is used for Chief Justice of the Court of Final Appeal

Note:
* Hong Kong but not England
# England but not Hong Kong
[1] From Law Society Circular 97–250 (PA) drawn to my attention by Michael Wilkinson

ANATOMY OF A REPORTED CASE

On the following five pages is a Hong Kong case. In fact, you will already know that it supplies an answer to question D in Unit 3.

224

Check Chor-ching   Appellant   A

AND

Wik Far East Ltd.   Respondent   B

C

(Court of Appeal)
(Civil Appeal No. 43 of 1991)   D

Fuad, V.-P., Penlington, J.A. and Jones, J.
12th June 1991.

Industrial law—employees' compensation—employee injured on public road walking from one bus to another, both provided by employer, on way home—whether accident happened while employee "travelling as a passenger by means of transport" within s.5(5A) of Employees' Compensation Ordinance (*Cap.* 282)—whether accident happened while in course of employment—observation on interpretation of this Ordinance.   E

The appellant was employed by the respondent who provided a free bus for employees, which they could use if they wished to and from work. On the relevant day the appellant climbed into one of the respondent's buses, thinking it served her home area, but before the bus started, she realized she was on the wrong bus. She then got off the bus and, while crossing the street to get into the respondent's other bus, she was knocked down and suffered injuries.   F

The appellant appealed the dismissal of her application for compensation under the Employees' Compensation Ordinance (*Cap.* 282). It was argued that she was entitled to compensation under s.5(5A) of the Ordinance.   G

Held :   H

1.   **As a matter of construction it is impossible to hold that, while walking on the road from one bus to another bus, the accident happened, in the words of the subsection "while she was travelling as a passenger" on either of the two buses from her place of work. (See p.227I.)**

2.   **At the time of the accident, the appellant was not in the course of her employment. (See p.228B-C.)**   I

3.   (*per* Penlington, J.A.). A very purposeful approach to this legislation may be taken bearing in mind s.19 of the Interpretation and General Clauses Ordinance (*Cap.* 1). (See p.228F.)

Appeal dismissed.

Annotations (margin):

Name of the person who brought the case to this court

Description of the party in this court. (Question: How was this party referred to in the court below?)

Description of party in this court (used in lower court too)

Name of the company against whom the case was brought

Name of the court and reference of the case in this court

Name of the judges in this court and date of hearing

Keywords

(Question: What was the name of the judge in the court below?)

Name of the Ordinance involved in this case

Summary of the facts of the case and what happened in the court below

Headnote

What this court decided (what it held)

Note of the outcome in this court

A   R. Pritchard, instructed by the Director of Legal Aid, for the appellant.
Miss A. Mok, instructed by W. K. To & Co., for the respondent.

B   **Cases cited in the judgment:**
Bremme v. Dubery [1964]1 WLR 119, [1964]1 All ER 193
Lo Kwai-chun v. Hong Kong Oxygen & Acetylene Co. Ltd. [1980] HKLR 420
Murphy v. Verati [1967]1 WLR 641, [1967]1 All ER 861

C   **Fuad, V.-P.:**

This is an appeal from the decision of Deputy Judge Peter Cheung (as he then was) dated 6th February 1991 (see [1991] HKDCLR 71) whereby he dismissed an application by Madam Check Chor-ching ("the applicant") for compensation under the Employees' Compensation Ordinance (*Cap.* 282) ("the Ordinance").

D   The applicant was employed by the respondents, Wik Far East Ltd., at their factory at No.399 Chaiwan Road which is at the junction of that road with San Yip Street. The respondents provided a free bus service for their employees, which they could use if they wished to and from work. One of their two buses served the Chai Wan area and the other the North Point area.

E   On 8th August 1988 the applicant had worked at the factory from 7 a.m. to 3 p.m. When she finished work, she intended to do some shopping at the market near where she was then living at Shau Kei Wan before going home. She climbed into one of the respondents' buses parked in San Yip Street thinking that it was the one which served the North Point area and would therefore pass Shau Kei Wan.

F   Before the bus started, the applicant realised from what one of her workmates told her that she was on the wrong bus. So she got off the bus and was crossing San Yip Street to get into the other bus belonging to the respondents when she was knocked down by a light goods vehicle. She received head injuries and, sadly, has lost the sight of one of her eyes.

G   The judge was invited by the parties only to decide the issue of the liability of the respondents to pay compensation under the Ordinance.

In his full and carefully reasoned judgment, the judge discussed the main submission made by counsel then appearing for the applicant, a submission which is maintained before us by Mr. Rodney Pritchard who now represents her: that she was entitled to compensation under the Ordinance by virtue of what is provided by s.5(5A) of the Ordinance. The sub-section is

H   in these terms:

I   "(5A)   Where an accident happens to an employee while he is, with the express or implied permission of his employer, travelling as a passenger by any means of transport to or from his place of work, such accident shall, for the purposes of this Ordinance, be deemed to arise out of and in the course of his employment if at the time of the accident the means of transport is being operated -

    (a) by or on behalf of his employer or by some other person pursuant to arrangements made with his employer; and

J   (b) other than as part of a public transport service."

Margin notes (left):

Barrister for Ms Check. Note that she was paid out of public funds.

Barrister and solicitor for Wik Far East

Judgment by Vice-President of the court

The story of the accident which gave rise to the claim

(Question: What does the word 'deemed' mean? If you don't know, look it up. Where? In a dictionary — an ordinary English dictionary would do.)

Margin notes (right):

Name and references of cases discussed in this case

Reference for this case in the lower court

(Question: What do you think HKDCLR stands for?)

Words of the sub-section to be interpreted in this case.

❖ Underline the words which cause the problem.)

A The judge observed that s.5(5A) had been enacted to overcome the difficulties illustrated by the case of **Lo Kwai-chun v. Hong Kong Oxygen & Acetylene Co. Ltd.** [1980] HKLR 420 and that its provisions had been closely modelled on s.53 of the Social Security Act of 1975 of the United Kingdom, which he set out. He drew attention to footnote no.4 to para.496 of vol.33 of *Halsbury's Laws of England*, 4th ed. where, of the U.K. provisions, it is said: "As

B this is an artificial extension of the course of employment, it must be strictly limited to the circumstances described." This is followed by references to a number of decisions by Social Security Commissioners on the application of those provisions and provisions which were in similar terms in earlier legislation, for example, s.9 of the National Insurance (Industrial Injuries) Act of 1946.

C The judge also cited the following passage from pp.80-81 of *Compensation for Industrial Injury* by Richard Lewis, where the learned author said:

> "The protection of s.53 only extends to employees travelling as a passenger by any

D > vehicle'. This means that the employee must be injured while actually being carried, for in R(I) 67/52 the phrase was taken to exclude injuries which occur as the claimant approaches the transport involved. Thus benefit was refused where the claimant was injured crossing the road to board the employer's bus in R(I) 79/51, and where the claimant was walking towards one bus having alighted from another in R(I) 48/54."

E The judge then said that he agreed that s.5(5A) gave an artificial extension to the meaning of the course of employment and that it must be construed narrowly. He held that the subsection would only apply if the applicant had been injured while she was actually being carried in the bus. Since she had not yet boarded it, she could not rely on the deeming

F provision to say that she was in the course of her employment at the time of the injury. He distinguished two English decisions (**Bremme v. Dubery** [1964]1 WLR 119 and **Murphy v. Verati** [1967]1 WLR 641) cited by the applicant's counsel in support of his submission that the word "travel" should be construed liberally. I mention here that in my view the judge was right to conclude that those cases are not in point.

G The judge then went on to deal with the submission made by counsel for the applicant on the position if she could not rely upon s.5(5A). There is no need for me to go into what the judge said about this part of the argument in view of the fact that Mr. Pritchard has conceded that he would not be able to submit that the appeal should be allowed if s.5(5A) had not been enacted.

H Mr. Pritchard, relying on s.19 of the Interpretation and General Clauses Ordinance, invited us to give a liberal interpretation to the words appearing in s.5(5A); otherwise, in his submission, an absurdity would result. He recognised that decisions in the United Kingdom by Commissioners on legislation broadly similar to ours were against him and he took us through the decisions mentioned by the author of Lewis's *Compensation for Industrial Injury* in the passage cited above.

I I find one particular case of great assistance. This is case R(I) 48/54 where the facts were that the claimant was travelling home from her place of employment. She was injured while walking a distance of two or three yards from one bus to another; both buses had been

J provided by her employer. The question which arose was whether whilst changing buses, she

---

Margin annotations:

An encyclopaedia of English law

Note that Hong Kong law is often modelled on English law. 'Act' in England is like 'Ordinance' here.

Quotation from an English book discussing the meaning of similar words in English legislation.

If previous cases are 'distinguished' the court means that they are different and do not apply to the present case.

Section 19 of the interpretation and General Clauses Ordinance says 'An Ordinance shall be deemed to be remedial and shall receive such fair, large and liberal interpretation as will best ensure the attainment of the objection of the Ordinance according to its true intent, meaning and spirit'.

Reference of decision of Social Security Commissioners.

Extract from the Commissioner's decision.

A   was covered by the precursor of s.53 of the Social Security Act of 1975. Reading from paragraphs 3, 4, 5 and 6 of the report, this is what the learned Commissioner said:

3.   In these circumstances, there is no doubt in my mind that her claim must fail. I disregard the fact that the claimant had an alternative route home, by using which she need not have approached anywhere near the place of her accident. It was clearly more convenient for her to travel along the route on which she met with her accident; that route was permitted - indeed it was provided - by her employers, and she was entitled to use it. The real question is whether during the period of changing from one bus to the other the claimant is covered by s. 9 of the National Insurance (Industrial Injuries) Act, 1946. In my judgment she was not so covered.

4.   I base my decision on the fact that the accident did not happen to the claimant while she was 'travelling as a passenger by any vehicle', within the meaning of s. 9. It is clear from decisions R(I) 79/51, R(I) 67/52 and R(I) 1/53 (to which the local appeal tribunal were referred) that s. 9 extends the course of a person's employment to cover the period 'while … travelling as a passenger' in his employers' transport (which would no doubt include the act of boarding or alighting), but does not cover the act of walking towards a vehicle for the purpose of boarding it, or indeed of walking away from it after alighting.

5.   The course of the claimant's employment ended when she left her place of work. It is artificially extended by s. 9 to cover an accident happening to her 'while … travelling as a passenger' in transport provided by the employers. It cannot be further extended to cover an accident which happened to her when she was about to become a passenger.

6.   The local appeal tribunal found in the claimant's favour on the ground that, since her transport was provided by her employers, she 'is therefore deemed to have been under the control of the employers the whole of the time from leaving [the place where she lived] until her return there'. In taking this view, the tribunal misdirected themselves. The section does not extend the employers' control to the journey for all the purposes of the employment. All that the section says is that an accident happening while an employee is travelling as a passenger shall be deemed to arise out of and in the course of the employment. This is a very different thing from extending the employers' control to the whole journey. And as I have already pointed out, the extension applies not to the whole journey, but only to the period 'while … travelling as a passenger'"

I respectfully adopt this reasoning. In my judgment the learned judge in our case correctly interpreted s.5(5A) of the Ordinance. As a matter of construction I find it impossible to hold that when this unfortunate lady was walking on the road from one bus provided by her employer to another such bus, that the accident happened, in the words of the subsection "while she was travelling as a passenger" on either of the two buses from her place of work.

Mr. Pritchard went on to submit that if his arguments on the true construction of that subsection were not accepted, the court should approach the question in this way; the purpose of enacting the new subsection was clearly to equate what he called "permissive" travel with "compulsory" travel. Although he was unable to find any authority directly in point, he submitted that it must be clear that if an employee were using a public street after leaving the factory on his way to "compulsory" transport he would certainly be in the course of his employment. Since this was so, to rule against compensation for an employee approaching a bus provided by his employer, would be to frustrate the very purpose for which s.5(5A) was inserted, by amendment, into the Ordinance.

I am bound to say that I cannot accept that this lady was in the course of her employment at the relevant time. As I have said earlier, the accident did not happen while she was travelling as a passenger on one of the buses provided by her employer and unless s.5(5A) applied, in my judgment she was not as matter of fact or in law in the course of her employment when she was knocked down and injured.

This is a most unfortunate case and everyone who knows the facts will have great sympathy for the applicant, but it would not be right to strain the language of s. 5(5A) so as to entitle the applicant to compensation which the legislature did not intend her to have by the words that it used.

The judge was clearly right and I would, therefore, dismiss the appeal.

Penlington, J.A.:

I also agree that this appeal should be dismissed. Mr. Pritchard, in his very attractive and well presented argument, must nevertheless persuade us that the words "travelling as a passenger" in sub-s.5A of s.5 of the Ordinance bear a meaning which certainly on a plain reading is difficult to reach. In another judgment delivered today I myself was certainly prepared to take a very purposeful approach to the interpretation of this legislation but even bearing in mind the provisions of s.19 of the Interpretation and General Clauses Ordinance, those words cannot in my view be read in the way Mr. Pritchard has suggested they should be.

Jones, J.:

I agree with the judgments of my Lords that this appeal should be dismissed.

Appeal dismissed.

D.J.P.

A NOTE ON HEADNOTES

You will see that the first item after the title and reference number in the reported case is a summary of the case, known as the headnote. This is prepared by the editor of the law report and not by the judge(s). The amount of information contained in headnotes varies from series to series. The *Check Chor-ching* case is from the *Hong Kong Law Reports* (HKLR), which usually have quite short headnotes. Those of the *Hong Kong Public Law Reports* (HKPLR) and *Hong Kong Cases* (HKC) are very much fuller. You may think that sometimes they become so full that they rather defeat the purpose of a headnote which is to convey quickly the main issues and decision in the case. Headnotes will usually include keywords or catchwords, which will be the words under which the case will be found in the index to the law reports. It will also include the cases cited in the judgments, and sometimes those cited in argument but not in the judgments. The HKPLR and HKC also include lists of other material cited, such as books.

❖ Compare the headnotes of the same case in the HKLR and the HKC, for example the contract case of *Kao, Lee & Yip v Koo Hooi Yan, Donald* in [1994] 2 HKC 228 and [1994] 1 HKLR 248.

☺ It should take you about 15 minutes to note a number of differences.

CASE NAMES

At first you may find the names of the cases puzzling.

The basic principle is that the party which is responsible for initiating the case in the first court will be the first party named — usually termed the **plaintiff** in civil cases and the **prosecution** in criminal cases. You should be wary of the possibility that the initiating party may be called something else: the **petitioner** in a divorce case, or the **applicant** (for example in a case under the Employees' Compensation Ordinance. This is also used when the Attorney-General applies for review of a sentence, or a convicted person applies for leave to appeal against conviction or sentence). (In Scottish law the parties are known as **pursuer** and **defender** rather than plaintiff and defendant.) When the initiator is called the applicant or the petitioner the other party will be called the **respondent**. This may cause confusion if the case goes on appeal, as the original respondent may be the **appellant** and the original applicant/petitioner the respondent for the purposes of the appeal!

Criminal Cases

UK: In UK criminal prosecutions the case is usually known as *R v ???*. *R* stands for *Regina* (Queen), and in the case of a King, for *Rex*. You will often see 'The Queen' actually spelled out. Occasionally a prosecution is brought by the Attorney-General or the Director of Public Prosecutions (sometimes A-G or DPP for short).

In UK in the magistrates court the prosecution is often brought by the individual police officer. If the case goes on appeal (which is the only situation in which the case will be reported) it will retain the names of the accused and the police officer (for example *Collins v Wilcock,* a case which you may have in tort). Confusingly this looks like a civil case but it is not. In Hong Kong this way of naming cases seems not to be used.

Hong Kong Before 1997

Prosecutions were brought by the Crown, and cases were known as *R v ???* as in the UK. The Attorney-General seemed to be named in appeals against sentence, in appeals by way of case stated at the instance of the Crown, and also in judicial review cases (which may arise out of either criminal or civil disputes).

Hong Kong After 1997

The Judiciary Administrator's Office has said that 'HKSAR' has been approved by the Chief Justice for law reporting purposes. This now seems to be standard, though initially one occasionally saw 'The HKSAR' or 'HKSAR Government' or even 'the Hong Kong Special Administrative Region'.

➤ It is quite common in secondary literature (books and journals) to refer to **criminal** cases by the name of the accused person alone. This is because the other party is really always the same — the Crown (R or in the future the Government of Hong Kong — see above). See for an example, Wilkinson, *Advocacy and the Litigation Process in Hong Kong* (2nd ed., Singapore: Butterworths, 1995)

Other Cases With 'R' in the Name

Also confusing is the fact that not every case which has R in the name is criminal. English judicial review cases will often be *R v [the government body whose decision is being reviewed] ex parte [the person who is seeking the judicial review]. Ex parte* means 'on the application of ...'. And cases in which the Crown is sued in tort or contract may also have R in the name (e.g. *May & Butcher v R* — a case in which the Crown was sued for breach of contract).

Maiden Names

You may have noticed that the full name of *Donoghue v Stevenson*, [1932] AC 562, is *M'Alister (or Donoghue) v Stevenson*. M'Alister was Mrs Donoghue's maiden name but the correct short version of the case name is as we know it. This only happens in Scottish cases.

Which Name Comes First?

One of the most confusing things is the order of names. In the past the tradition in civil cases in England was for the name of the plaintiff to remain first even if an appeal was brought by the defendant **unless the case went to the House of Lords**; in the House of Lords the name of the appellant to the House was given first. In 1974 the House ordered that this practice should stop [Practice Direction [1974] 1 WLR 305], so now you will find that even in the House of Lords the plaintiff's name appears first. The Judicial Committee of the Privy Council has not followed the approach of the House of Lords.

I found a recent criminal appeal from Hong Kong: *Chan Wai-keung v R* [1995] 1 WLR 251. The appellant is first. But in the *Hong Kong Criminal Law Reports* the case appears as *The Queen v Chan Wai-keung* at the top of the case, and as *Chan Wai-keung v R* on the cover! In *Hong Kong Cases* you will find that it is *Chan Wai Keung v The Queen* abbreviated to *Chan Wai Keung v R* in the index.

In fact in civil cases too, in Hong Kong, the name of the appellant is put first even in the Court of Appeal.

Other Oddities

All this is very confusing, and does not even mention the fact that occasionally you will find an anonymous case (*Re C* or *Re A Baby*), or a case named after a ship, or the fact that some English cases are called *Re a Company* (usually followed by the registration number of the company). In fact there are often cases called '*re*' something or someone, *Re* in short for '*in re*', Latin for 'in the matter of'. It will be found in cases involving wills and trusts, for example. Sometimes a quite different name will be used between one report and another, or between one stage of the litigation and another.

Although the unreported case of which you have just looked at the beginning describes it as being 'between' the plaintiff and the defendant, the usual short form of reference is plaintiff v defendant, v being short for the Latin word *versus*, meaning 'against'.

As it happens, the cases which I have chosen to illustrate the structure of 'cases' use different terminology to some extent. In the case on p. 26, the use of the expression 'plaintiff' and 'defendant' is rather odd. Mr Justice Barnett referred to City West etc. as 'applicants', which is the more usual expression for people bringing an action for a declaration. (See similar usage in *Check Chor-ching*.) Actually, the name of the case before the High Court was *In the matter of Building Appeal Case Nos. 55–93 and 70–93 and In the matter of Appearance by Mr Robert Neville Thomas Q.C.!*

(Keep your wits about you, take careful notes, and watch out for pitfalls!)

References

Unreported cases may be referred to only by their names and/or the reference numbers. An additional piece of information is the date of the judgment. The best practice is to use all three; so the case on p. 26 would be *City West Investment Ltd v Hong Kong Bar Association* Civ. App. 29 of 1994, 20 April 1994.

If the case has been reported you will be given (normally) the reference to the published law report. This will probably appear in a conventional abbreviated form (see the casenote below). See List of Abbreviations (Appendix III).

HOW TO READ A CASE

Should You Read the Headnote?

Any self-respecting student (by which I mean one who wants to save time) will probably respond: 'Don't be silly — of course I read the headnote'. OK, in a good series of law reports you can get a quick orientation by reading the headnote. The editor has absorbed the facts and identified the issues.

➤ **But** don't read only the headnote.

• Headnote writers are only human — they can make mistakes. Anyone involved in reading law reports for any length of time has encountered inaccurate headnotes.

❖ Go back to the case of *Check Chor-ching*. Read the part of the headnote which begins *per* Penlington JA. Compare it with what Penlington JA actually says. Do you think that the headnote correctly reflects what he says? ☺ No more than three minutes.

• Secondly, the headnote may simply not cover the point you are looking for.

• Thirdly, you may well, especially as a student, be asked to read a case in order to understand the way in which the judge(s) build up the reasoning, rather than simply looking for the result.

• Fourthly, if your purpose in reading the case is to attack it because it does not favour your client (or your side in a moot), you will only see possible weaknesses in the reasoning if you read that reasoning.

• Fifthly, even if the case favours you, you will only understand the way in which your opponent might seek to attack the case if you read the reasoning in detail.

So the headnote is useful but to be treated with caution. (It may also have the function of checking your understanding of the case; if you disagree with the headnote, you can at least ask which is right.) Another useful tool is the list of cases cited. You may be interested in the treatment of a particular earlier case. If you are already familiar with the area, the cases cited will give you a good idea of the line taken in argument.

'But time is limited'. True. You will learn only by practice the art of extracting the important issues from a case in an efficient fashion. ➤ Do not simply start at the beginning of the case and read through. If there is only one judge, skim the judgment to see the structure of his argument, and pick out the sections relevant to your purpose. If the judge quotes extensively from other cases which you are familiar, don't read these quotations — though do look to see whether the judge agrees with them! If there are several judges, they may have different emphases. Or they may be repetitious and you may find that much of one judgment can be ignored for your current purposes. Maybe you can read the main, in the sense of the fullest, judgment. This will often be the first judgment. Before you select a judgment be sure that is the fullest one **for your particular purposes**. ➤ In particular, don't fall into the trap of reading only a dissenting judgment (that is a judge who disagrees with his colleagues). You may end up getting quite the wrong idea!

Making a Casenote

Precisely what you note about a case will depend on why you are reading it. However, there are certain things which you should always note, and those have been emboldened in the list below.

An important aspect of making a casenote is deciding what is relevant: what is the legal point at issue, and what are the facts which are essential to understand the legal point. But you will come to realize that many cases are important for observations made by the judges which were **not** necessary to decide the case. And many cases involve several points of law, and sometimes you will only be interested in one.

➤ Whatever purpose you want to use it for, you must check whether it has been affected by subsequent developments: later legislation, or a case which amplifies, restricts or even overrules it. How to do this we shall come to later.

CONTENTS OF A CASENOTE

*   **Name**

*   **Reference**

*   **Court**
    (This may affect the value of the case as a precedent.)

- **Judges**
  (Why? Does it matter who the judges were? The answer may be 'Yes, the identity of the judge may affect the authority of the case'. Some judges attract more respect than others. Judges have been known to contradict themselves.)

- **History**
  (Which court(s) it had gone to before and the result there.)

- **Outcome** of the case in the present court.

- **Facts**
  (So far as they are relevant for your purposes.)

- **Issues**
  (So far as they are related to the reason why you are reading the case. Sometimes you may find out only a small part is relevant.)

- **Decision on issues(s) identified, and reasoning**
  (In most instances this is the heart of the matter, especially if you are reading the case for its value as a precedent. You should, naturally include the *ratio decidendi* (see box). This can be defined as 'the principle of law for which the case is authority'[5]. For immediate purposes you should note ➤ you may not find that any judge has stated the *ratio decidendi* very clearly in a sentence or two (**you** must extract it); ➤ a proper note of the reasoning may include more than the *ratio*: this depends on why you are reading the case.

- **Authorities relied on, or not relied on**
  (Include cases and statutes.)

- Other important things said
  (Which are not necessary to the decision (*obiter dicta*))

- Quotable quotes
  (Depending on what you want to use the case for. If it is an essay, you might find something you would like to quote in the actual words of a/the judge.)

- Comment
  (Again this depends on why you are reading — it may be a comment about whether you think the decision was right, or a thought you have, which you do not want to forget, about policy factors which you feel might have influenced the judge(s), or a reference to a comment on the case in a law review.)

---

5   For further reading on this topic, see Twining & Miers, Chap. 8.5, Holland & Webb, *Learning Legal Rules* (London: Blackstone, 1991) pp. 120–122, Farrar & Dugdale, *Introduction to Legal Method,* (3rd ed., London: Sweet and Maxwell, 1990), 90–98.

➤ Whenever you use the very words of a judge in your casenote, be sure to put the quotation marks (' ') round them. You may believe now that you will remember that these are not your own words, but weeks later, when you are rushing to finish an essay, you may forget, and write someone else's words as though they were your own. This is a serious piece of academic bad practice, or, to be blunt, in extreme cases, cheating.

Ratios and Dicta

You will find many discussions of what is precisely meant by the *ratio decidendi* of a case, and guidance as to how to identify one. Here are a few points to bear in mind:

1. What **is** the *ratio*? It must involve both a proposition of law and reference to the facts of the case. A finding of fact (such as 'the defendant was negligent') is not a *ratio decidendi*, nor is a pure proposition of law ('breach of a duty of care is necessary for liability in negligence'). A statement like 'where, as in this case, the defendant manufactured goods intended to be consumed by members of the public like the plantiff, and it was foreseeable that if the goods are manufactured negligently they may cause injury, there is a duty of care' is a *ratio decidendi*. If the judge could not have said 'as in this case' — in other words his remarks were not applicable to the facts of the case — this would be only an *obiter dictum*.

> *Obiter dictum*: this Latin phrase means literally 'a thing said by the way'. *Dictum* is a noun (plural *dicta*) and *obiter* is an adjective. It is, therefore, incorrect to use the word *obiter* as if it were a thing. You should not say 'This was an *obiter*'. You can say 'The remarks were *obiter*'.

2. It is not always possible to find some words of the/a judge which precisely encapsulate the *ratio* of the case. You may have to work it out for yourself, taking into account the facts of the case, and the actual decision as well as what the judges said.

3. The *ratio* is not something which is graven in stone. There is often room for argument about what the *ratio* was, and lawyers on each side of a later case may wish to argue for a particular interpretation of the earlier case. Always read the case bearing in mind what you are reading it for.

4. Strictly speaking it is only the *ratio* of a case which is binding on later courts (if anything is binding). But the distinction is sometimes not really drawn in later cases. For example, in the case of *Hedley Byrne v Heller* [1964] A.C. 465 which

(continued)

you will study in tort, the proposition for which the case is always cited is strictly speaking *obiter* but that argument was never raised in later cases. It showed the House of Lords' thinking, and that was enough. Similarly, *obiter* observations of distinguished individual judges may be treated with respect almost as great as a *ratio*.

Further reading: Zander, *The Law Making Process*. (Weidenfeld & Nicolson).

A Possible Note on *Check Chor-ching*

Name: *Check Chor-ching v Wik Far East Ltd*

Reference: [1991] 2 HKLR 224

Court: Court of Appeal (CA would do)

Judges: Fuad, Penlington, Jones (main judgment by Fuad)

History: Applicant failed in District Court

Outcome: Appeal dismissed

Facts: Applt. knocked over while walking between buses, provided by employer for transport home

Issues: Could applt. claim under ECO? Was she 'travelling as passenger' under s. 5 (5A)?

Decision: Applicant failed to show she was a passenger.

Reasoning:
(i)   Plain words of statute did not cover applt. So she could not be 'deemed to be in the course of employment'.
(ii) Artificial extension of employment — should not be construed broadly, could not do so even if took purposive approach (Penlington clearer on this)
(iii) Counsel for plf argued that if plf was **required** to travel on the bus she would have been covered, though no authority, and that legislation was intended to put non-required transport on the same footing. Rejected because language cannot support such construction.

Authority: Mainly English social security cases (identical language in Act). Interpretation and General Clauses Ordinance s. 19 could not support the broader interpretation sought.

Obiter dicta: Fuad agreed with judge that English cases on meaning of 'travel' could be distinguished. (Not clear whether counsel argued this point; anyway not poss. to see from Fuad how they were distinguished.)

Quotable quote: 'This is a most unfortunate case and everyone who knows the facts will have great sympathy for the applicant, but it would not be right to strain the language of s. 5 (5A) so as to entitle the applicant to compensation which the legislature did not intend her to have by the words that it used.' (Fuad p. 228)

Comment: Here you might comment on whether you think the decision is just; on other cases calling for interpretation of the ECO, and give a reference to any discussion of this case in the literature.

SELF-TEST QUESTIONS

⊘ Ten minutes.

1. If someone asks you 'Do I have a good case?', in which sense are they using the word case?

2. Why should you **not** rely on headnotes alone?

3. Assuming you are a law student: by the time you read this, for what purpose(s) have you been asked to read cases?

4. If you were to be asked to do the following essays, for what purposes might you need to read cases?

    Discuss the use of precedents other than those from Hong Kong and England in the courts of Hong Kong.

    'The law of defamation is very complex and confusing for judges and lawyers alike, not to mention litigants.' Discuss.

    Describe the law relating to offer and acceptance as applied in the courts of Hong Kong.

5. If you see a case name, such as *Chan v Smith*, which of the following words may be appropriate to describe the first named person: plaintiff, respondent, applicant, accused, appellant?

    For each word you have identified, think of one type of case where the first named person would be so described (for example, the first person would be the *plaintiff* in a *civil* case).

Unit 5   Law Reports

OBJECTIVES

By the end of this Unit you will:

- have a general understanding of how the system of law reporting developed, and the importance of a system of law reporting
- be familiar with the names and scope of all Hong Kong series of law reports and the major United Kingdom ones
- have an understanding of the principles on which cases are reported
- understand which law reports series to use if you have a choice

☺ Maybe as long as three hours if you go to the library and identify the law reports mentioned.

LAW REPORTS: THE DEVELOPMENT OF AN INSTITUTION

The common law is a system originally made by judges (although statutes are probably the most important source of law these days). Law reports make these cases available. Previously the only alternative was the hand written record of the case, or the recollection of the judge(s) who decided it, or of the lawyers who happened to be in court — not a very reliable way of developing a system of judge-made law.

Other systems of law do not give law reports such a central place. The law will be found in codes (systematic bodies of rules of law, often covering a very wide range such as the Indian Penal Code, the French Civil Code or the Chinese Criminal Procedure Code or General Principles of the Civil Law). Or the law will be found as much in the writings of distinguished jurists as in codes or cases (an example is Roman-Dutch law which applies, among other places, in South Africa and Sri Lanka).

Even before the days of printing there were collections of cases known as Yearbooks.[1] They were compiled by lawyers or even by students for their own purposes. Originally they were arranged under headings rather than chronologically. For obvious reasons it is impossible to tell exactly when they started, but the earliest known example dates from 1268.

After the invention of printing, Yearbooks began to be printed, old ones as well as the current ones. The earliest printing took place in 1481 or 1482. Towards the end of the Yearbooks period one can see that the courts are beginning to refer to older cases, so the Yearbooks are becoming more than student notebooks, and more like modern law reports. The Yearbooks ceased to appear in about 1535.

Why Should You Bother About Yearbooks?

You will occasionally find references to them in textbooks. For example I find that Winfield and Jolowicz's *Tort* in the chapter on 'Trespass to the Person' refers (indirectly) to a case in 1317. The reference is to YB 10 Ed II — the Yearbook in the 10th year of the reign of King Edward II. And occasionally a Yearbook is cited in court. Many of the Yearbooks have been printed in modern times by the Selden Society.[2] In 1987 the Society published *A Centenary Guide to the Publications of the Selden Society*, on pp. 31–2 of which you will find a list of all the Yearbooks published up to that date, and which volume they appear in. The case referred to in Winfield is to be found in Volume 54 of the Selden Society Series on p. 140, and is reproduced below:

---

37. RATTLESDENE *v.* GRUNESTON.[1]

Trespas devers un qe aprés q'il vendy un tonel de vyn il horstret le vyn et le muly de euwe salé ut ——.

Un A. porta bref de trespas vers B. et counta coment il avoit achaté[2] une tonele de vyn pur VI livres de mesme cely B. tel jour etc. en sa garde lessa etc. la vint B.[3] a force et armis et graunt partie de vyn horstret et le tonel repleny del ewe salé par qoy qe ele[4] devynt[5] purru[5] et perist countre la pees etc.

Ing. Jugement de Counte qar vous avez dit qe nous fumes seisi et qe nous venismes a force et armis qe ne put estre entendu et non valuit unqore jugement qar il n'ad dit en quele ville le trespas se fyt.

Scrop. Nous avoms dit en H.

Ingh. Vous avez dit qe la achat se fit en H. et ne mye le trespas etc.

[1] Reported by *Z*[1], *Z*[2]. Text from *Z*[2] collated with *Z*[1]. Headnote in *Z*[2].
[2] chace *Z*[1].   [3] C. *Z*[1].   [4] la vyn *Z*[1].   [5] purrust *Z*[2].

---

1   See further Winfield, *The Chief Sources of English Legal History*, p. 158ff; Holdsworth, *History of English Law* Vol. II, and (1906) XXII LQR 266–84, and Van Vechter Veeder 'The English Reports 1537–1865' in *Select Essays on Anglo-American Legal History* Vol. 2, p. 123.

2   Library Note: The publications of this society are held by the Law Libraries of the University of Hong Kong and the City University.

'Oh!', I hear you say, 'I can't understand that!'. It is Norman French (the language of the ruling classes after the Norman conquest and of the courts long after even the rulers started to speak a version of English). Some of the Yearbooks are in Latin. Here is the English translation which appears on the opposite page of the Selden Society volume:

---

37. RATTLESDENE *v.* GRUNESTON.

Trespass against one who after he had sold a tun of wine drew out the wine and mixed it with salt water, as appears.

One [Simon] brought a writ of trespass against [Richard and Mary] and counted how he had bought a tun of wine for six pounds from this same [Richard] on such a day etc. ; he left it in his custody etc. There came [Richard] with force and arms and drew out a great part of the wine and refilled the tun with salt water, wherefore it became rotten and perished, against the peace etc.

Ingham. Judgment of the count, for you have said that we were seised and that we came with force and arms, which is not to be understood and is worth nothing. Judgment again, for he has not said in which ville the trespass was done.

Scrope. We have said in [Orford].

Ingham. You have said that the buying took place in [Orford] and not the trespass etc.

Incidentally, are you wondering what the point of this case is? If you look at it carefully, you might wonder how someone could withdraw water 'with force of arms'! This allegation is made in order to bring the case under the class of 'trespass' for which such an allegation was a vital ingredient; the purpose of this was to bring the case in the Royal Courts.

Nominate Reports

The Yearbooks were anonymous, but from about 1537 there began law reports which were kept by known individuals. Hence they are known as the nominate reports. Even these it seems were originally kept for personal use. The earliest published was Plowden.[3]

The style of these varies enormously. Coke's reports are really a commentary on the law. Sometimes he was wrong, and sometimes he put down what he thought ought to be the law. In contract you will find *Pinnell's case* ((1602) 5 Co. Rep. 117a) which Coke reported in

---

3   There are apparently very large number of reports from this period which remain in manuscript form, never having been published. See Ibbetson, 'Law Reporting in the 1590s' in Stebbings, *Law Reporting in Britain* (London: Hambledon Press, 1995).

such a way that a mere *obiter dictum* appeared as though it were the law. (This was not really set right until 1946!)

The quality of the reports varied, much to the annoyance of some of the judges who thought the reports made them look fools. Some of the reports are treated with caution; and sometimes the same case will appear in more than one report and it can be useful to look at all the versions in order to get the fullest information about the case. Remember the cases are based upon notes taken in longhand (how good would a series of law reports be if it was based upon **your** notes of cases you listened to in court?)

From about 1756 standards greatly improved. Around the end of that century the practice developed of judges revising their reports of their decision, or supplying handwritten copies of their judgments to one reporter. These reports were described as 'authorized', meaning authorized by the judge.

Beginning of the Modern Era

In the nineteenth century various commercial series of law reports began to be published — for example, the *Law Times Reports*, the *Times Law Reports*, the *Law Journal*, the *Solicitors Journal*. As their names indicate, some of these had other things in them apart from reports of cases.

The Incorporated Council

In 1863 the Bar in England set up a committee which created a new system of reporting. The Incorporated Council of Law Reporting was set up, and it produced the series of reports we now call *The Law Reports.* By about 1895 this series was very well established and reckoned to be the best. They are still not 'official'. The Incorporated Council is not a government body. *The Law Reports* are revised by the judges and to that extent they have some special authority. ➤ Where there is a choice, therefore, *The Law Reports* ought to be cited in preference to other series. However, the next reports mentioned are also revised by the judges.

The All England Law Reports

This series began in 1936 and remained the most important general series after *The Law Reports*.

Reporting

In the US most decisions are reported, but the English system has always been much more selective. *The Law Reports* publish only about 7% of the cases decided in England; most of the ones reported are decided by appeal courts: the Court of Appeal or the House of Lords mostly.

How is the decision made to report a case? Clinch *Using a Law Library* (London: Blackstone, 1992)[4] reproduces the criteria adopted by the *All England Law Reports*:

> Does the case state new law?
> Or does it give a modern restatement of existing law?
> Does it clarify conflicting decisions?
> Does it interpret legislation?
> Does it clarify a clause commonly used in contracts etc.?
> Does it clarify an important point of practice or procedure?

> If it does one of these things, it will probably be reported.

There used to be a rule that a law reporter had to be a barrister. That has become very weak, and I notice that in the *Hong Kong Law Reports* the reporter is often a solicitor rather than a barrister.

The Doctrine of Precedent

First year students (for whom this book is mainly designed) will learn about this doctrine in their courses. In case they have not come to it before they read this chapter, or for other users who are not from the common law system, these few notes may be helpful.

The development of the common law has depended on courts making use of the decisions of earlier court — known as precedents. The basic idea is that the core elements of the legal reasoning (known as the *ratio decidendi* — see Unit 4) in the earlier case may be used to assist in the decision of the new case. Indeed, very often the common law system goes further and says that the decisions of **some** earlier courts **must** be followed. This is what is known as **binding** precedent. In brief, the decisions of a higher court within the same legal hierarchy must be followed in this way, and the decision of even the same court must be followed (provided that it is a court with more than one judge, such as the Court of Appeal). The House of Lords (the highest court in

(continued)

---

4   Page 91.

the English legal system) and the Judicial Committee of the Privy Council (the highest court in the Hong Kong system until 1997) do not have to follow their own decisions, however.

In actual fact the system does not operate as rigidly as this bald statement might suggest: courts will usually treat the decisions of earlier courts with respect even if not **bound** to follow them. They will prefer if at all possible to distinguish earlier cases (show how they differ from the present case) rather than to refuse to follow them. On the other hand, techniques of judicial reasoning do make it possible for the court very often to decide as they feel it right to decide, even if an earlier decision seems to stand in the way. Occasionally, however, a court does find it impossible to distinguish an earlier case — we can see this in the instances when the House of Lords has admitted departing from an earlier precedent of its own, e.g. *British Railways Board v Herrington* [1972] AC 877. On this whole question see Twining & Miers *How to Do Things With Rules*.

After 1997, the Basic Law says that the courts of Hong Kong will be free to apply the decisions of common law courts anywhere (BL Art. 84). In fact they are already free to do this, and the interesting question is whether English decisions will cease to have a special position (see Unit 2).

LAW REPORTS: WHAT YOU ARE LIKELY TO FIND IN A LAW LIBRARY

The rest of this Unit looks in a little more detail at the reports which you are likely to find in the libraries you will use as a student, and in practice.

Finding the Nominate Reports

You will not find many libraries which have copies of the original reports.[5] For most purposes, your best hope is that a case in the nominate reports was reprinted (or that it was also reported in one of the modern series, such as the *Law Journal*, but this will only help with nineteenth century cases).

There are two series of reprints of nominate reports.

---

5   Library Note: In the Supreme Court Library, however, there is a good collection of nominate reports. The HKU Library has a few specimen volumes, so that students can see them: they are not very old: the reports of Young and Jervis volumes 1–3, 1826–30, Cromption and Jervis, volumes 1 and 2, 1830–32, Cromption and Meeson volumes 1 and 2, 1832–34, and Crompton, Meeson and Roscoe volumes 1 and 2, 1834–35.

The Revised Reports

Around the end of the nineteenth century some of the nominate reports were reprinted in this series subtitled 'Reports of such cases in the English Courts of Common Law and Equity from the year 1785 as are still of practical utility'. The cases stopped in 1866, because the Incorporated Council reports had started by then.

The English Reports

Most of the nominate reports, going back to 1210, were reprinted in a series of fat volumes called the *English Reports* (ER), which also finish in 1866. Within each volume of these, you will find several volumes of the old reports, and, of course, the sizes of pages are different from the originals. The series is now available in CD-ROM format.

When you find a reference to one of these old cases in another case or in a textbook, I am afraid that very often they will give you only the old reference and not the reference in the *English Reports*: a very irritating habit (which sometimes indicates, I suspect, that the author has simply copied the case reference from some other source and has never actually read the case in the *English Reports*, otherwise why should they not help us out by giving the ER reference?) They are even less likely to give a *Revised Reports* reference.

See next Unit for information on finding a case in these reprints.

All England Reports Reprint

There is also a series called the *All England Report Reprint* which has reports from 1558–1935. It is a sort of modern *Revised Reports*. Cases were selected on the basis that they had been mentioned twice or more in the *All England Reports*. Work on this series began in 1968, and it runs up to the beginning of the *All England Reports*, and is published by the same publisher. (One odd feature of this series is that it does not seem to say what is the source of the original report; an old case may be reported by several old reporters, and in the *Law Journal* etc., but although the *All England Report Reprint* lists all these, it does not say which is the source of the reprint.)

Among older reports it is common to find the *Times Law Reports* (1884–1952), and the *Law Times Reports* (1859–1947). ➤ Be careful when taking notes not to confuse these! Also please note that there are also **summaries** of cases in the *Law Times* itself, to which the *Law Times Reports* were a supplement. ➤ So you need to be even more careful to distinguish between LT and LTR! An important English defamation case is *Blennerhasset v Novelty Sales Service Ltd.* for which you may see the reference as (1933) 175 LT 393 or 175 LTJ (meaning *Law Times*, journal as opposed to reports).

Other older English reports are the *Law Journal* reports (see below), also the *Solicitors Journal* (SJ). You may also find *Commercial Cases* (Com Cas) covering 1895–1941.

The Incorporated Council of Law Reporting Reports

The Incorporated Council of Law Reporting produces the closest to an authorized series of law reports available in the United Kingdom. They are not 'official' but they should be cited if available.

In the last third of the nineteenth century the English courts were reorganized several times, and the series of *The Law Reports* changed as well. This is very confusing. What happened was that before the reorganization there were three common law courts: the Court of Common Pleas, the Court of Exchequer and the Court of Queen's Bench. When the Incorporated Council began, there was a separate series of law reports for each court. When the Supreme Court was created these became divisions of the new High Court: Common Pleas Division etc. A few years later these were merged into the Queen's Bench Division. The form of citation changed each time the court structure changed. The situation for the other Divisions of the High Court was less complex, except for what is now called the Family Division. For many years this was the Probate Divorce and Admiralty Division, but in 1972 the Probate jurisdiction went to the Chancery Division and the Admiralty jurisdiction to the Queen's Bench Division. Here is a list of case citations which illustrate the different forms of reference, listed under the name of the present Court/Division.

House of Lords/Privy Council

McCormick v Grogan (1869) L.R. 4 H.L. 82	1965–75 (spines may say 'English and Irish Appeals')
Lyall v Jardine, Matheson & Co. (1870) L.R. 3 P.C. 318	1865–75 Appeals to Privy Council
Steuart v Robertson (1875) L.R. 2 Sc. & D. 494	1865–75 Scottish & Divorce appeals
Speight v Gaunt (1883) 9 App. Cas. 1	1875–90
Nocton v Ashburton [1914] AC 932	1891–

Note that the correct name of the series is now 'Appeal Cases'; ➤ you should remember that this covers only appeals to the House of Lords/Privy Council, **not** to the Court of Appeal.

Chancery

Jones v Lock (1865) 1 Ch. App. 25	1865–75 Lord Chancellor and Court of Appeal in Chancery
Re Kershaw's Trusts (1868) L.R. 6 Eq. 322	1865–75
Re Chesterfield's (Earl) Trusts (1883) 24 Ch.D. 643	1875–90
Re Best [1904] 2 Ch. 354	1891–

Queen's Bench

R v Curgerwen (1865) L.R. 1 C.C.R. 1	1865–75 Crown Cases Reserved (an old appeal court for criminal cases)

Mullett v Mason (1866) L.R. 1 C.P. 559	1865–75 Court of Common Pleas
Smith v Green (1875) 1 C.P.D. 92	1875–90 Common Pleas Division
Atkinson v Newcastle & Gateshead Waterworks Co. (1871) LR 6 Ex. 404	1865–75 Court of Exchequer
Household Fire Insurance v Grant (1879) 4 Ex. D. 215	1875–90 Exchequer Division (more than one volume bound together)
Smith v Hughes (1871) L.R. 6 Q.B. 587	1865–75 Court of Queen's Bench
Lowe v Dixon (1885) 16 Q.B.D. 455	1875–90 Q.B. Division
Burrows v Rhodes [1899] 1 Q.B. 816	1891–

Family

Banda and Kiswee Booty (1866) L.R. 1 A & E. 109	1865–75 Admiralty and Ecclesiastical
In the Goods of Daniel Saunders (1865) L.R. 1 P. & D. 16	1865–75 Probate and Divorce
Le Parlement Belge (1879) 4 P.D. 129	1875–90 PDA Division
The Annefield [1971] P. 168	1891–1971 Probate and Admiralty
Re St. Barnabas, Kensington (1988) [1992] Fam. 1	1972– Family and Ecclesiastical

The current position is that there are these series (listed last under each heading in the above table):

- **Appeal Cases** (AC) containing House of Lords and Judicial Committee of the Privy Council
- **Chancery** (Ch) containing reports of Chancery Division cases and Court of Appeal cases on appeal from that division
- **Queen's Bench** (QB) containing reports of cases in the Queen's Bench Division of the High Court and cases on appeal to the Court of Appeal
- **Family** (Fam) reports of cases in the Family Division, and those on appeal to the Court of Appeal

❖ Locate the volumes for the cases listed in the Table above, unless you have already used the series.

☺ It would take perhaps 30 minutes to locate them all.

In 1953 the council started another series called the ***Weekly Law Reports***. These can bring out cases much more quickly, but those cases have not been revised by the judges. There are about 42 weekly issues in the year, and in each issue you will probably find a pale green sheet dividing the cases. The first cases say they are in volume 1 *Weekly Law Reports* and the rest in either 2 or 3 *Weekly Law Reports*. When the reports are bound at the end of the year the binding of the case will correspond to this. Volume 1 contains cases which the editors think have no permanent interest; these will never be revised by the judges. Cases in

Volumes 2 and 3 will be revised by the judges and later reprinted in the AC, QB, Ch or Fam report, as appropriate. Because they have been revised these should always be cited in preference to the *Weekly Law Reports* if possible. The AC, QB, etc. also appear several time a year in paper covers and then are re-bound into hard cover volumes.

> Should you insert the ' . '? In other words, should there be a full stop in abbreviations? Traditionally there always was, of course. However, modern editors (not uninfluenced by the awareness that time is money I suspect) often seem to prefer a cleaner style with no full stops. For the purpose of essays, you should ensure that you are consistent.

Other Major Series

Butterworths still publish the **All England Law Reports** (see above). These also appear weekly and are re-bound usually into three volumes. However there is no distinction between the volumes (the judgments are all taken from the official transcripts and approved by the judges).

Most of these cases are civil cases. There is also an important series of English criminal cases: the **Criminal Appeal Reports**, and its sister the **Sentencing** series. These include cases from the Criminal Division of the English Court of Appeal. The abbreviation is CAR or Cr App. Reps with (S) in the case of the sentencing series.

These are still current. You may have occasion to use another major series of general law reports which is no longer being published, but is rather complicated:

Law Journal: This was published from 1832 until 1949. In the HKU Law Library:[6]

- 1832 to 1835 — 4 volumes:
  Within each bound volume there are separate sequences for a variety of courts: Chancery, Exchequer in Equity, Kings Bench, Common Pleas, Exchequer of Pleas and Exchequer Chamber (on appeal from Court of Exchequer), Court of Bankruptcy.

- 1836 to 1903 — vols. 5–72:
  Each year there are two volumes of the same number. One called 'Common Law' which contains essentially separate books, one for the Court of Queen's Bench, one for Court of Common Pleas, one for Court of Exchequer and Exchequer Chamber,[7] each with its

---

6   In other libraries you may find that the series is bound differently.

7   When the courts were recognized these first became divisions of the new High Court, and were then merged into the Queen's Bench Division; see also *The Law Reports* above.

own pagination starting from 1. The other is called 'Equity' and also covers more than one court, including the Court of Chancery, and the Privy Council and the Probate Divorce and admiralty Division.

- 1904 to 1949 — vols. 73–118:
  One volume each year including different sections.

Another now defunct series, in this case a specialist series, which is of some importance is: ***Butterworths Workmen's***[8] ***Compensation Cases***. You will not find this discussed in most books about law reports, since the legislation does not exist in the UK any longer (although, as you know, similar provisions appear in the Social Security Act — see Unit 4). You will find in most Hong Kong Law Libraries a copy of these reports which ceased publication in 1949. They go up to volume 41 (in Roman numerals XLI). In some volumes there is a Supplement, beginning from page 1 again, of Scottish and Irish workmen's compensation cases. The abbreviation was BWCC.

Modern Specialist Reports

In the past law reports were rarely specialized in the sense of concentrating on one area of the law, although they might be classified according to the courts or divisions involved. In most countries, however, there has been a marked trend towards specialist series. Sometimes these are restricted to one jurisdiction, but sometimes they are regional, or have cases from a wide range of jurisdictions. There will be some degree of overlapping with general series, which will typically publish the major cases in each area, but the bulk of the cases in a specialist series will probably not be found in the general series.[9]

Examples: you will find UK series such as:
- the *Family Law Reports*
- the *Construction Law Reports*
- the *Financial Law Reports*

Other countries have similar examples such as:
- the *Australian Tort Reports*

The UK based *Fleet Street Reports*, however, include intellectual property cases from many countries.

---

8   The Hong Kong legislation, too, was originally the Workmen's Compensation Ordinance, but the name was changed to Employees' Compensation Ordinance when the scope was expanded to all employees.

9   See the comment on the possible implications for the law of the development of specialist series of reports, in Cocks, 'Planning Law and Precedent: A Study in Twentieth Century Law Reporting' in Stebbings, above, p. 187.

Parts of a Volume of Law Reports

Different series of law reports vary slightly in the information which they contain. A good series ought to contain the following parts:

* list of cases reported in this volume (in alphabetical order)
* list of other cases which are cited or discussed in the cases reported
* list of statutes which are cited or discussed in the cases reported
* subject index — index of the topics which the cases reported are about

Occasionally there is more. To take two Hong Kong examples (see further below): *Hong Kong Cases* and the *Hong Kong Public Law Reports* each contain a list of other sorts of material cited or discussed, for example books and articles. *Hong Kong Cases* also includes a useful list of abbreviations.

HONG KONG REPORTED CASES[10]

General Reports

The Hong Kong Law Reports (and Digest)

This (with its supplement the *District Court Law Reports* (see below)) was the only general series of law reports produced in or for Hong Kong, until the publication of *Hong Kong Cases* began in late 1994.

The HKLR started in 1905. Until 1956 each volume had a separate number. Therefore the reference to a case would be in the form (1905) 1 HKLR until (1956) 40 HKLR. A few of the earlier volumes are bound together. (For explanation on the shape of brackets, see Unit 6.)

Since 1957 the year has been the key element in the reference, therefore [1957] HKLR. In one or two years you may find that the binder split a volume into two books. But inside you will find that there is no division and the pages run in one sequence throughout the year.

However, since 1988 there have been two volumes a year, each with its own sequence of numbers. Therefore now you would expect a reference to be in the form [1992] 1 HKLR or [1992] 2 HKLR, and so on.

From 1988 to 1996 there were two volumes a year each with its own sequence of numbers.

---

10 Prepared with helpful advice from Andrew Halkyard and Peter Wesley-Smith.

In 1997 the Law Reports joined with the *Hong Kong Law Digest* to form the *Authorised Hong Kong Law Reports and Digest.* When they were bound at the end of the year there was only one Law Reports volume (with 1393 pages). In 1998 there were two volumes again.

The District Court Law Reports

Since 1953 a few reports of District Court cases have appeared as a supplement to the HKLR (now divided from the Superior Court cases by a green sheet). At the end of the year these are bound separately. On its spine the volume says Hong Kong District Court Reports Supplement. But they are referred to simply as the 'District Court Reports'. The reference would be in this form: [1992] HKDCLR. Since 1958 Lands Tribunal cases also appeared in this series. The District Court Reports have ceased to have a separate existence.

Hong Kong Cases

This series, published by Butterworths, began publication in 1994. The first volumes to appear were two bound volumes for 1993. The intention of the publishers is both to produce volumes for recent years, and also to publish volumes of past cases, including from before 1905 when the HKLR began. Current issues appear fortnightly and are then bound at the end of the year into (at the time of writing) three volumes.

The correct form of citation for this series is as in the following example: *Yung Chi Kin Larry v Leung Tin Wai* [1993] 1 HKC 143 (a libel case).

On p. 56 is a page from the HKC. You will see that the layout is very much the same as for the HKLR (see Unit 4 pp. 29–33). ❖ How many differences can you see?

Specialist Reports

Criminal law

From the beginning of 1992 each monthly part of the *Hong Kong Law Reports* had a new section — the *Hong Kong Criminal Law Reports.* At the end of the year it is bound in a separate volume, with the reference [1992] HKCLR. Since 1996 the *Criminal Law Reports* have ceased to appear separately.

Public law

The *Hong Kong Public Law Reports* began publication in 1991. They are edited in the Faculty of Law at the University of Hong Kong. They include Bill of Rights cases, administrative law cases and so on. The form of reference is (1991) 1 HKPLR, (1992) 2 HKPLR and so on.

Since early 1996, these reports have been published by Butterworth and the cases appear initially at the end of the fortnightly parts of Hong Kong Cases. However, in 1998 no cases seem to have been identified as *Public Law Reports* cases.

ATTORNEY GENERAL v NGAN KAM MING & ANOR   A

COURT OF APPEAL – APPLICATIONS FOR REVIEW NOS 15 AND 17 OF 1995
POWER VP, LIU JA AND WONG J
29 FEBRUARY 1996

Criminal Law and Procedure – Sentencing – Possession of offensive weapon   B
– Youth offender – Detention in drug addiction treatment centre – Whether
imprisonment or detention in training centre mandatory – Public Order
Ordinance (Cap 245) s 33

刑法與刑事訴訟程序 – 判刑 – 管有攻擊性武器 – 年青被告 – 拘留於戒毒   C
所 – 是否必須判處監禁或拘留 –《公安條例》（第 245 章）第 33 條

The respondents, both 19 years' of age at the time of the offence, were
convicted of possession of offensive weapon contrary to s 33 of the Public Order
Ordinance (Cap 245) (the Ordinance). They were drug dependants and were
ordered to be detained in a drug addiction treatment centre. The Attorney General   D
applied for review of the sentences on the ground that s 33 of the Ordinance was
mandatory and left the court no option but to sentence an offender between 17 and
25 either to imprisonment or to a detention centre.

Held, allowing the applications: E
The provisions of s 33 of the Ordinance were mandatory. The intention of the
legislature was clear and could not be overridden except by some explicit provision
elsewhere in the law. *A-G v Wong Yiu Chung* [1973] HKLR 131 referred. *R v Ng
Yun Fong* [1978] HKLR 186 applied (at 178G-H).

Cases referred to   F
A-G v Wong Yiu Chung [1973] HKLR 131
R v Ng Yun Fong [1978] HKLR 186

Legislation referred to
Drug Addiction Treatment Centres Ordinance (Cap 244) s 4(1)   G
Hong Kong Bill of Rights Ordinance (Cap 383) art 6(3)
Interpretation and General Clauses Ordinance (Cap 1) s 19
Public Order Ordinance (Cap 245) s 33

Application for review
This was an application by the Attorney General for the review of sentences of   H
detention in a drug addiction training centre. Both respondents had been convicted
for possession of offensive weapon contrary to s 33 of the Public Order Ordinance
(Cap 245). The facts appear sufficiently in the following judgment.

IG Cross QC, WS Cheung and Denis Chan Fung Shan (Crown Prosecutor) for   I
the applicant.
Philip Dykes (Director of Legal Aid) for the respondents.

Hong Kong Conveyancing and Property Reports

The *Hong Kong Conveyancing and Property Reports* reproduce cases within the scope of the title only, which are also in *Hong Kong Cases*. Five volumes covered 1983–95. The series is produced in bound volume form only.

Lands Tribunal

There are three volumes of *Hong Kong Lands Tribunal Reports*: [1977] HKLTR
                                                                 [1978]
                                                                 [1979–80]

Each volume has an index at the back. From 1981 this series of reports was absorbed into the *District Court Reports*.

For the jurisdiction of the Lands Tribunal see Wesley-Smith, *The Hong Kong Legal System* (2nd ed.) pp. 62–64 and Lands Tribunal Ordinance. The Tribunal is presided over by a District Court judge.

Planning appeals

Recently the Government started to produce the *Town Planning Appeal Board Decisions*. The first volume is for 1992–93.

Tax

Hong Kong Board of Review Decisions: The first volume covered 1968–82, and the second 1982–87. During that period only selected cases were reported. Now they are published in A4 format without a year on the cover, but each volume covers about one year. Each A4 size 'volume' has been supplemented by as many as three supplements of equal size; these are bound together in files, all to be treated together as a volume. Page numbering runs throughout the 'Volume' and 'Supplements'. Within the volumes the cases are referred to by numbers, not by names. There is a cumulative index published with each part.

Hong Kong Tax Cases: These are published by the government and are reports of court cases. The format is rather like the Board of Review cases, but the page size is smaller. The reports appear a year or more in arrears.

CCH *Hong Kong Revenue Legislation*: CCH (Commerce Clearing House) is a US company originally which produces loose-leaf practitioner texts of various types (and a few other types of publication). *Hong Kong Revenue Legislation* is a loose-leaf publication one volume of which is Hong Kong tax legislation, but the other two of which constitute a loose-leaf collection of Hong Kong tax cases. One volume covers Board of Review cases and the other court cases. These cases appear quite quickly. CCH explain that the correct form of citation for their Board of Review cases would be, e.g., *Case B37* (1992) 1 HKRC ¶80–198. (The form of reference is CCH's idiosyncratic own.)

There is a list of cases (one for Board of Review cases and one for court cases) with page number and a brief note of the issue, and a subject index at the end of the volume. There is a list which relates the offical numbering of Board of Review cases to the CCH publication.

Other Reports in Which Hong Kong Cases May Appear

- Reports of the Judicial Committee of the Privy Council from Hong Kong may appear in *The Law Reports Appeal Cases* volume: [1992] AC and so on.

- *Law Reports of the Commonwealth* which appear in three volumes for each year: Constitutional and Administrative Law (since 1990 called Constitutional Law only), Commercial Law and Criminal Law. The first volume on commercial law is [1980–84] LRC (Comm); the first volume for the other two was in 1985, Reference: [1985] LRC (Constl) and [1985] LRC (Crim). From 1997 Hong Kong cases will no longer appear.

Most volumes have several Hong Kong cases, although most, if not all, of these will have been published elsewhere.

- Hong Kong cases (usually reported elsewhere) with international implications (such as those concerned with refugees or extradition) may appear in the *International Law Reports*.

- *Butterworths Human Rights Cases.*

- *Intellectual Property Reports*: This series is published in Australia. It started in 1982. It contains a very few Hong Kong cases.

- *Asian Intellectual Property Reports.*

- *Fleet Street Reports*: This is a UK series of intellectual property reports (copyright and so on). It also contains a few Hong Kong cases.

- *Lloyds Law Reports*: This UK series contains commercial cases with a shipping and insurance bias. Occasionally a Hong Kong case is reported.

Short Reports of Hong Kong Cases

No Hong Kong newspaper carries reports of the quality of *The Times* or the *Independent* in UK. The newspapers do report legal hearings and judgments, though with a bias towards what the public would wish to read rather than the profession. However, reports in short form may appear in *The Hong Kong Lawyer*; these vary in length, and may or may not be followed by a brief commentary.

- The <mark>*Hong Kong Law Digest*</mark> (in its annual form this is called the *Hong Kong Law Digest Yearbook*[11]) carries summaries of cases, some of which are or will be also reported elsewhere. Now called the *Hong Kong Law Reports and Digest*.

- *Bill of Rights Bulletin*: Edited by Andrew Byrnes and Johannes Chan, published informally by the Faculty of Law, University of Hong Kong since 1991. Includes summaries of HK Bill of Rights cases, sometimes with comment. Now called the *Basic Law and Human Rights Bulletin*.

- *The Commonwealth Law Bulletin*: This is published by the Commonwealth Secretariat, Legal Division. One of its sections deals with the 'Judicial Decisions'. These are summaries of cases, sometimes reported elsewhere, sometimes not, by topic and jurisdiction within the Commonwealth. (Reference [1992] CLB.) Since 1997 Hong Kong cases will presumably no longer be included.

- <mark>*The Digest*</mark>: This research tool carries the occasional summary (very brief) of a Hong Kong case. These would always be reported elsewhere.

Cases in Mainland China

The legal system of the PRC belongs to the civil law tradition and not to the common law. Cases do not have the same authority or binding force that they do in the common law tradition. However, it is not uncommon for the decisions of courts to be reported. The French courts do it, and the Supreme People's Court publishes reports of cases in its Gazette. They will not be used in the same way as in the Hong Kong system.

❖ Find the *China Law Reports* (published by Butterworths). This series begins with cases for 1991, and is a translation of cases decided in PRC courts. Compare the cases with those you would find in a common law volume of law reports. You will find that the cases do not refer to previous cases. There is no 'Index of cases referred to' in the volume. Also an individual case is literally a 'report' of what the court decided — it is not in the words of the judge(s). ☺ You might spend about 15 minutes on this.

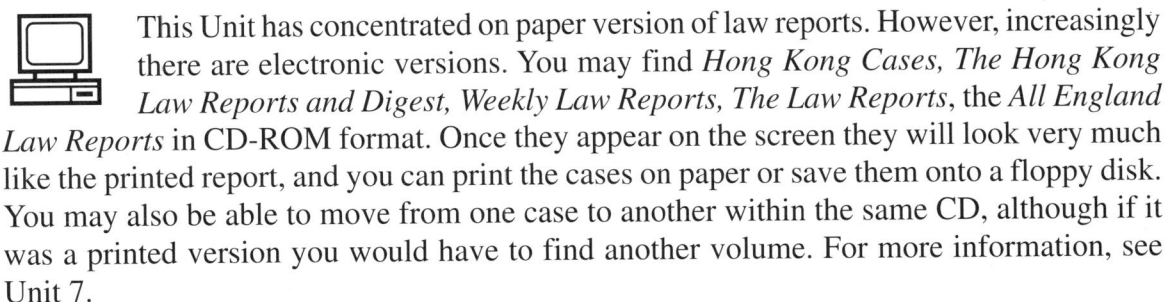 This Unit has concentrated on paper version of law reports. However, increasingly there are electronic versions. You may find *Hong Kong Cases, The Hong Kong Law Reports and Digest, Weekly Law Reports, The Law Reports*, the *All England Law Reports* in CD-ROM format. Once they appear on the screen they will look very much like the printed report, and you can print the cases on paper or save them onto a floppy disk. You may also be able to move from one case to another within the same CD, although if it was a printed version you would have to find another volume. For more information, see Unit 7.

---

11 The publication was originally known as *Hong Kong Current Law*. The *Yearbook* was just the *Hong Kong Law Yearbook* until 1994.

Full decisions of the Hong Kong Court of Final Appeal are available on the Internet at **<http://www.info.gov.hk/jud/guidezcs/html/cfa/jadmt/index.htm>.**

SELF-TEST QUESTIONS

🕐 Ten minutes.

1. What was a Yearbook?

2. What were the nominate reports and why are they so-called?

3. What are the names of the two series of reprints of nominate reports? Which is the more complete one?

4. What does the *All England Law Reports Reprint* contain?

5. What is the Incorporated Council of Law Reporting and when was it set up?

6. Who publishes the *All England Law Reports* and when did the series begin?

7. Which is the newest series of general Hong Kong reports?

8. At the time this Unit was written, which of the series of law reports were already or were soon to become available on CD-ROM.

Unit 6 　Finding Cases (I)

OBJECTIVES

By the end of this Unit you will:

- know the customary abbreviation for the major series of law reports you are likely to use as a student, and where to find the meaning of those which you do not know
- understand when square brackets and when round brackets are used in case (and journal) references
- be able to find within 3 minutes any case which is in the library if you have the correct reference, assuming the relevant volume is in its correct place on the shelf
- know how unreported Hong Kong cases are kept and how they are to be found

☺ If you do the exercises it could take you two hours or so.

Cases will generally be found in published law reports (although rather a lot of Hong Kong cases remain unreported and you can only get them in cyclostyled or photocopied form, though some are now appearing in CD-ROM format — see p. 74.

FINDING REPORTED CASES WHEN YOU HAVE A COMPLETE REFERENCE

Quite likely you will be faced with a reference which looks roughly like this:

Ng Chek-kok v Kiu Wai-ming [1992] 1 HKLR 5
　　　*1　　　　　　　　　　*2 　*3　　*4 *5

The various parts of this reference (with * and number) are:

*1　Case name
*2　Year of report
*3　Volume

*4 Abbreviation of name of series
*5 Page on which the case begins

There may be slight variations. You could be asked to find one of the following:

Pau On v Lau Ying Long [1980] AC 614
Hillas & Co Ltd v Arcos Ltd (1932) 147 LTR 503
The Satanita [1897] AC 59
Excomm Ltd v Guan Guan Shipping (Pte) Ltd, [1987] 1 Lloyd's Rep 330

❖ Before moving on, identify for yourself how each of these references differs from the first one. ☺ This should take only a few minutes.

I hope you noticed the following:

➤ Different structure of name of the case. You will note that I have not said 'name of the parties'. Very often the name of the case is the name of the parties, but sometimes it is not. For your immediate purposes it will rarely matter, except that sometimes the same case appears under different names in different series of law reports.

➤ Different shapes of brackets (see box).

➤ Different abbreviations. Not only will each series of law reports have its own abbreviation, which is what you would expect, but sometimes the same series have two abbreviations (for example, some people use All ER as the abbreviation for *All England Law Reports* and some use AER), and sometimes two completely different series have the same abbreviation (for example, in the HKU Library are four series for which the abbreviation is FLR — meaning either *Financial Law Reports* or *Family Law Reports* or *Fiji Law Reports* or *Federal Law Reports*).

It is also possible, not unnaturally, that you may find yourself with information that is incomplete or wrong — you may make an

Shapes of Brackets

References to reported cases and to articles in journals will very often contain a date and a volume number. Sometimes the date is in square brackets — [ ] — and sometimes in round — ( ).

If the date is in a **square** bracket the year is an essential part of the reference; without the year you will not find the volume. Very probably there are several volumes published each year, and if you note just 'volume 2', for example, you may find that there are many volume 2s. If the brackets are round the number alone would be enough to find the volume; in other words the number is unique. Sometimes a volume may cover more than one year, but the reference to a case may give only the year in which the case was decided, which will, therefore, not correspond precisely to what is on the spine of the book. If there is only one volume each year, it sometimes happens that the reference is that date only; there is no volume number. In this instance, since the year is essential, it will be in square brackets.

(continued)

incomplete note of the reference, or your teacher may give you incomplete information (incredible as it may seem, we do make mistakes!), or even a book may contain an error, while in some countries they are less fastidious than I would wish about references, especially about brackets (it is very difficult to convince a typist or a printer who is not a lawyer that this matters!). So you may find you have no case name, or the wrong bracket, or the wrong year, or no year or no page or the wrong volume number, and so on.

However, for the moment let us assume that you have the complete information. What are the stages of the process in finding the case?

The same conventions apply to the law journals as to the law reports. The more normal pattern is for the year to be in round brackets and the volume number to be different each year. There are a few examples of year-only citations, thus the year is in square brackets, for example, *Public Law*.

US Law Reports: The convention in the US is to give volume number, abbreviation, page followed by the year in round brackets.

– What does the abbreviation stand for? Try:
  • the list in Appendix III of this book,
  • the other sources mentioned in the box.

> Raistrick, *Index to Legal Citations and Abbreviations* (2nd ed. London: Bowker-Saur, 1993) is the fullest list.
>
> You will also find lists of abbreviations in Legal Dictionaries such as Curzon or Osborne.

❖ Look up FLR in Raistrick. How many meanings can you find for this abbreviation? How many of these reports are in your University Library? ☺ You should be able to do this in less than ten minutes.

– Is the series in the library?

– If yes, where are they?

➤ Watch out for the possibility that reports may be shelved somewhere unexpected, especially if they are part of a publication which combines a law journal with law reports. For example, in the past the *Australian Law Journal Reports* were bound together with the Journal; now they are bound, and should be shelved, separately. The *Malayan Law Journal* contains more cases than articles, but may be shelved with the journals, and the *Criminal Law Review*, which is mainly articles, but sometimes has the only report of a case (but this will be a summary, not a full report) is usually shelved with the journals.

Some law reports are part of large publications such as CCH Hong Kong Revenue Legislation.

– From there on it should be simple. ➤ Make sure you get the right volume if the year is in round brackets. Don't worry if the year you have been given is not the year on the spine of the book. The year may be that of the actual case. The volume number should be correct.

❖ If you are a first year student go **now** (or as soon as possible) and identify the location in your library of all the series of law reports. Identify the different jurisdictions. How are they arranged: alphabetically, or are countries in the same region of the world grouped together?

Within each jurisdiction: are the law reports in alphabetical order or arranged in some other way?

☺ You could not do this in less than 30 minutes.

Familiarize yourself with the law reports, especially with the series you are likely to use most often. The cases you are most likely to want to find will be in the:
Hong Kong Law Reports
Hong Kong Public Law Reports and Digest
Hong Kong Cases

and in the following series of English reports:
The Law Reports Appeal Cases
The Law Reports Chancery
The Law Reports Queen's Bench
The Law Reports Family
The Weekly Law Reports
The All England Reports

❖ To help get yourself oriented, as you go round try to find the first three cases listed near the beginning of this section. They should be quite easy.

Some Tips

You might wonder how you could distinguish between law reports with the same abbreviation! Take FLR (see above). If you have a case with this name:

Sherry v Sherry [1991] 1 FLR 307

how would you know which series it is in? Use your common sense! Is it very likely that you would be referred to the *Fiji Law Reports*? Is there not a good chance that you will know from the context whether the case is (a) about family law or (b) about financial matters or (c) from Australia and therefore likely to be in the *Federal Law Reports* even before you start looking? There may be other clues which you will learn to pick out, for example, that a case involving a company with (Pty) in its name is likely to be Australian. Or that in this case the parties both have the same name; this often indicates a divorce case, which means it is likely to be (as this one is) in the *Family Law Reports*.

Suppose you have lots of references to the same case like this:

> *Lam Chi-ming v The Queen* [1991] 2 AC 212, [1991] 2 WLR 1082, [1991] 3 All ER 172, (1991) 135 SJ (LB) 445, [1991] Crim LR 914, *Daily Telegraph* April 18 1991 (PC)

How would you know which one to go to first? As you will see from the section above on law reporting in England, the first one would be the first choice. After that the *All England Reports*, then the *Weekly Law Reports*. Go to the others only if desperate since they will be brief summaries, not full reports.

Note that this has a Chinese name and that the case was before the PC — the Privy Council. This suggests there is a good chance it is a Hong Kong case and you would also find it in the *Hong Kong Law Reports*. Indeed, there it is: [1991] 2 HKLR 191. (Try also the *Hong Kong Cases* or *Hong Kong Public Law Reports* as appropriate.) By the same token, if you are given the HKLR or HKC reference for a Privy Council case, there is a good chance it will also be in the *Law Reports Appeal Cases*, and therefore also in the *Weekly Law Reports*, at least. So if 100 students are all looking for the same case you may find it in a variety of places.

Finding the Reprinted Nominate Reports

Suppose you want to find one of those old cases? In 2 Crompton, Meeson & Roscoe on page 659, you would find this case (see p. 66):

MICHAELMAS TERM, 6 WILL. IV.   659

Exch. of Pleas,
1835.

NICOLLS *v.* BASTARD, Esq.

TROVER against the late sheriff of *Devonshire*, for divers cattle, goods, and chattels, to wit, thirty horses, thirty mares, thirty bulls, thirty cows, &c.; hay, corn, furniture, &c. Pleas, *first*, not guilty; *secondly*, that the cattle, goods, and chattels, in the declaration mentioned, were not, nor was any or either of them, the property of the plaintiff, in manner and form, &c.; *thirdly*, that one *J. Horne* was possessed of the said cattle, goods, and chattels, in the declaration mentioned, and in order to avoid an execution about to be levied upon his goods, fraudulently sold the same to the plaintiff; that a writ of execution against the goods of *Horne* (which was set out) being delivered to the defendant, he seized the cattle, goods and chattels, in the declaration mentioned, under such writ. Replication to the third plea, that *Horne* did not, for the purpose of fraudulently preventing the said cattle, goods, and chattels in the declaration mentioned from being taken in execution, sell them to the plaintiff: and issue thereon. The particular of demand comprised only " one cow." At the trial before *Gurney*, B., at the last *Devonshire* Assizes, it was proved that the plaintiff was the owner of a cow, which he had lent to *Horne*, to be kept in his pasture, where it was seized by the defendant under the execution. For the defence, the writ and proceedings under it were given in evidence; and it was proved that a great quantity of property was sold by auction by *Horne*, in order to avoid the execution, a large part of which was purchased by the plaintiff; that the plaintiff's cow was put into the catalogue, but was not sold; nor was any cow sold at all. The defendant's counsel contended, that the

In the case of the simple bailment of a chattel, without reward, it may be recovered in trover, either by the bailor or the bailee, if taken wrongfully out of the bailee's possession.

Trover for horses, cows, furniture, &c. &c. Plea, that *J. H.* was possessed of the cattle, goods, and chattels in the declaration mentioned, and fraudulently sold them to the plaintiff, to avoid an execution against the goods of *J. H.*, and that the defendant (the sheriff) seized them under such execution. Replication, that *J. H.* did not fraudulently sell the cattle, goods, and chattels in the declaration mentioned to the plaintiff; and issue thereon. The particular of demand was merely " one cow." It appeared that the plaintiff had lent a cow to *J. H.*; that the goods of *J. H.* were fraudu-

lently sold to avoid an execution, and the greater part of them bought by the plaintiff; that the plaintiff's cow was not sold, nor was any cow sold at such sale:—*Held*, that the plaintiff was entitled to a verdict on the above issue.

The plea of no property in the plaintiff, in trover, means no property *as against the defendant.*

This case was cited in a 1992 case.

O'Sullivan and another v Williams

COURT OF APPEAL, CIVIL DIVISION
FOX, STAUGHTON AND BELDAM LJJ
11 FEBRUARY, 6 MARCH 1992

Bailment – Damage to bailed chattel – Damage caused by third party – Separate claims by bailor and bailee – Claim by bailee against tortfeasor for loss or damage to bailed chattel – Bailor's motor vehicle damaged by third party while in bailee's care – Bailor and bailee bringing joint action against tortfeasor for loss of use of car – Bailor's claim settled – Whether bailee entitled to damages from tortfeasor for loss of use of car.

The first plaintiff allowed his girlfriend, the second plaintiff, to use his car while he was away on holiday. While the car was parked outside her home it was irreparably damaged when an excavator, which was on a trailer being towed by the defendant, toppled off the trailer onto it. The plaintiffs brought an action against the defendant in which the first plaintiff claimed £1,300 as the value of the car and damages for loss of use of the car since the accident at £25 per week and the second plaintiff claimed damages for nervous shock and other distress, and for inconvenience in not having the use of the car to get to work and for social purposes. The first plaintiff's claim was settled without prejudice to the second plaintiff's claim. The judge dismissed the second plaintiff's claim for damages for nervous shock and other distress but awarded her £400 damages for loss of the use of the car. The defendant appealed against that award.

Held – A bailee could not sue and recover damages arising from loss or damage to the bailed chattel if the bailor had already recovered damages against the wrongdoer in respect of the tortious damage to the chattel, since there could not be separate claims by the bailor and the bailee arising from loss of or damage to the chattel. If the bailor recovered damages and the bailee had some interest in the property enforceable against the bailor, then the bailor was required to account appropriately to the bailee. It followed that since the first plaintiff's claim in respect of loss of use of the car had been settled, the second plaintiff had no claim against the defendant. The defendant's appeal against the award of damages to the second plaintiff would therefore be allowed (see p 387 *j*, p 388 *a* to *c g h* and p 389 *a b*, post).

The Winkfield [1900–3] All ER Rep 346 and *Nicolls v Bastard* [1835–42] All ER Rep 429 applied.

Notes
For damage to chattels and loss of use of non-profit-earning chattel, see 12 *Halsbury's Laws* (4th edn) paras 1163, 1165, 1167.

Cases referred to in judgments
Brunsden v Humphrey (1884) 14 QBD 141, [1881–5] All ER Rep 357, CA.
Elliott Steam Tug Co Ltd v Shipping Controller [1922] 1 KB 127, CA.
Leigh & Sillavan Ltd v Aliakmon Shipping Co Ltd, The Aliakmon [1986] 2 All ER 145, [1986] AC 785, [1986] 2 WLR 902, HL.
Nicolls v Bastard (1835) 2 Cr M & R 659, [1835–42] All ER Rep 429, 150 ER 279.
Winkfield, The [1902] P 42, [1900–3] All ER Rep 346, CA.

Cases also cited
Caparo Industries plc v Dickman [1990] 1 All ER 568, [1990] AC 605, HL.

Here you will see the editor (or maybe the judge or counsel) has supplied the *English Reports* citation. But you will not always be so lucky. Let us suppose you do not have available either the original report or the citation in a reprint. You will remember that old cases are often reprinted in the *Revised Reports* or the *English Reports* (see previous unit). *Nicolls v Bastard* actually appears in both. ➤ It is better to try the *English Reports* first because they contain far more cases. However, there are some cases in the *Revised Reports* which are not in the *English Reports*.

(A) The English Reports

There are three ways to find a case in here.

1. Hanging up near the shelves which include the *English Reports,* you should find a chart which list the names of the old reports. Then there is the abbreviation, and then the volume of the ER in which this old volume is reprinted.

    This method has two drawbacks:

    (i) The first item is not the abbreviation, which is what you will be looking for, but the full name of the reports, which is sometimes a little different from the abbreviation (e.g. the reports produced by Lord Coke may be abbreviated as Co. Rep. or just as Rep. (They were so highly thought of that they were just known as The Reports!)
    (ii) ➤ Some abbreviations do not appear on the chart at all, even though the reports are actually there (e.g. *Viners Equity Abridgement* has several abbreviations, one of which, Vin Abr., does not appear on the chart). There is a better chart in *Where to Look for Your Law* (see below), but rather than searching for this, it is better to rely on method 2.

2. Find the Index volumes (vols 177 & 178) and look up the case name, and you will find the original report and the reference in the *English Reports*.

    Method 2 also has the advantage that you can see if there are other reports of the same case. It has the slight disadvantage that you have to pick up two heavy volumes before reaching your goal — and someone else might be using the Index volume!

3. Method 3 is to be used only by those familiar with the reports: each volume of the ER has on its spine a note of which old volumes it contains. If you know your way around you may be able to find the relevant volume pretty quickly by looking at the spine (this is helped by the fact that the *English Reports* are grouped so that all the volumes with, for example, King Bench cases, come in sequence). On the other hand, if you do **not** know your way around, this method can waste a lot of time!

An example: Go back to the case of *Nicolls v Bastard* for which, you will recall, the citation is (1835) 2 Cr. M. & R. 659. If you look in the chart (or in a bound version of the chart which is kept at the end of the set of reports) you will find:

TABLE OF ENGLISH REPORTS 7

Old Reports.	Volume in English Reports.	Abbreviation.	Period covered (approximate).	Series.
Common Bench, 1 & 2	135			
,, ,, 3–6	136			
,, ,, 7–9	137	C.B.	1845–1856	C.P.
,, ,, 10–13	138			
,, ,, 14–16	139			
Common Bench, New Series, 1–4	140			
,, ,, ,, 5–8	141			
,, ,, ,, 9–12	142	C.B. N.S.	1857–1866	C.P.
,, ,, ,, 13–16	143			
,, ,, ,, 17–20	144			
Comyns, 1 & 2	92	Com.	1695–1741	K.B.
Cooke	125	Cooke.	1706–1747	C.P.
Cooper C. P. or Cooper's Practice Cases	47	C. P. Coop. or Coop. Pr. Ca.	1837–1838	Ch.
Crompton & Jervis, 1	148	Cr. & J.	1830–1832	Ex.
,, ,, 2	149			
Crompton & Meeson, 1 & 2	149	Cr. & M.	1832–1834	Ex.
Crompton, Meeson & Roscoe, 1	149	Cr. M. & R.	1834–1835	Ex.
,, ,, ,, 2	150			
Cunningham	94	Cun.	1734–1736	K.B.
Curteis, 1–3	163	Curt.	1834–1844	Ecc. Adm. P. & D.

Column 1 gives the name and volume number of the original report, column 2 the corrsponding volume of the *English Reports*, column 3 the common abbreviation, column 4 the approximate period the reports covered and column 5 the sub-series of the *English Reports* (they are divided according to courts covered).

The Chart in *Where to Look for Your Law* (a rather elderly book, no new edition since 1963) is clearer:

```
Cromp.      .. Star Chamber Cases,
              by Crompton
Cromp. & Jer. Crompton & Jervis .. Ex. .. 2 1830–1832  148–9
Cromp. & M. Crompton & Meeson  Ex. .. 2 1832–1834  149
Cromp.,     Crompton, Meeson &
  M. & R.     Roscoe  ..    .. Ex. .. 2 1834–1836  149–50
Crow.       .. Crowther's  Reports,
```

Raistrick will also include the information, though perhaps slightly less clearly:

```
Cromp.Just.  Crompton's Office of        Cru.Us.  Cruise on Uses
   Justice of the Peace. 1637           Cruchaga  Cruchaga-Tocornal,
Cromp.M.& R.  Crompton, Meeson &           Nociones de Derecho internacional.
   Roscoe's Exchequer Reports               3ed. 1923–25
   (149–50 ER) 1834–5                    Cruise Dig.  Cruise's Digest of the Law
Cromp.R.& C.Pr.  Crompton's Rules          of Real Property. 4ed. 1835
   and Cases of Practice                 Crump Ins.  Crump on Marine
```

Go to Volume 150 of the ER.
The spine looks like this:

Inside you will find this page:

which it appeared that the action was on a promissory note for 30l.; that the bail were rejected because they were not described in the affidavit of justification as housekeepers, and stated themselves to be possessed, instead of worth, the requisite amount. No other bail had been perfected or put in. They now swore that they were housekeepers, and were worth the amount required. He contended that they were not, however, entitled to set aside the attachment; otherwise bail had only to give an imperfect description of themselves, and get rejected, in order to get rid of the proceedings against the sheriff.

Tyndale, contrà, referred to Tidd's Practice, 317 (8th ed.), where it is said, "The practice, when the sheriff has been fixed, is to move for a rule to shew cause why, on putting in bail, the proceedings against him should not be set aside, and to have the bail ready to justify when the rule is disposed of." The present rule was obtained on the terms of rendering the defendant, which is equivalent to justifying bail. [Parke, B. You can justify bail, [657] or render, and then move. There is a difference between the practice in proceedings on the bail-bond and in attachments against the sheriff; perhaps the passage you have cited has confounded them.] The reference there given, to the judgment of Buller, J., in *Williams v. Waterfield* (1 Bos. & P. 334), supports the statement as applying to the case of an attachment. [Parke, B. At all events, the rule must not be drawn up until the defendant has actually rendered. The practice has certainly been generally understood to be otherwise.]

Wightman suggested that this application was virtually the same as if it had been to set aside proceedings on the bail-bond; being made, not on behalf of the sheriff, but of the bail.

Some difficulty occurred in settling the terms of the rule, so as to secure the immediate render of the defendant; and

PARKE, B., said,—The difficulty of arranging the terms of the render shews the convenience of what we understood to be the practice. If we make this rule absolute, it is not to be understood as deciding that the same course is to be pursued in future.

Wightman urged, that if the Court thought a departure from that which had been considered to be the established practice would lead to inconvenience, it would be advisable not to introduce such a precedent. And ultimately the rule was

Discharged without costs.

[658] STAINES *v.* STONEHAM. Exch. of Pleas. 1835.—The plaintiff cannot have the bail-bond to stand as a security where he has not declared de bene esse, although he was prevented from declaring by the vacation.

[S. C. 1 Tyr. & G. 193; 4 Dowl. P. C. 678; 1 Gale, 327; 5 L. J. Ex. 15.]

A rule had been obtained to stay proceedings on the bail-bond on payment of costs, the defendant having been rendered; and the only question was, whether the bail-bond should stand as a security or not. The arrest was on the 2nd of October. The plaintiff had not declared de bene esse. The assignment of the bail-bond was taken on the 20th of October.

Blackburne, for the plaintiff, urged, that, inasmuch as by the 2 Will. 4, c. 39, s. 11, no declaration could be filed or delivered between the 10th of August and the 10th of October, and therefore it was impossible for the plaintiff to have declared de bene esse before he took the assignment of the bail-bond, the rule of Court could not apply to this case. The plaintiff had lost a trial through the defendant's irregularity.

But per Curiam. The rule of Court entitles the plaintiff to have the bail-bond to stand as a security only where he has declared de bene esse. He has not complied with the condition, because he could not; he cannot, therefore, entitle himself to the benefit. He brought upon himself the loss of the trial, by taking an assignment of the bail-bond.

Rule absolute.

⇨ [659] NICOLLS *v.* BASTARD, ESQ. Exch. of Pleas. 1835.—In the case of the simple bailment of a chattel, without reward, it may be recovered in trover, either by the bailor or the bailee, if taken wrongfully out of the bailee's possession.—Trover for horses, cows, furniture, &c. &c. Plea, that J. H. was possessed

(B) The Revised Reports [1]

It is easier to find a case in the *Revised Reports* simply by looking at the spine: the spines give not only the names of the reports reprinted but the dates covered by the volume. However, there is a volume which lists all the cases reprinted, just as with the *English Reports*. Incidentally, there are also two subject index volumes to the *Revised Reports*. (There is also a 'Preface' to each volume written by the principal editor, Frederick Pollock, containing his sometimes entertainingly expressed comments on a few of the cases in the volume.)

You will find *Nicolls v Bastard* in the *Revised Reports* (volume 41 page 814), and you could do this by either of the methods mentioned above.

It may not have escaped your notice that there in another reference for this case in the 1992 case: [1835–42] All ER Rep 429. This refers to the *All England Reports Reprint*. As it happens the case was also reported by two other series of reports at the same time as Crompton Meeson and Roscoe reported it: 1 Gale 295 and Tyr & Gr 156. The last report is by Tyrwhitt & Granger, and some of this volume is reprinted in the *Revised Reports*, but not this case. It is not reprinted at all in the *English Reports*, while Mr Gale's report was not thought worthy of reprinting in either series.

❖ Find the following cases with a friend or two. ☺ It may well take you 45 minutes.

> *Levy v Attorney-General* (1987) 90 ILR 412
> *Re: A Lawyer's Professional Negligence* [1990] 3 CMLR 415
> *R v Depardo* (1807) 9 RR 693, 127 ER 739, 168 ER 723
> **Barnes v Addy* (1874) LR 9 Ch App 244
> **Jenkins v Deane* (1933) 103 LJKB 250
> *R v McCarthy* (1982) 4 Cr App R (S) 364
> *Wong v Cook* (1979) 102 DLR (3d) 61
> *Michigan Dept of State Police v Sitz* (1990) 110 L Ed 2d 412

Maybe you will notice the following peculiarities: a Hong Kong case in an unexpected place; reports which contain cases from a large number of jurisdictions; there are three reports of *R v Depardo* — are they all the same? Maybe LR 9 Ch App was a bit difficult to find? What type of cases does Cr App R (S) contain? I hope you noticed that *Wong v Cook* is in the 3rd series of the DLR! Incidentally, does anything surprise you about the date (1979)? What is the date on the spine of 103 LJKB? And what does 'L Ed' mean in the final reference?

---

1   📖 The *Revised Reports* are available in the HKU Library but not the City U Library.

UNREPORTED JUDGMENTS

Until now the majority of Hong Kong cases have remained unreported. This is improving as the new series *Hong Kong Cases* is published. The publishers are determined to publish a far higher proportion of cases.

➤ Before you accept the necessity to find an unreported Hong Kong case, make sure it is not reported. If it is you will save yourself a lot of trouble, and have a more informative version of the case. You will probably find occasionally a reference to a case as though it is unreported even though it is in fact reported. Why? Probably because the author found the case when it was still unreported and failed to check later whether it had been reported. ➤ Even quite old cases may have been reported quite recently in *Hong Kong Cases*, so it is worth checking there. Try the Index volume if it is available (or, even better, the *Consolidated Index of All Reported Hong Kong Decisions* which covers the *Hong Kong Cases* **and** the *Hong Kong Law Reports* up to 1995).

It may well be easier to find a case using the number rather than the name. If you have a name only, you could try to find the number through the CD-ROM of the *Hong Kong Law Digest*.

You can find the actual cases in two forms: in paper form, and in one CD-ROM of *Hong Kong Cases* (only from 1996) — see p. 74.

The judgments are made available in A4 photocopied form. This means that they may be organized differently in different libraries. They may be bound into volumes or kept in files. The way of organizing them may vary — by case number, the reference number at the top of the case, or by date of decision.

In the box below you will find a note on how the various Hong Kong law libraries organize these cases:

📖 Organizing the Unreported Judgments

In HKU Library and City U Library from 1977 to 1988, the cases are bound into volumes in series:

Lands Tribunal Rating Appeals	Bankruptcy
Lands Tribunal (Other)	Court of Appeal Criminal Cases
Admiralty	Inland Revenue Appeals
High Court Civil Actions	Appeal Cases: Divorce
Court of Appeal Civil Appeals	Miscellaneous Prceedings
Commercial List	Privy Council Appeals
Probate	Stamp Appeals [Stamp duty]
Small Claims Tribunal Appeals	Labour Tribunal Appeals

and organized by case number.

(continued)

City U Law Library since 1988 — The cases are in loose-leaf binders, not divided as above, and in case number order.

Supreme Court Library — The cases are bound into volumes (divided into series):

Criminal Appeals	High Court Sentencing
Civil Appeals	Personal Injury
High Court Civil Actions	District Court
Admiralty	Miscellaneous

Within each volume each case is given a Folio Number, and there is a list in order on the front of each volume. The cases themselves are not rigidly in order, but are roughly in order of judgment. There is a card index of case numbers, from which you can find the volume and folio numbers.

A similar system has been adapted in the University of Hong Kong Library for more recent judgments.

ELECTRONIC ACCESS TO UNREPORTED JUDGMENTS

 However, some unreported judgements are now available on the *Hong Kong Cases* CD-ROM — I suppose you could say they are reported in electronic format.

The publisher says:

'4. Citations of unreported judgments — HKCU

To facilitate reference to unreported judgments which appear on this CD-ROM, the Publisher has devised and added a citation system for unreported judgments as follows:
[1998] HKCU 1

where the year in brackets refers to the year of judgment, HKCU refers to Hong Kong Cases Unreported and 1 refers to the case reference number under this citation system.'

Note also the judgments of the Court of Final Appeal at
<**http://www.info.gov.hk/jud/guide2cs/html/cfa/judmt/index.html**>.

SELF-STUDY QUESTIONS

◷ Fifteen minutes.

1. What do the following abbreviations stand for: WLR, AC, All ER, HKC, HKCLR, HKPLR, QB, FLR?

2. If you have a reference to a case in each of the following, which series will you prefer to find the case in, and why? — All ER, QB, WLR.

3. Give three ways of finding an unreported Hong Kong case of which you have the name and a rough idea of the date.

4. Are you more likely to find a case from a nominate report in the *English Reports* or the *Revised Reports*?

Unit 7 Finding Cases (II)

OBJECTIVES

By the end of this Unit you will:

- be able to find a case even though you have only the name and not the full citation
- be able to trace how later courts have dealt with a case
- be able to find a case on a particular topic

☺ It may take you as long as three hours if you do the exercises.

FINDING A REFERENCE TO A CASE WHEN YOU KNOW THE NAME

Occasionally you will want to find the reference to a case when you have only its name. By and large this should not happen, since it means someone (you or another) has given or noted incomplete information. It can happen if you have a vague recollection of a case which you have learned about or read but do not have the source of your information handy.

The most usual technique is to use a textbook. This may seem so obvious as not to be worth saying, but the fact is that unless the case is obscure it is likely to be discussed in some standard work on the area of law. ➤ I would recommend that you go to a **practitioner** text. In most areas of the law there are books written for the lawyer rather than for the student. These are expensive (because lawyers can pay!) and detailed. This extends to the table of cases, which will usually contain the reference to the report as well as the name of the case, whereas a student text will often just give the case name and you then have to go to the page in the text to find the reference.

❖ Take a look at the table of cases of a practitioner text and you will see what I mean. ☺ It should only take a few minutes.

Standard practitioner texts include Clerk & Lindsell on **Tort**, Chitty on **Contracts**, Gatley on **Libel and Slander**, Charlesworth on **Negligence** (they are shelved with other books, and you will just have to learn by experience which are the practitioner and which the student books; you should also note ➤ which are English books, as opposed to Australian, Canadian, etc., and the title does not always indicate this). There are fewer practititioner books on Hong Kong law (e.g. Sihombing & Wilkinson on **Conveyancing**) and the volumes of *Halsbury's Laws of Hong Kong* will also be helpful.

For Hong Kong cases also try:

- *The Consolidated Index to the Hong Kong Law Reports for 1905–1967* and the Supplementary volume for 1968–70.

- *Consolidated Index to Hong Kong Cases*. The first volume of this publication covered 1946–1995. Eventually there will be a set of volumes covering the entire period which the law reports series will cover, namely from 1843.

- Addison: a judge who compiled a number of indexes to Hong Kong cases:
  A Digest of Hong Kong Civil Case Law 1954–1968
  A Digest of Hong Kong Civil Case Law 1969–1975
  A Digest of Hong Kong Civil Case Law 1976–1980
  A Digest of Hong Kong Civil Case Law 1981–1991
  A Digest of Hong Kong Criminal Case Law 1905–1967
  A Digest of Hong Kong Criminal Case Law 1968–1973
  A Digest of Hong Kong Criminal Case Law 1974–1977
  A Digest of Hong Kong Criminal Case Law 1978–1980
  A Digest of Hong Kong Criminal Case Law 1981–1985
  A Digest of Hong Kong Criminal Case Law 1986–1988
  Supplement 1990 and 1991
  Digest and Consolidated Index of the District Court Law Reports of Hong Kong 1953–1971
  Digest and Consolidated Index of the District Court Law Reports of Hong Kong 1972–1973

- If the case falls outside these periods, try the annual volumes of the HKLR.

- The *Consolidated Index to All Hong Kong Reported Decisions* covers both major series to the end of 1995 as well as the other series of Hong Kong law reports and other series which include Hong Kong cases such as *Appeal Cases, Fleet Street Reports, Lloyd's List Law Reports*. (Most of these report Privy Council cases.)

- If the case is unreported, try the *Hong Kong Law Digest*. (To find the actual text see Unit 6.)

For English cases:

- You could also use the *Current Law Case Citator* (but see * below). ➤ The purpose of this publication is to show in which later cases a case has been cited. But it is also useful to find the reference to the report of any case which has been cited. For some cases it does not seem to give all the references to the reports of a case (which you might want to see if your classmates are using all the obvious reports of a case, or if your library does not have the report for which you have the citation).

  You will find *Current Law Case Citator 1947–76* which gives every case reported or cited in those years, and many of those cited will be much older. This is followed by *Current Law Case Citator 1977–88*. Each year since then there has been a volume, covering 1989 onwards.

- * The current editions do not give the full citation to the original case, unless it is itself reported in the same period. To see what I mean, look at the two extracts from the Citator below on the case of *Anns v Merton*. The earlier one is from the 1977–88 volume. The other is from the 1989–1994 volume. This does not give you the main reference for *Anns*, only the year. You could clearly now find the case, but an extra stage is involved. (The only citations given for *Anns* are to new reports published since the 1977–88 volume was published.)

CASE CITATOR 1977–88   **ANT**

Anna Ch., The. *See* Islamic Republic of Iran Shipping Lines v. Royal Bank of Scotland;
    Anna Ch., The.
Anna Maria, The [1980] 1 Lloyd's Rep. 192 ....*Digested,* 80/**76**
Annamunthodo v. Oilfields Workers' Trade Union [1961] ....*Distinguished,* 79/**14**
Annandale and Hartfell (Earldom of) [1986] A.C. 319, H.L. ....*Not digested*
Annangel Glory Compania Naviera S.A. v. Golodetz, Middle East Marketing Corp.;
    Annangel Glory, The. 1988 PCC 37; [1988] 1 Lloyd's Rep. 45 ....*Digested,* 88/**301**
Annangel Glory, The. *See* Annangel Glory Compania Naviera S.A. v. Goldetz (M.)
    Middle East Marketing Corp. (U.K.) and Hammand (C.R.); Annangel Glory, The.
Annefield, The [1971] ....*Considered,* 84/3156: *Referred to,* 83/3389
Annen v. Rattee (1984) 17 H.L.R. 323; [1985] E.G.L.R. 136; (1984) 273 E.G. 503, C.A. ....*Digested,* 85/**1898**
Anness v. Grivell [1915] 3 K.B. 685 ....*Followed,* 87/1818
Annie Hay, The [1968] ....*Applied,* 81/2506
Anns v. Merton London Borough Council [(1987) 137 New L.J. 794]; [1978] A.C. 728;
    [1977] 2 W.L.R. 1024; (1977) 121 S.J. 377; (1977) 75 L.G.R. 555; [1977] J.P.L.
    514; (1977) 243 E.G. 523, 591; [1977 L.G.C. 498]; [1987] L.S. 319]; *sub nom.*
    Anns v. London Borough of Merton [1977] 2 All E.R. 492, H.L.; affirming *sub*
    nom. Anns v. Walcroft Property Co. (1976) 241 E.G. 311, C.A. ....*Digested,* 77/**2030**:
                             Applied, 78/1550, 2067; 79/213, 1865, 2570; 80/198; 81/1837, 1860, 1849, 1859;
                   82/2134, 339; 83/2531, 2638, 2746; 84/2337, 3044; 85/952, 2303; 86/210;
                             87/241, 242, 2579, 2857, 3153; 88/2442:
                  Considered, 80/1878; 82/2266; 84/2298, 2300, 2566; 85/2305, 3549;
       86/2252, 2259, 87/2580, 2586, 2591, 3466; 88/2418, 2433, 2435, 2444, 2457, 3409, 3410:
                         Distinguished, 78/1547; 83/2523; 87/2709a:
   Followed, 78/2062; 80/1879; 82/766, 2125, 2133: *Referred to,* 78/2074; 79/1866, 1884;
                           83/2521; 87/3582: *Not followed,* 86/2274

(From the *Case Citator 1977–88*.)

Annibale Culin v. E.C. Commission (C–343/87) [1990] ECR I–225, European Ct.
Anns v. Merton London Borough Council [1977] [(1990) 6 P.N. 158]; [(1988) 4 Const.L.J.
100]. . . . . : . . . . *Considered,* 89/259, 469, 2559, 2564, 2566; 90/3270;
Distinguished, 92/3197; *Overruled,* 90/3288; 91/2661

(From the *Case Citator 1989–94*.)

- Try the Index volumes of *The Law Reports*. Each main volume covers ten years, and then it is supplemented by pink issues which appear several times a year. They are then consolidated into red, soft-cover volumes which cover the years since the last, main, hardback volume (thus you will find 1981–1990, a main volume, then 1991–1994, etc. to be replaced by 1991–1995). These cover only the major series of English reports. If the case you want was decided earlier, you can look at the table of 'Cases judicially considered'. This serves the same purpose as the *Current Law Case Citator*, but still gives the full citation for the cited case. Below is an extract from the 1990–1993 volume. Again this shows *Anns v Merton* and where it has been cited. It also give the reference for *Anns*.

Cases Judicially Considered

Anglo-Persian Oil Co. Ltd. v. Dale [1932] 1 K.B. 124; 16 T.C. 253, C.A. **Applied,** *Lawson v. Johnson Matthey Plc.* [1992] 2 A.C. 324; [1992] 2 W.L.R. 826, H.L.(E.)

Anisminic Ltd. v. Foreign Compensation Commission [1969] 2 A.C. 147; [1969] 2 W.L.R. 163; [1969] 1 All E.R. 208, H.L.(E.). **Considered,** *R. v. Cornwall County Council, Ex parte Huntington* [1992] 3 All E.R. 566, D.C. **Distinguished,** *Daisystar Ltd. v. Town & Country Building Society* [1992] 1 W.L.R. 390, C.A.

Annangel Glory Compagnia Naviera S.A. v. M. Golodetz Ltd. [1988] 1 Lloyd's Rep. 45. **Applied,** *Care Shipping Corpn. v. Itex Itagrani Export S.A.* [1993] Q.B. 1; [1991] 3 W.L.R. 609

Anns v. Merton London Borough Council [1978] A.C. 728; [1977] 2 W.L.R. 1024, [1977] 2 All E.R. 492, H.L.(E.). **Not applied,** *Department of the Environment v. Thomas Bates and Son Ltd.* [1991] 1 A.C. 499; [1990] 3 W.L.R. 457, H.L.(E.). **Departed from,** *Murphy v. Brentwood District Council* [1991] 1 A.C. 398; [1990] 2 W.L.R. 944, C.A.; [1991] 1 A.C. 398; [1990] 3 W.L.R. 414, H.L.(E.)

Other series of law reports also have index volumes periodically, so if you know that it is a shipping case, for example, you might well find it in the index volume of the *Lloyds Reports*.

- Another source is Volume 54 of **Halsbury's Laws of England** — the 'Consolidated Table of Cases'. This gives references to all cases cited in that legal encyclopaedia (except for recent ones). It has the disadvantage that it does not give the citation in that volume, but sends you to the relevant volume of the encyclopaedia, where you will find the citation. Thus for *Anns v Merton* you find in the Consolidated Table of Cases references to a number of volumes, for example Vol. 1 (I) 27, 28, 199, 205. You could find the full citation in any one of the places.

- The **Digest** is not recommended for this purpose. You will be sent from the Consolidated Table of Cases to the index of a particular volume, which will refer you to the individual case summary where you will finally find the citation!

In Summary: Finding a Case Knowing Only Its Name (Paper Resources Only)

All cases (especially if you are vague about the date of the case):
- a practitioner's text — table of cases

Hong Kong cases
- *Consolidated Index*
- Digest/yearbook
- Addison's

UK cases
Before 1865:
- Index volumes to *English Reports*
- *Current Law Case Citator*

After 1952, and you can pinpoint the year to within ten years:
- *Index to the Law Reports*

Any cases:
- 'Cases judicially considered' in *Index to Law Reports*
- *Current Law Case Citator*
- Volume 54 of Halsbury

➤ A good deal of frustration may be saved by thinking about the case before you try to search for it. You may well have some clues as to where and when it was decided.

➤ Using Electronic Sources

You may feel that these are more fun to use, but if you are looking for just one case it will almost certainly be quicker to find the case from paper sources. It is also easier to read a case on paper than on a screen. Finding cases by name alone is becoming much easier with the development of CD-ROMs. However, try not to let this persuade you to be lazy about noting citations. It is an irritating waste of time to have to find a case without a citation, even if it is possible.

TRACING THE HISTORY OF A CASE AFTER IT IS FIRST DECIDED

Many cases are decided, reported (though not always, especially in Hong Kong) and then are never referred to in later cases. But often a case is referred to by lawyers arguing a later case, and then by the judges, who may, as we have seen, rely upon it, follow it — which is really the same thing; they may consider it without having to follow it, they may cite it, quote from it, or may decide that it is not relevant to the case before them (distinguish it); they may decide that it was wrong and, if they have the authority to do so, overrule it. If a case goes on appeal to a higher court, which thinks the decision of the court below was wrong, they may reverse the earlier decision.

Obviously you want to know if a case has received any such treatment before you make use of it to advise a client, prepare a case, or write an essay. How do you do this?

- Use the *Current Law Case Citator**; this is precisely what it is intended for. Look back at the extract above — you will see that in the 1989–94 volume it says after the name of *Anns*: 'Considered 89/259, 469, 2559, 2564, 2566, 90/3270'. This means that *Anns* was considered in later cases which you will find digested in the *Current Law Yearbook* for 1989 para. 259, 469, etc. and in the *Yearbook* for 1990 para. 3270. In order to find the name of those cases you then have to go to the relevant Yearbook and paragraph. You may therefore find the next item more useful.

- Use the *Index to the Law Reports**, the section on cases judicially considered. ➤ I actually think this more helpful than the previous publication; it tells you a little more clearly how the earlier case was treated, and gives you the citation to the later case straight away, rather than sending you to the relevant volume and paragraph of *Current Law* as the citator does. ➤ The disadvantages are that only certain law reports are covered, mainly the Incorporated Council reports and the *All England Reports*, and it seems to omit certain cases cited even in those reports.

- If you want to know what has happened to a case **in Hong Kong** (whether the case you are interested in is itself a Hong Kong case or from somewhere else), you will find a 'Cases judicially considered' section in the Index to the HKLR and in *Hong Kong Cases* including in the *Consolidated Index* and in the *Hong Kong Law Digest* (previously called *Hong Kong Current Law*) and its annual version the *Hong Kong Law Digest Yearbook**. (See the extract on p. 83 from the *Consolidated Index* of the *Hong Kong Cases*.) ➤ You will see that this is less useful than a case citator, since it just says where the earlier case was cited, not whether it was followed, distinguished, etc.

However, you will find that the earlier editions of the *Index to the Hong Kong Law Reports* are more helpful. Those for 1905–67 and 1968–75 do indicate whether a case was applied, distinguished, etc. That for 1976–83 does not. Now the individual issues and the annual volumes contain a 'Noter-up' which gives this information but ➤ it does not cover all cases mentioned in the cases reported.

From the Index Volume to *Hong Kong Cases*

TABLE OF CASES CITED

A-G v Chan Chi Man [1987] HKLR 221 152
A-G v Chan Tak King [1989] 2 HKLR 428 555
A-G v Cheung Pit Yiu [1989] 2 HKLR 12 555
A-G v Fong Chin Yue [1995] 1 HKC 21 53
A-G v Lee Ching Kwong [1987] 2 HKC 563 555
A-G v Lee Kwong Kut [1993] AC 951 53
A-G v Lui Kam Chi [1993] 1 HKC 215 747
A-G v So Chin Chiu [1994] 1 HKC 131 152
A-G v Tsui Kwok Leung [1991] 1 HKLR 40 24
A-G v Tuen Shui Ming [1995] 2 HKC 798 152
A-G v Wan Wing Tak [1994] 1 HKCLR 191 457
A-G v Wong Kwai Lok [1984] HKLR 364 90
A-G v Wong Kwok Wai [1991] 2 HKLR 384 751
A-G v Wong Sai Cheong (AR 1/85, unreported) 457
A-G v Yau Wing Hong [1995] 3 HKC 95 751
Abouloff v Oppenheimer & Co (1882) 10 QBD 295 444
Air 2000 Ltd v Secretary of State for Transport [1989] SLT 698,
    [1990] SLT 335 209
Allen v Flood [1898] AC 1 461
Allen v Sir Alfred McAlpine & Sons Ltd [1968] 1 All ER 543 95

There are similar publications for other jurisdictions, which may be available. *Canadian Current Law*, the *Australian Digest,* are examples. There is also an *Australian and New Zealand Citator of English Cases** cited in those two countries, published by Butterworths.

It **may** be worth using electronic searching means to find out the subsequent history of a case (see next section). In fact, since the Citators in the Hong Kong paper publications are not as good as those in the UK ones, it may be more useful to use the Hong Kong CDs. If you are looking for the history of cases in the UK, it is almost certainly as quick to use the paper version of the Citators discussed above.

Unit 12 gives details about the use of reference materials such as *Halsbury's Laws of England*, *The Digest*, the *Hong Kong Law Digest*, the *Canadian Abridgement*, the *Australian Legal Monthly Digest* and so on.

❖ Find each of the publications referred to above which has an asterisk (*) against it. In each case find the list of 'Cases cited' or 'Cases referred to' — except in the case of the *Current Law Case Citator*, which has no other function. See how they could be used in the following ways: to provide you with a reference when you have only the name of the case, and to show you how later cases have dealt with the case.

◷ It will take just a few minutes for each publication.

FINDING A CASE ON A PARTICULAR TOPIC

Suppose you are writing an essay or preparing for a moot, or even for a class, and you need to find cases on a topic, but you have no idea where to begin. You can approach this in a number of ways, some of which you have encountered in this Unit or the previous one, and some of which will be discussed in more detail later (see Unit 12).

- If you just need basic cases, and the point you are interested in does not seem very obscure, try a student textbook.

- For something rather more detailed try a practitioners' book (see first section in this Unit). Or try the practitioners' encyclopaedias, such as *Halsbury's Laws of England* or *Halsbury's Laws of Hong Kong* (See Unit 12).

For Hong Kong:

- *The Consolidated Index to all Reported Hong Kong Decisions* Vol. 2 (1998) contains a Subject Index to cases reported in Hong Kong and UK law reports until the end of 1997, arranged under the same subject headings as *Halsbury's Laws of Hong Kong* (see p. 172).

- The various sources listed above for finding cases by name also have subject indexes: the index volumes of the *Hong Kong Law Reports*, of *Hong Kong Cases*, and the various *Digests* by Addison. (Now *Hong Kong Cases* has a Chinese subject index.)

- The *Hong Kong Law Digest,* which is discussed in detail in Unit 12, is also designed mainly to be used as a topic-by-topic summary of recent developments including cases.

For the UK:

- Again the sources mentioned above, especially the *Law Reports Index* will be useful, and *Current Law* (see Unit 12).

Finding Hong Kong Unreported Judgments by Subject

- The best method is through the *Hong Kong Law Digest/Yearbook* (see Unit 12).

- Secondly Addison's *Digest*. Some of the Digests include a few unreported cases, namely:

    - Criminal: 1968–73, 1974–77, 1978–80, 1981–85, 1986–89. Not, therefore, the 1990 and 1991 *Supplement.*
    - Civil: 1981–91

Note: you can use this *Digest* to search for cases by subject, or, if you know the name, to find the summary using the list of cases at the beginning of the volume.

- The *Basic Law Bill of Rights Bulletin* has full reports and summaries of Bill of Rights cases.

- Beginning with 1996 there are now some unreported decisions in the *Hong Kong Cases* CD-ROM — see p. 74. You can carry out a search on the full text of these.

 It is for finding reported cases by topic that electronic resources will be most useful. There are now several series of law reports available in CD format, and more will no doubt become so. Here is some information about two Hong Kong series and one from the UK.

Hong Kong Cases on CD-ROM

To see how this works, ❖ try to see how many cases there have been in Hong Kong on nervous shock, at least as reported in the *Hong Kong Cases*. Follow these steps (⊘ 20 minutes):

Click on the little icon called Query (along the top). In the Box which opens, type "Nervous shock". You will be told how many times each word appears and how many times as the phrase you have asked for. If you use quotation marks it searches for one phrase. If you don't it looks for all cases in which both words appear.

Click OK. The first 'hit' will appear on the screen.

However, you may want to see just what you have found before you start to look at individual cases. So click on the icon called 'Contents'. You should then see a screen saying something like:

7 + Hong Kong Cases on CD-ROM

7 being the number of hits — it may be more by the time you do it.

Click on the + and you will see a list of all the volumes of law reports in the database with a number indicating how many hits in each volume if any. For example, I found:

3 + [1994] 1 HKC

Click on the + and you will see a list of all the cases in the volume. Scroll down until you see the name of a case with a number beside it indicating how many hits in the case. If you do it for [1994] 1 HKC you will come across a case with 3 hits.

➤ 3 hits in one case? So a hit is not a case? No, it is an occurrence of your search word. The number of hits therefore is little help in deciding how many actual cases include the word or phrase.

Click on the + again and you will see a list of the parts of the case with an indication of the number of hits in each, headnote, judgments, etc.

Then click on the part of the case you would like to see, or click on the first part of it and work your way through the case.

If you click on the word "SEARCH" in the top line, a list of possibilities open including a proximity search which asks for certain words near each other, and you can say how near. You can search for a case reference — the way Hong Kong cases are often cited.

If you click on the "Template" icon you will be able to search for names or parties, specific judges, lawyers, cases referred to, legislation referred to, as well as a free text search.

❖ Try your own search. Look for cases on "stare decisis" — is there any other phrase which might produce similar cases?

Try looking for any Hong Kong case that has cited *Donoghue v Stevenson*. Do you think it is actually very useful to be able to search cases cited?

Was there any case in which Hunter J mentioned "economic loss"?

Hong Kong Law Reports and Digest

This now combines these two elements which were until 1997 quite different (published by different publishers). It uses a different software from *Hong Kong Cases*. As soon as you enter you will be faced with a template — a form — to fill in which asks for a phrase or word. You may indicate that you are looking for precisely that phrase (exact entry) or for the same words but in any order ('composite entry' — you might want negligent misstatement or any record which includes negligent and misstatement).

You may ask to search all the text, or just catchwords, or just digests, or digest and judgments, or party names.

What you get as a result list is a series of brief summaries. Some of them, especially those which come from the older issues of the Digest, are very brief, even just a word or two. You can click on the brief summary and you will be taken to the full entry in the Digest or a headnote of a fully reported case. If what you then see is too long for you to be able to identify the word you searched for, you can click on Find on the left and then ask for the word. If what you have in front of you is the headnote of a case, you may find that the button for ⬚ Full ⬚ is available — again on the left. If you click this it will bring up the full version of the report. If the Full button is faded this means that the headnote or summary is all that is available.

You may click on one button to move to the next hit — occurrence of a word you searched for, or another to move to the next record.

You will notice that the screen in front of you is a bit like a set of index cards. One is for Digests and one for Results list etc . To get back to the list of brief summaries click on results list.

ENGLISH LAW REPORTS

All the major series are now available in CD-ROM format — and all in different formats!

The Electronic Law Reports

This covers all the main Incorporated Council of Law Reporting reports since 1865! It covers

> First Series: Admiralty and Ecclesiastical cases; Common Pleas; Crown cases reserved; Equity cases; Privy Council; Chancery Appeal cases; Exchequer; Probate & Divorce; Queen's Bench: Scotch and Divorce Appeals; House of Lords.
>
> Second Series: Appeal Cases; Chancery Division; Common Pleas Division; Exchequer Division; Probate Division; Queen's Bench Division.
>
> Third Series: Appeal Cases; Chancery; Probate; Family; and, Queen's (King's) Bench.

Not the *Weekly Law Reports*, therefore (see below). You need two CDs; one contains the Index and the other the case reports. ➤ Check the date because you may well have to check a few issues published since the CD came out. It appears about twice a year, but the Law Reports are issued in unbound volumes more frequently.

There are three main types of Search: Quick enables you to search party names, catchwords or "Publication Reference" — the citation. ➤ Be careful — D & F Estates produced nothing — I had to type D. & F. Estates. If there is more than one response you will find a set of summaries, called profiles. You can click on any one to get the full document. You can toggle (switch) back and forth between the profiles and the document you select by clicking on the relevant icon.

Along the bottom you will find a row of buttons:

< ⬚ Hits ⬚ >   < ⬚ Terms ⬚ >   < ⬚ Page ⬚ >   < ⬚ Find ⬚ >

The first will move you to the next or previous case, the second to the next occurrence of one of your search words etc.

The second type of search is "Form" which provides a template or form for you to fill in and you can search for Court, Parties, in the Headnote, in the Catchwords, the Argument, for a Year, or for words in the text; you may fill in as few or as many as you please. I tried my defamation and ridicule search; it produced far too many when I typed "(libel or slander or defamation) and ridicule". A much better search was "libel or slander or defamation" in the catchwords box and "ridicule" in the free text box.

The last sort of search is "General" and gives you a big box in which you can type, and the possibility of identifying any Field in which you might find your search text — including Facts, Counsel, Order, Opinion etc.

The Weekly Law Reports

This is in a DOS format rather than Windows. You find a search space to type in; you can use a **BOOLEAN SEARCH**. Across the top is a series of indictors of how to use the F keys. For example, you can press F4 and you will then see a list of possible fields — title, headnote etc. Indicate the one you want and then you can type your query into a pair of square brackets [ ]. When the search is done you can ask for the results in chronological order or reverse order. You can scroll down or press F5 and move from one appearance of your words to another. F10 enable you to clear your query, or save it and move on or exit.

All England Law Reports

This series uses a system known as Books on Screen. You can choose the *All England Law Reports*, or the European Cases from 1995 or the Case Index. You can ask for words next to each other or in the same paragraph or in the same case.

The results come up in two forms — a small box opens in the centre of the screen with the case names in a list (you can click on them), and behind the box the text of the first case appears.

You can click on a button called Guide and it will help you to search for the name of a judge, or a barrister etc.

You can also choose to go straight to a particular volume of the reports.

The English Reports

This is the newest CD. It offers rather exciting possibilities for research into these old cases (one wonders whether more of them will be cited in court in future). It uses the Folio Views system with a full range of possibilities. The only problem is that in the University of Hong Kong Library you have to search the two CDs separately. The first is for volumes 1–90 and the second for the rest. Each CD has an Index ➤ but it covers only the cases on that CD.

There is a list of the original reporters, and a list of the volumes of the ER with the original reporters in each one — and if you are using the right CD you can go straight to the beginning of the particular reporter.
There is even a list of the dates of the Kings and Queens of England!

You can click on Contents and see the full list of volumes, and unpack it by clicking on a cross to see the original reports, and then again to see the cases within the volumes.

You can click on the word Search and then choose to search the page number, or the original report page number, or the case name or cases by date; there is an "advanced search" which is the same as the basic search discussed earlier under Hong Kong Cases.

SELF-STUDY QUESTIONS

☺ Fifteen minutes.

1. Give the two most efficient ways of finding a case when you have only its name and know that it is an important English case in a particular area of the law but cannot remember its date.

2. Suppose the case was a Hong Kong rather than an English case.

3. Where would you go to find out how an English case has been treated in Hong Kong courts?

4. Do you understand what is meant by the following words applied to the treatment of a case — reversed, overruled, distinguished, applied, considered? If not, take steps to ensure you are familiar with them (there is a brief dictionary in Appendix III).

Unit 8　Introduction to Legislation

OBJECTIVES

By the end of this Unit you will:

- understand in broad terms the nature of legislation
- understand the distinction between an Act and an Ordinance
- understand the distinction between a statute and a delegated legislation
- understand what elements will be found in a statute
- have some understanding of why you might need to read a statute

⊘ Perhaps about 90 minutes.

LEGISLATION

Legislation as a word is actually from 'proposing law' (from Latin). The word refers to the process of making law and to the resultant law itself. Because, as you will by now know, judges do make law, we also talk of 'judicial legislation', but the word 'legislation' taken alone means law made by a body (or in some systems a person) who has the power to lay down rules applying generally (judges will lay down rules only in the context of a particular dispute, although thereafter they will, or may, depending on the operation of the doctrine of precedent, apply generally). In Hong Kong the Governor (and from 1997 the Chief Executive, see BL Arts. 48–50) signs legislation passed by the

---

Legislation

'Legislation' is a sort of collective noun, rather like pottery or royalty. You cannot therefore say 'a legislation' any more than you can say 'a pottery' to mean a pot. If you wish to use the word 'legislation' when referring to an Ordinance, Act, etc., you have to say 'a piece of legislation', as you would say 'a piece of pottery' or a 'member of royalty' or a 'royal person'. Equally, you cannot say 'legislations'. You must say 'pieces of legislation' or 'legislation'.

Legislative Council.[1] Other people or bodies may be given the power to make laws; this power will itself be given by legislation. Since this involves giving someone else power normally exercised by the legislature, we often call this second type '**DELEGATED LEGISLATION**'. Sometimes it is known as '**SUBORDINATE LEGISLATION**' — subordinate, or lower than the **main** legislation. A general term for main legislation is **STATUTE**.

You will be mostly concerned with Hong Kong legislation, and to a lesser extent UK legislation. From 1997 UK legislation no longer has the same significance as previously, though it retains considerable importance, as we shall see later. Certain Chinese legislation will then become important. How much we cannot yet know, but when Hong Kong is a Special Administrative Region of China the Chinese Constitution will be important, and, of course, so will the Basic Law of the Hong Kong SAR, which is itself an enactment of the Chinese legislature, the National Peoples' Congress. Annex III of the Basic Law will apply the Nationality Law of the PRC to Hong Kong.

Who Makes Legislation?

Within Hong Kong, principal legislation is made by the Legislative Council and the Chief Executive. A piece of such legislation is known as an **ORDINANCE**.

In the UK the equivalent legislation is made by Parliament and signed by the Queen. Each piece is known as an **ACT**.

A third type of legislation was relevant to Hong Kong (until 1997): **ORDERS IN COUNCIL**. These are made by the monarch; the Council is the Privy Council — though not the Judicial Committee of that council, the final court of appeal (until 1997) for Hong Kong. Sometimes such Orders are examples of the exercise of the Royal Prerogative (the inherent power of the monarch); more often, these days, specific authority is given by statute to the monarch. I suppose one might think of a prerogative Order as primary legislation, but the other sort seems more like delegated legislation.

Delegated legislation may be made by all sorts of people. In Hong Kong it may be made by one of the Secretaries (Home Affairs, Planning, Environment and Lands, etc.) depending on the topic; sometimes the Chief Justice may make a piece of such legislation, and sometimes even the Legislative Council (some Ordinances say that certain things may be done by Resolution of the Legislative Council). Delegated legislation is usually published in the

---

1   For student readers: you will discuss in Constitutional Law, and perhaps in Legal System, courses who initiates the proposals for legislation, and whether the Governor/Chief Executive **must** sign, and so on — see Wesley-Smith, *An Introduction to the Hong Kong Legal System* (2nd ed.) pp. 74–85; *Constitutional and Administrative Law in Hong Kong* (2nd ed.) pp. 186ff.

form of **LEGAL NOTICES** in Hong Kong. Each piece of such legislation will be known as **REGULATION** or **RULES** or **ORDER** or **RESOLUTION** as appropriate. In the UK most delegated legislation is published as **STATUTORY INSTRUMENTS**, although some are not, and may be more difficult to get hold of. However it is published, it all has the force of law.

Legislation must be distinguished from other forms of Government Publications , some of which, like Codes of Practice, or Circulars, may contain rules but do not have the force of law.

What Do You Read a Statute for?

As with reading a case, you might want to look at a statute for a number of different reasons.

- You might want to explore the statute as a whole: what changes in the law was it intended to bring about?

- You might want to write an essay or advise a client or prepare a moot for which a particular provision of the statute is important.

- What you are looking for will depend on your purpose — it may be that you will find out that the statute is quite clear, and changes the law in a way which is favourable, or not favourable, to your case. You might find that the statute is open to argument about interpretation — it is not clear quite how it affects your case. It may be that you wish to argue that correctly interpreted the statute is not relevant at all. You might even wish to argue that the statute is invalid, because it conflicts with the Bill of Rights, or (after 1997) with the Basic Law.

- You might think that this statute, and the interpretation it has been given by the courts, will help in understanding another statute.

What Do You Do With Legislation?

What are the skills which you have to acquire? Teachers are prone to bewail the fact that 'students can't read statutes'. By this they do not mean the students are illiterate! They mean that students have not developed the skills of handling statutory material. The skills involved seem to be:

- Reading the legislation — that is getting the sense out of the words in front of you without any outside assistance.

- Finding the material — where to find the text of a statute when you have its name, etc.

- Making sure that you have the latest version of the statute.

- How to find out whether a piece of legislation that has been passed is actually in force.

- Finding the relevant legislative material on a particular topic.

- Being able to find your way around an individual statute, and locate the part(s) of it which are relevant.

- Understanding the meaning of the legislation by the use of the principles and rules of statutory interpretation.[2]

- How to find the material that will enable you to interpret the legislation: other statutes (in Hong Kong or even elsewhere), existing cases interpreting the legislation or similar legislation or words, dictionaries, **HANSARD**, Law Reform Committee reports, etc.

- Tracing the history of a piece of legislation — what it was like as a **BILL** (or even a draft Bill); what it provided as originally **ENACTED**; how it has been changed or **AMENDED**.

This is a statue, not a statute!

---

2 There is a brief summary of the topic in the next unit.

Life Cycle of an Ordinance[3]

Stage	*Physical manifestation*
Proposals for change in the law (this may come from the Government, the Law Reform Commission or business or other organization)	E.g. Law Reform Commission report, Government White Paper or Green Paper; consultation document may be published by many departments, and may be on Internet <http://www.info.gov.hk/consult.htm>
Draft Bill (a very specific form of proposal for change)	May be sent to interested parties for comment; occasionally published in *Gazette*
Bill	Published in *Gazette Supplement No. 3* (blue); text may also be on Internet — see next page
First Reading Second Reading	**Hansard** — Proceedings of the Legislative Council (Speech introducing legislation published in *Daily Information Bulletin* of HKG — on Web at <http://www.info.gov.hk/gia/general/>) also Hansard
Committee	Hansard if Committee of whole house
Third Reading	Hansard
Chief Executive's Assent	Published Ordinance says so
Ordinance published	In *Gazette Supplement No. 1* Appears on BLIS within about 2 weeks Reprinted in Loose-leaf Edition of *Laws of Hong Kong*
Comes into force (if does not do so when published in *Gazette*)	Legal Notice — Commencement Notice, published in *Gazette Supplement No. 2*. Version of Ordinance in Loose-leaf Edition gives date and LN number.
Amended	Amending Ordinance published in *Gazette*; revised version of principal Ordinance published in *Laws of Hong Kong* and BLIS (when the amendments come into force)
Repealed	Repealing Ordinance published in *Gazette*; repealed Ordinance disappears from *Laws of Hong Kong*

---

3   On the legislative process in Hong Kong see also Cheek-Milby, *A Legislature Comes of Age: Hong Kong's Search for Influence and Identity* (Hong Kong: Oxford UP, 1995) pp. 147–9 **and the footnotes.**

HONG KONG

ORDINANCE No. 80 of 1992

I assent.

(L.S.)

Christopher PATTEN,
Governor.
5 November 1992

An Ordinance to provide for safety standards for children's toys and safety standards for specified chattels used in association with children, and to provide for other powers to enhance the safety of children.

[   ]

Enacted by the Governor of Hong Kong, with the advice and consent of the Legislative Council thereof.

PART I

PRELIMINARY

1. Short title and commencement

(1) This Ordinance may be cited as the Toys and Children's Products Safety Ordinance.

(2) This Ordinance shall come into operation on a day to be appointed by the Governor by notice in the Gazette.

2. Interpretation

In this Ordinance, unless the context otherwise requires—

"advertise" (宣傳) includes issuing a catalogue, circular or price list that is intended for the general public;

"authorized officer" (獲授權人員) means an officer specified in Schedule 1 to the Customs and Excise Service Ordinance (Cap. 342) or an officer appointed by the Commissioner under section 19 to be an authorized officer;

"children's product" (兒童產品) means a product listed in the Schedule and, for the purposes of Parts IV to IX, includes a product designated by regulation to be a children's product;

CHAPTER 424

TOYS AND CHILDREN'S PRODUCTS SAFETY

An Ordinance to provide for safety standards for children's toys and safety standards for specified chattels used in association with children, and to provide for other powers to enhance the safety of children.

[1 July 1993]   *L.N. 240 of 1993*

PART I

PRELIMINARY

1. Short title

(1) This Ordinance may be cited as the Toys and Children's Products Safety Ordinance.

(2) *(Omitted as spent)*

2. Interpretation

In this Ordinance, unless the context otherwise requires—

"advertise" (宣傳) includes issuing a catalogue, circular or price list that is intended for the general public;

"authorized officer" (獲授權人員) means an officer specified in Schedule 1 to the Customs and Excise Service Ordinance (Cap. 342) or an officer appointed by the Commissioner under section 19 to be an authorized officer;

"children's product" (兒童產品) means a product listed in the Schedule and, for the purposes of Parts IV to IX, includes a product designated by regulation to be a children's product;

Authorized Loose-leaf Edition, Printed and Published by the Government Printer, Hong Kong

THE ANATOMY OF AN ORDINANCE

On the opposite page are two versions of the first page of a Hong Kong Statute. One is as it appeared in the *Gazette*; the other is as it appears in the Looseleaf Edition of the *Laws of Hong Kong*. Below are comments corresponding to the Numbers with asterisks (*). Names of the parts of the statute are emboldened.

*1. Page of the *Gazette Supplement No. 1* for 1992 (before this page there were contents pages of the Ordinance).

*2. Number of the Ordinance in 1992 (each Ordinance is given a number in order of enactment).

*3. Statement by the Governor that he assents to the Ordinance, reflecting statement on the original document.

*4. Represents the Public Seal of the Colony which must be placed on the original and the copy which is sent to the Queen (see Letters Patent IV and Royal Instruction XXVIII). LS stands for *Locus Sigilli*, Latin for the Place of the Seal.

*5. Date of Signature of Governor. Publication in *Gazette*, upon which the Ordinance became law, was the following day.

*6. **Number of Ordinance** in the collected *Laws of Hong Kong*. It will keep this number.

*7. **Long title of the Ordinance.**

*8. In the original this blank space indicates that the Ordinance was not yet in force. When it was published in the *Laws of Hong Kong* Issue 7 it had been brought into force on 1 July 1993, so the empty brackets had been filled. It had been originally published as part of Issue 5 before it was brought into force.

*9. The reference number of the Commencement Order, the piece of subsidiary legislation which brought the Ordinance into force (published in *Gazette Supplement No. 2*).

*10. The constitutional formula which reflects the true position in a colony like Hong Kong (see Letters Patent VII (1) (and Wesley-Smith *Constitutional and Administrative Law* p. 120).

*11. **Section** 1 provides the *short title* by which the Ordinance can be conveniently known: The Toys and Children's Products Safety Ordinance.

*12. Section 1 **sub-section** (2), providing that the Ordinance is to come into force when the Governor appoints; not reproduced in the 7th issue of *Laws of Hong Kong* version as it had fulfilled its purpose.

*13. Interpretation section specifying the meaning in which certain words or phrases are used for the purposes of this Ordinance, or even part of it — see the definition of 'children's product' here.

*14. Note how you cannot have even a full understanding of the Ordinance as it is in front of you without referring to at least one other Ordinance!

*15. The **Schedule** is added at the end of the Ordinance, and often contains detailed lists and regulations which might unduly clutter up the main part of the Ordinance. It will be referred to in the Ordinance, but even if this is not done, it has the force of law by virtue of the Interpretation and General Clauses Ordinance (s. 12, see p. 120). See the Control of Exemption Clauses Ordinance for examples of Schedules (p. 105).

*16 The issue of the Loose-leaf Edition of the *Laws of Hong Kong* in which this appears (having initially been published as part of Issue 5).

BILLS

Legislation is presented to the Legislative Council in the form of a Bill. Bills are published in the *Gazette Supplement No. 3*, which is printed on blue paper. The normal practice is for the Bill to be published in the *Gazette* on the Friday before it is presented to Legco on Wednesday.

There is a list of Bills on the Legco World Wide Web page. It gives the date on which each Bill was introduced into Legco, and the date it was passed. The Legco Web site address is **<http://legco.gov.hk/>.**

You will find the full text of Bills as well. You can find some material from the Provisional Legislative Council and the last colonial Legco, too.

Amending UK and Hong Kong Statutes

There is a difference in the technique used for the publication of amendments to statutes in the two jurisdictions. This will become immediately apparent if you look at a topic such as criminal law. There are in the current *Halsbury's Statutes of England*, Volume 12 1994 Reissue 9 statutes (or parts of 9 statutes) each called Criminal Justice Act. This will never happen in Hong Kong. If a statute is amended the amending Ordinance will be called (Amendment) Ordinance, if it has the same name as the Ordinance it is amending. And as soon as possible the principal Ordinance will be reissued incorporating the changes. There is only one statute of any one name in the *Laws of Hong Kong*.

It sometimes becomes necessary to add sections in the middle of existing Ordinances. This is why there are often sections called something like s. 23A. Sometimes it goes as far as 25L or even further through the alphabet! This is the cost of the Hong Kong system of amendment. The idea is that users get used to one section and it would be confusing to change the section number.

What usually happens in the UK is that over a long time a statute may be added to and amended until the situation become very unwieldy. Then the whole lot will be repealed and replaced by one new statute. This is called a consolidating Act. For example, the main Company Law statute was for a long time the Companies Act 1948. There were Companies Acts in 1967, 1976, 1980, 1981. Then all these were repealed and replaced by the Companies Act 1985. Then the whole process began again the next year when the Insolvency Act amended the 1985 Companies Act!

DELEGATED LEGISLATION

Below you will find a section of the Criminal Procedure Ordinance giving the power to make delegated legislation, followed by a piece of legislation made under the authority of that section. Notes follow the extracts.

---

*1 9A. **Legal aid in criminal cases**

(1) The Chief Justice may, with the approval of the Legislative Council, make rules providing for the granting of legal aid in criminal cases to persons of limited means which rules, in particular, may—

(*g*) prescribe the scale of fees and costs which shall be paid to solicitor or counsel acting for an aided person (or submitting any opinion for the purpose of the rules);

L. S. NO. 2 TO GAZETTE NO. 13/1995 ***3**   **L.N. 119 of 1995**   B455

*2 **L.N. 119 of 1995**

LEGAL AID IN CRIMINAL CASES (AMENDMENT) RULES 1995 ***4**

(Made under section 9A of the Criminal Procedure Ordinance
(Cap. 221) with the approval of the Legislative Council)

1. **Commencement**

These Rules shall come into operation on 1 April 1995.

2. **Solicitor and counsel fees**

Rule 21(1) of the Legal Aid in Criminal Cases Rules (Cap. 221 sub. leg.) is amended—
   (*a*) in subparagraph (*a*), by repealing "$5,000", "$620" and "$3,250" and substituting "$6,010", "$740" and "$3,910" respectively;
   (*b*) in subparagraph (*aa*), by repealing "$6,750", "$850" and "$4,350" and substituting "$8,100", "$1,020" and "$5,230" respectively;

Explanatory Note

These Rules increase, with effect from 1 April 1995, the scale of fees payable to solicitors and counsel assigned under the Legal Aid in Criminal ***5** Cases Rules (Cap. 221 sub. leg.) to represent persons receiving legal aid.

B454   **L.N. 118 of 1995**   L. S. NO. 2 TO GAZETTE NO. 13/1995

L.N. 118 of 1995

CRIMINAL PROCEDURE ORDINANCE

RESOLUTION OF THE LEGISLATIVE COUNCIL   ***6**

Resolution made and passed by the Legislative Council under section 9A of the Criminal Procedure Ordinance (Cap. 221) on 29 March 1995.

RESOLVED that the Legal Aid in Criminal Cases (Amendment) Rules 1995, made by the Chief Justice on 8 March 1995, be approved.

Ricky FUNG Choi-cheung,
Clerk to the Legislative Council.

29 March 1995.

*1. The Chief Justice is given power to make Rules. Note these must be approved by the Legislative Council. This is not the case for all types of delegated legislation. See generally Wesley-Smith, *Constitutional and Administrative Law* 163ff.

*2. Reference number of the Legal Notice in which these Rules were published.

*3. Issue of *Supplement No. 2 to the Gazette* in which it appeared.

*4. Note these Rules amend existing Rules.

*5. Explanatory Note: this is customary for delegated legislation. In the case of Ordinances there is no such explanatory note. However, when the Bill is published, an explanatory statement is attached which sets out what changes in the law the Bill will bring about.

*6. A copy of the Resolution of Legco approving the Amendment to the Rules.

> ### Ultra Vires
>
> Delegated legislation made by anyone — the Chief Justice, a policy Secretary or even a resolution of Legco — must not go beyond the scope of the powers given by the Ordinance. Any regulation, order or whatever which exceeds those powers has no legal effect. The Latin phrase used to describe this situation is '*ultra vires*' meaning simply 'beyond the powers'.

SELF-STUDY QUESTIONS

⊘ Ten minutes.

1. Suggest 2 places to find the text of Bills and 3 places to find the text of an Ordinance.

2. What is the difference between the Ordinance being passed and its coming into force?

3. An Ordinance may be signed on one day, become law on another, and come into force on another. Why is this so? How can you find out what the relevant dates are for any particular Ordinance?

4. What does it mean to say that a piece of delegated legislation is 'ultra vires'?

Unit 9   Reading a Statute

OBJECTIVES

By the end of this Unit you will:

- have read carefully one statute
- be beginning to overcome your fear of reading statutes
- understand why it is important to get a sense of the whole of any statute and not just concentrate on sections which appear relevant at first sight
- have taken your first steps in developing the skill of applying a statute to a set of facts
- know some of the things which the Interpretation and General Clauses Ordinance does
- understand where, within and outside the bounds of an individual statute, you may be able to find help in understanding it

☻ If you read this carefully and try the exercises it may well take as long as three hours.

N ow that you have some idea of what legislation is, we need to consider how you go about reading it. The following piece of good advice comes from Bradney et al., *How to Study Law.*

> Statutes should be read carefully and slowly. The general rule is that a statute means precisely what it says. Each word is important. Because of this, some words which we use loosely in ordinary conversation take on special significance when found in a statute. For example, it is important to distinguish between words like "may" and "shall," one saying you can do something and the other saying you must do something. Conjunctives, such as "and," joining things together, must be distinguished from disjunctives, such as "or," dividing things apart.

On the next page but one begins a copy of the Control of Exemption Clauses Ordinance. (In order to save space I have reproduced only the English version. In the *Laws of Hong Kong* you will find the Chinese language version also.)

Beside the sections I have commented on aspects which you ought to note — these are points which are more generally relevant to reading statutes, not just to this one. I have chosen this one because it is quite a complex example and illustrates well some of the difficulties of reading a statute.

A few words of introduction: this statute is relevant both to contract and to tort. It is designed to protect people who find that they have entered into a contract, or accepted the implications of a notice, which takes away a right they would otherwise have had, for breach of the contract, or for tort. Here is a problem question, of the sort that you might have to discuss in a tutorial class, or answer in an examination. From it you will see what is meant by 'exemption clauses'. When you have looked through the Ordinance with the help of my marginal comments, try to answer the problem question.

> Lily went to a concert at a hall owned and run by the Urban Council. She bought a ticket saying 'The Council accepts no responsibility for any injury or loss to the person or property of those attending functions at this venue, whether resulting from negligence or otherwise'. During the concert, the chair on which Lily sat collapsed and she was injured. Also, her dress was torn on a broken piece of the seat when she fell. It is obvious that the chair was negligently maintained.
>
> After this unpleasant event, Lily went to the bar to get a restorative drink. She took a mouthful of her drink and then noticed that there was a piece of broken glass in the drink. She was not hurt, but she went to demand her money back. The staff refused to give her the money, pointing to a large notice which said, 'No Liability. No refund.' which Lily admits she had seen before she bought the drink.
>
> The Council refuses to compensate her for the injury to herself or her dress, or to refund the money for the drink, claiming that they had excluded their liability. Do you think the Ordinance helps Lily?

Note:
The number of the statute in the *Laws of Hong Kong*.

Look at the overall structure:

It is divided into Parts. What is the rationale for this division? What does Part I contain? Part II? and so on ...

Is there an interpretation section? Or more than one? Look at them. Does each one apply to the whole Ordinance or is there anything which applies to only part of the Ordinance?

Section 20 and Schedule 3 deal with amendments of other legislation by this Ordinance.

CHAPTER 71

CONTROL OF EXEMPTION CLAUSES ORDINANCE

CONTENTS

PART I
PRELIMINARY

Section

1. Short title
2. Interpretation and application
3. The "reasonableness" test
4. "Dealing as consumer"
5. Varieties of exemption clause
6. Power to amend Schedules 1 and 2

PART II
CONTROL OF EXEMPTION CLAUSES

Avoidance of liability for negligence, breach of contract, etc.

7. Negligence liability
8. Liability arising in contract
9. Unreasonable indemnity clauses

Liability arising from sale or supply of goods

10. "Guarantee" of consumer goods
11. Seller's liability
12. Miscellaneous contracts under which goods pass

Other provisions about contracts

13. Effect of breach on "reasonableness" test
14. Evasion by means of secondary contract
15. Arbitration agreements

PART III
CIRCUMSTANCES WHERE CONTROL DOES NOT APPLY

16. International supply contracts
17. Choice of law clauses
18. Saving for other relevant legislation
19. Application

PART IV
CONSEQUENTIAL AND OTHER AMENDMENTS

20. *(Omitted)*

Schedule 1. Scope of sections 7, 8, 9 and 12
Schedule 2. "Guidelines" for application of reasonableness test
Schedule 3. *(Omitted)*

CAP. 71   *Control of Exemption Clauses*

CHAPTER 71

CONTROL OF EXEMPTION CLAUSES

To limit the extent to which civil liability for breach of contract, or for negligence or other breach of duty, can be avoided by means of contract terms and otherwise; and to restrict the enforceability of arbitration agreements.   ——— The long title

[1 December 1990] *L.N. 38 of 1990* ———
The date it came into force.
The number of the Legal Notice containing the Commencement Order.

PART I

PRELIMINARY

1. Short title

This Ordinance may be cited as the Control of Exemption Clauses Ordinance.

2. Interpretation and application

(1) In this Ordinance—
"business" (業務) includes a profession and the activities of a public body, a public authority, or a board, commission, committee or other body appointed by the Governor or Government;
"goods" (貨品) has the same meaning as in the Sale of Goods Ordinance (Cap. 26);
"negligence" (疏忽) means the breach—
    (*a*) of any obligation, arising from the express or implied terms of a contract, to take reasonable care or exercise reasonable skill in the performance of the contract;
    (*b*) of any common law duty to take reasonable care or exercise reasonable skill (but not any stricter duty);
    (*c*) of the common duty of care imposed by the Occupiers Liability Ordinance (Cap. 314);
"notice" (告示) includes an announcement, whether or not in writing, and any other communication or pretended communication;

Note the difference between a definition which says 'a word or expression **means** something' and 'one which says it **includes** something'. See for example s. 2 of CECO. 'Business' **includes** a profession and the activities of a public body ... it also includes other things. But 'negligence' **means** the breaches specified: if the breach involved in a particular case is not one of these it is not negligence for the purposes of this Ordinance.

This Ordinance is a particularly tricky example in which some parts of the Ordinance do not apply in particular situations. Here is the first of a number of examples:

In the case of contract and tort (and I am not sure that there can be any other situations relevant here), sections 7-12 only apply to 'business liability' — see s. 2 (2).

But — there is a qualification to even this — 'except where the contrary is stated in s. 11 (4)'.

And note how 'business liability' is defined — but immediately recreational and educational purposes are excluded — and another exception introduced to that exception!

Note that after most sections there is a reference in square brackets to *1977 UK c.50*. This is a reference to the English Act — Unfair Contract Terms Act — from which this Ordinance is mainly copied.

Section 3 says that Schedule 2 applies to deciding whether under s. 11 or 12 the requirement of 'reasonableness' is satisfied.

---

4   CAP. 71   *Control of Exemption Clauses*

"personal injury" (人身傷害) includes any disease and any impairment of physical or mental condition.

(2) In the case of both contract and tort, sections 7 to 12 apply (except where the contrary is stated in section 11(4)) only to business liability, that is liability for breach of obligations or duties arising

(a) from things done or omitted to be done by a person in the course of a business (whether his own business or another's); or

(b) from the occupation of premises used for business purposes of the occupier,

and references to liability are to be read accordingly; but liability of an occupier of premises for breach of an obligation or duty towards a person obtaining access to the premises for recreational or educational purposes, being liability for loss or damage suffered by reason of the dangerous state of the premises, is not a business liability of the occupier unless granting that person such access for the purposes concerned falls within the business purposes of the occupier.

(3) In relation to any breach of duty or obligation, it is immaterial whether the breach was inadvertent or intentional, or whether liability for it arises directly or vicariously.

[*cf. 1977 c. 50 ss. 1 & 14 U.K.*]

3. The "reasonableness" test

(1) In relation to a contract term, the requirement of reasonableness for the purposes of this Ordinance and section 4 of the Misrepresentation Ordinance (Cap. 284) is satisfied only if the court or arbitrator determines that the term was a fair and reasonable one to be included having regard to the circumstances which were, or ought reasonably to have been, known to or in the contemplation of the parties when the contract was made.

(2) In determining for the purposes of section 11 or 12 whether a contract term satisfies the requirement of reasonableness, the court or arbitrator shall have regard in particular to the matters specified in Schedule 2; but this subsection does not prevent the court or arbitrator from holding, in accordance with any rule of law, that a term which purports to exclude or restrict any relevant liability is not a term of the contract.

(3) In relation to a notice (not being a notice having contractual effect), the requirement of reasonableness under this Ordinance is satisfied only if the court or arbitrator determines that it would be fair and reasonable to allow reliance on it, having regard to all the circumstances obtaining when the liability arose or (but for the notice) would have arisen.

(4) In determining (under this Ordinance or the Misrepresentation Ordinance (Cap. 284)) whether a contract term or notice satisfies the requirement of reasonableness, the court or arbitrator shall have regard in particular (but without prejudice to subsection (2) to whether (and, if so, to

Section 4 (1) defines 'dealing as consumer'; don't stop there:

If you go on to sub-section (2) you will see that a person who buys goods at auction or by competitive tender is not dealing as consumer.

And note sub-section (3), saying who must prove whether or not the person is a consumer; we call this the 'burden of proof'.

Section 5 clarifies the extent of the Ordinance in the sense of the types of exclusion clauses it covers.

CAP. 71   *Control of Exemption Clauses*

what extent) the language in which the term or notice is expressed is a language understood by the person as against whom another person seeks to rely upon the term or notice.

(5) Where by reference to a contract term or notice a person seeks to restrict liability to a specified sum of money, and the question arises (under this Ordinance or the Misrepresentation Ordinance (Cap. 284)) whether the term or notice satisfies the requirement of reasonableness, the court or arbitrator shall have regard in particular (but without prejudice to subsection (2) or (4)) to

(a) the resources which he could expect to be available to him for the purpose of meeting the liability should it arise; and
(b) how far it was open to him to cover himself by insurance.

(6) It is for the person claiming that a contract term or notice satisfies the requirement of reasonableness to prove that it does.   [cf. 1977 c. 11 s. 11 U.K.]

4.   "Dealing as consumer"

(1) A party to a contract "deals as consumer" in relation to another party if

(a) he neither makes the contract in the course of a business nor holds himself out as doing so;
(b) the other party does make the contract in the course of a business; and
(c) in the case of a contract governed by the law of sale of goods or by section 12, the goods passing under or in pursuance of the contract are of a type ordinarily supplied for private use or consumption.

(2) Notwithstanding subsection (1), on a sale by auction or by competitive tender the buyer is not in any circumstances to be regarded as dealing as consumer.

(3) It is for the person claiming that a party does not deal as consumer to prove that he does not.   [cf. 1977 c. 50 s. 12 U.K.]

5.   Varieties of exemption clause

(1) To the extent that this Ordinance prevents the exclusion or restriction of any liability it also prevents—

(a) making the liability or its enforcement subject to restrictive or onerous conditions;
(b) excluding or restricting any right or remedy in respect of the liability, or subjecting a person to any prejudice in consequence of his pursuing any such right or remedy;
(c) excluding or restricting rules of evidence or procedure,

Issue 3   Authorized Loose-leaf Edition. Printed and Published by the Government Printer, Hong Kong

Section 6 gives Legco the power to amend the schedules — it creates a power to make Delegated Legislation.

Section 7, as we have already seen, only applies to business liability, but there is nothing here to tell you this.
Section 7 also uses the expression 'requirement of reasonableness', but Schedule 2 does not apply to this section. There is nothing in s. 3, or in Schedule 2 itself to apply it to s. 7.
If you look at Schedule 1 you will see that s. 7 does not apply to insurance contracts, or contracts about land, or about intellectual property, or about companies or securities. There is nothing in s. 7 to warn you of this.

Section 8 (1) makes it clear that this section only applies in certain circumstances.
Schedule 2 does not apply to s. 8 any more than to s. 7.
Section 8 also does not apply to certain types of contracts, by virtue of Schedule 1, and there are other limitations on the reach of s. 7 and s. 8 there too.

---

6 **CAP. 71**   *Control of Exemption Clauses*

and (to that extent) sections 7, 10, 11 and 12 also prevent excluding or restricting liability by reference to terms and notices which exclude or restrict the relevant obligation or duty.

(2) An agreement in writing to submit present or future differences to arbitration is not to be treated under this Ordinance as excluding or restricting any liability.

[*cf. 1977 c. 50 s. 13 U.K.*]

6. Power to amend Schedules 1 and 2

The Legislative Council may by resolution amend Schedules 1 and 2.

PART II

CONTROL OF EXEMPTION CLAUSES

Avoidance of liability for negligence, breach of contract, etc.

7. Negligence liability

(1) A person cannot by reference to any contract term or to a notice given to persons generally or to particular persons exclude or restrict his liability for death or personal injury resulting from negligence.

(2) In the case of other loss or damage, a person cannot so exclude or restrict his liability for negligence except in so far as the term or notice satisfies the requirement of reasonableness.

(3) Where a contract term or notice purports to exclude or restrict liability for negligence a person's agreement to or awareness of it is not of itself to be taken as indicating his voluntary acceptance of any risk.

[*cf. 1977 c. 50 s. 2 U.K.*]

8. Liability arising in contract

(1) This section applies as between contracting parties where one of them deals as consumer or on the other's written standard terms of business.

(2) As against that party, the other cannot by reference to any contract term—

(a) when himself in breach of contract, exclude or restrict any liability of his in respect of the breach; or

(b) claim to be entitled—

(i) to render a contractual performance substantially different from that which was reasonably expected of him; or

Section 9 is also limited in its scope by Schedule 1.

Watch out also for the distinction between **and** and **or**. It may be of great importance to see whether someone has to satisfy only one of a list of requirements or all of them for example.

See s. 10 (1) which applies if **both** requirements are satisfied:

the loss or damage arises from the goods being defective in consumer use **and** it results from negligence.

Under s. 10 (3) the rest of the section does not apply between parties to a contract under which possession or ownership of the goods passes. You might have thought this was exactly the sort of contract in which you would expect to find a guarantee! It is aimed at the relationship between the **manufacturer** and the consumer, where the guarantee might create a contractual relationship, but also try to restrict certain rights of the consumer.

CAP. 71 *Control of Exemption Clauses*

(ii) in respect of the whole or any part of his contractual obligation, to render no performance at all,

except in so far as (in any of the cases mentioned above in this subsection) the contract term satisfies the requirement of reasonableness.

[cf. 1977 c. 50 s. 3 U.K.]

9. Unreasonable indemnity clauses

(1) A person dealing as consumer cannot by reference to any contract term be made to indemnify another person (whether a party to the contract or not) in respect of liability that may be incurred by the other for negligence or breach of contract, except in so far as the contract term satisfies the requirement of reasonableness.

(2) This section applies whether the liability in question—

(a) is directly that of the person to be indemnified or is incurred by him vicariously;

(b) is to the person dealing as consumer or to someone else.

[cf. 1977 c. 50 s. 4 U.K.]

Liability arising from sale or supply of goods

10. "Guarantee" of consumer goods

(1) In the case of goods of a type ordinarily supplied for private use or consumption, where loss or damage—

(a) arises from the goods proving defective while in consumer use; and

(b) results from the negligence of a person concerned in the manufacture or distribution of the goods,

liability for the loss or damage cannot be excluded or restricted by reference to any contract term or notice contained in or operating by reference to a guarantee of the goods.

(2) For these purposes—

(a) goods are to be regarded as "in consumer use" when a person is using them, or has them in his possession for use, otherwise than exclusively for the purposes of a business; and

(b) anything in writing is a guarantee if it contains or purports to contain some promise or assurance (however worded or presented) that defects will be made good by complete or partial replacement, or by repair, monetary compensation or otherwise.

(3) This section does not apply as between the parties to a contract under or in pursuance of which possession or ownership of the goods passed.

[cf. 1977 c. 50 s. 5 U.K.]

Remember you need to look at Schedule 2 about the requirement of reasonableness.

---

11. Seller's liability

(1) Liability for breach of the obligations arising from section 14 of the Sale of Goods Ordinance (Cap. 26) (seller's implied undertakings as to title, etc.) cannot be excluded or restricted by reference to any contract term.

(2) As against a person dealing as consumer, liability for breach of the obligations arising from section 15, 16 or 17 of the Sale of Goods Ordinance (Cap. 26) (seller's implied undertakings as to conformity of goods with description or sample, or as to their quality or fitness for a particular purpose) cannot be excluded or restricted by reference to any contract term.

(3) As against a person dealing otherwise than as consumer, the liability specified in subsection (2) can be excluded or restricted by reference to a contract term, but only in so far as the term satisfies the requirement of reasonableness.

(4) The liabilities referred to in this section are not only the business liabilities defined by section 2(2), but include those arising under any contract of sale of goods.

[*cf. 1977 c. 50 s. 6 U.K.*]

12. Miscellaneous contracts under which goods pass

(1) Where the possession or ownership of goods passes under or in pursuance of a contract not governed by the law of sale of goods, subsection (2) to (4) apply in relation to the effect (if any) that the court or arbitrator is to give to contract terms excluding or restricting liability for breach of obligation arising by implication of law from the nature of the contract.

(2) As against a person dealing as consumer, liability in respect of the goods' correspondence with description or sample, or their quality or fitness for any particular purpose, cannot be excluded or restricted by reference to any such term.

(3) As against a person dealing otherwise than as consumer, that liability can be excluded or restricted by reference to such a term, but only in so far as the term satisfies the requirement of reasonableness.

(4) Liability in respect of—

(a) the right to transfer ownership of the goods, or give possession; or

(b) the assurance of quiet possession to a person taking goods in pursuance of the contract,

cannot be excluded or restricted by reference to any such term except in so far as the term satisfies the requirement of reasonableness.

[*cf. 1977 c. 50 s. 7 U.K.*]

Under s. 15 (2) the scope of sub-section (1) is restricted.

Under section 16 **the whole Ordinance** does not apply in the case of exclusion clauses in an international supply contract.

CAP. 71   *Control of Exemption Clauses*

Other provisions about contracts

13. Effect of breach on "reasonableness" test

(1) Where for reliance upon it a contract term has to satisfy the requirement of reasonableness, it may be found to do so and be given effect accordingly notwithstanding that the contract has been terminated either by breach or by a party electing to treat it as repudiated.

(2) Where on a breach the contract is nevertheless affirmed by a party entitled to treat as repudiated, this does not of itself exclude the requirement of reasonableness in relation to any contract term.

[cf. 1977 c. 50 s. 9 U.K.]

14. Evasion by means of secondary contract

A person is not bound by any contract term prejudicing or taking away rights of his which arise under, or in connection with the performance of, another contract, so far as those rights extend to the enforcement of another's liability which this Ordinance prevents that other from excluding or restricting.

[cf. 1977 c. 50 s. 10 U.K.]

15. Arbitration agreements

(1) As against a person dealing as consumer, an agreement to submit future differences to arbitration cannot be enforced except

(a) with his written consent signified after the differences in question have arisen; or

(b) where he has himself had recourse to arbitration in pursuance of the agreement in respect of any differences.

(2) Subsection (1) does not affect—

(a) the enforcement of an international arbitration agreement within the meaning of section 2(1) of the Arbitration Ordinance (Cap. 341); (*Replaced 76 of 1990 s. 2*)

(b) the resolution of differences arising under any contract so far as it is, by virtue of Schedule 1, excluded from the operation of section 7, 8, 9 or 12.

PART III

CIRCUMSTANCES WHERE CONTROL DOES NOT APPLY

16. International supply contracts

(1) The limits imposed by this Ordinance on the extent to which a person may exclude or restrict liability by reference to a contract term do not apply to liability arising under an international supply contract.

Here there is another definition, especially for the purposes of this section.

Section 17 says that if the parties have deliberately chosen to make the contract covered by Hong Kong law, the whole Ordinance does not apply. On the other hand, the Ordinance will apply to the contract, even if it is bound by the law of another country, in two specified circumstances — one of these circumstances protects people in an unequal bargaining position, the other is a consumer protection measure.

---

10   **CAP. 71**   *Control of Exemption Clauses*

(2) The terms of an international supply contract are not subject to any requirement of reasonableness under section 8 or 9.

(3) For the purposes of this section, an international supply contract means a contract—

(a) that is either a contract of sale of goods or a contract under or in pursuance of which the possession or ownership of goods passes;

(b) that is made by parties whose places of business (or, if they have none, habitual residences) are in the territories of different States or are in and outside Hong Kong; and

(c) in the case of which—

(i) the goods in question are, at the time of the conclusion of the contract, in the course of carriage, or will be carried, from the territory of one State to the territory of another, or to or from Hong Kong from or to a place outside Hong Kong; or

(ii) the acts constituting the offer and acceptance have been done in the territories of different States or in and outside Hong Kong; or

(iii) the contract provides for the goods to be delivered to the territory of a State other than that within whose territory the acts constituting the offer and acceptance were done; or

(iv) the acts constituting the offer and acceptance were done in Hong Kong and the contract provides for the goods to be delivered outside Hong Kong; or

(v) the acts constituting the offer and acceptance were done outside Hong Kong and the contract provides for the goods to be delivered to Hong Kong.

[*cf. 1977 c. 50 s. 26 U.K.*]

17. Choice of law clauses

(1) Where the proper law of a contract is the law of Hong Kong only by choice of the parties (and apart from that choice would be the law of some other country) sections 7 to 12 do not operate as part of the proper law.

(2) This Ordinance has effect notwithstanding any contract term which applies or purports to apply the law of some other country, where (either or both)—

(a) the term appears to the court or arbitrator to have been imposed wholly or mainly for the purpose of enabling the party imposing it to evade the operation of this Ordinance; or

(b) in the making of the contract one of the parties dealt as consumer, and he was then habitually resident in Hong Kong, and the essential steps necessary for the making of the contract were taken there, whether by him or by others on his behalf.

[*cf. 1977 c. 50 s. 27 U.K.*]

Issue 3   Authorized Loose-leaf Edition, Printed and Published by the Government Printer, Hong Kong

Section 19 makes it clear that the Ordinance does not apply if the contract was made before the Ordinance came into force, even if the breach of contract occurred later.

Under Schedule 1 s. 7, 8 and 9 do not apply to insurance contracts, or contracts about land, or about intellectual property, or companies, or securities.

CAP. 71 *Control of Exemption Clauses*

18. Saving for other relevant legislation

(1) Nothing in this Ordinance removes or restricts the effect of, or prevents reliance upon, any contractual provision which—

    (a) is authorized or required by the express terms or necessary implication of an enactment; or

    (b) being made with a view to compliance with an international agreement which applies to Hong Kong, does not operate more restrictively than is contemplated by the agreement.

(2) A contract term is to be taken for the purposes of this Ordinance as satisfying the requirement of reasonableness if it is incorporated or approved by, or incorporated pursuant to a decision or ruling of, a competent authority acting in the exercise of any statutory jurisdiction or function and is not a term in a contract to which the competent authority is itself a party.

(3) In this section—

"competent authority" (具有法定裁判權的主管當局) means any court, arbitrator or public body;

"enactment" (成文法則) means any Ordinance and any instrument having effect by virtue of any Ordinance; and

"statutory" (法定) means conferred by an enactment.

[cf. 1977 c. 50 s. 29 U.K.]

19. Application

Nothing in this Ordinance applies to contracts made before the date on which it comes into force but, subject to this, it applies to liability for any loss or damage which is suffered on or after that date.

[cf. 1977 c. 50 s. 31(2) U.K.]

PART IV

CONSEQUENTIAL AND OTHER AMENDMENTS

20. (*Omitted as spent*)

SCHEDULE 1   [ss. 6, 7, 8, 9, 12 & 15]

SCOPE OF SECTIONS 7, 8, 9 AND 12

1. Sections 7, 8 and 9 do not apply to—
    (a) any contract of insurance (including a contract to pay an annuity on human life);
    (b) any contract so far as it relates to the creation or transfer of an interest in land, or to the termination of such an interest, whether by extinction, merger, surrender, forfeiture or otherwise;

Issue 5   Authorized Loose-leaf Edition, Printed and Published by the Government Printer, Hong Kong

Under Schedule 1 Para. 2, s. 7 (1) applies to certain types of contract, but the rest of s. 7, and ss. 8 and 9 only apply to someone dealing as consumer.

Under Para. 3 the application is similarly restricted in the case of goods carried by ship or hovercraft.

Under Para. 4 s. 7 (1) and (2) applies to contracts of employment only in favour of the employee.

CAP. 71   *Control of Exemption Clauses*

(c) any contract so far as it relates to the creation or transfer of a right or interest in any patent, trade mark, copyright, registered design, technical or commercial information or other intellectual property, or relates to the termination of any such right or interest;

(d) any contract so far as it relates—
   (i) to the formation or dissolution of a company (which means any body corporate or unincorporated association and includes a partnership); or
   (ii) to its constitution or the rights or obligations of its corporators or members;

(e) any contract so far as it relates to the creation or transfer of securities or of any right or interest in securities;   (*Amended 68 of 1992 s. 20*)

(f) any contract so far as it relates to a person specified in that contract being a participant within the meaning of section 2 of the Securities (Clearing Houses) Ordinance (Cap. 420), and includes any other contract entered into by that person —
   (i) which is required by that first-mentioned contract to be so entered into; and
   (ii) so far as it relates to the activities of that person as such a participant.   (*Added 68 of 1992 s. 20*)

2. Section 7(1) applies to—
   (a) any contract of marine salvage or towage;
   (b) any charterparty of a ship or hovercraft; and
   (c) any contract for the carriage of goods by ship or hovercraft,
but sections 7(2) and (3), 8, 9 and 12 do not apply to any such contract except in favour of a person dealing as consumer.

3. Where goods are carried by ship or hovercraft in pursuance of a contract which either—
   (a) specifies that as the means of carriage over part of the journey to be covered; or
   (b) makes no provision as to the means of carriage and does not exclude that means,
then sections 7(2), 8 and 9 do not, except in favour of a person dealing as consumer, apply to the contract as it operates in relation to the carriage of the goods by that means.

4. Section 7(1) and (2) does not apply to a contract of employment, except in favour of the employee.

[*cf. 1977 c. 50 Sch. 1 U.K.*]

SCHEDULE 2   [ss. 3(2) & 6]

"GUIDELINES" FOR APPLICATION OF REASONABLENESS TEST

The matters to which the court or arbitrator shall have regard in particular for the purposes of sections 11(3) and 12(3) and (4) are any of the following which appear to be relevant—
   (a) the strength of the bargaining positions of the parties relative to each other, taking into account (among other things) alternative means by which the customer's requirements could have been met;
   (b) whether the customer received an inducement to agree to the term, or in accepting it had an opportunity of entering into a similar contract with other persons, but without having to accept a similar term;
   (c) whether the customer knew or ought reasonably to have known of the existence and extent of the term (having regard, among other things, to any custom of the trade and any previous course of dealing between the parties);
   (d) where the term excludes or restricts any relevant liability if some condition is not complied with, whether it was reasonable at the time of the contract to expect that compliance with that condition would be practicable;
   (e) whether the goods were manufactured, processed or adapted to the special order of the customer.

[*cf. 1977 c. 50 Sch. 2 U.K.*]

Issue 5   Authorized Loose-leaf Edition. Printed and Published by the Government Printer, Hong Kong

❖ Now see how you would get on in answering the problem printed earlier using only the words of this Ordinance. ☺ I would expect this to take you over a hour.

Think about the problem yourself, and discuss it with your colleagues. Then consider my remarks below:

1. You probably had no difficulty in finding S. 7 and thinking that it would apply to Lily and her dress, sub-section (a) to the injury to Lily and sub-section (b) to the damage to the dress.

2. But did you then recall that under S. 2 (2) s. 7 applies only to 'business liability'?

3. What is 'business liability'? S. 2 defines 'business'. Does it include the Urban Council?

4. Under s. 7 (1) liability cannot be excluded. But under s. 7 (2) liability can be excluded so far as the 'requirement of reasonableness' is satisfied.

5. What does this mean? See s. 3, headed 'The "reasonableness" test'. Think about whether this notice in the ticket satisfied this test.

6. Now to the drink: there is no damage here so there is no possibility of an action in tort. If anything Lily is complaining in contract.

7. You could think that there are two possible sections which apply here — s. 8 about contracts, and s. 11 about seller's liability. Since the second is more neatly suited to the case, rely on that. (It is because this might be so that you should get a sense of the whole Ordinance before you try to apply it, so that you do not miss any relevant bit by stopping too soon.)

8. Ignore s. 10 — a guarantee is the sort of piece of paper you get with goods giving you an undertaking that if they go wrong within a certain time you can send them back etc. This is not the case here; there is no such guarantee.

9. Section 11 (2) is the most relevant. You can work this out because it refers to the Sale of Good Ordinance (surely drink is 'goods'). It refers to undertakings as to quality or fitness for purpose of goods (surely a drink with glass in it is not fit to drink!).

10. Under s. 11 (2) the liability for breach of the Sale of Goods Ordinance cannot be excluded by reference to any contract term; note however, the statement in the first line — 'As against a person dealing as consumer'. Was Lily 'dealing as consumer'?

11. Section 4 deals with the meaning of 'dealing as consumer'. This requires that three tests must be satisfied if Lily is to be held to 'deal as consumer' and therefore get the benefit of s. 11 (2). She must (a) not make the contract in the course of a business, (b) the other

party must make the contract in the course of a business and you have already thought about whether this is so in connection with 'business liability' and, (c) in a sale of goods cases, as here, the goods must be of a sort usually supplied for private use or consumption. Does her drink satisfy this test?

WAYS OF DEALING WITH STATUTES

Breaking up Sections

It might even be helpful when trying to understand a complex section to write it out in a different form. Let us take s. 9 (1) of CECO. We could set it out like this:[1]

(Here you could move down each requirement, and if it does not apply to your situation decide the section was not applicable. At two points, where I have placed the words in *italics*, you would have to go elsewhere in the Ordinance for a definition.)

A person dealing as
consumer

        cannot by reference to
        any contract term

                be made to indemnify
                another person (whether
                a party to the contract or
                not)

                        in respect of liability
                        that may be incurred by
                        that other for negligence
                        or breach of contract

                                except in so far as the
                                contract term satisfies
                                the requirement of
                                reasonableness

---

1   With acknowledgements to Twining and Miers, *How to Do Things With Rules* Appendix II.

Algorithms

A more complex way of setting out the provisions of legislation would be in a algorithm. (See Twining & Miers, *How to Do Things With Rules.*) Here is an example applied to attempt to exclude liability for negligence — s. 7 (1) and (2):

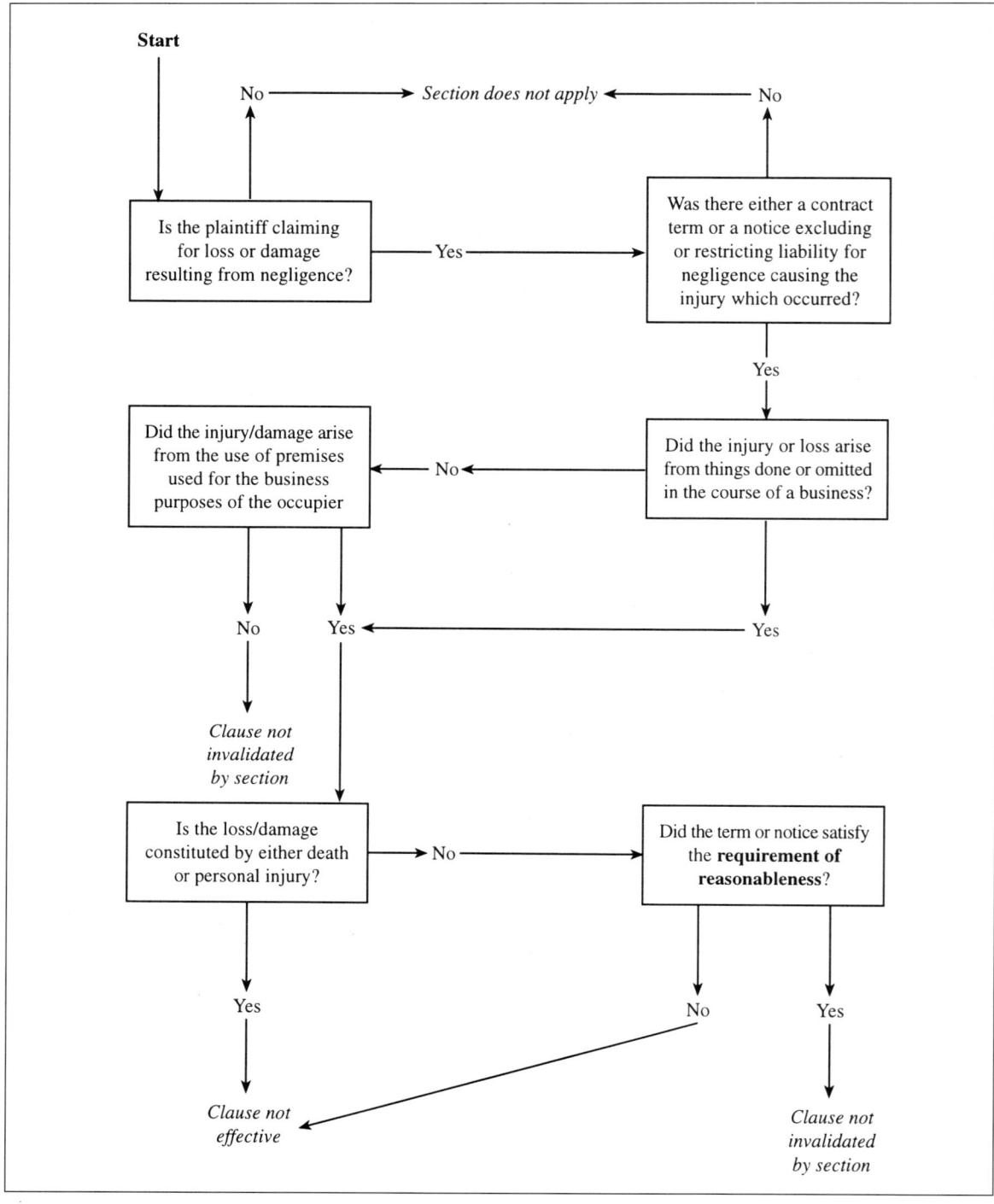

Note: this leaves something to be desired, since 'requirement of reasonableness' still needs to be 'unpacked'.

INTERPRETATION AND GENERAL CLAUSES ORDINANCE CAP 1

The Long Title of this Ordinance (IGCO), originally passed in 1966, is:

> To consolidate and amend the law relating to the construction, application and interpretation of laws, to make general provisions with respect thereto, to define terms and expressions used in laws and public documents, to make general provision with regard to public officers, public contracts and civil and criminal proceedings and for purposes and for matters incidental thereto or connected therewith.

It is the equivalent of the Interpretation Act in the UK, but is much longer.

- Section 3 gives definitions for a long list of words and phrases that occur quite often in legislation. In any piece of legislation any of these words and phrases will have the meaning assigned in the IGCO unless in the individual Ordinance the word or phrase is defined differently. Below is an extract from that section:

> "person" (人、人士、個人、人物、人選) includes any public body and any body of persons, corporate or unincorporate, and this definition shall apply notwithstanding that the word "person" occurs in a provision creating or relating to an offence or for the recovery of any fine or compensation;
>
> "personal name" (個人名字) means the names other than a surname which a person most commonly adopts in conjunction with his surname or, in the case of a person having no surname, the names which he commonly adopts;
>
> "pier" (碼頭) includes every quay, wharf or jetty of whatever description connected to and having direct access to the shore and used or intended to be used for the purposes of a pier, quay, wharf or jetty;
>
> "police officer" (警務人員) and terms or expression referring to ranks in the Royal Hong Kong Police Force shall bear the meanings respectively assigned to them by the Police Force Ordinance (Cap. 232);   *(Amended 29 of 1969 s. 2)*
>
> "power" (權、權力) includes any privilege, authority and discretion;
>
> "prescribed" (訂明) and "provided" (訂定), when used in or with reference to any Ordinance, mean prescribed or provided by that Ordinance or by subsidiary legislation made under that Ordinance;
>
> "prison" (獄、監獄) means any place or building or portion of a building set apart for the purpose of a prison under any Ordinance relating to prisons;

There is a very large number of other provisions (the Ordinance runs to over 100 sections).

- The best-known example is that which says that words like 'man' and 'he' include 'woman' and 'she' (as well as that words in the singular include the plural and vice versa) — s. 7.

- There are important provisions relating to legislation in both English and Chinese (ss. 10B–10E). Also to the making of subsidiary legislation, providing that such legislation must not conflict with the Ordinance under which it is made (which would be so even without the IGCO), and that contraventions of rules under such legislation may be made offences punishable by up to $5000 or 6 months imprisonment (s. 28); and the procedure for placing subsidiary legislation before Legco (s. 34).

- There is a provision allowing public officers to delegate their functions — something which might otherwise be beyond their powers (s. 43), a power in the Governor to appoint committees and other bodies (s. 47A).

- There is a provision to the effect that if a company commits an offence under any Ordinance any director of the company or other person involved in its management with whose consent or connivance the offence was committed is also guilty. (A company is counted as a separate legal person, which is, also by virtue of the IGCO — s. 3 — is included in the word 'person') (s. 84).

- It says that marginal notes and section headings in statutes shall not have the effect of law (s. 18), and that schedules to Ordinances have effect as part of the Ordinance — it is not necessary for them to be referred to in any section of the Ordinance (s. 12).

- Section 90 specifies the penalty for criminal offences where the Ordinance which creates them does not provide for a specific penalty.

- Another important section is 19, which provides:

  > An Ordinance shall be deemed to be remedial and shall receive such fair, large and liberal construction as will best ensure the attainment of the object of the Ordinance according to its true intent, meaning and spirit.

  This has no counterpart in UK law, but is to be found in the Interpretation Act of New Zealand.[2]

The Interpretation and General Clauses Ordinance has been an important tool in amending Hong Kong's laws to comply with the Basic Law and generally to effect changes necessitated by the change of sovereignty. Changes to the IGCO were introduced by the Hong Kong Reunification Ordinance (Ordinance No. 110 of 1997) and the Adaptation of Laws (Interpretative Provisions) Ordinance No. 26 of 1998. There is a new schedule added by s. 6 of the Reunification Ordinance: Schedule 8 deals with the construction of various words and phrases in pre-Handover Ordinances — such as 'Her Majesty', 'the Crown', 'Supreme

---

2   For a discussion of this section see *ibid*. Chap. 14.

Court', 'alien'. It may seem strange, when you look at BLIS or the *Laws of Hong Kong* that there are still a few Ordinances with names like Crown Proceedings Ordinance (at least as of January 1999). You need to look at the new schedule to IGCO to understand what words should now be used. Ordinance 26 of 1998 introduced a large number of new definitions in s. 3, and amending existing ones. Many other sections were repealed, amended or replaced.

➤ It should be obvious that this is an important Ordinance, which covers things other than the sorts of interpretation problems which would naturally occur to a reader of Ordinances. **Lawyers should be familiar with its contents.**

OTHER HELP IN UNDERSTANDING THE WORDS IN A STATUTE

You may use a good dictionary: the best one is the *Oxford English Dictionary*, which is in many volumes, and now on CD-ROM also. If this is not available, you should use the best dictionary available.

Dictionaries of Legal Definitions

You may want to look up how a particular word or phrase has been used by judges or in legislation. Remember how in Unit 1, question D you needed to know whether someone who has not yet got onto a bus could be described as a passenger. Maybe you can find your way to a precisely relevant case, such as *Check Chor-ching*. But if not you may want to see how the expression has been used in other situations. The 'Words and Phrases' sections of the law reports Index and *Hong Kong Law Digest* etc. will help you find such references. And see "Words and Phrases" the Table of Words and Phrases in the *Annotated Ordinances of Hong Kong* see Unit 10. This is available in CD-ROM format.

There are two other major collections of definitions.

Stroud's Judicial Dictionary

This gives you ways in which **judges** have interpreted words.

Words and Phrases Legally Defined

This covers **statutory definitions** as well as what judges have said about words.

➤ These two publications give you the definitions, rather than just referring you to the case or statute where the definition occurs, as 'Words and Phrases' indexes in law reports etc. do.

❖ Look up 'passenger' in each of these works. ☺ Should take less than ten minutes.

Interpretation of Statutes

The function of interpreting legislation is performed in the common law system by the courts. Apart from the material which is discussed in this Unit, the following rules or principles are relevant to the interpretation of legislation:

- The words of a statute should be given their ordinary meaning if possible. The courts will if necessary use a dictionary to help in this process, such as the *Oxford English Dictionary* — the most authoritative. This is the 'Literal Rule'.

- If the meaning of a statute is ambiguous, then the court should use the meaning which makes the most sense (the so-called 'Golden Rule').

- Again only in cases where the meaning is not clear, the courts should interpret a statute in the light of the mischief which the statute was intended to remedy — the 'Mischief Rule'.
  It has been said that in effect this has been made part of Hong Kong's law by the IGCO s. 19 (see above — see the observations in the case of *Wharf Cable v Attorney-General* 1995 MP 1493 March 25 1996 (Sears J.). It can, however, be argued that the IGCO is designed to encourage a more purposive approach than the mischief rule.

- It is now permissible to look at the legislative history of a statute (see *Pepper v Hart* [1993] AC 593, applied in Hong Kong in *Canon Kabushiki Kaisha v Green Cartridge Co.* [1996] 2 HKC 180).

- The Law Reform Commission has recommended in its *Report on the Use of extrinsic Materials as an Aid to Statutory Interpretation* (1997) that the rule in *Pepper v Hart* should continue to apply in Hong Kong, and that it should be included as new s. 19A of Cap 1; the proposal is based on the Australian Acts Interpretation Act s. 15AB

- The doctrine of precedent applies to the interpretation of statutes in the same way as other decisions made by the courts.

LEGISLATIVE HISTORY

You might want to know why a statute was enacted. Maybe for an essay topic. Maybe now even for use in court. It used not to be possible to cite the debates about a statute as an aid to its interpretation. Since the case of *Pepper v Hart* [1993] AC 593, this is permitted if the statute itself is unclear (see box on p. 122).[3] It may be necessary to read not so much the proceedings of the Hong Kong Legislative Council (Hansard) as those of the UK Parliament in order to understand why a Hong Kong piece of legislation was passed. Hong Kong Ordinances have often been copied from UK ones with very little discussion or amendment. And Hong Kong Legco debates are far less detailed than those in the UK Parliament. However, ➤ watch out for differences between the Hong Kong legislation and its UK original. The differences are likely to be significant.

Background to Hong Kong Legislation

There may be a Law Reform Commission report that preceded the Ordinance, or even another report — of a Select Committee of Legco or some other committee. These are rare in Hong Kong. Try the *Hong Kong Law Journal* for any note on the statute, or an earlier article discussing the necessity to change the law. Go to Hansard (see **Government Publications**) for the Legco debates.

You can now find minutes of some Bills Committees on the World Wide Web which may help in the interpretation of legislation (these are available very much sooner than Hansard, the report of proceedings of the whole LegCo, is available); the url is **<http://legco.gov.hk/yr98–99/english/bc/bc.htm>** for the current year. Reports of the Law Reform Commission may also be available on the Web; for example the Statutory Interpretation report is at **<http://www.info.gov.hk/justice/related/2/index.htm>**.

Background to UK Legislation

Here you are likely to find some help in the annotations to the original Act in *Current Law Statutes Annotated.* This will tell you why the Act was passed and refer you to Law Commission and other committee/commission reports. Also try journal articles (look in *Legal Journals Index*, statute section).

You can now find much material, including Hansard, on the Web:
For Bills: **<http://www.parliament.the-stationery-office.co.uk/pa/pabills.htm>**
For various House of Commons papers including Hansard, Committes etc.:
    <http://www.parliament.the-stationery-office.co.uk/pa/cm/cmpubns.htm>
For the House of Lords:
    <http://www.parliament.the-stationery-office.co.uk/pa/ld/ldpubns.htm>
For recent Law Commission publications including reports see
    <http://www.gtnet.gov.uk/lawcomm/library/library.htm>

---

3   See Wesley-Smith, *The Sources of Hong Kong Law*, Chap. 15.

SELF-STUDY QUESTIONS

⊘ Ten minutes.

1. You have found a word in a statute which is important to the point of law you are researching but which is unclear or ambiguous. Can you suggest seven ways in which you might be able to get guidance about how to interpret the word?

2. What does it mean to say that 'or' is to be construed disjunctively?

3. How can you find out why a statute was passed?

Unit 10 Finding Legislation and Related Matters

OBJECTIVES

By the end of this Unit you will:

- be able to find the text of a statute as it was passed by the Legislature
- be able to find the text of a statute as amended to-date or at a particular point in the past
- be able to find subsidiary legislation
- be able to find out whether a statute has been cited in a case
- be able to find out whether a piece of UK legislation has been copied in Hong Kong
- be able to find out whether a piece of legislation is in force

⊘ At least three hours if you go to look at the material in the library.

Now you know what to do with a statute when you have one in your hand. You need to learn how to find statutes. This is not a particularly difficult task, **provided** that all you want is the text of a new Ordinance, which does not amend an earlier Ordinance. But that may not be good enough. You may want to find the text of the statute **as amended**. If you are using UK legislation, it is quite easy to find the text of statutes as they pass through Parliament, but more difficult to find a text which incorporates amendments. In Hong Kong, on the other hand, it is quite easy to find the amended text of a statute, but the original text, before amendment, may be less ready to hand! Even more difficult will be the intermediate stages (say, to locate how a 1980 statute stood by 1990 when you are in 1998).

HONG KONG LEGISLATION

Gazette

All Hong Kong legislation is first published in a *Supplement to the Government Gazette* (see Government Publications). This has been so ever since 1844. Periodically, revised editions of the laws have been published: bound, up-dated collections. There were editions in 1904,

1912, 1924, 1937 and 1950, as well as the two editions discussed in more detail below. In between new editions it was necessary to go to the *Gazette* supplement version, which is also published as an annual volume of the *Laws of Hong Kong*.

The Loose-leaf Edition

From 1991 a new Loose-leaf Edition began to appear. It is loose-leaf in the sense that a single sheet can be removed and replaced with amendments, whereas in the most recent Revised Edition the whole Ordinance had to be replaced. Some of the Ordinances appear in Chinese as well as English versions. Ordinances which appear in both Revised and Loose-leaf editions have the same number in each.

By mid-1998, 42 volumes of Ordinances had been published in 14 batches (or issues). Naturally the higher number volumes include the more recent Ordinances where these were not simply amending earlier Ordinances. Each time there is a fresh issue, new sheets can be issued for existing Ordinances. Amendments will usually be included only when they come into effect. Whole new Ordinances will be reprinted in the Loose-leaf Edition even though they are not yet in force.

* Early in Volume One you will find a list, on blue pages, of the Ordinances showing how up-to-date each one should be if all replacement pages have been properly filed. This list changes every time there is a new issue of loose-leaf pages.
* The first volume now contains Constitutional Documents and National Laws that apply in Hong Kong, beginning with the Constitution of the PRC, followed by the Basic Law, various NPC Decisions, the Joint Declaration, etc.
* There is an index of Short Titles, which lists **all** Ordinances and their numbers with subsidiary legislation. It is a bi-lingual list, and appears in two versions, Chinese first and then English — in effect a contents list of the edition.
* There is a chronological list of all Hong Kong Ordinances since 1844, giving the original number when enacted, the current number (if any) and date of repeal (if any). This is now Appendix 1 in the final volume.

There is a pink sheet before each Ordinance which should show you when the version was published, and gives the legislative history of the Ordinance (when it was passed and when it was been amended). There is an example on the next page.

The penultimate volume contains Ordinances with Cap. numbers over 1000. These relate to individual institutions, and to charities, such as the University of Hong Kong Ordinance, Cap. 1053.

▶ The Basic Law is not an enactment of the Hong Kong legislature but of the National People's Congress of the PRC (see above and p. 146).

Here is a specimen pink page which appears before an Ordinance in the Loose-leaf Edition.

Check List and Instructions for the

PENSION BENEFITS ORDINANCE
(CAP. 99)

See the Master Check List (in the Contents and Index Volume) to verify that this is the latest issue referred to in that list. To determine how up to date this enactment is, see page 1 of the Master Check List and Instructions in Volume 1.

Withdraw pages	Insert pages	You should now have pages	Issue number
		1 - 2	6
		3 - 4	9
		5 - 8	6
		9 - 12.1	9
		13 - 16	6
		17 - 18	7
19	19	19	10

Enactment History

Originally 36 of 1987 — R. Ed. 1987, 61 of 1988, 86 of 1988, R. Ed. 1988, L.N. 23 of 1991, L.N. 295 of 1992, 54 of 1992, 3 of 1993, 4 of 1993, L.N. 411 of 1993, 98 of 1994, L.N. 66 of 1995

The following are not yet in operation —

Amendment to s. 15(3) — see 21 of 1995 s. 40 (in operation on 1.7.1995)

Issue 10

Authorized Loose-leaf Edition, Printed and Published by the Government Printer, Hong Kong

After the Ordinance comes the subsidiary (delegated) legislation. There is a green sheet which lists all the legislation. Before each individual piece of subsidiary legislation is a pink sheet like that which appears before Ordinances.

Below is the list of subsidiary legislation for the Ordinance which you have just seen the pink sheet. In this case the list of subsidiary legislation is quite short.

➤ Note three different types of delegated legislation under this Ordinance: Regulations, Notices and Orders. Another type sometimes found is Rules.

CAP. 99

SUBSIDIARY LEGISLATION

		Page
1.	Pension Benefits Regulations	**A** 1
2.	Pension Benefits Ordinance (Established Offices) Order	**B** 1
3.	Pension Benefits (Prescribed Ages) (Directorate Ranks) Notice	**C** 1
4.	Pension Benefits (Prescribed Ages) (Senior Rank and Rank and File Grades) (Correctional Services Department) Order	**D** 1
5.	Pension Benefits (Prescribed Ages) (Senior Rank and Rank and File Grades) (Customs and Excise Department) Order	**E** 1
6.	Pension Benefits (Prescribed Ages) (Senior Rank and Rank and File Grades) (Fire Services Department) Order	**F** 1
7.	Pension Benefits (Prescribed Ages) (Senior Rank and Rank and File Grades) (Immigration Department) Order	**G** 1
8.	Pension Benefits (Prescribed Ages) (Senior Rank and Rank and File Grades) (Royal Hong Kong Police Force) Order	**H** 1
9.	Pension Benefits (Prescribed Ages) (Senior Ranks) (Government Flying Service) Notice	**I** 1

The Revised Edition

The most recent revised edition was just known as: the *Revised Edition of the Laws of Hong Kong*. It did away with the periodical reprinting of the entire set of statutes. It consisted of separate booklets bound together in binders. Periodically Ordinances were reprinted, incorporating all amendments, and the new version was inserted into the binders of the revised Laws, as well as being available as a separate booklet. Pending such reprinting, the copies in the binders were updated manually, by handwritten additions, and slips of paper stuck in.[1] A second copy of these amendments appeared in Volume 31, called 'Minor Amendments'. The updating ceased in 1990 when the Loose-leaf Edition began. This system could have been permanent, but the Loose-leaf Edition was thought to be more flexible.

There are several Appendices, of which only Appendix I is (as at early 1996) reproduced in the Loose-leaf Edition:

- Appendix I: contains the *Letters Patent and the Royal Instructions, the Standing Orders of the Legislative Council,* and a miscellaneous collection of regulations and instruments applicable to Hong Kong usually under English legislation

- Appendix II: a list of English Acts which apply in Hong Kong, plus the actual text of the British Nationality Act 1981, and the Hong Kong Act 1985 (providing for the end of sovereignty in 1997)

- Appendix IIA: the text of certain UK Acts which apply to Hong Kong under the Application of English Law Ordinance, including the Habeas Corpus Acts

- Appendix IIB: (see p. 138)

- Appendix III: Orders in Council and rules made under UK Acts and applying in Hong Kong

- Appendix IV: various constitutional documents, treaties etc., including the Treaty of Nanking and the Lease of Kowloon

In order to find out which volume an Ordinance is to be found in, look in the separate Index Volume.

Legislative history

In the Revised Edition there is a marginal note which tells you the date of the original Ordinance and of amendments.

---

1   There is at least one firm which will carry out this service for subscribers in the case of the Loose-leaf Edition.

The Annotated Ordinances of Hong Kong

In 1996 the first elements of this new venture appeared. This is published by Butterworths, and contains Ordinances and subsidiary legislation bound together into individual booklets. There is a separate 'Finder Binder' which includes indexes and updating tools. The elements contained in the Finder Binder, as contained in the first issue, are:

- Subject Index: ➤ This is the first time such an index is available for Hong Kong legislation. The official editions have only the lists of the names of the Ordinances.

- Lists of Short and Long Titles of Ordinances: There are two lists: one in the order of Chapter Number, and the other in English alphabetical order. ➤ If you want a list which is organized by Chinese title, you will have to go to the Loose-leaf Edition.

- Noter-up: This says it 'lists Ordinances and items affecting Ordinances which are not published in Issue 9 of the Loose-leaf Edition of the Laws of Hong Kong, up to 31 October'. More precisely, in the first Issue (Issue 0 as with some other loose-leaf publications) the bulk of the Noter-up is a list of all Ordinances too recent to appear in Issue 9, and all Ordinances changed by some instrument which is too recent to appear in Issue 9, with a note of the repealing or amending instrument and the date it was passed or came into effect. This list was up-to-date to the end of October 1995. There are also lists of 1995 Ordinances and 1995 Bills. ➤ The noter-up is presumably intended to provide information supplementary to the most recent issue of the Loose-leaf Edition, and to the information contained in individual Ordinance booklets.

- Words and Phrases Defined and Judicially Considered: This includes definitions and interpretations both in Ordinances and in Hong Kong cases (reported and unreported). It does not seem to aim to be comprehensive so far as Ordinances are concerned, but is the first index of statutory definitions produced in Hong Kong.

- Legislation Judicially Considered.

An individual booklet of an Ordinance will contain:

- a statement of the date up to which the information is current
- a table of cases cited in the annotations to the Ordinance and Regulations in the booklet
- a table of legislation (other than the legislation actually reproduced) mentioned in the annotations
- a table showing which sections of the English legislation the Hong Kong sections are based on
- a table of other sources cited in the annotations, e.g. books, articles, Law Reform Commission reports, Hansard
- if the Ordinance has a Chinese version, a glossary of Chinese equivalents of English terms, derived from that version
- a brief introduction to the Ordinance — what it is intended to achieve, its history, etc.

- the text of the Ordinance annotated section by section
- the text of subsidiary legislation similarly annotated

➤ In case of any doubt the official government version of the legislation is to be relied on. It is wise to check any information with the official version.

Using the Annotated Ordinances

Suppose you are interested in the law of libel (a tort). You might look up in the Subject Index in the Finder Binder and find this:

LIBEL

Generally .... Defamation Ordinance (Cap 21)

The Defamation Ordinance was in fact one of the first to be reproduced for this publication. ➤ You may well find that the Ordinance indicated in response to other searches is not yet in the publication.

If you turn to the individual booklet of the Ordinance, you will find each of the items listed above except subsidiary legislation for this Ordinance.

Here is a specimen section with notes:

> **[22. Broadcast statements**
>
> For the purposes of the law of libel and slander, the broadcasting of words shall be treated as publication in permanent form.]
>
> NOTES
>
> This section was added pursuant to s 11 of the Defamation and Libel (Amendment) Ordinance 1961 (33 of 1961), commencing 4 August 1961.
>
> **UK** The wording of this section is the same as s 1 of the Defamation Act 1952.
>
> **Broadcasting of words by means of wireless telegraphy** For the construction of these words, see s 2 above, and the notes thereto.
>
> **Permanent form** A false defamatory statement in permanent form gives rise to an action for libel. That the permanent form need not consist of writing or print has been long established: see *Monson v Tussauds Ltd* [1894] 1 QB 671, [1891-4] All ER Rep 1051, CA and *Youssoupoff v Metro Goldwyn Mayer Pictures Ltd* [1934] 50 TLR 581, 78 SJ 617, CA.
>
> **Slander of title, etc** For the application of this section to actions for slander of title etc, see s 24 below.
>
> **Definitions** For 'broadcasting' and 'words', see s 2 above.
>
> **Glossary** For Chinese equivalent of 'broadcast', 'broadcasting', 'libel', 'permanent form', 'publication', 'slander', 'statement' and 'words', see *Glossary of Chinese Words and Phrases* above.

The notes here are quite clear. They could perhaps have been fuller — e.g., they do not really state what the law was before the section was passed: that there was some uncertainty, but unscripted broadcasts were perhaps slander and those using a script were libel.

HOW TO UPDATE HONG KONG LEGISLATION

It is very important to ensure that one has the latest version of the law. In the case of Ordinances, this process is now much simpler, since the Loose-leaf Edition of the *Laws of Hong Kong* has been completed. Ordinances are published first in the *Government Gazette Legal Supplement No. 1* (LS No. 1). This is the official, authorized text. Subsequent amendments, repeals etc. are all published in LS No. 1. The Supplements are published weekly and contain the full text of legislation passed during the week. (Occasionally an Extraordinary Gazette is published.) Every month a set of Indexes to each Supplement is published which shows what has happened since the current pink sheet at the front of each Ordinance or piece of subsidiary legislation was printed.

Here is the beginning of a recent *Gazette Supplement No. 1* list of new Ordinances, since the most recent issue of the Loose-leaf Edition was printed:

INDEX OF NEW ORDINANCES AND AMENDMENTS TO ORDINANCES NOT YET PUBLISHED IN THE LOOSE-LEAF EDITION OF THE LAWS OF HONG KONG AS UPDATED BY ISSUE 14
(To 30.9.1998)

This index lists new Ordinances and amendments to Ordinances which are not published in the Loose-leaf Edition as updated by the most recent issue (i.e. Issue 14). The index is published monthly, and for new Ordinances or amendments to Ordinances published later than the index, users should refer to the individual Legal Supplements to the Gazette.

2.   Part 1 lists new principal Ordinances. Part 2 lists Ordinances that have been amended, repealed or otherwise affected; following each item is the Ordinance or the Legal Notice that effected the amendment or repeal, etc.

N.B.   (*a*)   Items arising from legislation enacted in September 1998 are printed in bold type.

      (*b*)   Material is included whether or not it is in operation, but is not included when it is shown (as not yet in operation) in the pink Check Lists of the Loose-leaf Edition.

      (*c*)   No attempt is made to address repeals of the nature referred to in s. 3(2) of the Hong Kong Bill of Rights Ordinance (Cap. 383).

PART 1

New Principal Ordinances

(For amendments to these, see Part 2)

Chinese Nationality (Miscellaneous Provisions) (128 of 1997)

Electoral Affairs Commission (129 of 1997)

Hong Kong Special Administrative Region Passports (127 of 1997)

Land (Compulsory Sale for Redevelopment) (30 of 1998)

Legislative Council (134 of 1997)

Prevention of Copyright Piracy (22 of 1998)

Road Traffic (Validation of Collection of Fees) (7 of 1998)

Step by Step for Updating Using Paper Material

It is now better to use BLIS since this is usually up-to-date to only a few days ago.

1. Find the Ordinance. Amendments, repeals, etc. up to the date of publication will be included in the text.

2. Check how up-to-date the version in the Loose-leaf Edition is. At the beginning of Volume 1 are the blue sheets containing Master Check List and Instructions for the latest Issue of pages which are in your copy. It will tell you that, ➤ assuming the filing has been done properly, the edition will be up-to-date to a certain date, except for some Ordinances listed which are up-to-date to different dates. (For example, when preparing this page, I was asked by someone else about updating the Crimes Ordinance. The Ordinance was up-dated to Issue 10. When we looked at the Filing Instruction we found that Issue 10 generally up-dated the Loose-leaf Edition to 1 October 1995; but the Crimes Ordinance was listed as being up-dated to 31 August 1995 only.)

    ➤ It is unwise to assume that the filing has been done properly. Look at the pink sheet before the Ordinance — it will tell you which sheets you should have and from which issue they should come (see the specimen in the box on p. 127).

3. Go to *Government Gazette Legal Supplement No. 1* latest monthly Index. As well as the list of new Ordinances (see above), you will also find an Index of all amendments to Ordinances since the most recent Issue of the Loose-leaf Edition. Here is an extract from this showing a list of those Ordinances which have been amended since Issue 11 with the name and citation of the amending Ordinance or subordinate legislation.

PART 2

AMENDMENTS, REPEALS, ETC.

(N.B. This Part does not include commencement notices)

Administrative Appeals Board (c. 442)—46 of 1996, 51 of 1996

Air Passenger Departure Tax (c. 140)—LN 122/96, 30 of 1996

Airport Authority (c. 483)—LN 391/96

Amusement Game Centres (c. 435)—LN 372/96 s. 3(2)

Amusement Rides (Safety) (c. 449)—LN 372/96 s. 3(2)

Animals and Plants (Protection of Endangered Species) (c. 187)—LN 204/96

Antiquities and Monuments (c. 53)—LN 372/96 s. 3(2)

Banking (c. 155)—LN 70/96, LN 336/96

Bankruptcy (c. 6)—LN 139/96

Betting Duty (c. 108)—15 of 1996, 31 of 1996

(Note that a citation consisting of a number and a date only indicates an Ordinance. LN followed by a number indicates a Regulation or other subsidiary legislation, the text will be found in *Legal Supplement No 2*.)

4. Check any individual *Gazette Supplements No. 1* since the date of the monthly list, ➤ and *Supplement No. 2* in case there has been any amendment by way of LN and not by amending Ordinance!

5. If the Ordinance is not in the Loose-leaf Edition, check whether it is in the *Gazette* — first by using the list of new Ordinances (see the box on p. 132), and then by checking individual issues since.

Subsidiary legislation is included in full after its parent Ordinance in each version of the Laws. As with the Ordinances, there may be later ones, which must be looked for in *Gazette Supplement No. 2*.

❖ Try updating the Employees Compensation Ordinance. Begin by finding out the number of the Ordinance from Volume 1 of the Loose-leaf Edition, and then see what amendments there have been right up to the most recent *Gazette* you can find. ☺ About 40 minutes.

The *Hong Kong Law Digest* also contains notes of amendments to Ordinances.

The most recent issue of *Hong Kong Law Digest* contains a Cumulative Table of Amended Legislation (cumulative for the current year). ➤ The most recent issue is at least one month behind the *Government Gazette*.

The *Annotated Ordinances of Hong Kong* will include in the Noter-up revisions ➤ after the date of the individual booklet and before the date of the Noter-up. Here is an extract from the Noter-up as it refers to the Defamation Ordinance (see p. 131, upper box).

DEFAMATION ORDINANCE (CAP 21)

s 6   *Rep:* Administration of Justice (Miscellaneous Provisions) (No 2) Ordinance (68/1995, 1 September 1995)

s 10   *Am:* Administration of Justice (Miscellaneous Provisions) Ordinance 1995 (13/1995, 1 April 1995)

Finding the Statutory Position at a Point in the Past

Suppose you need to find out what the position was at some point in the past, with respect to a piece of legislation which has been amended.

Why would you want to do this?

You might need to know what the law was at a time when a contract was made, but are aware that an Ordinance which affects the contract has been amended, or come into force, **since** the contract was made.

If what you need to know is the original version of an Ordinance, that should be easy, as all Ordinances were published in the *Gazette*, and then are bound together as an annual volume of the Ordinances of Hong Kong, going right back to 1844.

If what you want is before 1989, you should be able to see from the Revised Edition when the slips of paper were added, or the annotations written, and work back to the earlier position. There will be at a date on the individual booklet of the statute telling you when it was printed.

There are also binders of superseded statutes of the Revised Edition, themselves full of slips of paper and handwritten annotations, which will take the process back to the earlier booklets. Always look at the date when the booklet was printed. The earliest booklets in the Revised Edition will be dated 1966.

➤ Always cross check with the issues of the *Gazette*, in case the slips have become detached, or the handwritten additions were incomplete.

If what you want is between the beginning of 1990 and the present day, things will be rather more tedious, as you may not find superseded individual pages of the Loose-leaf Edition preserved — at least in a way which is easy to find and use. You will have to go back to the Revised Edition and then work your way through the *Gazette* until you have updated the Ordinance to the crucial date.

BLIS makes it possible to find any version between 30 June 1997 and the present. It does not give the text of any version before 30 June 1997, unless that text was still in force on that date.

Is It in Force?

Some Ordinances come into force on the day they are published in the *Gazette*. Others will come into force on a day specified in the Ordinance itself. Commencement Notices are delegated legislation and are printed in the *Gazette*.

In the Loose-leaf Edition of the Laws, the pink sheet before each Ordinance tells you whether there was any part which was not in force **at the time the pink sheet was issued**. Periodically there is a list in *Gazette Legal Supplement No. 2* of Commencement Notices **published in the current year**.

The necessary steps are:

1. Find the Ordinance.
2. Look at the pink sheet. It will tell you whether the operation of any part of the Ordinance, as printed in the Loose-leaf Edition, was not in force at the date of the pink sheet, and what was the Commencement Date of any section brought into operation before the pink sheet.
3. If the section in which you are interested was not in force (or the date when it would be in force was not indicated) at the time the pink sheet was printed, go to the *Gazette Supplement Number 2*. Find the most recent Monthly List of Commencement Notices. Here is an extract from such a list.

70 INDEX TO COMMENCEMENT NOTICES	*Date of Gazette*	*L.N. No.*	*Page*
Professional Accountants (Amendment) Ordinance 1995 (85 of 1995) in operation on 2 August 1996	2. 8.96	364	B1558
Residential Care Homes (Elderly Persons) Ordinance (Cap. 459)—			
Section 6 in operation on 1 June 1996	1. 3.96	121	B554
安老院條例（第 459 章）——			
第 6 條在 1996 年 6 月 1 日實施	1. 3.96	121	B555
Road Traffic (Amendment) Ordinance 1996 (13 of 1996) in operation on 1 August 1996	14. 6.96	266	B1148
1996 年道路交通（修訂）條例（1996 年第 13 號）在 1996 年 8 月 1 日實施	14. 6.96	266	B1149
Sex Discrimination Ordinance (Cap. 480)—			
Sections 63, 64, 67, 68 and 69 and Schedule 6 in operation on 20 May 1996	10. 5.96	185	B858

4. Check the individual *Gazette Supplements No. 2* after the Monthly list for any further Commencement Notices.
5. Note that the Monthly list covers only the current year. Is there any risk that there is a gap between the publication of the pink sheet and the beginning of the current year? If so, you will have to go to the list in the *Gazette Supplement No. 2* at the end of December of the previous year, to check the list of Commencement Notices there too.

➤ BLIS includes a note of any provisions not yet in force.

THE RELATIONSHIP BETWEEN HONG KONG AND FOREIGN LAW

If you want to know which English legislation has formed the basis for a Hong Kong Ordinance, you will find that in the marginal or end note in the Hong Kong legislation, though this is not necessarily complete, as we shall see.

It is more difficult to find out whether an English Act has a Hong Kong counterpart. If they have the same name it is pretty easy. But this is not always the case. There is in theory a scientific way of doing it. At the end of Volume 28 of the Revised Laws you will find Appendix IIB which lists the UK legislation which is referred to in Hong Kong legislation (i.e. in the notes saying where the Hong Kong provisions come from). If these notes were complete and up-to-date, this Appendix would answer our question. But the Hong Kong note may simply be referring to the **original** English provision, although what you may be interested in is a more recent English amendment.

To take an example I encountered when teaching Tort: the Hong Kong equivalent of s. 148 (3) of the Road Traffic Act 1972 (now s. 149 (3) of the Road Traffic Act 1988!) is s. 12 (2) and (3) of the Motor Vehicles Insurance (Third Party Risks) Ordinance Cap. 272. As it happens, I found this out by using some guesswork. The English provision was originally introduced by the Motor Vehicles (Passenger Insurance) Act of 1971 (this can be found from, for example, *Current Law Statutes Annotated* — see p. 142). That at least could give me a clue that I was looking for legislation connected with insurance. But neither the 1972 nor the 1971 Act appears in Appendix IIB (or in the note after s. 12 of cap. 272 which gives only the Road Traffic Act 1934, an Act which has been totally repealed in England!). So Appendix IIB may be of some use, but if you don't find the English Act for which you are looking, **don't give up**.

I reproduce below the beginning of Appendix IIB. You will see that you need to know the year (regnal or calendar depending on the date) plus the cap. number in order to identify the English legislation.

REFERENCES TO UNITED KINGDOM STATUTES IN THE ORDINANCES OF HONG KONG AS AT 31.12.88

1351	c. 2	(25 Edw. 3, St. 5)		Cap. 200, s. 2(1)(*a*), (*b*), (*c*), (*d*), (*e*)
1361	c. 1	(34 Edw. 3)		Cap. 88, Schedule
1540	c. 32	(32 Hen. 8)	s. 1	Cap. 352, s. 2
			s. 2	s. 4(3)
	c. 37			Cap. 88, Schedule
1666	c. 11	(18 & 19 Car. 2)		Cap. 88, Schedule
1670	c. 10	(22 & 23 Car. 2)		Cap. 88, Schedule
1679	c. 2	(31 Car. 2)		Cap. 88, Schedule
1689	c. 5	(2 Will. & Mary)		Cap. 88, Schedule
1695	c. 3	(7 & 8 Will. 3)	s. 6	Cap. 200, s. 4(1)
1698	c. 22	(10 Will. 3)		Cap. 88, Schedule
	c. 7	(11 Will. 3)	ss. 7, 8	Cap. 200, s. 20
1707	c. 72	(Ruffhead c. 18) (6 Ann.)		Cap. 88, Schedule

➤ There is no equivalent of Appendix IIB in the Loose-leaf Edition.

Sometimes Hong Kong legislation is based on that of somewhere other than the UK, for example, Australia. How would you know that this is so? Maybe you could find out from a Law Reform Commission Report, or from Hansard. ➤ *The Annotated Ordinances* **may** help. Occasionally there is a note about non-UK legislation in the Loose-leaf Edition: s. 81A of the Criminal Procedure Ordinance says [*cf. New Zealand Crimes Acts s. 383*]. The Bill of Rights refers to the International Covenant on Civil and Political Rights.

➤ It may not matter so much where the legislation was derived from; you may find it helpful to know that a similar phrase has been used in another jurisdiction and how the courts have interpreted it. The Index of Words and Phrases in the law reports of a possible relevant country may help, as may, increasingly, electronic sources which enable you to search the whole text of statutes and cases for words and phrases.

Statutes Judicially Considered

We are not as well served in Hong Kong as those in the UK (see below). There is no equivalent of the *Legislation Citator* which lists amendments etc., **and** cases considering the legislation all in one place. The *Annotated Ordinances of Hong Kong* has what will eventually be the most comprehensive legislation citator in Hong Kong. The *Hong Kong Law Digest* has a statute citator for the current year only. Some series of law reports also have such indexes/citators. Addison's *Digest* does not.

However, now the *Consolidated Index to all reported Hong Kong Decisions* Vol. 2 (1998) contains an 'Index of Legislation Referred To' in Hong Kong cases reported in Hong Kong and UK Law reports to the end of 1997.

Here is an extract from the 1996 *Hong Kong Law Digest*.

LEGISLATION JUDICIALLY CONSIDERED
CUMULATIVE (1996)

The following Hong Kong Ordinances and subsidiary legislation have been judicially considered in 1996. Ordinances are printed in bold typeface; subsidiary legislation in ordinary typeface. References are to paragraph numbers in [1996] HKLD.

Amusement Game Centres Ordinance (Cap.435)

S.5(4)(a). See *Cheng Chun Chon v Commissioner for Television and Entertainment Licensing,* E133

S.9(2)(d). See *Cheng Chun Chon v Commissioner for Television and Entertainment Licensing,* E133

Architects Registration Ordinance (Cap.408)

S.22. See *Leung Siu Kwong v An Inquiry Committee Established under s.22 of the Architects Registration Ordinance, Cap.408,* D82

BLIS

This stands for Bi-lingual Laws Information Service. This is on the Internet at **<http://www.justice.gov.hk/>**.

Below you will find a very brief description of how to find an Ordinance. There is more detail in Unit 18.

You will find a list of Ordinances beginning with Cap 1 and down the left side a frame allowing you to choose Ordinances [default position] or Subsidiary Legislation or Ordinances **and** Subsidiary Legislation; ○ English [default position] or Chinese; and Versions: current or current and past (for an explanation of this last choice see Unit 18. Th panel says:
Go to Chapter row (the box says 1 which you replace with your choice.)

At the bottom it says │ View Now │ ➤ In order to carry out the changes of choice you have made you must click this button.

This is the usual way to find the complete text of a statute of which you know the Cap number.

1. Fill in its number in the Chapter row box (click on the ○ next to Ordinances and Subsidiary Legislation if you want both) and click | View Now |

   You will probably find you see a list of Ordinances which begin **approximately** with the one you want!

2. Click on the blue arrow pointing to the Ordinance you want. If you have clicked Ordinances and Subsidiary Legislation you will now see a list of titles of that Ordinance and its Subsidiary Legislation. Click on the blue arrow next to the one you want to see more of, and you will see a list of sections/regulations. If the section you want does not yet appear on the list click on "Next List" until it does.

3. Then click on the blue arrow next to the section you want. To move to the next section click on "Next Section".

UNITED KINGDOM LEGISLATION

Your first question might be — why is UK legislation so important? The fact is that much Hong Kong legislation is based upon UK legislation, sometimes being, like the Control of Exemption Clauses Ordinance, a simple copy. Other legislation will use phrases and words which have been used for many years in drafting UK legislation. So you might want to look at UK legislation for the following reasons:

England or UK?

You might wonder whether there is any logic to the use of these two expressions. There should be! England (and Wales but it tends to get missed out in casual reference, except by Welsh people) has a separate legal system from Scotland. The latter has a civil rather than a common law system, and the cases may be somewhat different. Not always — *Donoghue v Stevenson* was a Scottish case. But there is no such thing as an **English** Parliament (has not been since 1707); statutes are the product of the Parliament of the United Kingdom. On the other hand, statutes very often apply to part of the UK only, which will sometimes be clear from the name. Northern Ireland is also part of the UK.

- because all or part of a piece of Hong Kong is copied from the UK legislation and English cases might help to interpret it
- because you might find the Hong Kong legislation differs slightly, and deliberately, from UK legislation, and the comparison might help you to understand the former
- because you are involved in a case which involves English law

- because you have to write an essay which involves suggesting changes in Hong Kong law
- because you are advising the Hong Kong government about possible changes in the law (one day this may be the case!)

Form of Reference to UK Legislation

We saw that Hong Kong Ordinances are given a number in the year in which they are enacted, and then receive their permanent number on being reprinted in the *Laws of Hong Kong*. The position in UK is a little more complicated:

Modern system   Since 1962 the correct form of citation has been the Short Title of the Act followed by the calendar year. Sometimes you may see the Chapter number (Cap. ?? or c. ??) within that year also referred to — e.g. see the references in the Control of Exemption Clauses Ordinance to *1977 c.50 UK* which means the Unfair Contract Terms Act. This brief and cryptic form of reference is also used in publications such as the *Chronological Table of the Statutes* (see p. 144).

> ### A Historical Oddity
>
> In 1752 England changed its calendar (to fall in line with the rest of Europe, not to mention Scotland, so that the year began on 1 January instead of 25 March (which is why, for the curious, the name of October is derived from eight when it is the tenth month). Earlier statutes passed in the months of January to March therefore changed year! An example is the Bill of Rights 1688 or 1689. See 24 Geo 2 cap 23.
>
> (With thanks to Peter Wesley-Smith who reminded me to put this in.)

In the past   The reference was to the parliamentary session within which the Act was passed, identified by the regnal year (the year of the reign) of the monarch. A Parliamentary session is usually about a year long, but may be less or more depending on the timing of elections. For example, 6 & 7 Vict. cap. 80: the eightieth statute passed during the parliamentary session which straddled the 6th and 7th years of the reign of Queen Victoria. Less obvious abbreviations include Geo. for George and Car. for Charles (actually for the Latin version Carolus).

You may find a set of statutes known as the *Statutes at Large* which has this form of reference on the spines of the volumes. These go up to 1865; they are not comprehensive, at least until the end of the reign of Queen Anne (1714); and the number in the pre-1714 volumes may not be those of the 'official' system. A gentleman called Ruffhead seems to have been responsible for this. He made his own collection, not including all statutes, and he gave them his own numbers. There is another version known as the *Statutes of the Realm*, the first official collection of English legislation, which began publication in 1810, but did not include statutes more recent than 1714. A table showing the relationship between Ruffhead's edition and the *Statutes of the Realm* edition appears in the *Chronological Table of the Statutes* (see p. 144). There are other private collections including Chitty, *Statutes of Practical Utility*.[2]

Finding an English Statute

Since 1996 all new statutes are available on the Internet at **<http://www.hmso.gov.uk/ acts.htm>**.

If you know the name of the statute and you simply want to see what it says, you may use one of the following: *The Law Reports — Statutes* edition, published by the Incorporated Council of Law Reporting since 1866, or *Public General Acts* as published by HM Stationery Office, the offical series. There is also another offical series, a looseleaf version called *Statutes in Force*.

➤ Better is probably *Current Law Statutes Annotated*. This prints statutes with comments (about the origin of the statute, possible interpretations etc. That is what is meant by 'annotated'). Firstly they bring out a copy very quickly, printed on blue paper without annotations. This is in a current service file. The blue version is replaced by a white version with annotations. Annually all the statutes are replaced by a bound volume, annotated. This system is very quick.

If you want to know what legislation there is on a particular topic, use *Halsbury's Statutes*. This is also annotated (➤ but often not as fully as the *Current Law* version); it will if necessary split up a statute and put part of it in one volume and part in another if it deals with different subject matter. This makes this publication less useful if you simply want the words of a statute for which you have the reference. There are 50 volumes. Periodically a volume will be reprinted in a revised version (and will say so on its spine; for example, the volume on *Criminal Law* says '1994 Re-issue' on its spine — use that rather than an earlier version if you want to be up-to-date). There is also a *Cumulative Supplement* which explains the effect of all new Acts, Statutory Instruments and Cases. The Cumulative Supplement (a new one is published each year) is itself supplemented, until the replacement is available, by the 'Noter-up'.

Finally there are two binders of new statutes, filed in a way which corresponds to the organization of the 50 main volumes.

Further reading: *Butterworths Legal Research Guide* para. 3.39ff.

---

2   See Grossman, *Legal Research, Historical Foundations of the Electronic Age* (New York: Oxford UP, 1994) Chap. 3.

Is It in Force?

One of the things which is most difficult in the UK is to work out whether an Act is actually in force: sometimes an Act may be brought into effect in many different stages.

This has been made much easier in recent years. *Halsbury's Statutes* includes a separate volume called *Is It in Force?* which deals with this, and this is updated in the Noter-up binder mentioned above.

Current Law Statutes has a binder called 'Current Awarness' which includes a list of Commencement Orders for the current year. The same information is to be found in the *Current Law Monthly Digest*.

Judicial Consideration

The other thing you may wish to know is whether the legislation has been discussed in any cases. This you can also find from the *Current Law Legislation Citator* which is published annually, consolidating information which is published monthly in both the *Current Law Statutes Service Binder* and *Current Law* monthly parts. It is also to be found out from the *Law Reports Index*.

Here is a brief extract from the *Current Law Legislation Citator*:

I have chosen an extract from the *Legislation Citator* 1989–93, which shows what has happened to existing legislation **during that period**. You will see that it includes both statutory changes and cases which refer to the legislation. It organizes the statutes chronologically. To save space the new, amending or repealing, Acts are referred to by their chapter number only, not titles.

SLR means 'Statute Law Reform Act' — occasionally one of these is passed, to tidy up the statute book and remove old, no longer useful, statutes.

Current Law is now part of the collection on the *Current Legal Information* CD-ROM.

CAP.

18 & 19 Vict. (1855)—cont.
111. **Bills of Lading Act 1855.**
repealed: 1992, c.50, s.6.
s. 1, see *Future Express, The* [1992] 2 Lloyd's Rep. 79, H.H. Judge Diamond, Q.C.; *Mitsui & Co. v. Novorossiysk Shipping Co.; Gurdermes, The* [1993] 1 Lloyd's Rep. 311, C.A.

19 & 20 Vict. (1856)
29. **National Gallery Act 1856.**
repealed: 1992, c.44, sch.9.
43. **Hereditary Revenues Act 1856.**
repealed: S.L.R. 1989.
56. **Exchequer Court (Scotland) Act 1856.**
ss. 10, 21, repealed: Act of Sederunt 86/1937.

20 & 21 Vict. (1857)
31. **Inclosure Act 1857.**
s. 12, see *R. v. Durham City Justices, ex p. Croxdale and Hett Parish Council*, June 20, 1989, D.C.
43. **Summary Jurisdiction Act 1857.**
repealed: S.L.R. 1993.
s. 6, see *Griffith v. Jenkins* [1992] 2 W.L.R. 28, H.L.
44. **Crown Suits (Scotland) Act 1857.**
ss. 1–3, 5, see *MacDonald of Keppoch, Petr.*, 1989 S.L.T. (Lyon Ct.) 2.

Other Useful Things

There is a two volume list of all the Statutes ever passed, called the *Chronological Table of the Statutes*. This tells you what happened to every statute, and thus mentions statutes wholly repealed, unlike the *Statute Citator*. ➤ Note this is very behind — the volumes covering 1235 to 1994 were published in 1997 and the next version will cover up to 1997. Here is an extract.

```
1833 (3 & 4 Will. 4).
    c. 41    ..   Judicial Committee.
                  appl.—Dentists, 1957 (c. 28), s. 29 (1);Federation of Malaya Indepen dence,
                       1957 (c. 60), s. 3 (3);Professions Supplementary to Medicine, 1960
                       (c. 66), s. 9 (3); Singapore, 1966 (c. 29), s. 3 (3); Veterinary Surgeons,
                       1966 (c. 36), s. 17 (1); Republic of the Gambia, 1970 (c. 37), s. 2 (3);
                       Trinidad and Tobago Republic, 1976 (c. 54), s. 2 (4); Medical, 1978
                       (c. 12), s. 11 (6); (Dominica) S.I. 1978/1030.
                  appl. (mod.)—Seychelles, 1976 (c. 19), s. 6 (5); (Malaysia) S.I. 1978/182;
                  Kiribati, 1979 (c. 27), s. 6 (4).
                  r. in pt.—S.L.R. (No. 2), 1888.
                  ext.—Medical, 1983 (c. 54), s. 40 (6); Dentists, 1984 (c. 24), s. 29 (2); Mauritius
                       Republic, 1991 (c.45), s.2(5).
                  preamble r.—S.L.R., 1890.
                  mod.—S.I.1991/1716.
                  s.1 r. in pt.—S.L.R., 1874; S.L.R. (No. 2), 1888; S.L.R., 1890.
                     ext.—Appellate Jurisdiction, 1887 (c. 70), s. 3.
                     2 r.—Colonial Cts. of Admiralty, 1890 (c. 27), s. 18: see S.R. & O.
                       1911/440 (Rev. IV, p. 1697: 1911, p. 19).
                     3 appl.—H. of C. Disqualification, 1975 (c. 24), s. 7 (2).
                     5 r. in pt.—Ct. of Chancery, 1851 (c. 83), s. 16.
                     9 r. in pt.—(E.). Perjury, 1911 (c. 6), s. 17; S.L.(Reps.), 1981 (c. 19), sch. 1
                       pt. VIII.
                     10–12 r.—Courts, 1971 (c. 23), s. 56 (4), sch. 11 pt. IV; (N.I.) S.L.R.
                  (N.I.) 1980 (c. 59), s. 1, sch. pt. I.
                     15 am.—Judicial Committee, 1843 (c. 38), s. 12.
                     20 expld. ("colony")—S.I. 1957/1364 (1957 I, p. 202), art. 4 (1).
                     22, 25–27 r.—S.L.R., 1861.
                     28 r. in pt.—Judicial Committee, 1843 (c. 38), s. 6.
                     29 r.—S.L.R., 1875.
                     30 r.—Appellate Jurisdiction, 1929 (c. 8), s. 1(7).
    c. 42    ..   Civil Procedure.—r., Admin. of Justice, 1965 (c. 2), s. 34 (1), sch. 2.
    c. 43    ..   Holyhead road.*
```

Note:

am	=	amended
excl.	=	excluded
ext.	=	extended
appl.	=	applied.
r.	=	repealed
r. in pt.	=	repealed in part
SI	=	statutory instrument (delegated legislation)
Short titles **emboldened**	=	statute still at least partially in force
short title in *italics*	=	statute repealed

There is also an *Index to the Statutes*, which gives an indication of which statutes deal with which topics. Below is the entry for Hong Kong. ➤ These volumes tend to be a few years out of date.

```
HONG KONG
    1985 c.15   Hong Kong (26:16A)                    1990 c.34   British Nationality (Hong Kong)
                                                                  (87)

    Ending of British sovereignty and jurisdiction over Hong Kong: 1985 c.15 s.1
    Short title and supplementary provisions: 1985 c.15 s.2,sch.
    Acquisition of British citizenship; selection schemes; registration of spouses and minor children:
                                                                  1990 c.34 s.1,schs.1,2
    Consequential nationality provns.: 1990 c.34 s.2(1)(3)
    Procedure: 1990 c.34 s.3
    Governor's annual report: 1990 c.34 s.4
    Expenses and receipts: 1990 c.34 s.5
    Short title, savings, commencement and extent: 1990 c.34 s.6
```

1985 c. 15 incidentally is the Hong Kong Act 1985.

➤ Note that neither of these last publications gives you the names of cases in which the statutes have been cited, unlike the statute citator.

There is an alphabetical list of every UK statute passed in the *Current Law Statutes Service Binder*. It is no more than a list of names and dates.

Delegated Legislation

You are unlikely to need UK delegated legislation very often (though it may be that this is copied in the Hong Kong legislation occasionally — probably because the statute under the authority of which it is made is itself copied in Hong Kong). *Halsbury's Statutory Instruments* contains statutory instruments. This is a better format than the official government version which tends to be slow in publishing. ➤ Not every SI appears in this collection, however. Now SIs are published on the Internet at **<http://www.hmso.gov.uk/stat.htm>**.

📖 The Supreme Court and Legal Department Libraries have the official versions of the UK Statutory Instruments.

There is a list (not text) of the current year's SIs in the *Current Law Statutes* annual binder, and in the *Current Law Monthly Digest*. There is a *Statutory Instruments Citator* (indicating which SIs have been cited in cases) in the *Statute Service* binder only.

Transitional Issues

Very little change in the substance of Hong Kong law was necessitated by the handover. In the event most of the existing law was adopted — in other words not rejected by the Standing Committee of the National People's Congress on the basis that they were not compatible with the Basic Law — see Basic Law Art. 160. It was adopted by a resolution of the Standing Committee of the National People's Congress on 23 February 1997 which has been included as Cap. 1570 of the *Laws of Hong Kong*.

The Reunification Ordinance became law immediately after the return of sovereignty, and carries out a number of changes in terminology necessitated by the constitutional change. The Adaptation of Laws (Crown Land) Ordinance No. 29 of 1998 renamed the Crown Lands Ordinance as the Land (Miscellaneous Provisions) Ordinance and amended a large number of Ordinances in which references to Crown land, or Crown leases or other references to the Crown in connection with land appeared. The Adaptation of Laws (Courts and Tribunals) Ordinance No. 25 of 1998 also made changes to a large number of Ordinances (324 Ordinances or sets of subsidiary legislation!) to bring them into line with the Basic Law, including changing the Supreme Court Ordinance (Cap 4) to the High Court Ordinance. Several other such Ordinances have been or will be passed — about 35 in all.

National Laws Applying in Hong Kong

National Laws are laws of the Central People's Government; according to the Basic Law Annex III various laws such as the Nationality Law, apply in Hong Kong, and these were added to in 1997 by a decision of the Standing Committee of the National People's Congress (included as Cap. 1562 of the *Laws of Hong Kong*). The Basic Law itself is a national law, of course, for it was enacted by the NPC. In fact BLIS includes a number of national laws (in many instances these English translations are not 'official' and do not have the force of law in Hong Kong, though the original Chinese version is law in Hong Kong). They include the Constitution of the PRC, the Basic Law, the February 1997 Decision of the Standing Committee of the National People's Congress on Treatment of the Laws Previously in Force in Hong Kong in Accordance with Article 160 of the Basic Law and the Hong Kong Reunification Ordinance. They have, for the sake of convenience, been given numbers beginning with Cap. 1553 (the Basic Law). In the paper version of the *Laws of Hong Kong* these documents appear in Volume 1.

UK Legislation Applying in Hong Kong

The NPC decision in February 1997 (Cap. 1570) said that various Ordinances were not to be adopted. One of these was the Application of English Laws Ordinance. This has been treated as having been repealed by the NPC decision (although rather oddly it remained on BLIS for some months after the transfer). By the time of the transfer of sovereignty there were only a small number of Acts left in the Schedule; repeal is unlikely to have a serious impact on Hong Kong law. It can in fact be argued that the effect will be negligible in view of the principle that repeal of legislation does not (at least in some circumstances) revive the pre-existing legal position. On this complex question see Wesley-Smith, *Sources of Hong Kong Law* Chap. 8.

The Reunification Ordinance introduced as part of Cap. 1 new section 2A which says this:

> (e) provisions applying any English law may continue to be applicable by reference thereto as a transitional arrangement pending their amendment by the Hong Kong Special Administrative Region through the Legislature thereof, provided that they are not prejudicial to the sovereignty of the People's Republic of China and do not contravene the provisions of the Basic Law.

This would cover the various other Ordinances which apply English Acts, such as the Jury Ordinance — which was eventually amended by Cap. 25 of 1998.

SELF-STUDY QUESTIONS

☺ Thirty minutes.

1. How would you find out whether a Hong Kong Ordinance is in force?

2. How would you find out the same information about an English Act?

3. How do you find out whether there is a Hong Kong equivalent of an English Act?

4. Where do you find an old Ordinance — one which is no longer in force?

5. What are the steps you must take to ensure you have the up-to-date version of an Ordinance?

6. How can you find the text of an English Act which applies in Hong Kong?

Unit 11 Approaching Research

OBJECTIVES

By the end of this Unit you will:

- have given some more thought to the types of research you may find yourself engaged in
- know something about the different types of secondary literature which you may wish to use
- have an idea about breaking down problems and research topics
- be able to use your imagination to think of words and phrases which you might want to look up in catalogues and indexes

☺ It may take you up to one hour.

Previous Units have been mainly concerned with how to read primary legal material (cases and legislation), as well as with how to find that material when you have a fairly clear idea of which items you are looking for. In this Unit we shall be looking at secondary sources and works of reference which will give you a discussion of the topic, help you find which cases and legislation are relevant to your work, and offer criticism of the cases, legislation or general state of the law. One could say that we are now beginning to look at something which could genuinely be called 'research'. These are the tools you will need to find something out, as opposed to finding what someone else has suggested that you find. We look first at the works of reference which are the research tools of the practising lawyers. But before that we look briefly at the intellectual tasks you must undertake when faced with any new question: what is it that you are looking for? How do you formulate your question in a way which will extract the material you need from the literature?

UNPACKING YOUR SUBJECT

You have a task which will involve the use of primary materials: cases and/or statutes, or other sorts of literature. How do you get into a new topic?

However you do it, you will need to give some thought to precisely what your subject is. Let us take one or two examples:

You want to write an essay on the control of corruption. Leaving aside, for the moment, the likelihood that you will want to read something about the phenomenon of corruption which may lead you to books by sociologists and political scientists, how do you find the statutes and the cases, if any, on corruption?

You have a practical problem (either as a problem question or in practice for a client): *A* is injured due to defective premises while he is at work.

Your first task, which goes beyond the scope of this book, is to take apart the question. You will learn how to analyse a problem question by practice in class, and maybe by reading, or by more formal instruction in the process. There are now some books on problem solving generally, or on problems in different aspects of the subject.[1]

You need to categorize your question, not necessarily into **one** category — indeed that is precisely what I am suggesting you should avoid. But in order to find the right books, or to look the right words up in indexes, etc. you need to know:

- what you are looking for
- how other people (text writers, indexers, etc.) might classify this.

(It is a bit like going to a strange supermarket: first of all you have to make your own shopping list.Then you have to work out how the supermarket managers classify the stock — which is not always the way you would have done it yourself!)

To go back to the corruption question, or the injured worker problem. You might feel you should clarify the following:

- What 'branch of the law' does this fall under?
- Do I want to look only at Hong Kong law or will the law of other countries be helpful?
- What sorts of words might I look up in an index?

What Branch of the Law?

The branches of the law are to a large extent artificial divisions created by textbook writers and curriculum developers — boundaries have to be set somewhere to accommodate them! But these considerations should not set the boundaries of your research project and still less of seeking the arguments for a client. It would be professional negligence to treat something which has a tort dimension as simply a contract question because you only thought of looking at contract books!

---

1   For example, Beale, *Solving Problems in Constitutional and Administrative Law* (London: Cavendish, 1995).

The corruption question: is corruption a criminal law question? Yes, but you will find that in many books on criminal law it does not figure. Why not? Because student textbooks don't have the room to discuss what is not usually taught in courses. A practitioners' book on criminal law will discuss it. There is at least one English practitioners' book on fraud which has a chapter on corruption. But you might find something about corruption in books on administrative law, because it is very often corrupt practices by civil servants that are the main problem, or books on the police and the law.

➤ You will already have some idea of the so-called 'branches of the law' from looking at the syllabus for the degree you are working on. But don't forget that no law school can teach everything. A good example might be Air Law. Only a postgraduate degree would have a course on this, but there are books. If you have a problem which involves an aviation accident, you will find that a book on air law will have a detailed discussion of the various situations, and all sorts of cases which would never find their way into a general book on the law of tort or contract etc., even though they are in fact tort or contract cases.

What are the issues to be discussed? Which are the investigatory powers available in dealing with corruption? Does this touch on privacy? What branch of the law is privacy? Tort — it is sometimes included in a tort course. But is that what you are looking for here? Human rights, maybe. There is something on privacy in the Bill of Rights.

And how about the injured worker question? Maybe tort? Negligence? Employees' compensation? Books on employment law? Contract? Who occupied the premises? Occupiers' Liability, maybe?

Which Jurisdiction?

For your corruption essay it would be very helpful to look at the experience of other countries. There are four main reasons, it seems to me, for choosing to look at the law of another country:

- If it faces similar problems or needs.

- If it has experience in the area of the law from which lessons can be drawn — they may be lessons of how to achieve something, or even mistakes which can be learned from.

- Because the law of Hong Kong is derived from that of the other country, so that may help you to understand the reasons for the Hong Kong law; you may find cases and other material from that other country which can help you interpret the law here.

- Sometimes there may be a foreign element to the problem in front of you — take the injured employee case: suppose he is employed by a foreign company, or is himself a foreigner and his contract of employment was made in another country.

Most of the Units in this book are designed to help you find material from Hong Kong and the United Kingdom, for obvious reasons. Unit 16 introduces the material of a few other jurisdictions, and there you will find some introductory information about different types of legal system, and some hints from which might be useful for certain purposes.

Words, Words, Words!

Even when you have identified a book in the right area you need to think about the words to look up in the index. Try **corruption**. Suppose this doesn't cover the sort of corruption you are interested in? Try **bribery, corrupt practices, misconduct**, etc.

➤ **Think** before choosing your words. It is all too easy, especially for students, to take the words which someone else has given them and try to use them for finding material. I have seen a student who was asked to write an essay on 'Sanctity of Contract'; she looked up that phrase in the Library catalogue, and came up with just one book published in 1959. But all sorts of other books discuss the issue even though the phrase does not appear in the title. I have also come upon the computer terminal where a student has obviously given up in despair — having typed in effectively the whole of an essay title, only to be told, naturally enough, that there is no book of that name in the Library (this is perfectly true — I have seen it more than once!).

This business of thinking of related words is likely to crop up constantly. Here are a few other examples of related words/phrases:

Defamation, slander, libel, reputation, honour, dignity, personality, criminal defamation, defamatory

Human rights, civil liberties, civil and politicial rights, economic social and cultural rights, rights, United Nations Charter, fundamental rights

Family, divorce, marriage, children, separation, matrimonial, fertility, infertility, dowry, brideprice (I am sure no one pays brideprice in Hong Kong but in some societies they do. In some societies it is called dowry, but arguably they are different), **conjugal**

Environment, pollution, ecology, conservation, water pollution, air pollution, waste control, pigs (Pigs! What am I talking about? A major source of water pollution in Hong Kong is waste from pigs!)

In order to make sure you have got:

- the right books and
- the right part of the book, or
- the right cases or
- the right statutes

you need to be sure you are looking up the right words and phrases. You will see from the groups of words and phrases above that one starts from one word and then thinks of others that:

* mean the same as the first one (synonyms — but ➤ very few words actually mean exactly the same as other words)
* are narrower words than your first word (e.g. slander is a sort of defamation)
* are wider words than the first one
* overlap in meaning with the first word
* mean something almost opposite to the first word (conservation could be said to be almost an antonym of pollution)

➤ Of course, if you don't start with the right word or concept, any number of other words, narrower, wider, etc. will probably not help you find the relevant material!

A Word on Indexes

➤ Just because you have found one word in the index of a book does not mean that you will not find the other words as well, and the various words will not necessarily produce the same material. A good index ought to say 'see also' and list related entries, but not all indexes are good. For example, you might find that the index of a book contains both 'Defamation' and 'Libel'. It is wise to check both to see that you have traced all references.

Not all books have indexes — regrettably the series *Law Lectures for Practitioners* published by the Hong Kong Law Journal does not.

Some books have poor indexes; indexing is a skilled professional task, but some authors or publishers evidently take short cuts.

Having thought about the nature of your problem, it is time to decide where to go to find your sources. ➤ Remember that you may have to adjust your ideas about the topic in the light of the material you find. Don't be too constricted by the original ideas you had. On the other hand, you must call a halt somewhere: don't go on and on collecting new material of increasingly marginal importance.

Where you go next may depend upon the extent of your ignorance when you begin! If you have some idea of the topic already you can go straight to the law reports and statutes. But you may feel you want an introduction to the subject, as well as something which indicates what the most important cases are. If so, it makes sense to read some sort of book — a student textbook, or a practitioners' book, etc. first. If it is a very new topic you might find the best approach is to locate a journal article.

❖ Think of words related to each of the following: child, pigeon, bicycle, fishing.

DIFFERENT TYPES OF BOOKS

There are a number of different types of law books, and which you go to will depend upon the nature of your research topic. Here is a list of types, and an indication of the pros and cons of using each.

Student Texts

These should not be ignored even when you are in practice. Many textbooks written for students have become classics of the literature in their own field. There are also books which are in no way classics but will give you a good introduction to a topic. There are also **bad** student books which may mislead by being wrong, while others are not wrong but are so elementary that they may mislead by oversimplifying. Points to bear in mind about student textbooks are:

- they are designed to explain to people who are not already familiar with the material;
- they will not deal with the more obscure corners of the topic which are unlikely to appear in courses;
- they are geared to discussing the issues and stimulating interest and ideas and criticism (good textbooks anyway) and not at providing neat answers (➤ remember there are very rarely neat answers anyway);
- a good textbook should refer you to the main cases and to other literature such as journal articles on a topic;
- you may find you are looking at a textbook not from Hong Kong or even from England but from Canada or Australia. This is not to be discouraged, since there are a number of excellent books from these countries. But never rely exclusively on one of these because sometimes the law may have taken on a dynamic of its own in that country which is a little different from England — and Hong Kong courts are more used to dealing with English cases. And the statutory law will be quite different.

➤ **Never** assume that a statute which applies in England has a Hong Kong counterpart.

➤ Even worse is to forget that you are in Hong Kong — in the sense that you write about the 'Unfair Contract Terms Act' for example, just because you find it discussed in an English textbook! That Act does have a Hong Kong counterpart — as you know.

There is now a very wide range of textbook styles. Years ago it was not so — there were just good books and not-so-good books. But now you will find some books which aim to be just an exposition of the law, and even take the view that law students should not take a critical view of the law! Others try to place the law in its historical, economic and social context.[2]

Specialist Books

There are also specialist books on smaller topics which may be designed for students, but because they deal with narrower topics in greater detail, they may be useful for practitioners too. Take contract as an example: as well as books on **contract**, you will also find books on **exclusion clauses, mistake and misrepresentation, consideration, sale of goods, retention of title clauses**. All these deal with aspects of the law of contract. There are also books which deal with more than contract, or with contracts in specific situations, for example: **damages, air travel, banking, carriage of goods by sea, insurance**. If there is such a book which covers the category into which your problem neatly fits, use it. But remember,
➤ many problems do not fit neatly into categories. Also, sometimes you might want something briefer, and the general textbook would be better.

Monographs

These are likely to go even deeper into the topic, and sometimes discuss in greater depth the history and philosophy of topics. But the borderline between these and the previous category is not easy to draw. Some of these books will cross traditional boundaries. Examples of books in the area of contract and tort which would fit into this category would be: Atiyah, *The Rise and Fall of Freedom of Contract*, Hart and Honoré, *Causation in the Law*. Books like this would not be used by practitioners except for especially abstruse problems, but might be useful to a student. One might include in this category a huge range of books which take a theoretical approach to law — a feminist view, or an economic theory approach, or a marxist approach, a liberal constitutionalist approach, or which study how law and legal institutions work in society by means of empirical research.

Books on Comparative Law

By this I mean books which look at the law of more than one country. They themselves may concentrate on on area of law, or on one theoretical approach, or they may try to illuminate the nature of law in different types of society. They may be by one author, but very often they are actually collections of writings by a number of people, each of whom contributes a chapter on the problem under consideration in his or her own country.

---

2   The series known as 'Law in Context', of which several of the books I have mentioned are part (including Atiyah's *Accidents, Compensation and the Law*) was created for this very purpose.

Practitioners' Books

By these I mean books like Clerk and Lindsell on *Tort*, Gatley on *Libel and Slander*. There are examples now in most areas of the law. Like student textbooks, they may cover all or most of a traditional subject like contract or criminal law, or they may be more detailed. For example, in criminal law you will find books on drugs, sexual offences, fraud, offences against the person, theft, offences against property as well as books on criminal law as such. When looking at practitioners' texts, bear in mind the following:

- they are more detailed than student texts
- they may be more up-to-date (but on the other hand they are expensive to produce and sometimes new editions come less frequently than student texts)
- they should deal with difficulties and uncertainties in the law, but not with philosophical debates
- they may have appendices with the texts of relevant statutes
- sometimes they may not be easy for a student to follow since they may assume some knowledge of the law

Loose-leaf Texts

These are relatively new development, and are practitioners' texts. They vary a lot in style. Some have fuller coverage than others, while others explain more fully.

- They should all be good sources of references to cases and statutory materials.
- Some have law reports attached.
- Some have statutory materials included.
- They are very expensive and occasionally you may find a loose-leaf in a library which is not being updated for this reason.
- Some loose-leafs may be quite difficult to use, while others are very easy and clearly set out.

Encyclopaedias

These may be comprehensive like *Halsbury's* or topic-based like *Simon's Taxes*. If topic-based they are like practitioners books (and may also be loose-leaf) and will be detailed.

Updating

There are different ways of updating books. It goes without saying that you should ➤ always look for the latest edition. (However, if the law in England has changed and the law in Hong Kong has not, you might actually want to look at an older edition of an English book.) Updating may be done in the following ways:

- Loose-leaf — individual sheets or sections are removed and replaced. ➤ Look for the dates indicating when the pages or sections were replaced.
- Supplements — separate little (or not so little) books updating the main book by reference to pages or paragraphs. This technique is more often used for practitioners than student books, but has been used by Fleming on *Torts* and Gower *Modern Company Law*. Nowadays they are often superseded by loose-leaf versions.
- Pocket parts — supplements that slip into a pocket in the back cover. More used in the US and still used for the *United States Code Annotated*, and *American Law Reports*. Sometimes the parts (which are cumulative) outgrow the pocket!

TYPES OF ELECTRONIC RESOURCES

You will already have some familiarity with non-paper resources. You will have used the catalogue of your University library, and, if you have followed the advice given earlier in this book, should have experimented with the Internet, and with CD-ROMs, as well as wrestled with INFOLAW. In future, as you will be framing your own searches, it is important to understand the different types of resources, and what they can offer. It is necessary to make various distinctions between different types of electronic media, depending on the material which they contain, the ways in which they can be searched, the methods by which you get access to them, and how up-to-date they are likely to be.

Content

- **Full text:** Some media contain the full text of cases or statutes, or articles or other sources.
- **Indexes:** Others are simply indexes (or perhaps abstracts or summaries as well).

The latter simply tells you where to find the material, but you will then have to go to the paper version (this is just the way paper versions of indexes work, of course). You can also use a full-text database as an index too, which may be more convenient when the electronic database is either expensive (like LEXIS) or cumbersome (like INFOLAW).

Relationship With Print Media

Electronic versions of print media

You will find that some items which appear in print also appear in electronic format. Essentially what you get in the latter format is the same as in the former, although new ways of getting access to the material are possible. Examples of this are the *Hong Kong Law Digest, Hong Kong Cases, Weekly Law Reports, Laws of Australia*. Some journals are available in electronic and paper format. You may find that a library may have either one or both versions of a particular resource.

Electronic only

Some sources are developed for electronic media only. This is true of some journals which are available only through the Internet for example, and also of teaching materials which are specially designed for computer use.

Electronic Format

Sometimes the format is that of a single CD-ROM. Sometimes, depending on the resources of the particular library, a CD-ROM may be mounted on a network, so that the same CD may be 'accessed' from a variety of computers within the library. Sometimes the actual material is located somewhere completely different, and access is obtained through a computer and a modem, and ultimately via the telephone network. In that case the actual computer containing the information may be far away.

Electronic sources can be, to some extent, turned into paper ones by printing their contents.

Updating

CD-ROM

If a CD is supplied by a commercial company, it will probably be replaced at quite frequent intervals. This may be monthly, or three monthly, for example.

On-line database

A remote database which you have to access via a telephone system may be updated constantly. This is the case with LEXIS for example, where you may sometimes be told that new material has been added while you are carrying out a search. On the other hand, many databases which can now be accessed through the Internet are not maintained by commercial organizations, and are not all as up-to-date as you might wish.

Who Maintains Them?

It has become easier and easier for non-commercial organizations to keep databases. After all, a database simply means a collection of information kept on a computer, or in computer-readable format. Now individuals can store their own databases on computer hard or soft disks, or on CDs. (Law firms will often have their own databases, of conveyancing and other precedents, and of client information and perhaps of other information too.) It is not only commercial concerns that make their databases available to the public these days, but all sorts of organizations: university law schools, courts, research institutions and even individuals. This is all the more possible because of the development of Internet, and the easy access to it via the World Wide Web.

Cost of Use

If you use a CD-ROM you will not have to pay for time spent on using it, and nor will the institution to which it belongs (apart from a little extra on the electricity bill!). The CD is purchased outright, or more usually on a subscription basis. (The subscription fee will be higher if more than one person can use it at the same time on a network, sometimes a lot more expensive. This is why a library will keep some or all of its CDs separate, so that only one person can use them at a time.)

Some remote databases are free, though it may be that there is a substantial cost of connecting to them. For academic institutions the cost of connecting through the Internet is not high, but non-educational institutions will have to pay to a commercial service through which they link up to the Internet.

Other remote databases will require a password before you can use them, and will be charged for each use. The charge may be once for each 'visit', or for each item searched for, or according to the length of time, and there may be a different rate if you want to download documents (that is bring them home to your own disk, as it were) or print them. For commercial databases the cost may be high, and it will be a requirement if you are in practice, and, to say the least, socially responsible otherwise, to be conscious of how much money you are likely to spend, even if it will not come out of your own pocket!

➤ While this has enormously expanded the resources available to those who have access to good computer resources, which students in Hong Kong have, it does mean that you have to be aware of who is producing the database at which you are looking. Notice how up-to-date it is. Also, when using the World Wide Web: virtually any one can set up a Web site, and something which at first sight looks as though they are official may turn out to be the project of a private individual who may have a personal axe to grind, or simply not have the motivation to keep the site up-to-date.

The variety of electronic sources makes it very difficult to generalize about them. The various sorts are constantly merging into each other as well.

FRAMING SEARCHES

How best to go about searching for the precise material you want will depend upon two factors: what material the database contains, and what search tools you have.

Undigested or Pre-digested?

Some sorts of material, indexes, abstracts and summaries have already been processed for you: someone has categorized the material as a lawyer. So you can use the sorts of words that you would use in looking things up in an index. But some full-text material is full-text of, especially, cases. Judges tend to use legal language, but they do not necessarily use precisely the terms that you might expect in an index. You therefore have to think about the sorts of words they might have used in the sorts of cases in which you are interested.

Search Tools

The searches you are able to do may range from very simple, one word, ones to very complex combinations. These days you are most likely to find one-word searches only on the Internet. Even there you may find complex searches are possible. What you are likely to want are combinations of words, and possibly of dates as well. Many resources will permit you to use the Boolean search.

Boolean Search

A Boolean search is one which permits you to specify the following:

>   one word or phrase **and** another
>   one word or phrase **or** another
>   one word or phrase **and not** another

Here are some examples:

>   Hong Kong **and** law
>   Hong Kong **and** law **and** environment
>   Hong Kong **and** law **and** (environment **or** pollution)
>   (Hong Kong **or** China) **and** law **and** (environment **or** pollution)
>   (Hong Kong **and** China) **and** law **and** (environment **or** pollution)
>   (China **and not** Hong Kong) **and** law **and** (environment **or** pollution)

I tried this as a 'keyword' search on the University of Hong Kong Library catalogue which permits Boolean searches. This was the result:

Hong Kong **and** law	1227 hits
Hong Kong **and** law **and** environment	6 hits
Hong Kong **and** law **and** (environment **or** pollution)	18 hits
(Hong Kong **or** China) **and** law **and** (environment **or** pollution)	28 hits
(Hong Kong **and** China) **and** law **and** (environment **or** pollution)	1 hit
(China **and not** Hong Kong) **and** law **and** (environment **or** pollution)	not possible

In most of the sources similar types of search can be carried out. You can ask for a single word or phrase to be searched for or a combination. Sometimes it is possible to specify that two words or phrases should appear within a certain distance (Donoghue within three words of Stevenson for example). In the case of some resources you will have to begin with one word and then you will be invited to introduce new elements to refine the search (you may only be invited to do this if your initial word produced many 'hits').

It is extremely important that you think carefully before you search. In the case of some databases time is money. Most important is the effective use of your time, and the retrieval of the fullest and most accurate information.

➤ You will waste a lot of time if you type in mis-spellings. Try to type accurately.

➤ These days most sources are Windows-based (see Unit 1).

SUMMARY

Whatever type of research you are about to embark on you should ask yourself the following questions:

- What areas of the law am I looking for?

- Am I looking for Hong Kong law only or that of other jurisdictions as well?

- Am I looking for the law as it is, or am I to be critical of the law?

- What concepts, words and phrases shall I be searching for?

- Where should I begin to look for the law: is it very new, so I am likely to find it discussed only in law journals, or is it a topic on which there might be a useful discussion in student textbooks, or is it rather technical and I should go straight to practitioners' books?

- Am I looking only for law books and books about law, or does the topic require that I find material about society, or theory, or history, for example?

Unit 12 General Works of Reference

OBJECTIVES

By the end of this Unit you will be able to use the following works of reference:

- *Hong Kong Law Digest/Yearbook*
- *Current Law Hong Kong*
- *Halsbury's Laws of Hong Kong*
- *Current Law*
- *Halsbury's Laws of England*
- *The Digest*

☺ As long as four hours if you look at the material and do the exercises.

T his Unit is concerned with a certain type of publication directed at the practitioner mainly, though of use to the law student and teacher as well. These are works of reference which do not specialize in any branch of the law, but set out to cover the full range. You should realize what you are likely to find in the various publications. One can divide practitioners works into:

- the specialist and the non-specialist
- the updatable and the non-updatable and those which are serial publications
- those which contain summaries of cases and those which contain descriptive statements of the law
- those which are mainly intended to provide current awareness and those which are long-term works of reference

As we shall see, it is now impossible to divide the publications into watertight compartments.

HONG KONG

Hong Kong Law Digest

This is a non-specialist, serial publication which contains summaries of material, and is a current awareness tool.

This publication is modelled fairly closely on *Current Law* (see below) and used to be called *Hong Kong Current Law*. For some years it was called *The Hong Kong Digest* and the annual consolidation the *Hong Kong Law Digest Yearbook*.[1] Now it is merged with the *Hong Kong Law Reports* and the whole called *The Authorized Hong Kong Law Reports and Digest*.

Monthly parts: the 'Hong Kong Law Digest'

There are 11 monthly parts each year. The paragraphs are prefaced by a letter — 'A' for January, B for February and so on (a very irritating format, since it does not come naturally to anyone to think of July as G and so on.) Since mid-1998 each monthly Part has included its name and letter on the spine.

Within each monthly part you will find the paragraphs divided by topic, and a contents page at the beginning. However, ➤ it is probably just as good if not better to look at the Index at the back, especially if what you want is within a broad topic (such as 'Practice and Procedure' which takes up 15 pages). The Index is cumulative, that is each month's index covers also the previous months of the same year. So ➤ look at the most recent month, don't bother to look at the index of each part separately.

In the issue for May 1995 there is a case on negligence, involving some damages points. You could find it by:

* Looking in the Index:

> **Tort**
>   Negligence,
>   accident at construction site, E42
>   duty of care, E42
>   industrial accident, D104

E is the fifth letter of the alphabet, so this means May.

* Or by going straight to the Tort paragraphs:

---

1   This rather cumbersome title applied since 1994; before then the Yearbook did not include the word 'Digest'.

TELECOMMUNICATIONS

E133   Office of the Telecommunications Authority Trading Fund

RESOLUTION OF THE LEGISLATIVE COUNCIL (L.N.162 of 1995), made under the Trading Funds Ordinance (Cap.430) ss.3, 4 and 6, gazetted on 12 May 1995, establishes the Office of the Telecommunications Authority Trading Fund under the Trading Funds Ordinance for the operations of the Office of the Telecommunications Authority.

Schedule 1 to the Resolution specifies the services to be provided under the trading fund, and Schedule 2 sets out the assets to be appropriated to the trading fund.

TORT

E134   Accident at construction site — claim based on negligence and breach of statutory duty — duty of care — contributory negligence

See TSE HOI CHEUNG v HIP HING CONSTRUCTION CO LTD & OTHERS, E42

TRADE AND INDUSTRY

E135   Industrial Training (Clothing Industry) (Amendment) (No.2) Ordinance 1995 (No.31 of 1995)

See EMPLOYMENT, E49.

- Or by going to the paragraphs on Damages — one of which is E42 — where you find quite a long summary of TSE HOI CHEUNG v HIP HING CONSTRUCTION CO LTD HCA Nos A7930 of 1988 and 5903 of 1989, 20 February 1995, Barnett J.

Each monthly part also includes the following indexes, also cumulative:

- Legislation, including subsidiary legislation and commencement dates (for an example see Unit 10 on Legislation)
- Amended Legislation (as mentioned earlier, the *Gazette* version is fuller since it covers all amendments since 1990)
- Legislation Judicially Considered (for example see Unit 10 on Legislation)
- Index of cases digested in the current year

- Cases judicially considered (this does not say whether those cases were followed, distinguished, etc.)

The case digests are often a page long or more, reflecting the fact that many cases are reported late or not at all.

➤ Other things to note which might be useful: the section on Legislation lists (Royal — until 1997) assents received, and Bills presented during the month. Also monthly there is a table of quantum (amount) of personal injury damages awards.

'Words and phrases judicially considered' appear as the last paragraph in each monthly issue (unless, I suppose, there were some item like zoos coming later in the alphabet!). This information is cumulated throughout the year.

➤ The correct way to cite the monthly Digest is [1996] HKLD G69, for example.

On the next page is a specimen page. Here are some comments (for others see after the specimen page).

*1 Heading of Section

*2 Paragraph number and key words/issues (G means that it is the July issue)

*3 UK cases distinguished

*4 Name of the case with citation. The reason it has been digested a second time is that it has now been reported [a little wasteful?]

 The alert reader will see that the judgment appears to have been given after the child had the operation! Presumably, in view of the urgency, Kaplan J. gave his decision immediately, and his reasons later.

*5 Summary of delegated legislation (bylaws are usually used to refer to local authority legislation, here both Regional and Urban Council)

*6 Summary of delegated legislation amending schedule of Ordinance

*7 Beginning of another case summary. (The Life Assurance Act 1774 is a UK statute applying in Hong Kong under the Application of English Law Ordinance.)

Undertakings (Suspended Working Platforms) Regulation (L.N.393 of 1994).

FAMILY LAW

G69 **Infant — wardship — whether court should overrule parents' refusal to consent to operation on 15-day-old child who would die without it**

C was 15 days old. Shortly after birth she suffered an attack of cyanosis whilst feeding. She was found to have bilateral broncho-pulmonary foregut malformation or sequestrations with oesophageal connection, ie she had an extra pair of rudimentary lungs which were attached to the oesophagus. She also had other congenital abnormalities, namely patent ductus arteriosus, bifid vertebrae at T7 and T8 and hemi-vertebra at L2 level. As a complication of the foregut abnormality, the child developed septicaemia which was treated with antibiotics, ventilation, and exchange transfusion. Her treatment was stabilised and likely that the extra lungs were the probable source of the sepsis. Further, because the abnormality was connected to the oesophagus, there existed a point of entry for gut organisms. Without any surgical intervention the child would die in a short time. It was a rare case and the operation the doctor would carry out had not been performed before in Hong Kong. He believed that the operation would be successful in which case the child would only be left with her spinal problems which were in no way life threatening and could be dealt with later by orthopaedic treatment. The longer the delay before surgical intervention, the more chance there was of damage to her main lungs. In addition an angiogram would be required which carried only a small risk. There was no chance of survival unless the infected lungs were surgically removed. She could die during the operation. However, there was an even chance that the operation would be a success, and if so, she would be able to lead a relatively normal and healthy life thereafter. The parents refused to consent to the operation. They preferred to allow the child to die from natural causes than risk surgery with possible complications and further suffering thereafter, were unhappy at the prospect of the child being handicapped and suffering therefrom, and were not prepared to risk the operation.

Held, making the child a ward of court and ordering the operation, that (1) the question was what was in the best interest of the child. Although it was a very serious matter to overrule the wishes of the child's parents who had carefully weighed up all the factors before refusing to consent to an operation, it was the court's duty to consider what was in the child's best interest; (2) nothing was certain in life and the court could give the parents no more guarantee than the doctors. Neither could the parents be assured as to the level of support they might receive if the child was handicapped. However, the evidence was that if the operation was successful, she would not be handicapped as a result of any condition which gave rise to the operation in consideration; (3) there was no doubt that it was in the child's best interests to undergo the angiogram and operation. There was a real chance that she might survive and enjoy a normal life and she would not be condemned to a certain death without giving the doctors a chance to correct nature's imperfections. If she did not survive, then everyone concerned would know that everything possible was done to give her a chance of a relatively healthy life (*Re B (A Minor: Wardship — Medical Treatment)* [1981] 1 WLR 1421 and *Re C (A Minor) (Wardship: Medical Treatment)* [1989] 3 WLR 240 distinguished).

Postscript: as at 20 May 1993 C's progress after the operation was satisfactory.

*RE C (A MINOR) (WARDSHIP: MEDICAL TREATMENT) [1994] 1 HKLR 60, 28 May 1993, Kaplan J.
*[This case was previously digested at [1993] HKLD F63.]

FOOD AND DRUGS

G70 **Food business — control of water quality**

FOOD BUSINESS (REGIONAL COUNCIL) (AMENDMENT) (NO.2) BYLAW 1994 (L.N.447 of 1994), made under the Public Health and Municipal Services Ordinance (Cap.132) s.56, operative on 22 July 1994, amends the principal Bylaws (Cap.132, Sub.Leg.) by adding bylaw 10A which controls the quality of water in which live fish or shell fish intended for human consumption may be kept. S.2 amends bylaw 35(1)(a) by including the new bylaw 10A(1) in it so that the penalty provision in by-law 35(3)(b) applies.

FOOD BUSINESS (URBAN COUNCIL) (AMENDMENT) (NO.2) BYLAW 1994 (L.N.448 of 1994), made under the Public Health and Municipal Services Ordinance (Cap.132) s.56, operative on 22 July 1994, amends the principal By-laws (Cap.132, Sub.Leg.) by adding by-law 10A which controls the quality of water in which live fish or shell fish intended for human consumption may be kept. S.2 amends by-law 36(1)(a) by including the new by-law 10A(1) in it so that the penalty provision in by-law 36(3)(b) applies.

INSURANCE

G71 **Classes of insurance business**

INSURANCE COMPANIES ORDINANCE (AMENDMENT OF FIRST SCHEDULE) REGULATION 1994 (L.N.398 of 1994), made under the Insurance Companies Ordinance (Cap.41) s.59, operative on 1 July 1994, amends the First Schedule to the principal Ordinance to —
• define the term "party" in order to clarify the persons whom that term is meant to refer to in long-term business of the nature specified in classes G and H in that Schedule;
• empower the Insurance Authority to specify, by notice in the *Gazette*, that certain occupational retirement schemes within the meaning of the Occupational Retirement Schemes Ordinance (Cap.426) shall not be retirement schemes within the meaning of that Schedule; and
• clarify that long-term business of class I excludes general business of class 1 or 2.

G72 **Employees' compensation insurance — agent of employer named as the insured in policy — whether undisclosed principal can sue on policy**
[Life Assurance Act 1774 (c.48), ss.1, 2]

Around 9 September 1983, typhoon "Ellen" struck Hong Kong and the barquentine "Osprey" sank at sea. Crew members, X and Y, were killed. The plaintiffs, their dependents and personal representatives, were awarded employees' compensation and common law damages against Axelson, the owners of the vessel and the employers of X and Y. Axelson went into liquidation and the judgments in favour of the plaintiffs were never satisfied. An insurance policy issued by Eastern

➤ Warning:

The General Index is not very imaginative:
- The *Re C* case is indexed only under Family Law — not, for example, under a separate heading of Children.
- The items in para. G70 appear under a separate heading Food Business or as a sub-heading to Public Health and Urban Services. They do not appear under, for example, a separate heading of Fish or Water.

Use **your** imagination!

You could, of course, get to the case of *Re C* by looking up either the name of that case in the Cases Digested index, or *Re B* or *Re C* in the Index of Cases Judicially Considered, as well as under Family Law in the General Index.

Yearly volume of Hong Kong Law [Digest] Yearbook

This has all the same features as the monthly parts, consolidated for the whole year. Paragraphs no longer have letter prefixes, naturally.

➤ Although the Indexes are (at least in some years) called 'Consolidated Indexes' this is misleading. Of course they are consolidated for the year — you would hardly expect otherwise! But they do not include material from previous years — which is what I would expect to be the meaning of this expression used to describe the index in a volume.

➤ The correct way to cite the Yearbook is [1994] HKLY 299 (for example) (the number being the paragraph).

❖ This is not so much an exercise as a suggestion of one or two things to look up which will help you learn your way around the publication, and warn you against pitfalls. ☺ About 15 minutes.

Look at the Index to the annual volume for 1992. Suppose you are interested in Defamation cases. Is there a heading on 'Defamation'? No? Try 'Tort'. Is there a defamation case? Yes? Is it the only one? Turn over the page. What do you find? Go to the relevant paragraphs. Are they both libel cases?

Go to the Index for 1996 (if this is still 1996 go to any of the monthly parts and find the Cumulative Index). Look up 'Tort'. How many cases? Now try 'Damages — Personal Injuries'. Look up the case on 'Multiple Injuries'. Is it a case about damages only? No. Why is it listed only under 'Damages'? I have no idea!

➤ At least the CD-ROM version should make it possible to be free from the inadequacies of indexes.

CD-ROM version of Hong Kong Law Reports and Digest

The electronic version of the *Hong Kong Law Digest* is essentially just that. What you see on the screen is similar to what you see in the printed version. When you start up you will be in the Search screen. You can type in your search, using Boolean terms if you wish. You may shorten (truncate) a word by using an asterisk (*); or ? to replace a single letter (e.g. wom?n)

You may also choose whether to search everything, or only the catchwords, or party names. This faces you with the usual dilemma (it is the same in a book but you do not have the choice of searching the whole text other than by reading it!). On the one hand if you use the keywords you are dependent on the quality of the indexers who decided on the keywords — so you may miss important items. On the other hand, if you search the whole text you may get many things which are not relevant. For example, I tried 'divorce' as a search term, and found that one item was a case summary in which the judgment said one could not divorce one issue from another — not what I had in mind!

➤ But if you are using technical legal terms you may do best to search the whole text. I tried the following: 'Defamation'. Searching the whole text there were 84 hits. Searching only the catchwords produced only 44.

In fact, you will probably realize by this time that this was a very primitive search! I also tried 'Defamat*' — since this would include defamation and defamatory (but not defamed!). This produced 105 hits. But when I added 'or libel or slander' the number of hits was increased to 157.

➤ if you want alternative words, or a phrase not just as you type it, remember to click "composite entry" not "exact entry."

You may also limit the search in terms of years. The CD contains all the years since 1985[2] and you might want to restrict yourself to one or more years.

Once your list of 'hits' is seen, you should double-click on any item of which you want to see the full version (as you would see it in the paper version). You may click on a Next or Previous button to move through the list of hits.

The screen is designed to look like a set of file index cards. If you want to go back from the full version of an item to the list of hits, you can click on the card called 'Search List'. If you want to carry out a fresh search, click on the one called 'Search'.

Current Law Hong Kong

This publication started in 1996 and was designed for the practising commercial lawyer. Most of it ceased to exist in 1998. Although published by the same company as *Current Law* in the UK, it was organized rather differently. It contained the following sections:

Current Law Hong Kong

There are summaries under the following heading:

- cases (taken from the *Hong Kong Law Reports*, *Hong Kong Cases* and the *Hong Kong Law Digest*)
- Legislation
- Press releases — government announcements explaining new developments such as Bills

Here is a case summary from the May 1996 issue:

Keywords ────────

13. Compensation – personal injury – loss of earnings capacity – whether court should apply s.9(1A) of the Employees' Compensation Ordinance.

[Employees' Compensation Ordinance (Cap 282) ss.9, 9(1A), 10, 10, Sch 1].

The applicant had been injured when engaged in plastering work in the course of his employment. He applied for compensation under ss.9, 10 and 10A of the Employees' Compensation Ordinance (Cap 282), (the Ordinance). Under dispute was the calculation of compensation under s.9 of the Ordinance.

Held, that the applicant's employment history, qualifications, training and experience did not give rise to 'special circumstances' under s.9(1A)(b) of the Ordinance, which would have lead the Court to apply different percentages for calculation of the compensation than those given in the first schedule to the Ordinance. The Court held that discretion should not be exercised in this case.

Names of parties ────────

CHEUNG WAN SUN v. LAI WAI MAN (T/A WAI MAN DECORATION AND DESIGN ENGINEERING CO);

District Court, Employee's Compensation Case No.

Case number ────────

288 of 1993, February 16, 1996. Kwan DJ. [1996]1

Report ────────

H.K.C. 657-662.

Current Law Case Citator

This lists cases in alphabetical order and indicates where cases have been cited in later cases, and where they have been discussed in articles. It also indicates where a case has been summarized in *Current Law Hong Kong* itself. Below is the entry in the *Case Citator* for the case summarized above:

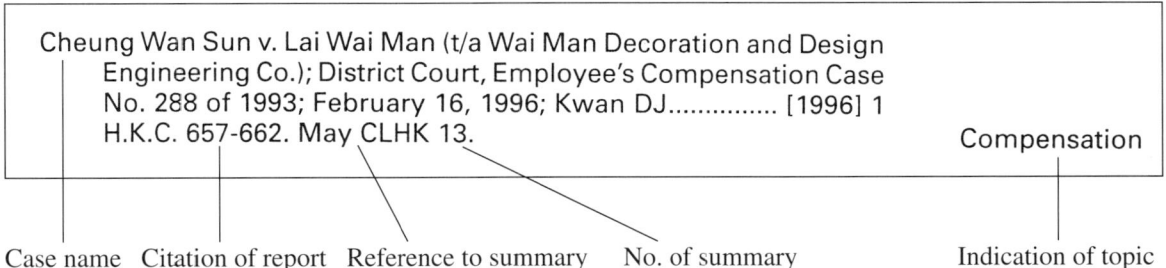

Cheung Wan Sun v. Lai Wai Man (t/a Wai Man Decoration and Design Engineering Co.); District Court, Employee's Compensation Case No. 288 of 1993; February 16, 1996; Kwan DJ............... [1996] 1 H.K.C. 657-662. May CLHK 13.

Compensation

Case name   Citation of report   Reference to summary   No. of summary   Indication of topic

Asian Legal Journals Index

This survived, at least temporarily, the demise of the rest of *Current Law Hong Kong* and provides brief descriptions of articles in regional journals directed mainly at the profession: such as the *Asian Business Law Review* and the *New Gazette* (though it so far includes the *Asia Pacific Law Review*, but not the *Hong Kong Law Journal*). It also includes articles about the region from journals published in the UK. It contains:

- Subject Index — each item may appear under several different keywords
- Index of Cases considered in Articles and Index of Legislation considered in Articles.

Here is an item from the subject index about Hong Kong in the *Cambridge Law Journal*.

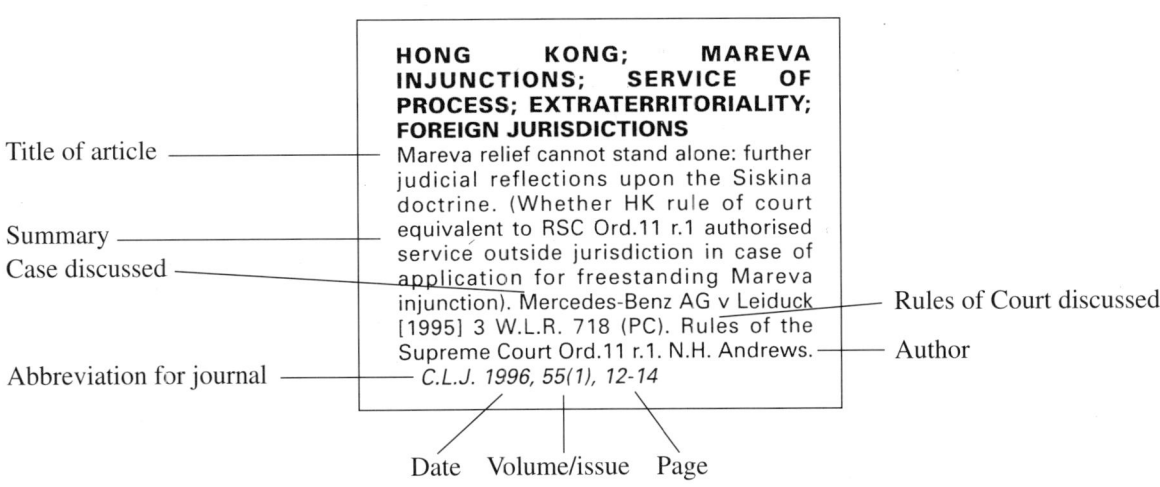

Title of article

HONG KONG; MAREVA INJUNCTIONS; SERVICE OF PROCESS; EXTRATERRITORIALITY; FOREIGN JURISDICTIONS

Summary
Case discussed

Mareva relief cannot stand alone: further judicial reflections upon the Siskina doctrine. (Whether HK rule of court equivalent to RSC Ord.11 r.1 authorised service outside jurisdiction in case of application for freestanding Mareva injunction). Mercedes-Benz AG v Leiduck [1995] 3 W.L.R. 718 (PC). Rules of the Supreme Court Ord.11 r.1. N.H. Andrews.

Abbreviation for journal

C.L.J. 1996, 55(1), 12-14

Rules of Court discussed

Author

Date   Volume/issue   Page

Halsbury's Laws of Hong Kong

This is an encyclopaedic work which began publication at the end of 1995. It falls into the category of descriptive, non-specialist work, and will eventually be updated by loose-leaf service. There is also a plan for a CD-ROM version.

The model is that of *Halsbury's Laws of England* (see below). In other words, it will be a series of treatises on aspects of Hong Kong law, to be published in over 20 volumes, and each volume will in most instances contain more than one topic. Probably over a long period it is intended that volumes will be reissued with updating material and, where it becomes necessary, new titles. There will also eventually be separate volumes which have indexes for the whole publication: a General Index, a Consolidated Table of Cases, and a Consolidated Table of Statutes.

Below is the list of titles as envisaged by early 1996, and the volumes in which they will appear. (One of the hazards of planning such a mammoth enterprise is shown by the fact that although initially it was intended that Volume 10 should include Education, Elections and Employment, by the time Volume 10 did appear (it was the second volume to be published) it had either become apparent that this was too much material to include in one volume or it proved impossible to get all three titles ready simultaneously. So now Volume 10(1) includes Education and Elections, and Volume 10(2) will have Employment.

Halsbury?

Lord Halsbury was Lord Chancellor at the time the first edition of the English version was published. To honour him, the new publishing venture was named after him. Later editions bear the name of the Lord Chancellor at the time the new edition was commenced.

It may seem a trifle odd, one might think, that on the eve of the return of Hong Kong sovereignty to China a new work should be published, which is designed to continue into the indefinite future, bearing the name of a former (colonial) Lord Chancellor! The publishers, Butterworths are evidently capitalizing on the asset they have in the form of a name associated with a well-known publication. Incidentally, there is also a *Halsbury's Laws of Australia*.

Title scheme

Note that the title numbering allows for the additon of new titles as necessary.

Volume 1
[10] Administrative Law
[15] Agency
[20] Animals
[25] Arbitration
[30] Auction

Volume 2
[35] Bailment and Lien
[40] Banking and Finance
[45] Bankruptcy

Volume 3
[50] Betting, Gambling and Lotteries
[55] Bills of Exchange and Other Negotiable Instruments
[60] Bribery, Corruption and Organised Crime
[65] Building and Construction

Volume 4
[70] Carriers
[75] Charities
[80] Citizenship
[85] Civil Aviation

Volume 5
[90] Civil Procedure

Volume 6
[95] Companies and Corporations

Volume 7
[100] Conflict of Laws
[105] Constitutional Law
[110] Contempt of Court
[115] Contract

Volume 8
[120] Coroners
[125] Courts and Judicial System

Volume 9
[130] Criminal Law and Procedure

Volume 10(1)
[135] Education
[140] Elections

Volume 10(2)
[145] Employment

Volume 11
[150] Energy and Resources
[155] Entertainment, Hotels, Sport and Tourism
[160] Environment
[165] Equity
[170] Estoppel

Volume 12
[175] Evidence
[180] Family Law

Volume 13
[185] Firearms, Weapons and Explosives
[190] Foreign Relations
[195] Gifts
[200] Guarantee and Indemnity

Volume 14
[205] Health and Safety
[210] Human Rights
[215] Immigration

Volume 15
[220] Insurance
[225] Intellectual Property

Volume 16
[230] Land

Volume 17
[235] Landlord and Tenant
[240] Legal Practitioners
[245] Limitation of Actions

Volume 18
[250] Maritime Law
[255] Media and Communications

Volume 19
[260] Medicine, Pharmacy and Drugs
[265] Mental Health
[270] Military Forces
[275] Misrepresentation and Fraud
[280] Mortgages and Securities

Volume 20
[285] New Territories
[290] Partnerships and Joint Ventures
[295] Personal Property
[300] Police and Emergency Services
[305] Primary Industry
[310] Prison and Detention

Volume 21
[315] Professions and Trades
[320] Public Health and Municipal Services

Volume 22
[325] Rating
[330] Registration concerning the Individual
[335] Religion
[340] Remedies

Volume 23
[345] Road Traffic
[350] Roads and Tunnels
[355] Sale of Goods
[360] Social Welfare and Services
[365] Statutes

Volume 24
[370] Taxation and Revenue
[375] Time

Volume 25
[380] Tort
[385] Town Planning
[390] Trade and Labour

Volume 26
[395] Transport
[400] Trusts
[405] Urban and Regional Councils and District Boards
[410] Voluntary Associations
[415] Water

Volume 27
[420] Weights and Measures
[425] Wills, Probate, Administration and Succession

Consolidated Index

Tables

➤ The Hong Kong Halsbury's differs from the UK original in one respect — that each title has a number, as you will see from the list. In the Index at the end of each volume, and presumably in the ultimate Consolidated Index, reference will be to title numbers, not to volume numbers.

A worked example:

Volume 1 as you will see, includes the topic Animals. If you look at the Index at the back of Volume 1 you will ➤ find that the index is divided so there is in effect a separate index for Administrative Law, for Agency, etc. Under Wild Animal you find this: ⇨

offence—
  contravening—
    restrictions on import and export, of,
     [20.044], [20.047]
    Wild Animals Protection Ordinance,
     [20.053]
  destroying nest or egg of protected
    wild animal, of, [20.046]
  entry into restricted area, of, [20.049]

Here is part of para. 20. 049:

> **[20.049] Entry in restricted areas** No person may, except in accordance with a permit in writing granted by the Director of Agriculture and Fisheries, enter into or be within any area specified as a restricted area[1]. This restriction does not apply to a public officer[2] or a member of Her Majesty's forces on duty within any such area[3], a person engaged on public works within any such area[4] or a person ordinarily resident in such specified area[5]. A person who lawfully enters or is within a restricted area may not be in possession of any arms[6], unless he is a police officer or a member of Her Majesty's forces or the Customs and Excise Service on duty[7], may not be in possession of any hunting appliance[8] and may not hunt any wild animal[9]. A person who contravenes these provisions is guilty of an offence and liable on conviction to a fine[10].
>
> 1 Wild Animals Protection Ordinance (Cap 170) s 13(1). Areas specified as restricted areas are Fung Shui wood (from 1 April to 30 September, both days inclusive) and the Mai Po Marshes (at all times): Sch 6.
>
> 2 'Public officer' means any person holding an office of emolument under the Crown in right of the Government of Hong Kong, whether such office be permanent or temporary: Interpretation and General Clauses Ordinance (Cap 1) s 3.

In the looseleaf, current service volume you will find that this paragraph was updated in Issue 3, 31 July 1998:

> **[20.045]–[20.054]** Note the amendments to the Wild Animals (Protection) Ordinance (Cap 170) by the Wild Animals (Protection) (Amendment) Ordinance 1996 (No 77 of 1996) as from 1 February 1997.
>
> **[20.049]** Note 1. The restricted area of the Mai Po Marshes has been extended to include the intertidal mud flats and shallow waters of Inner Deep Bay as from 5 July 1996: Wild Animals Protection Ordinance (Amendment of Sixth Schedule) Order 1996 (LN 19 of 1996).
>
> Note 2. *Substitute the following*: 'Public officer' means any person holding an office of emolument under the Government, whether such office be permanent or temporary: Interpretation and General Clauses Ordinance (Cap 1) s 3 (amended by the Adaptation of Laws (Interpretative Provisions) Ordinance (No 26 of 1998) s 4).

ENGLAND

Current Law

This is the major UK publication for keeping up-to-date with the law. The *Hong Kong Law Digest* is modelled on it. It is non-specialist, contains summaries, and is periodical.

Current Law Monthly Digest contains:

- Summaries of cases †
- Summaries of statutes †
- Summaries of statutory instruments (delegated legislation) †
- Lists of new books and journal articles †
- Statute Citator — cases in which English statutes have been cited during the year*
- Dates of Commencement of Statutes*†
- Table of Cases — listing cases digested (names in CAPITALS) and those from any jurisdiction which have been cited during the year* so far
- Words and Phrases judicially defined during the year*†
- Table of the progress of Bills through the UK Parliament*
- Index *†

(* Items marked with an asterisk are cumulative lists/indexes. Look for the latest one and it will give you the information for the whole year so far.)

The body of *Current Law* consists of material under headings in alphabetical order, so you could go straight to the relevant paragraph instead of using the index. ➤ The disadvantage is that this will only show you this month's entries, whereas the index will refer you to entries for the previous months in the same calendar year.

Current Law Yearbook: This reproduces the information from the year's Monthly Digests in one volume. All the material marked † in the above list is reproduced. The list of books and articles is separate at the back, although still divided by subject matter.

The Yearbook used to consolidate its indexes periodically, but this has been overtaken by the volume of legal development. There were consolidations in 1956, 1961, 1971, 1986 and 1989, but now each yearbook only tells you about that year. (The CD-ROM version will help here.)

Current Law Case Citator and the *Current Law Statute Citator* which consolidate the Tables of Cases judicially considered and the Legislation judicially considered have been considered earlier.

Here is a simple example of the use of *Current Law* and its Index.

Suppose you want to find out whether interference with another person's televison reception is a 'nuisance'. You may think it is worth looking up (in the Index of the latest monthly Digest in 1996) 'television'.

Or nuisance:

⇨
television
    interference with reception
        private but not public nuisance, Apr 792
    licences
        fees, Apr 504

⇩

nuisance—*cont.*
    environmental health
        landlord and tenant
            articles, Jan 371
    eviction, Jan 360
    harassment
        exclusion order prohibiting from designated
            area, Jan 553
    interference
        locus standi
            articles, Feb 714
    locus standi
        occupation of property as home, Apr 792
    noise
        local authorities, Jan 212
        person responsible, Feb 286
    repairs
        owner's liability for costs, Jan 557
    television reception
        interference by tall buildings, Apr 792

So I looked for paragraph 792 in the April Monthly Digest as an example, and I found this:

⇩

792. **Nuisance—whether interference with TV reception by tall building action-able in private nuisance—BBC's duty to broadcast did not give viewers rights against third parties—whether planning consent gave immunity in nuisance—whether interference with reception actionable in negligence without proof of physical damage**

Held, dismissing the application, that the plaintiff and hundreds of others who complained of interference with television reception following the construction of the Canary Wharf Tower could not claim damages because (1) interference by tall buildings was not capable of constituting private nuisance. Analogy with loss of prospect applied and the BBC's duty to provide signals did not confer rights against third parties; (2) CW could not rely on the defence of statutory authority. Planning consent did not include immunity in nuisance; (3) interference with TV reception was not capable of being public nuisance use; (4) a substantial link between those enjoying the use and the land was necessary for a claim in private nuisance, eg. occupation of property as a home and (5) a deposit of dust during the construction process was capable of constituting an action in negligence dependent on proof of physical damage.

HUNTER v. CANARY WHARF LTD; HUNTER v. LONDON DOCKLANDS DEVELOPMENT CORP [1996] 1 All E.R. 482, Neill, L.J., CA.

 Current Law is now available in CD-ROM format, as part of Current Legal Information. It works just the same way as *Legal Journals Index* which is in the same collection (see p. 197). However, there is also an on-line version which works slightly differently.

❖ Try the same search as for the *Hong Kong Law Digest* — namely look in the Index for a Yearbook and see what you can find on Defamation. Is this a separate heading or does it appear under 'Tort'? Does the index distinguish between Libel and Defamation? Are there cross-references? ☺ About 15 minutes.

Halsbury's Laws of England

This is an encyclopedia of the law of England. It describes the law and gives references to the relevant cases and English legislation. It consists of the following elements:

- Main volumes (Volumes 1–52, but some of these have been subdivided, e.g. Criminal Law which is Volume 11 is actually 11(1) and 11(2) now)
- Consolidated Index (2 Volumes — Volume 55 and 56)
- Consolidated Table of Cases (Volume 54)
- Consolidated Table of Statutes (Volume 53)
- Annual Abridgement
- Cumulative Supplement (2 annual volumes)
- Current Service (2 loose-leaf binders)

Each main volume contains one or more broad topic, and you may find it simplest to pick up the volume which seems most relevant to your topic. (But this may be a bit risky if some material relevant to your topic has actually been placed in another volume — as Clinch points out, in *Using a Law Library*. An example would be Negligence, for which the main entry is Volume 34, but on which there is material in Volumes 4, 11, 12, 19, 22, 23, 24, 27, 30, 38 and 43!) Periodically a volume may be reissued — if so it will say it is a reissue on its spine. So some volumes are quite elderly and some can be quite up-to-date. ➤ Make sure you get the most recent one or you may miss some material.

If you cannot see the relevant volume quickly, use the consolidated index (2 volumes).

If you know you want to find a discussion of a particular case or English statute, you can look them up in the Consolidated Table of Cases or Consolidated Table of Statutes — separate volumes.

The Index, whichever one you use, will refer you to a volume number and paragraphs (maybe more than one volume).

Having found the main discussion of the topic in question, you will probably want to make sure you get the up-to-date law. Halsbury's now has a number of additional elements which make it possible to do this:

- **Annual Abridgements:** These summarize cases and legislation which have happened since the Main Volumes were published. They are a bit like the Annual Volumes of *Current Law*. Like the latter they give references to secondary material, books and articles, as well.

- **Cumulative Supplement:** This is published every year. As its name suggests, it includes all the material (up to the end of the previous year) which updates the main volumes, organized in the same order as the main volumes.

- **Current service:** This is for any developments since the last cumulative supplement. It consists of two binders:

  Binder 1: **Monthly Review** — summaries which will eventually be consolidated into the Annual Abridgement. It is a bit like *Current Law* monthly parts.

  Binder 2: **Noter-up** is also organized in the same order as the main volumes, and will give you references to the latest cases and legislation on the topics.

➤ Be sure to note the volume number, the broad subject, and the paragraph number from the main volume in order to find the updating material in the Cumulative Supplement and the Noter-up.

You may sometimes find it useful to look at previous editions of Halsbury. Sometimes Hong Kong's law is more like some older English law than current English law. A good example is Employees' Compensation for which you would need to use the Second Edition.

Worked example

Suppose you have an interest in provocation, especially in the context of murder.

Go to the Consolidated Index Volume No. 56 and look up Provocation. There is no mention of murder there, so go to the entry on Murder and you will find: ➪

MURDER. *See also* HOMICIDE; MANSLAUGHTER
  meaning, 11(1), 426
  absence of body, 11(1), 459
  alternative verdicts, 11(2), 1030
  attempted, penalty, 11(1), 75
  bail restriction, 11(2), 886
  burden of proof, 11(1), 426, 453
  charge. *See under* LEGAL AID
  circumstantial evidence, 11(1), 459
  complicity, 11(1), 435

  prevention of crime, defence of, 11(1), 455
  property, in defence of, 11(1), 457
  provocation as defence, 11(1), 438, 439

So find Vol. 11(1) paras. 438 and 439: you will find this:

438. Provocation as defence to murder charge. Provocation may reduce a charge of murder[1] to one of manslaughter[2]. It consists of conduct[3] which would cause in any reasonable person, and actually causes in the accused, a sudden and temporary loss of self-control[4], making him so subject to passion that he is not the master of his mind[5]. Where on a charge of murder there is evidence on which the jury can find that the person charged was provoked[6], whether by things done or by things said[7], or by both together, to lose his self-control, the question whether the provocation was enough to make a reasonable man do as he did must be left to be determined by the jury[8]. In determining that question the jury must take into account everything both done and said according to the effect which, in the jury's opinion, it would have on a reasonable man[9].

1 Provocation may be a defence only to a charge of murder: *R v Cunningham* [1959] 1 QB 288, 43 Cr App Rep 79, CCA; *R v Bruzas* [1972] Crim LR 367.

2 The defence of provocation is available even though there exists in the accused's mind such malice as would support a charge of murder: see *A-G of Ceylon v Kumarasinghege Don John Perera* [1953] AC 200 at 206, [1953] 2 WLR 238 at 243, PC; *Lee Chun-Chuen v R* [1963] AC 220, [1963] 1 All ER 73, PC; *Parker v R* [1964] AC 1369, [1964] 2 All ER 641, PC; *R v Martindale* [1966] 3 All ER 305, 50 Cr App Rep 273, C-MAC. If the facts are not in dispute, it is open to the judge to direct the jury that it may return only a verdict of murder or manslaughter, ie it may not return a verdict of not guilty: *R v Larkin* as reported in [1943] 1 All ER 217, CCA.

3 Conduct constituting provocation may include spoken words: see infra. It is not essential that the conduct be directed at the accused himself. A man may be provoked by finding another raping his wife (1 Hale PC 486; *R v Millward* (1931) 23 Cr App Rep 119, CCA), or committing an unnatural offence with his son (*R v Fisher* (1837) 8 C & P 182), or committing an assault on a member of his family (*R v Harrington* (1886) 10 Cox CC 370). Adultery may also constitute provocation: see 1 Hale PC 486; *R v Manning* (1671) T Raym 212; *R v Pearson* (1835) 2 Lew CC 216. In general provocation is a defence when it causes the accused to kill the person giving the provocation (see *R v Simpson* (1915) 84 LJKB 1893, 11 Cr App Rep 218, CCA), but it may provide a defence even where it causes him to kill a third person (see *R v Davies* [1975] QB 691, 60 Cr App Rep 253, CA; and see also the Homicide Act 1957 s 3: see infra). As to self-induced provocation see para 439 text and note 7 post.

4 It is essential to the defence that the accused should in fact have lost his self-control at the time of the killing. In considering whether there was such a genuine loss of self-control the jury may have regard to the time elapsing between the provocation and the killing (*R v Hayward* (1833) 6 C & P 157; *Kwaku Mensah v R* [1946] AC 83, PC; *R v Duffy* [1949] 1 All ER 932n, CCA; *R v Ibrams* (1981) 74 Cr App Rep 154, CA), and to the manner of the killing itself which may support or negative contrivance or design (1 Hale PC 454; Fost 291; 1 Hawk PC c 13 s 42; 1 East PC 235; *R v Thorpe* (1829) 1 Lew CC 171; *R v Shaw* (1834) 6 C & P 372; *R v Thomas* (1837) 7 C & P 817; *Mancini v DPP* [1942] AC 1, 28 Cr App Rep 65, HL; *R v Gilbert* (1977) 66 Cr App Rep 237, CA). See also *R v Cocker* [1989] Crim LR 740, CA (husband gave way to wife's entreaties that he should kill her; loss of self-restraint but not of self-control; no evidence of provocation).

5 See *R v Duffy* [1949] 1 All ER 932n, CCA, approving the direction given to the jury by Devlin J; *R v Whitfield* (1976) 63 Cr App Rep 39 at 42, CA.

But you want to make sure you are up-to-date. So find the Cumulative Supplement. There you will find this:

---

2 Ibid, s 36A(1), (6).
3 Ibid, s 36A(2). "Officer" means a person commissioned by the commissioners: s 36A(6). In the case of the death, removal, discharge or absence of the officer in whose name any proceedings for a specified offence were commenced, those proceedings may be continued by another officer: s 36A(3).
4 Ibid, s 36A(4), referring to an assigned matter within the meaning of the Customs and Excise Management Act 1979 (see s 1(1)).
5 1986 Act, s 36A(5).

411   Disclosure of information held by government departments
TEXT and NOTES—As to procedure generally, see paras 1312–1325 post.
NOTE 2—1986 Act, s 33 repealed: Land Registration Act 1988, ss 1(2)(f), 2, Schedule.

Part 3.   Offences against the Person

426   Definition and proof
NOTES—As to extended territorial scope of murder or manslaughter in the case of acts in relation to or by means of Nuclear Material, see Nuclear Material (Offences) Act 1983, Vol 16, para 415A post.

428   Person under the Queen's peace
NOTES—As to extended territorial scope of murder or manslaughter in case of acts in relation to or by means of Nuclear Material, see Nuclear Material (Offences) Act 1983, Vol 16, para 415A post.

430   Causation
NOTE 3—See also *R v Le Brun* [1991] 4 All ER 673, CA (victim's head hitting pavement caused fatal fracture to skull after defendant had knocked her to ground).
NOTE 7—See *R v Williams* [1992] 2 All ER 183, CA (victim jumped from moving car to his death when other occupants allegedly tried to rob him).
NOTE 10—See *R v Cheshire* [1991] 3 All ER 670, CA (hospital staff's negligence in treatment of victim immediate cause of death, but medical complication was direct consequence of accused's acts, which remained a significant cause of death).

435   Joint enterprise
NOTE 4—See also *Hui Chi–ming v R* [1991] 3 All ER 897, PC.
NOTE 5—See also *R v Hyde* [1990] 3 All ER 892, CA; *R v Roberts* [1993] 1 All ER 583, CA.

436   In general
NOTES—As to extended territorial scope of manslaughter in case of acts in relation to or by means of nuclear material, see Nuclear Material (Offences) Act 1983, Vol 16, para 415A post.

437   Penalty for manslaughter
NOTE 1—*R v Eaton*, cited, reported at (1989) 11 Cr App Rep (S) 475, CA.
As to appropriate sentence for manslaughter of baby where mother (defendant) was suffering from diminished responsibility, see *R v Lewis* (1989) 11 Cr App Rep (S) 578, CA.

438   Provocation as defence to murder charge
TEXT and NOTES—See *R v Clarke* [1991] Crim LR 383, CA; *R v Richens* [1993] Crim LR 384, CA.
NOTE 4—See also *R v Thornton* [1992] 1 All ER 306, CA; *R v Ahluwalia* (1992) Independent, 4 August, CA.
NOTE 8—The issue of provocation must be left to the jury even where the evidence of provocation is tenuous: *R v Rossiter* (1992) 95 Cr App Rep 326, CA.

You will see that there have been some more cases. This is the 1995 Supplement. Is it worth going further? Let's try the Noter-up (Current Service Binder 2). There you will find this:

1219A.3 (Supplement)   Disposal of human remains
NOTE 5—1981 Act, Schedule, para 10 amended: Local Government (Wales) Act 1994, s 66(6), Sch 16, para 60.

Volumes 11(1), (2) (reissue)

CRIMINAL LAW, EVIDENCE AND PROCEDURE

In the MONTHLY REVIEWS material updating this title appears under three titles: CRIMINAL EVIDENCE AND PROCEDURE, criminal law and sentencing.

The revised title CROWN PROCEEDINGS AND CROWN PRACTICE will be published in due course in Vol 12 (reissue). Until then, the revised title in its entirety is included in the 1996 *Cumulative Supplement* following the title CRIMINAL LAW, EVIDENCE AND PROCEDURE.

As to legal aid in criminal proceedings, see now Vol 27(2) (reissue).

Volume 11(1) (reissue)

14   Recklessness and foresight
NOTE 4—See *R v Merrick* [1996] 1 Cr App R 130, CA.

20   Mistake or general ignorance of law
NOTE 1—1946 Act, s 3 amended: Statutory Instruments (Production and Sale) Act 1996, s 1.

24   Duress; compulsion
NOTE 9—See *R v Bowen* [1996] 2 Cr App R 157, CA.

438   Provocation as defence to murder charge
NOTE—See *Thiet-Thuan v R* [1996] 2 Cr App Rep 178, PC.
NOTE 4—*R v Thornton*, cited, reversed on appeal: [1996] 2 Cr App R 108, CA.
NOTE 8—See *R v Humphreys* [1995] 4 All ER 1008, CA.

439   Provocation; the criterion of the reasonable man
NOTE 2—See *R v Dryden* [1995] 4 All ER 987, CA; *R v Humphreys* [1995] 4 All ER 1008, CA.; *Luc v R* [1996] 2 All ER 1033, PC. *R v Thornton*, cited, reversed on appeal: [1996] 2 Cr App R 108, CA.

488   Assault and battery
NOTE 9—See *R v Ireland* [1996] 3 WLR 650, CA.

490   Assault occasioning actual bodily harm
NOTE 2—See *R v Ireland* [1996] 3 WLR 650, CA.

494   Consent to assault
NOTES 2, 3—See *R v Wilson* [1996] 3 WLR 125, CA.

522   Indecent assault on a woman
NOTE 13—See *R v Allen* [1996] 2 Cr App R (S) 36, CA.

548   Property belonging to another
NOTE 3—See *R v Wain* [1995] 2 Cr App R 660, CA.

632   Extension by statute or by the prerogative
NOTE 9—See also the Territorial Sea (Amendment) Order 1996, SI 1996/1628, which revokes the 1979 Order in Council.

672A (Supplement)   Material relevant to overseas investigation
NOTE 3—See *R v Central Criminal Court, ex p Propend Finance Property Ltd; R v Secretary of State for the Home Department, ex p Propend Finance Property Ltd* [1996] 2 Cr App R 26.

685   Seizure of property
TEXT AND NOTES—See *Sutcliffe v Chief Constable of West Yorkshire* (1995) 159 JP 770, CA.

768   Method of identification
TEXT AND NOTES—See *R v Hickin* [1996] Crim LR 584, CA.

786   Limitation of time in criminal proceedings
NOTE 6—See *R v Wilkinson* [1996] 1 Cr App Rep 81, CA.
NOTE 7—See also *R v E (John)* [1996] 1 Cr App R 88, CA.

So it is worth it! Note when the Noter-up was published (bottom left-hand corner).

Now you should go to the law reports ideally. But if you cannot do this (for example because the case referred to is in a series of reports not available to you), you can at least look in Binder 1 of the Current Service, and in the Monthly Review you will find this (you can find this by looking at the Index pages filed at the back of the binder):

95/1046   Murder—defence—provocation—question for determination by jury
When the appellant's wife was found dead he told the police that he had thrown her onto a bed. Her injuries were consistent with impact to a wooden bed end but there were too many injuries to have resulted from a single fall. The appellant's principal defence was one of accident, in that the injuries occurred when he restrained his wife from leaving home because he believed she would commit suicide. The issue of manslaughter was also raised on the basis that excessive force had been used by the appellant. His counsel did not invite the jury to consider provocation because it was inconsistent with the defence but the judge gave a direction upon it. The appellant was convicted of murder and, on appeal, he submitted that the judge gave the jury no assistance on the evidence relevant to the issue of provocation. *Held*, it was well established that the judge had to leave the jury to decide if there was evidence which suggested that the accused had been provoked, even if the defence did not raise the issue and would prefer not to do so because it was inconsistent with the primary defence. Where the judge had to do so, he should indicate, unless it was obvious, what evidence might support the conclusion that the accused lost his self-control. This was particularly important where counsel had not raised the issue. In the present case, the judge had not given any such assistance to the jury and that amounted to a non-direction. However, on the evidence there had not been a miscarriage of justice. Accordingly, the appeal would be dismissed.
   R v Stewart [1995] Crim LR 66 (Court of Appeal: Stuart-Smith LJ, Kay and Dyson JJ).
R v Rossiter (1992) 95 Cr App Rep 326, CA (1992 Abr para 798) and *R v Cambridge* [1994] 2 All ER 760, CA considered.

Halsbury's Laws, Vol 11(1) (reissue), para 438

The Digest

This is a digest of cases from England and other Commonwealth jurisdictions. **On the whole this is a research tool I should not encourage you to use**. You should get into the habit of reading full case reports. However, it may be useful to put you onto cases you can then read in more detail elsewhere, or which are not available to you in any other form, or it may be used to find the references for cases for which you have the name but no citation — but *Current Law Citator* is better for this purpose if it includes the case you want.

The Digest is in some ways like Halsbury's Laws. It has:

- Main volumes divided by topic
- Consolidated Index
- Consolidated Table of Cases
- Cumulative Supplement
- Quarterly Survey

The volumes are periodically reissued. They will usually say so on the spine (and certainly inside). There have even been second reissues of most volumes.

For some areas of the law in which there are many cases the volume are split into two parts. In the case of criminal law, the two volumes have each been further split into two — 14(1) and (2), and 15(1) and (2).

The Consolidated Index and Consolidated Table of Cases are now being reissued annually. Every year there is a Cumulative Supplement, which replaces the previous year's supplement.

A recent development is the **Quarterly Survey**. The first appeared in September 1995. The idea is that rather than waiting for a whole year for new material, it will be available sooner. It is arranged in the same order as the main volumes. ➤ It is not cumulative, so you have to look at each Survey.

A worked example

Let us take an example. It should be simple, but does reveal some of the problems about the Digest. Suppose you are interested in the line of cases which began with *Wilkinson v Downton*. If you look it up in the Index of Cases you will find this:

> Wilkinson v Cummins (1853) **9(2) Coys**
> Wilkinson v Dent (1871) **20 Eqy**
> Wilkinson v Detmold (1890) (AUS) **40 S Land**
> Wilkinson v Downton (1897) **17(2) Damgs; 34 Misre**
>   **46 Tort**
> Wilkinson v Duncan (1857) **41 Settlmts**

(Note that it gives only the volume, and to find the paragraph you need to look in the list of cases in the individual volume (here Volume 17(2) on Damages). ➤ Incidentally, if you looked up 'nervous shock' in the Consolidated Index, it would supply paragraph as well as volume numbers.)

When you go to the relevant paragraph in Volume 17(2) you will find this:

844 Pain and suffering—Nervous shock
Defendant, by way of a practical joke, falsely represented to plaintiff a married woman that her husband had met with a serious accident whereby both his legs were broken. Defendant made the statement with intent that it should be believed to be true. Plaintiff believed it to be true, and in consequence suffered a violent nervous shock which rendered her ill: *Held* these facts constituted a good cause of action.

Wilkinson v Downton [1897] 2 QB 57; [1895–7] All ER Rep 267; 66 LJQB 493; 76 LT 493; 45 WR 525; 13 TLR 388; 41 Sol Jo 493
ANNOTATIONS **Consd** Dulieu v White [1901] 2 KB 669 Janvier v Sweeney [1919] 2 KB 316; Hambrook v Stokes (1924) 41 TLR 125

845 Pain and suffering—Nervous shock
Damages for a nervous shock occasioned by fright unaccompanied by any actual impact may be recoverable in an action for negligence if physical injury has been caused to plaintiff.
Dulieu v White & Sons [1901] 2 KB 669; [1900–3] All ER Rep 353; 70 LJKB 837; 85 LT 126; 50 WR 76; 17 TLR 555; 45 Sol Jo 578, DC
ANNOTATIONS **Apprvd** Hambrook v Stokes (1924) 41 TLR 125 **Consd** Owens v Liverpool Corpn [1939] 1 KB 394; Smith v Leech Brain & Co Ltd [1961] 3 All ER 1159; Chadwick v British Transport Commission [1967] 2 All ER 945

846 Pain and suffering—Nervous shock False words and threats calculated to cause, uttered with the knowledge that they are likely to cause, and actually causing, physical injury to the person to whom they are uttered are actionable. Defendants were two private detectives. One of them wished to inspect certain letters, to which he believed plaintiff, a maidservant, had means of access. He instructed the other defendant, who was his assistant, to induce plaintiff to show him the letters, telling him that plaintiff would be remunerated for this service. The assistant endeavoured to persuade plaintiff by false statements and threats as the result of which plaintiff fell ill from a nervous shock. In an action by plaintiff against defendants for damages: *Held* the assistant was acting within the scope of his employment and both defendants were liable.
Janvier v Sweeney [1919] 2 KB 316; [1918–19] All ER Rep 1056; 88 LJKB 1231; 121 LT 179; 35 TLR 360; 63 Sol Jo 430, CA
ANNOTATION **Consd** Hambrook v Stokes (1924) 41 TLR 125

There you see summaries of *Wilkinson* and of two other oldish cases including *Janvier v Sweeney*.

But now you want to be sure you are up-to-date. Try the latest Annual Cumulative Supplement, looking for the part which updates Volume 17(2). You will find this: ⇨

Part 3 — THE MEASURE OF DAMAGES IN TORT

828 Consd Hunt v Severs [1993] 4 All ER 180

846 Apld Khorasandijian v Bush [1993] 3 All ER 669

854 Apld McFarlane v EE Caledonia Ltd [1994] 2 All ER 1

855a Pain and suffering — Nervous shock — Explosion on oil rig — Whether duty of care owed by owners of oil rig to bystander or witness The plaintiff was employed as a painter on an oil rig in the North Sea owned and operated by

---

You will see that it says *Janvier* was applied in *Khorasandjian v Bush*. You will also see the beginning of a new digested case (No. 855a) which is in fact *McFarlane v EE Caledonia Ltd.* [1994] 2 All ER 1.

Finally you would now go to the *Quarterly Survey*. In the issue for December 1995 you will find:

DAMAGES Vol 17(2) (2nd Reissue)

LIST OF NEW CASES

	CASE
Page v Smith	35
Sivakumaran v Yu Pan	36

ANNOTATIONS

848 Consd Page v Smith [1995] 2 All ER 736

849 Dbtd (dictum Denning LJ) Page v Smith [1995] 2 All ER 736

852 Apld (dictum Geoffrey Lane J) Page v Smith [1995] 2 All ER 736

1303 Consd Jaggard v Sawyer and another [1995] 2 All ER 189

DIGESTS

Part 3 — The measure of damages in tort

35 Damages claim for nervous shock — Factors to be considered — Plaintiff directly involved in accident and not mere bystander — Plaintiff alleging that trauma of accident aggravated symptoms of myalgic encephalomyelitis
The plaintiff was involved in a collision with the defendant when the latter failed to give way when turning out of a side road. The plaintiff was physically unhurt in the collision, but the accident caused him to suffer the onset of myalgic encephalomyelitis (ME) from which he had suffered for about 20 years but

Case 35 (in the particular issue of the Survey), of which you can see the beginning, is *Page v Smith*. ➤ Oddly enough there is another nervous shock case in the Survey, under negligence. Please note that *Page v Smith* is also summarized in the September Survey, but only in the Court of Appeal.

❖ Here are some research topics:

- Telephone tapping
- Is it contempt of court to reveal the deliberations of a jury?
- Do patients have a right of access to their medical records?
- What are the rights of prisoners?

Choose one of them and use each of the following:

- *Halsbury's Law of England*
- *Halsbury's Laws of Hong Kong* (if it has reached the topic!)
- *The Digest*
- *The Hong Kong Law Digest*

Find the relevant part of the Main volumes (in the case of the first three items). Then try to find out the most recent legal position (in the case of *Halsbury's Laws of England* and *The Digest*). In the case of the last item, just try to find relevant material in the **current year**.

☺ Probably 90 minutes at least.

SELF-STUDY QUESTIONS

☺ Fifteen minutes.

1. On what publication is the *Hong Kong Law Digest* based?

2. What is the difference between *Hong Kong Current Law* and the *Hong Kong Law Digest*?

3. If you looked in the Index of the *Hong Kong Law Digest* and found this reference — H27, what does it mean?

4. What is *Halsbury's Laws of England Monthly Review*?

5. Which part of *Halsbury's Laws* contains the most up-to-date information?

6. What is a cumulative index?

7. Where would you find the annual statute citator of *Current Law*?

8. *Current Law* contains some sorts of material about UK law which the *Hong Kong Law Digest* does not contain about Hong Kong law. Which?

9. Which part of *The Digest* contains the most up-to-date material?

❖ Make sure you look at all these materials in the library. Note what colour each of the bindings is (being able to recognize a publication quickly in a new library enhances your ability to find what you want quickly).

Unit 13　Journals

OBJECTIVES

By the end of this Unit you will:

* understand the various purposes that a law journal may serve and the sorts of material it may contain
* know the names of the main journals you are likely to encounter, at least as a first year student
* know how to locate articles in the journals
* know how to use the paper versions of indexes to legal periodicals
* know how to use the electronic versions of the same indexes

☺ About three hours.

Students are more familiar with textbooks than with journals. But you will realize that textbooks are almost bound to be more out-of-date than a journal, do not have space to go into the details of issues and individual cases, and are directed mainly at people new to the field, or at least they must be comprehensible to such readers. Journals can be more current, more detailed, more controversial and more sophisticated — indeed they ought to be all of these.

➤ It is wise to learn what types of journals there are. This will mean that if you see a reference to an article in a journal you will be able to guess what type of article it might be, and therefore whether it is likely to be useful to you. Or you may go straight to the recent issues of a certain journal or type of journal knowing that it is likely to have material of interest.

VARIETIES OF JOURNALS

❖ To get a sense of the different types of journals, I suggest you go **now** (or as soon as possible) to the current issues rack in your library. ☺ Take at least 20 minutes.

Look, for example, at the most recent issues of the *Law Quarterly Review*, the *Cambridge Law Journal* or the *Modern Law Review*. These all have certain features in common:

- they are published, or at least edited, by law faculties
- they contain material mainly written by academics
- they contain 'articles' each of about twenty pages dealing with a wide variety of topics
- they are not specialized in a particular field of law
- they also contain notes of cases (**CASENOTES**), **NOTES ON STATUTES** and book reviews, and possibly shorter notes which are not necessarily about a single case or statute.

By way of contrast look at the *Harvard Law Review*, the *Yale Law Journal* or the *Columbia Law Review*. There are certain similarities between these and the earlier ones. They are American and produced in the great US law schools. They also include articles, shorter articles, book reviews, etc. They are much fatter than the English ones! They are edited not by teachers but by students. The best law students in the US all aim to be put on the law review. Many of the articles in the review will be written by students, too. You will notice a different style in US legal literature. There is a fashion for enormously long and multitudinous footnotes (often containing a valuable bibliography of the existing literature).

Now look at the *Hong Kong Law Journal* and *Asia Pacific Law Review*. Which of the other journals you have just looked at do these resemble most? Can you see any differences in content or approach between these two Hong Kong journals?

Take a look now at the *New Law Journal* or the *Solicitors Journal* or the *Gazette*. These are A4 size, with shorter articles, often with practice notes (sometimes on different colour paper). They are written for the profession, although others read them too. They will have notes of latest cases and statutes too. The authors are usually a mixture of academic and practising lawyers. One might call these 'magazines' for the legal profession.

Now look at *The New Gazette* (a Hong Kong publication): how does it compare in content and style with the three English journals mentioned in the last paragraph?

You will notice other journals the titles of which indicate a degree of specialization in their subject matter: the *Journal of Business Law*, *Public Law*, the *Law Teacher*. There are journals which specialize in virtually every field of law, and since there is no sacred and pre-ordained classification of legal topics, as new areas draw the attention of lawyers and writers, there will be new journals. There is at least one journal for each of the subjects which figure in a typical LL.B. subject (unless a particular law school has a very new or unusual course). Since course contents vary even if the names are similar, a journal with a name like that of a course you are studying may not cover entirely the same ground, and there will be relevant articles in many other journals too. But it may well worth looking at the journal(s) with the name most close to the name of a course for articles discussing the latest developments and controversies in that field. For some courses, you will find many journals, for example, human rights law.

❖ When you are looking at the journals, also notice how old they are — you will find that some journals have been published for over 100 years. Others are in their first volume or have only been published for a few years. This will probably be an indication that it is either published by a new institution such as new law school, or that it is on a new topic.

Some journals are more commercial ventures than others, which probably means they are directed at the practitioner (not always the solicitor or barrister), and the articles are more practically oriented and less theoretical. Then there are specialized journals which are aimed primarily at the legal profession (often A4 size too). An example would be *Professional Negligence*.

Even within the broad categories there are differences. For example, there are journals mainly contributed by academics which have a particular bent, or are more likely to have a particular bent. The *Journal of Legal Studies* is published by the University of Chicago, and has an emphasis on the economic approach to law (and the Chicago School approach which is rather conservative). There is the *International Journal of Law and Economics* which is its British equivalent, but less conservative. The *Journal of Law and Society* is a British journal with an interest in sociology and law. The *Medico-Legal Journal* is self-explanatory, as is the *American Journal of Legal History*. Other differences are more subtle. There is the *Oxford Journal of Legal Studies* which is more likely to have articles which are theoretical or historical, and the *Anglo-American Law Journal* which has a slight comparative bias. The *Modern Law Review* was given that name to distinguish it from older publications, especially the *Law Quarterly Review*; it tended to abjure historical articles, and some of the more antiquarian topics which the LQR used, especially in the past, to favour. It still has a slightly more radical image.

Hong Kong Based Journals

Except for the *Hong Kong University Law Journal* (1926–27) and the *Hong Kong University Journal of Law and Commerce* (1928–40), the most venerable journal is the *Hong Kong Law Journal* (abbreviation HKLJ) which was started in 1971. It has articles mainly but not exclusively about Hong Kong law, case and statute notes, short notes, items on Chinese law, damages and sentencing (not found in the academic journals in England because there this is done by publications like *Current Law*).

The Law Society of Hong Kong has its own publication: the *Hong Kong Lawyer*. There are also a number of journals intended for legal practitioners with an interest in this region. The emphasis is on short, topical articles. Examples are *IPAsia, Asia Law*.

The *Asia-Pacific Law Review* is published by the Law School at the City University of Hong Kong. This, as its name suggests, emphasizes regional material as much as that about HK specifically. The *Chinese and Comparative Law Review* is also published by City U, and contains articles in both Chinese and English.

The *Hong Kong Student Law Review* is published by students at the University of Hong Kong. In the 1980s there was a student written and edited journal called *Justitia*.

Other Countries

A similar pattern is found in other countries. Most of those you will find in Hong Kong will be the university-edited journals, such as the *Osgoode Hall Law Journal*, the *University of New South Wales Law Review*, the *Victoria University of Wellington Law Review* — to take a Canadian, an Australian and a New Zealand example.

➤ Journals tend to be much less parochial than student and practitioner texts which are usually restricted to the law of one country. You are very likely to find articles about Hong Kong in the journals of other countries. It is also common to have comparative articles, which compare the law of the 'home country' of the journal with that of one or more other jurisdictions.

Regional Journals

There are a number of journals published in Asia which might be of interest, but which textbooks written in England are unlikely to refer you to. Apart from the very large number of Indian journals, most of which are not easily accessible and are often irregular (although there are some excellent ones such as the *Journal of the Indian Law Institute* — which is like, for example, the *Modern Law Review*, with articles, notes, book reviews — and also specialist Indian journals such the *Indian Journal of International Law*), there are journals from Singapore, Malaysia and Japan in English. There are, of course, many journals in Chinese and Japanese.

The *Singapore Journal of Legal Studies* used to be called the *Malaya Law Review*. It is published and edited by the Faculty of Law of the National University of Singapore. It contains mostly articles about Singapore law, though not exclusively. Some of the issues which are important in Singapore may be so in Hong Kong too, and this journal may be quite useful to you. It also contains material on Malaysian and Singapore legislation, and on ASEAN. The *Singapore Law Review* is edited by the students of the Law Faculty at the National University of Singapore. The articles themselves are by a mixture of students and staff.

The *Jernal Undang-Undang* or *Journal of Malaysian and Comparative Law* is published by the Faculty of Law of the University of Malaya, Kuala Lumpur. Some of the articles are in Bahasa Malaysia. Although it has mainly articles on Malaysian law this is not so entirely. The *Malayan Law Journal* is mainly directed at the profession, and consists more of law reports than articles, and should really be shelved with the law reports! The *Current Law Journal* is also from Malaysia, and has mainly cases with a few short articles.

Lawasia is currently published by the Faculty of Law of the University of Technology in Sydney. It usually contains a range of articles on different topics and dealing with the law of various countries in the Asia/Pacific region. It is not specialized in topic, just in region.

The *Philippine Law Journal* is a publication of the University of the Philippines and deals with mainly, though not exclusively, Philippines issues. It reflects the concerns of Philippines lawyers and there is some bias towards constitutional law articles.

The *China Law Reporter* is local in its focus although it is produced by the American Bar Association. The *Journal of Chinese Law* is also published in the USA.

Law in Japan is an annual publication in English dealing with a wide range of topics in connection with Japanese law.

WHY WOULD A LAW STUDENT READ JOURNALS?

Sometimes they will contain discussion of topics which are relevant to an essay. You may also find that case notes on difficult cases help you to understand both the facts and decision of the case and the implications and criticisms. Journal articles may give you a useful survey of the existing law, with references to cases and to previous articles and statutes. In brief, various types of journals may provide you with the following information:

- discussion of a broad area of law, especially of the 'recent developments in ...' type
- analysis of narrower questions, perhaps from a particular perspective, theoretical, feminist, economic, etc.
- a general survey of a topic in a particular country; ➤ it sometimes happens that there is an article reviewing an area of the law in Hong Kong, written for a foreign audience, but which may be useful to you if there is no textbook in the field
- summary and analysis of recent decisions
- discussion of the background and purposes, as well as critique of, recent legislation
- critical analysis of law (good articles should do this)
- tables of sentences or tables of damages awards (certain types of journals only)
- reviews of books on legal topics

References to journals usually use abbreviations. You will find some of these in the list in Appendix III of this book.

THE STRUCTURE OF JOURNALS

Journals are relatively uncomplicated. Note the question of brackets in the box. Journals appear at various intervals ranging from weekly (such as the *Solicitors' Journal*), fortnightly, monthly, bi-monthly, quarterly, every four months, twice a year to annual. Many journals are rather irregular and you sometimes find two or three issues rolled into one!

Usually there is one volume a year. But 'volume' now tends to refer not to physical volume, but is more of a concept. If they appear monthly, say, the 12 issues will be bound together at the end of the year. The pagination runs all through the volume (or year); it does not begin again with each monthly issue. Some of US journals have become so fat that they have to be bound in two parts (➤ this also happens with clumsy sets of journals like the *Solicitors Journal* and the *New Law Journal*, published in the UK). They will usually say on their spines what pages each book covers. ➤ When looking for these, therefore, make a note of the page number as well as the volume number before leaving your seat for the bookshelves.

Brackets for Journals

It is more common to have a new volume number each year, so the reference will usually have its date in **round brackets**. Thus (1966) 56 MLR 520 would be a reference to the *Modern Law Review* (Volume 56 published in 1966, p. 520). There are a few oddities. *Public Law* uses only the date — [1966] PL. The *Cambridge Law Journal* is inconsistent: it uses the date in square brackets and the volume number! Sometimes you see a citation using the date and sometimes one using the volume number!

HOW TO FIND OUT WHAT ARTICLES EXIST — INDEXES

There are several sources of titles, of which the most obvious is a textbook; some of these make a point of referring to useful articles. For example, Dias and Markesinis on *Tort Law* has lists of articles at the beginning of each chapter — an admirable practice.

But there are more specialized sources:

Current Law lists recent articles in a paragraph at the end of each broad topic each month: so the last paragraph under the topic 'Contract' will be a list of recent articles. In the *Yearbook* this is consolidated

Journals and Articles

I have found students getting confused about the meaning of these two words. The journal is the entire publication: the *Hong Kong Law Journal*, for example; inside are articles.

Other sorts of publications which come out at intervals, such as the *Laws of Hong Kong* or loose-leaf encyclopaedias etc. are not journals.

into a separate index of periodical articles. The *Annual Abridgement* and *Monthly Review* of *Halsbury's Laws of England* also give references to journal articles. There are a number of publications which are solely concerned with indexing journals. There is a separate section on most of these. However, in brief:

For	**Use**
Articles/notes/casenotes in English journals	*Legal Journals Index*
Articles in English journals	*Current Law, Monthly Review/Annual Abridgement of Halsbury* *Index to Legal Periodicals* (major periodicals and longer articles only)
Articles/notes/book reviews in US journals	*Index of Legal Periodicals*
Articles in major Australian journals	*Australian Current Law*, Index to Legal Periodicals*
Articles in all Australian journals	*Australian Current Law**
Articles in Australian journals not in *Index of Legal Periodicals*, only if *Australian Current Law* unavailable	*Index to Foreign Legal Periodicals*
Articles in major Canadian journals	*Index to Legal Periodicals*
Articles in all Canadian journals	*Index to Canadian Legal Literature**
Articles in *Hong Kong Law Journal*	Index volumes to journal (or *Index to Foreign Legal Periodicals*) or, since 1994, *Legal Journals Index*
Articles in *Asia-Pacific Law Review*, or *Journal of Chinese and Comparative Law*	Index volumes to journals, or *Index to Foreign Legal Periodicals*
Articles in Singapore and Malaysian journals until about 1984	*Index to Singapore/Malaysian Legal Periodicals 1972-1984*
Other articles in Singapore, Malaysia, Phillippines, Chinese, Japanese journals	Index volumes to journal or *Index to Foreign Legal Periodicals*
Articles on law of European Union	*European Current Law*

---

* For information on these, see Unit 16.

➤ The categories in the left-hand column refer to the country of the journal, not to the country which is discussed in the article. You will find many articles about Hong Kong indexed in the *Index to Legal Periodicals*, for example, because they appear in US journals. See also *Asian Legal Journals Index* on p. 171.

Legal Journals Index

This is a specifically British resource. It covers all the law journals published in the UK and ➤ indexes the items there even if they are very short, as many casenotes etc. are. Twelve issues appear during the year, and they are consolidated every three months and then at the end of the year.

There are five indexes:

- subject
- author
- cases (reports of cases in journals, as well as notes on cases)
- legislation
- book reviews

Here is a small extract from the subject index:

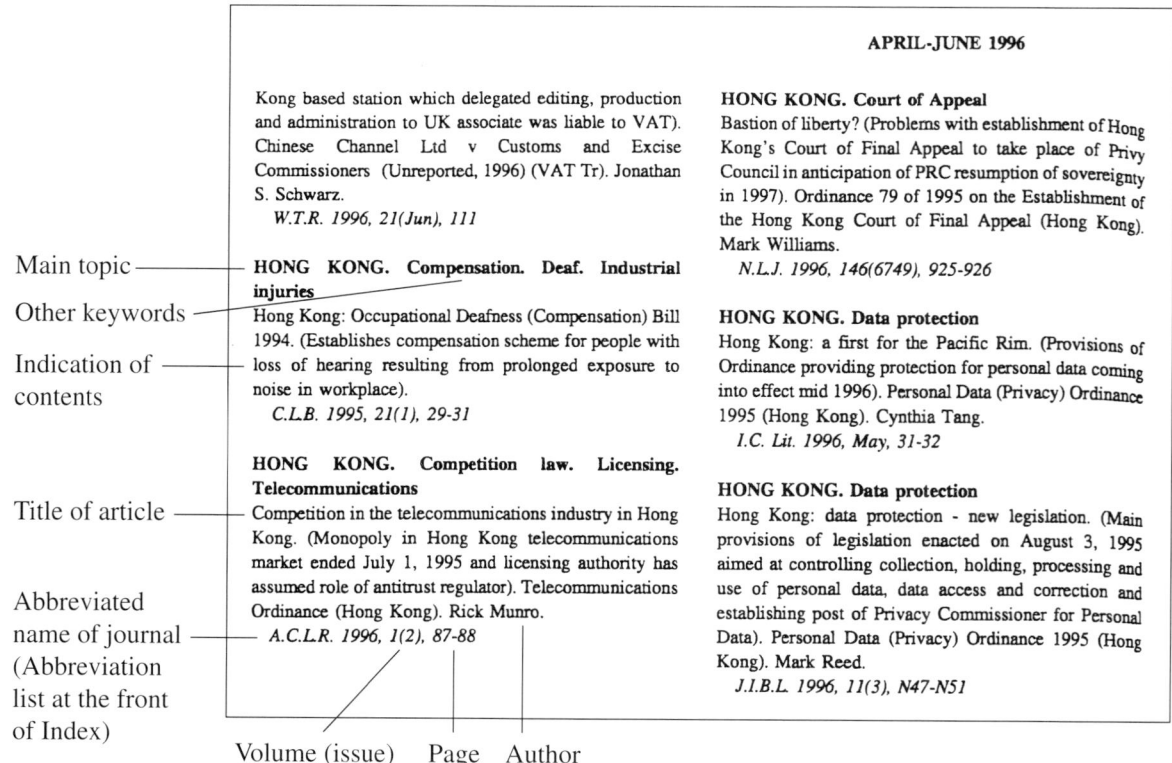

APRIL-JUNE 1996

Kong based station which delegated editing, production and administration to UK associate was liable to VAT). Chinese Channel Ltd v Customs and Excise Commissioners (Unreported, 1996) (VAT Tr). Jonathan S. Schwarz.
W.T.R. 1996, 21(Jun), 111

Main topic — **HONG KONG. Compensation. Deaf. Industrial injuries**

Other keywords —
Indication of contents —
Hong Kong: Occupational Deafness (Compensation) Bill 1994. (Establishes compensation scheme for people with loss of hearing resulting from prolonged exposure to noise in workplace).
C.L.B. 1995, 21(1), 29-31

HONG KONG. Competition law. Licensing. Telecommunications

Title of article — Competition in the telecommunications industry in Hong Kong. (Monopoly in Hong Kong telecommunications market ended July 1, 1995 and licensing authority has assumed role of antitrust regulator). Telecommunications Ordinance (Hong Kong). Rick Munro.

Abbreviated name of journal — A.C.L.R. 1996, 1(2), 87-88
(Abbreviation list at the front of Index)

Volume (issue)   Page   Author

HONG KONG. Court of Appeal
Bastion of liberty? (Problems with establishment of Hong Kong's Court of Final Appeal to take place of Privy Council in anticipation of PRC resumption of sovereignty in 1997. Ordinance 79 of 1995 on the Establishment of the Hong Kong Court of Final Appeal (Hong Kong). Mark Williams.
N.L.J. 1996, 146(6749), 925-926

HONG KONG. Data protection
Hong Kong: a first for the Pacific Rim. (Provisions of Ordinance providing protection for personal data coming into effect mid 1996). Personal Data (Privacy) Ordinance 1995 (Hong Kong). Cynthia Tang.
I.C. Lit. 1996, May, 31-32

HONG KONG. Data protection
Hong Kong: data protection - new legislation. (Main provisions of legislation enacted on August 3, 1995 aimed at controlling collection, holding, processing and use of personal data, data access and correction and establishing post of Privacy Commissioner for Personal Data). Personal Data (Privacy) Ordinance 1995 (Hong Kong). Mark Reed.
J.I.B.L. 1996, 11(3), N47-N51

For fuller details of this publication see *Butterworths Legal Research Guide* 2.19ff.

❖ Go back to the topic you looked up in general works of reference in the previous Unit. Find the *Legal Journals Index*. Look for any article related to that topic. ☺ About 15 minutes to do it carefully.

Take a little longer to get a sense of the general purposes of the publication. Also, look up 'Hong Kong' in the Index. You may be surprised how many articles there are.

Legal Journals Index is available in CD-ROM format, as part of the Current Legal Information collection. The underlying software is 'Folio Views' which is used for several other databases which you may already have tried including *Hong Kong Cases* and *Weekly Law Reports*.

Brief instructions for the Windows version are:

after you have loaded the programme from the CD you will see a list of contents:
    More information
    Browse what's new this month
    Browse table of cases
    Browse table of legislation
    Browse list of journals indexed
    Search table of cases/legislation
    Search whole database

These are pretty self-explanatory and you can click on the one you are interested in. If you click on 'what's new', you will find a list of topics. Click on one of these and you will see the summaries of new items for the current month (the current month of the Index, that is, of course, not the journals indexed!).

Summaries of items look very much like those in the printed version, except that they go across the screen instead of being in columns.

Suppose you want to search by topic or author. Click on Search whole database. You will then see a screen inviting you to type in your search terms (as you type you will see words in a small window change — so as you type 'po' for example, words beginning with 'po' will appear; if you add 'l' words like 'pollution' will appear: when you see the word you want you can click on it. ➤ I am not sure if this is any faster than typing the words you want though it does save typing errors. You can continue to type in words, and the software will search for items with all the words you specify. I tried Hong Kong environment; the screen showed:

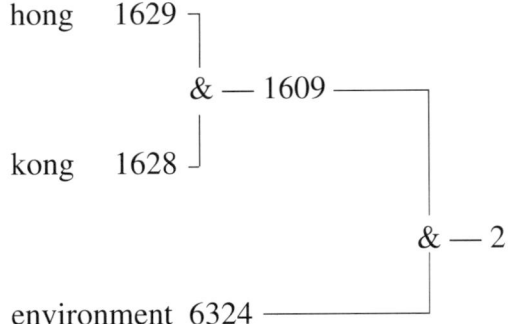

You can also use **BOOLEAN SEARCHES** — so you could type 'Environment OR Pollution' for example. You can also truncate words — so environment* includes environmental.

To see the results of your search click on OK and the summaries will appear.

If you want to find what an abbreviation means, click on it and a "pop-up" window should appear with the full title of the journal.

If you have a long list of summaries but you only want to print some, you can click on Tag which will mark the current summary. You can then click on Print and you will be invited to choose whether to print all the summaries which were 'hits' in response to your query, or only those you have marked. ➤ Clicking on Clear Tag clears them all and not just the one that you might have inserted by mistake!

❖ Try repeating the search you did in the paper version using the CD and compare how long it takes.

There is an Internet version of the same publication. The process is slightly different, and it will almost certainly be more up-to-date than the CD version.

Index to Legal Periodicals

This is a US-published resource and therefore has a US bias. It indexes all the law journals in the United States, and the major ones in Canada, the UK and Australia. The paper version is only an index. It gives author, title and reference only. It appears several times a year and then is reprinted as a consolidated annual version.

At the beginning it lists the headings and the abbreviations used for the journals, and publication details of the journals. Many of the headings are cross-referenced. The main body of the index covers both subjects and authors. Below is a short extract.

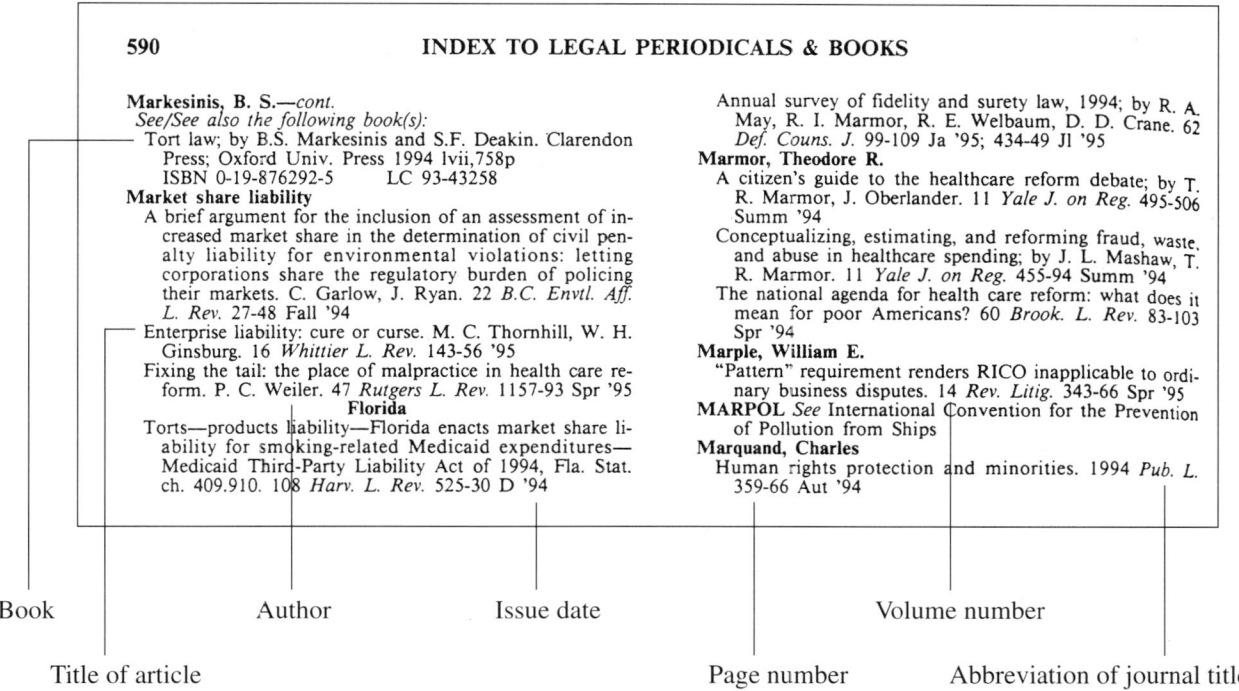

590   **INDEX TO LEGAL PERIODICALS & BOOKS**

Markesinis, B. S.—*cont.*
See/See also the following book(s):
— Tort law; by B.S. Markesinis and S.F. Deakin. Clarendon Press; Oxford Univ. Press 1994 lvii,758p
ISBN 0-19-876292-5   LC 93-43258
Market share liability
A brief argument for the inclusion of an assessment of increased market share in the determination of civil penalty liability for environmental violations: letting corporations share the regulatory burden of policing their markets. C. Garlow, J. Ryan. 22 *B.C. Envtl. Aff. L. Rev.* 27-48 Fall '94
Enterprise liability: cure or curse. M. C. Thornhill, W. H. Ginsburg. 16 *Whittier L. Rev.* 143-56 '95
Fixing the tail: the place of malpractice in health care reform. P. C. Weiler. 47 *Rutgers L. Rev.* 1157-93 Spr '95
           Florida
Torts—products liability—Florida enacts market share liability for smoking-related Medicaid expenditures—Medicaid Third-Party Liability Act of 1994, Fla. Stat. ch. 409.910. 108 *Harv. L. Rev.* 525-30 D '94

Annual survey of fidelity and surety law, 1994; by R. A. May, R. I. Marmor, R. E. Welbaum, D. D. Crane. 62 *Def. Couns. J.* 99-109 Ja '95; 434-49 Jl '95
Marmor, Theodore R.
A citizen's guide to the healthcare reform debate; by T. R. Marmor, J. Oberlander. 11 *Yale J. on Reg.* 495-506 Summ '94
Conceptualizing, estimating, and reforming fraud, waste, and abuse in healthcare spending; by J. L. Mashaw, T. R. Marmor. 11 *Yale J. on Reg.* 455-94 Summ '94
The national agenda for health care reform: what does it mean for poor Americans? 60 *Brook. L. Rev.* 83-103 Spr '94
Marple, William E.
"Pattern" requirement renders RICO inapplicable to ordinary business disputes. 14 *Rev. Litig.* 343-66 Spr '95
MARPOL *See* International Convention for the Prevention of Pollution from Ships
Marquand, Charles
Human rights protection and minorities. 1994 *Pub. L.* 359-66 Aut '94

Book   Author   Issue date   Volume number

Title of article   Page number   Abbreviation of journal title

➤ If you are frustrated by being unable to work out which heading to look for, look at the list of headings near the beginning.

Index to Legal Periodicals and Books: The CD-ROM version

These days most people make use of the electronic version of this Index. You will find that frustratingly often your library does not have the journals in which there seems to be something interesting! (Usually because it is an American one and Hong Kong libraries can only stock a small proportion of US journals.)

➤ Even when the journal is not available, I find it is useful to find important US cases on particular issues. It will indicate the cases discussed by casenotes, and give the case citation, so even if you can't find the journal you can probably read the case, at least if it is a Supreme Court case.

There are three types of search:

- The first one (first listed on the initial screen) is called 'Browse'. This asks you to type in your main subject search, and press 'return'. You will then see a list of topics with yours highlighted if it appears on their list of subjects. If the topic is recognized but no entries listed, there will be a * before the item. Press the F8 key for related topics.

- The second type of search (number 2, or subject search) gives you the chance to ask for keywords — those that may appear in the title or in the keywords under the main part of the entry. You can ask for one word **and** another, or one word or phrase **or** another etc. You can also ask for items by a particular author, in a particular journal etc. You can also truncate words: if you ask for Drug? it will look for drug and for drugs. You do not have to complete every field. If you want the search to start before every field is filled, press the End key and then the return (enter ↵) key.

- The third type of search is called 'Wilsonline' (by the company which produces the disk). This is very much like the search in the OPAC library catalogue. You can do 'Boolean searches' including 'and not' and truncations which include # standing for any letter in the middle of a word — such as wom#n for woman or women.

In the case of each type of search you will find you get a screen full of short references — just enough to tell whether the article is likely to be relevant. If you want to know full details, press the down arrow (↓) until the cursor is beside the article, and press the space key to mark the item. Go through the list marking all those which look interesting (Press PgDn to get a new list if there are too many to fit on one screen). Then press ↵ to begin to the see the full details. What you will see is a bit like the entry in the paper version. However, it also has a few keywords indicating the topics covered by the article, which may be more informative than the title alone. (See the example below.)

I tried all three searches in 1994:

- Using the first method I tried Hong Kong as a topic. This produced 58 items under the Hong Kong subject heading.

- Second method: I tried 'or Hong Kong Hongkong' — in order to get both spellings. This gave me 161 items. ➤ You see how much more material you are likely to find this way than by the 'browse' approach. This might be too many! If so, you can modify your search. Press Esc and then 2 (for 'modify a search') and then return. You can then add something else. To take an example, I knew there was at least one article on the death penalty in Hong Kong. So I added 'Death' on the second subject line. This produced only one article:

```
1 ILP
AUTHOR:              Scobell, Andrew
TITLE:               Strung up or shot down?: the death penalty in Hong Kong
                     and China and implications for post 1997
SOURCE:              v 20 Case Western Reserve Journal of International Law
                     (ISSN 008-9254) pp. 147-67 Winter '88
SUBJECTS COVERED:    Capital punishment
```

(ISSN means International Standard Serial Number, the equivalent of the ISBN which every book has these days.)

I knew there was another article. What had I done wrong? I tried 'Capital punishment' rather than 'Death' and found the other item I wanted.

- For the third method I tried 'Hong Kong' again. I also tried just 'Kong' — why waste effort and run the risk of making a typing error and getting nothing? A very odd thing happened. 'Hong Kong' produced 112 items, and 'Kong' produced 158. I am unable to explain this! I thought maybe there were people called 'Kong' — I went through every item and in each case the 'Kong' referred to Hong Kong!

➤ The moral of this story is — keep trying.

➤ Note also that the second type of search produced more records than the third. We cannot understand this but it does suggest that the second type is probably the best for many purposes.

Incidentally, if you want to amend an existing search when using the third type of search, press the F10 key and your previous search will be repeated and you can make amendments.

When doing the second type of search (keyword), note that you may request items other than subject, and may need to do so. While I was preparing these pages a student was looking for an article by Fiona Burns on the *Barclays Bank v Quistclose* case (an important Trusts case). Entering Burns and Quistclose in the subject sections produced nothing. Entering Burns as 'Person's name' and Quistclose as 'case name' produced precisely the right response.

Index to Foreign Legal Periodicals

This publication complements the *Index to Legal Periodicals*. 'Foreign' means not domestic US, or major UK, Canadian or Australian. It includes journals published in those countries but with a foreign or comparative bias, like the *American Journal of Comparative Law*. It also includes non-English language articles (transliterated if not originally in the Roman alphabet). ➤ The *Hong Kong Law Journal* is indexed in this publication.

It appears four times a year and is cumulated annually. The main index is by subject. There are also author, book review and geographical indexes. Here are three extracts from the 1995 cumulation: one from the Hong Kong entry in the Geographical Index, one from the Author Index and then the corresponding section from the Subject Index.

Geographical Index

HONG KONG
Administration of justice
Administrative & political divisions
Admissions & confessions
Air law & aviation
Arbitration: commerce, incl.
   foreign
Artificial procreation
Capital punishment
Carriers
Civil rights
Comparative law
Constitutional law
Criminal procedure
Cultural property (protection of)
Customary law (international)
Divorce, separation & annulment
Environmental protection: air
Executors & administrators
Family provision (incl. legitimate
   portion)

Author Index

Abi-Saab, G.
International disputes
Interpretation & construction

Abraham, G.
Church & State—South Africa
   (Republic)
Freedom of religion—South Africa
   (Republic)

Abrahamson, D.N.
Capital punishment—Hong Kong
Criminal procedure—Hong Kong

General Index

Subject Index

D'Agostino, F.
"Porte aperte": la pena di morte come problema.
Riv Intern Filos Dir 69:393–403 '92

Schreuer, C.
Capital punishment and human rights.
Rudolf Bernhardt collection, 563–577

China (People's Republic)
Shen De-Yong, *et al.*
Dui qiang jie zui shi yong si xing wen ti de tan tao he jian yi.
Faxue Pinglun no.2:55–57 '94

Wang Ming-Hu
Jian chi yi Mao Zedong ren min min zhu zhuan zheng si xing guan zhi dao si xing li fa yu si fa.
Faxue Pinglun no.1:9–15 '94

Wu Ping
Dui pan chu si xing fan bo duo zheng zhi quan li zhong shen gui ding de zhi yi.
Faxue Yanjiu no.2:36–40 '95

Hong Kong
Abrahamson, D.N.
Capital punishment in post-colonial Hong-Kong: issues, answers, and options.
NYU J Intl L & Pol 24:1219–1252 '92

Kazakhstan
Novikov, I.
The death penalty in Kazakhstan: problems and perspectives.
Rev CEE L 20:699–705 '94

The electronic version is quite easy to use. You type in the words you are looking for — you may use a Boolean search. For example: I thought I would look for articles on Freedom of Speech or Freedom of Expression in Hong Kong. I tried 'Freedom and (speech or expression) and Hong Kong'. Result — 0! I should have added 'or press' inside the brackets and I would have found one.

❖ Try looking for articles by your teachers. I suggest you choose one with an unusual surname. ➤ Incidentally, it will not accept Wesley-Smith — it requires Wesley Smith!

After you press ⏎ (or click on Search), the information about the articles, if any, will appear at the bottom of the screen. You may choose to see a brief form of the entry (showing only Author, Title, Source — that is journal — and Geographical Area. Or a full version giving keywords.

If you want to print the list or articles, or save it to a disk, and it seems very long and contains irrelevant items, you can go through it marking the useful ones (move the mouse so the little arrow on the screen points to the little book at the beginning of the item; it will then change into a pencil ✐ ; click and a red line will appear beside the item entry. You can then print or save the marked items.

❖ Try 'Capital Punishment and Hong Kong'. You will find both the articles I finally found from the *Index of Legal Periodicals*. What is the item by Glofcheski doing there?

➤ Don't use 'Kong' instead of Hong Kong in this database — you will find a lot of Kong words transliterated from Chinese!

Index to Periodical Articles Related to Law

This publication indexes **non**-law journals which contain law-related items. It is produced in the US, but has articles from elsewhere also. In the natural course of things it is most useful for material with a political or social science angle, and you are likely to find constitutional law, environmental law and policy issues, criminology and so on. You would be unlikely to find a black letter analysis of legal rules.

It is published four times a year, and cumulated annually. There is also a 30-year cumulation: 1958-1988, and a three-year cumulation is imminent.

Here is a short extract:

INDEX TO PERIODICAL ARTICLES RELATED TO LAW • 11

I

INFORMED CONSENT (MEDICAL)

Informed consent. the whole truth for patients? Lantos, J. *Cancer.* 72(9 Suppl.):2811-2815. November 1, 1993.

INTERNATIONAL LAW

Cross-border disputes: a legal quagmire. Goyens, Monique. *Consumer Policy Review.* 3:92-97. April, 1993.

INTERNATIONAL RELATIONS

Pre-law prerequisites: a guide to the post-socialist world. DeBow, Michael; and Clegg, Roger. *Policy Review.* 67:74-79. Winter, 1994.

Electronic Journals

You may have heard talk of the 'paperless office' — the idea that electronic means of communication are replacing paper ones. Perhaps with these CD-ROM databases you are beginning to think there could be a 'bookless library'! One development you are unlikely to use during your first year as a student, but might find useful later is the electronic journal — or the journal available in electronic form.

Some publishers are now making their journals available 'on-line' (see Unit 18). A library may choose to subscribe to the paper version, or the on-line version, or may offer access to both. At this point (1996) there are very few **law** journals available like this.

There are, however, a few journals available through the Internet — specially created for the Internet, not just On-line versions of paper journals. As you can imagine, there is something of a tendency for such journals to focus on computer and the law, and similar technological topics, but there is no reason why this should be so and there are some more general ones. Let me just mention two:

(continued)

E Law is produced at the Murdoch University Law School in Australia. It is not restricted to technology matters. Its address is: **<http://www.murdoch.edu.au/elaw/>.**

Journal of Information Law and Technology (JILT) is a joint production of two UK law schools, Warwick and Strathclyde. It does have a technology bias, as its name suggests. Its url (address) is: **<http://ltc.warwick.ac.uk/elj/jilt>.**

➤ I would suggest that you try to identify the core of the url address; for example in the one above you could stop at *uk*. This would have taken you as far as the Law Technology Centre of the University of Warwick, where it would be possible to click on the journal. The more you type the more mistakes you can make!

You may find it easier to start with the Home Page of a Law School or Law Library, even your own, and then click on a list of other schools or resources. Or you might go to the **List of Law-Related E-Journals and Periodicals** to be found at: **<http://www.usc.edu/dept/law-lib/legal/journals.html>**

Some of the journals on this list are full-text, some contain summaries of articles, some are indexes.

➤ url's (addresses) have a tendency to change. In all sorts of other ways this whole area of publishing could be said to be up in the air, if you will excuse the pun.

SELF-STUDY QUESTIONS

⊘ Ten minutes.

1. What sorts of items would you expect to find in the *Hong Kong Law Journal*?

2. And in the *Solicitors' Journal*?

3. Which index would you go to to find articles in the following journals: the *Hong Kong Law Journal*, the *Anglo-American Law Journal*, the *University of Melbourne Law Review*, the *Malaya Law Journal*?

4. What is wrong with this citation: Yash Ghai, 'Back to basics: the provisional legislature and the Basic Law' [1996] 25 HKLJ 2? (Actually there are two things wrong with it, one of which you should be able to see without looking at the journal.) Would you still be able to find the piece, even though there are faults in the citation?

Unit 14　Government Publications

OBJECTIVES

The purpose of this Unit is to introduce you to publications of the Hong Kong Government (and very briefly to those of the UK).

⊘　About one hour.

PUBLICATIONS OF THE HONG KONG GOVERNMENT

Hong Kong Government Gazette

This publication contains official notifications from the government to the community; very often publication of certain information in this form is required in an Ordinance. The *Gazette* comes out at least once a week. The first section consists of notifications of various appointments, or made under pieces of legislation such as the Town Planning Ordinance.

Then there are a number of Supplements:

- Legal Supplement No. 1 contains the text of Ordinances
- Legal Supplement No. 2 contains the text of Regulations made under Ordinances (subsidiary legislation)
- Legal Supplement No. 3 (printed on blue paper) contains the text of Bills when they are presented to the Legislative Council
- Special Supplement No. 4 tends to contain lists of people authorized to perform certain functions under Ordinances: e.g doctors, travel agents, and (once a year) public transport routes and fares.
- Special Supplement No. 5 is where you would find the text of agreements between the Government of Hong Kong and that of other governments, but it contains other items, for example in 1992 the 'Rules and Directions for the Questioning of Suspects and the Taking of Statements', historically known as the 'Judges' Rules'
- Supplement No. 6 is called 'Public Notices'; these are mainly under the Companies Ordinance or referring to subjects such as trademarks
- Special Supplement No. 7 contains the Chinese text of Ordinances previously in English only

All the supplements appear only if needed.

Occasionally there is an *Extraordinary Gazette*, if some public notice needs to be given when a regular *Gazette* is not due to appear. Sometimes this is just the Appointment of an Acting Governor/Chief Executive, but it may be something bigger than this, even a new piece of legislation.

Monthly a list of Ordinances or of Regulations is issued; this will also contain details of amendments to existing Ordinances or Regulations since the most recent issue of the Loose-leaf Edition of the Laws of Hong Kong. See Unit 10.

Periodically also there is a list of bills for the year, as part of Supplement No. 3.

In libraries you will usually find that the *Gazette* is bound each year, as are the supplements, each in a separate series.

Codes of Practice

Relatively recently governments, including that of Hong Kong, have begun to publish various forms of guidance notes and codes of practice. The oldest is the Road Users' Code, the legal effect of which is spelled out in the Road Traffic Ordinance s. 109, which also refers to the preparation of codes for loading vehicles and for lighting road works. Some other codes also have a legal effect which is partly spelled out in legislation. This is so of Codes of Practice under the environmental legislation. If the statute does not say anything, one would look to the ordinary principles of the law and say that these publications offer evidence, quite strong evidence, of what is reasonable behaviour. Failure to comply might therefore lead to liability, for example in negligence or nuisance (torts).

A very recent example is the Code of Practice for Overall Thermal Transfer Value in Buildings 1995, which is concerned with energy conservation, and will be used by the Building Authority in deciding on applications from developers/construction companies under the new Building (Energy Efficiency) Regulation.

Hansard

The official name is the *Official Report of Proceedings in the Legislative Council*. Hansard was an authorized printer of the reports of the UK parliament in the early nineteenth century.

The HK Hansard is now published in English and Chinese. The necessity for translation means that there is quite a delay in publication (in UK the first version of Hansard is produced overnight).

Hansard contains the debates on legislation (usually rather brief), debates on particular topics, and reports of questions asked orally or in writing by members of Legco.

There is an issue for each sitting (once a week). Annually (for each Legco year which runs from November) Hansard is bound (into three volumes now). There is no index.

You can also find the date when the Bills were introduced into the Legco, and when they received the Assent which makes them law from the *Hong Kong Law Digest*. This will help you pinpoint the period in which the Debates took place. Here is an extract from the February 1996 issue:

LEGISLATION

B74 **Assents**

The following Ordinances received Assent on 22 February 1996:

- Bank of Tokyo-Mitsubishi Ordinance (No.1 of 1996)
- The Bank of Tokyo-Mitsubishi (Merger of Subsidiaries) Ordinance (No.2 of 1996)

LEGISLATIVE COUNCIL

B75 **Bills**

The following Bills were presented to the Legislative Council but were not enacted during February 1996:

- Buildings (Amendment) Bill 1996
- Dutiable Commodities (Amendment) Bill 1996
- Evidence (Amendment) Bill 1996
- Insurance Companies (Amendment) Bill 1996
- Legal Practitioners (Amendment) Bill 1996
- Public Bus Services (Amendment) Bill 1996

❖ Select a recent Ordinance which you are aware of. Find the Ordinance and the date when it was first passed.

Go to the Hong Kong Hansard and find the volumes for the relevant year (remember when the legislative year is). Find the Contents pages for that year and locate the second reading of the Bill. (Why the Second Reading? Because this is where the major debate tends to occur on the principle of the Bill.) Note the date of the introduction of the Bill and the page number in the volume.

☺ About 30 minutes.

However, in recent years it has been possible to find Hansard and even Bills Committees on the Internet. Go to **<http://legco.gov.hk/>** and click on "meetings".

Proceedings of the Urban and Regional Councils

These are also published, like a small Hansard.

Committees of Legco

For example there are regularly reports of the Public Accounts Committee which discusses the Audit Report, and interviews officials about topics covered in the Audit Report.

Apart from standing committees, there may be ad hoc committees. For example, in July 1986 there was published the *Report of the Select Committee on the problems involved in the prosecution and trial of complex commercial crimes*. There are two volumes, one containing the Report and the other the Evidence.

A great deal of LegCo material is available on the Internet.

White Papers

White Papers are statements of Government policy. These are not particularly common in Hong Kong. There was quite a major White Paper on Social Welfare Policy. In 1989 there was a White Paper on Environmental Protection called: *Pollution: A Time to Act*. (There have also been three subsequent reviews of progress on the implementation of the White Paper.) There was an annual White Paper submitted to the UK Government by the Hong Kong Government.

Consultative Documents

Consultative documents (sometimes known as Green Papers) are published for the comments of the Public. The most important HK example was the Green paper on Constitutional Reform in 1987. On the other hand, consultative documents are not always termed Green Papers (nor are they necessarily green!) — for example the Committee on the Reform of the Town Planning Ordinance published a consultative document which was so called and was beige. The Law Reform Commission quite often produces consultative documents. Consultative documents are often available on the Internet, either at **<http://www.info.gov.hk/consult.htm>** or at the home pages of relevant departments.

➤ There is no system of numbering Hong Kong Government publications.

Law Reform Commission

These contain the proposals of the Commission for the reform of the law. They will usually contain a review of the existing law and an analysis of its shortcomings. Occasionally they produce a Working Paper, or consultative document inviting public comment — for example the Privacy Sub-committee published one on *Reform of the Law Relating to Information Privacy*. There have been reports in recent years on Arrest, Loitering, Divorce, Illegitimacy, Bail, Copyright.

There have been previous law reform bodies, e.g. the Company Law Revision Committee which produced reports in 1971 and 1973.

The Law Reform Commission's Internet site is **<http://www.info.gov.hk/justice/related/2/content.htm>**

Commissions of Inquiry

There have been a number of Commissions of Inquiry reports, e.g. into the Kowloon Disturbances in 1966, the Fire at the Jumbo Floating Restaurant in 1972, the 1972 Landslides, the Prevention of Bribery Ordinance, Mr Justice Woo's report on the new airport (see **<http://www.info.gov.hk/iairport/report/htm>**)

Departmental Reports

Some government departments are required to produce annual reports, and others may do so. Reports of the Commissioner for Administrative Complaints (ombudsman) and of the ICAC, for example, do appear. The former, the reports of COMAC, are particularly interesting, as they contain reports on many of the particular investigations carried out by the office. In 1995 COMAC also started to produce separate reports of major investigations (rather than complaints which affect individuals) — the *Investigation of Unauthorised Building Works*, and *Investigation on Overcrowding Relief in Public Housing* have been produced. About 50% of government departments produce reports. The Report of the Judiciary contains some, rather undetailed, statistics about the numbers and types of cases. The Reports of the Environmental Protection Department, called *Environment Hong Kong 1995* and so on, are informative. The Housing Department, the Police Complaints Commission, the Town Planning Board are among others which are of interest to lawyers. Much of this informtaion is on the Internet.

Other Publications

There is a constant flow of government publications of a statistical nature, e.g. the *Monthly Review of Statistics*. The Government produces a leaflet: *How to Obtain Statistics*, available free from the Government Bookshops. There are studies of environmental and planning issues, such as the Metroplan or the Port and Airport Development Strategy, the Territorial Development Strategy, the Sewage Strategy, the Waste Disposal Plan, regular studies of Water Quality.

The Annual Speech by the Governor at the Opening of the Legislative Council is published. This sets out the programme for the coming year. In 1995 it was supplemented by a *Progress Report* on how far the Government has implemented commitments made in previous Addresses, by *Policy Commitments* setting out new commitments, and by a summary of *Legislative Commitments*. Another area in which you may find publications setting out the government's view of its achievements is in human rights. For example, in 1995 the Government published a report, nominally from the British Government, to the United Nations Human Rights Committee: *Fourth Periodic Report by Hong Kong under Article 40 of the International Covenant on Civil and Political Rights.* (A current issue of some concern is what will happen to the reporting obligations under this Covenant, as well as the Covenant on Economic, Social and Cultural Rights, after 1997.) ➤ Do remember that the purpose of these publications is to present the Government's point of view. That is not to say that they are intended to mislead, but they are bound to be coloured by their origin, and should be read with this in mind, just like the Annual Report by the Government, *Hong Kong 1995*, etc. (For a mildly corrective view of the latter see *The Other Hong Kong Report* each year; for another view of the Government's human rights record, see publications of the HKU Law Faculty, such as Byrnes, Fong and Edwards, *Hong Kong's Bill of Rights: Two Years On* (1994).

📖 Location
You will not necessarily find all these in the law section of your library, but they will appear somewhere in a university library. ➤ Try the Internet, too.

PUBLICATIONS OF OTHER GOVERNMENTS

Less often you may want to consult the publications of other governments, maybe the UK Hansard to understand the original of a Hong Kong Ordinance, or the Report of the Law [Reform][1] Commission of some other country, like England, Ontario, Australia, New Zealand. There are major reports on the reform of the law in the UK which are produced by bodies other than the Law Commission. There are also quite a lot of UK government publications in recent years which concern Hong Kong. The UK Hansard is becoming available on CD-ROM too, and on the Internet at **<http://www.parliament.the-stationary-office.co.uk/pa>**.

It may be useful for you to understand that publications by the UK government very often have a reference number preceded by an abbreviation which is short for Command Paper. Between 1833 and 1869 there was no prefix to the number; since then the abbreviation has changed over the years: C (1870-99), Cd (1900-1918), Cmd (1919-1956), Cmnd (1956-86) and now Cm. (See Clinch, *Using a Law Library* p. 162.)

---

1   This word does not appear in the titles of the UK bodies.

SELF-STUDY QUESTIONS

⊘ Fifteen minutes.

1. Where would you find a Bill which has been introduced into the Legco but not yet passed? Two suggestions, please!

2. Do you think a code of practice is 'law'?

3. What was the original meaning of 'Hansard'?

4. What does 'Hansard' mean in Hong Kong?

Unit 15 Other Law-Related Materials

OBJECTIVES

By the end of this Unit you will be familiar with:

- works of reference of particular relevance to practitioners in Hong Kong
- some other sorts of material which may be of use to lawyers and law students
- the sorts of information published by the legal profession itself

☺ About 90 minutes if you try to locate the materials discussed.

OTHER LEGAL REFERENCE MATERIALS

There is a wide and growing range of other sorts of reference materials for lawyers which you are unlikely to need as first year students, but of the existence of which you ought perhaps, in general terms, to be aware. Some of these things have already been mentioned:

Tariffs

In some areas of the law certain types of decision have to be made very frequently and it is useful to know what previous decisions have been made, even if these decisions are ones of fact in the individual case and cannot be used as a precedent in the technical sense. This is particularly true of sentences in criminal cases and damages in personal injury cases. Justice, after all, is said to consist in treating like cases alike (and unlike cases differently). Although each individual is different and each crime or accident is different, it is only right that there should be some degree of consistency. Indeed, appeal courts do lay down guidelines in more general terms as well, as you will discover in your tort and criminal law courses.

➤ It should always be remembered, however, that a court must look at the individual circumstances in a particular case when exercising a discretion.

Lists of sentences: A number of publications give summaries of sentences imposed in criminal cases. You will find these in the *Criminal Law Review* (in the form of brief case summaries), and for Hong Kong in the *Hong Kong Law Journal.*

Personal injuries awards: Again it is not uncommon to find lists or tables of personal injury damages awarded. See *Current Law* (for the UK), and The *Hong Kong Law Digest*. Here is an example from the April 1995 issue of the latter:

QUANTUM OF DAMAGES
PERSONAL INJURIES OR DEATH

The table below is a cumulative guide to quantum of damages cases reported in [1995] HKLD. Damages for bereavement and funeral expenses are not included. All figures rounded to the nearest dollar.

Personal injuries/ Fatal accident	Age at accident and trial/sex/multiplier/ loss of earning capacity			Pre-accident occupation	Award PSLA	FAO/LARCO	Plaintiff's name	Court. date of judgment	Ref. No.
Burns and scars	2 1/2–8	F	—	—	—	$500,000	—	Chui Wing Lai	Master O'Donnell, 17 March 1995	C37
Elbow	48–54	M	5	$50,000 (discounted by 25% to $38,500)	Steel binder	$300,000 (discounted by 25% to $225,000)	—	Cheung Fat Tim	Findlay J, 17 Jan 1995	A35
Fingers	33–43	M	10	—	Window frame maker	$125,000	—	Sung Fuk Wah	Master O'Donnell, 13 March 1995	C38
Foot	56	M	—	—	Coolie	$50,000	—	Wong Sam Mui	Master O'Donnell, 17 March 1995	C39

Precedents

Many documents involved in legal practice have to follow a certain format. It is thus a waste of effort for a lawyer to start from scratch each time he or she wants a conveyance or a writ or a certain type of contract, or even a letter. Indeed, since sometimes language has been approved by the courts, it may be risky in the sense that the lawyer may run the risk of being held negligent if he or she does not use approved forms or formulae!

The biggest example is *The Encyclopaedia of Forms and Precedents*, and encyclopaedic works on more specific topics also contain precedents. *Halsbury's Laws of England*, Noter-up, has precedent **letters** for certain purposes.

Practitioner's Texts

Books written for practising lawyers may be rather like textbooks, only bigger and sometimes more detailed. They are unlikely to pursue issues of the social implications of law, though they may be concerned with areas of doubt, or even questions of justice.

Some of them contain legislation, annotated or not. Others, depending on the field of law involved, may include international treaties relevant to the area.

Some are loose-leaf. ➤ When using any publications, including loose-leaf ones, always check the date of publication, or even the date of the pages you are looking at. They will not necessarily be very up-to-date.

Here is a page of Wilkinson & Sihombing on *Hong Kong Conveyancing Law*. This is in two volumes, one 'sets out the law' and the other is 'cases and materials'. The latter has now got so fat that it has been divided into two, the second of which is called 2A.

The system of numbering pages and paragraphs is very confusing at first sight. As often happens, to allow for expansion, there are some numbers not yet used.

➤ The important thing is always to know whether you are looking for a page or a paragraph.

Chapter numbers (**bold**)

Planning Control by Way of Crown Leases or Conditions **III[42]**

(6) During the process of resumption there was neither statutory nor any other duty, on the part of the LDC, the Secretary or the Governor to consider possible alternatives to resumption which had not been canvassed by the appellants.

Their Lordships will accordingly humbly advise Her Majesty that the appeal should be dismissed.

1 (1993) Civ App No 197/92.

End of case

Paragraph numbers in [ ] (Paragraph numbers in Vol. 1 do not correspond)

PLANNING CONTROL BY WAY OF CROWN LEASES OR CONDITIONS

Restrictive terms in Crown leases/conditions

[38]–[40]

There are usually restrictions upon use in Crown leases/conditions that can be enforced by the Crown irrespective of any designation of land use in the draft or approved Zoning Plans.

Consideration by courts of terms that have been construed as restrictive of user

[41]

'Detached or semi-detached residential premises of European type': construction of block of flats not permitted.

Wong Bei-Nei v The Attorney-General

[1973] HKLR 582 (HCt)

See **II**[121].

Cross reference to this case which is reproduced in para. [121] of Vol. 2

[42]

'Not more than one residence': construction of block of flats not permitted

Loi Po Investment Co Ltd v Real Reach Co Ltd

[1986] HKLR 643 (HCt)

See **II**[131].

Chapter number; page number in chapter (not in [ ])

Brief title of book, volume number

Issue number (the initial publication was 0 so this is a replacement page)

And here is a short section from Bruce and McCoy *Criminal Evidence in Hong Kong*:

Table of Statutes

References are to Division and paragraph numbers

ORDINANCES OF HONG KONG

Banking Ordinance .... **XII** [403]
Bill of Rights Ordinance .... **III** [101], [255], [301], **V** [751], **VII** [803]
   Art 10.. **I** [401]
   Art 11(1) .... **III** [203], [255], [301], [303], [453]
   Art 11(2)(b) .... **I** [401]
   Art 11(2)(e) .... **XII** [952]
   Art 11(2)(g) .... **III** [203], [453]

And here is the beginning of one of the paragraphs discussing the Bill of Rights:

III[301] *Burden and Standard of Proof*

[301]
In *R v Sin Yau-ming* (above), Kempster JA held that the meaning of 'law' in Article 11(1) was not the domestic law of Hong Kong but rather more universal notions of justice. He noted that presumptions operate in every legal system and the provisions of the Bill of Rights does not prohibit presumptions *per se*. (See to the same effect Mortimer J in *R v Wong Hiu-chor & Ors* [1993] 1 HKCLR 107, 121. There he held that 'presumptions are frequently reasonable and even necessary feature of criminal law if it is to fulfil its function of balancing the needs of society with the protection of the individual accused'.) Kempster JA endorsed the approach adopted by Dickson CJC in *R v Oakes* (1986) 26 DLR (4th) 200. The effect of this was to determine if the legislative provision offended the Bill of Rights. If it did, this approach then required consideration of whether such a provision was justifiable derogation of the guarantees in the Bill of Rights. In *A-G v Lee Kwong-kut; A-G v Lo Chak-man & Anor* [1993] 3 WLR 329, Lord Woolf noted that the Canadian approach had been further refined in

---

➤ Loose-leaf publications are far from ideal for the use they get in a library. They are usually printed on thin paper and are very vulnerable to being torn. Please use them with care!

❖ Identify what other loose-leaf publications there are on Hong Kong law. ☺ Ten minutes.

Annotated Codes of Procedure

Court rules have become so complex that they are the subject of their own annotated encyclopaedic works. The classic English one is known as the *Supreme Court Practice*, or colloquially the 'White Book' and covers the Rules of the Supreme Court. (There is also one for the County Court which is green.) There is now a loose-leaf Hong Kong annotation of the *English White Book*, Clarke et al., *Hong Kong Supreme Court Practice* (inevitably known as the Hong Kong White Book although it is not white!). Here is a page:

Discovery and inspection of documents **II[8036]** ——— Chapter and [para] number

documentary evidence. A notice under this rule is an appropriate step to take where correspondence has failed to correct what the issuing party believes to be omissions in discovery.

[8034]
3. Order for discovery (O. 24 r. 3)

(1) Subject to the provisions of this rule and of rules 4 and 8, the Court may order any party to a cause or matter (whether begun by writ, originating summons or otherwise) to make and serve on any other party a list of the documents which are or have been in his possession, custody or power relating to any matter in question in the cause or matter, and may at the same time or subsequently also order him to make and file an affidavit verifying such a list and to serve a copy thereof on the other party.

(2) Where a party who is required by rule 2 to make discovery of documents fails to comply with any provision of that rule, the Court, on the application of any party to whom the discovery was required to be made, may make an order against the first-mentioned party under paragraph (1) of this rule or, as the case may be, may order him to make and file an affidavit verifying the list of documents he is required to make under rule 2 and to serve a copy thereof on the applicant.

(3) An order under this rule may be limited to such documents or classes of document only, or to such only of the matters in question in the cause or matter, as may be specified in the order.

Text (**bold**)

[8035]
This rule is identical to the English provision. ——————

[8036]
Stage at which discovery may be ordered

Commentary

In *Dragages et Travaux Publics v Lau Ching Kit t/a Man Shun Construction & Decoration Co & Ors* HCA No 6414 of 1980, discovery was ordered in advance of the defence being served. The registrar had ordered discovery of two classes of documents by the plaintiffs and granted the fourth defendants leave to file a defence out of time within seven days after inspection of the documents ordered to be disclosed. On appeal Liu J found:

> These defendants have set a course for their defence in this action, and they do not seem to be on any fishing expedition. The documents ordered in the discovery are limited in nature, and no difficulty should be expected by the plaintiff. A peripheral indication, if acceptable as a pleading, would inevitably necessitate extensive amendments and incur unwarranted litigation costs. The information sought from the documents desired, so counsel concluded, were necessary for disposing fairly of the controversy between the parties ... These contentions are formidable. In the circumstances, the exercise of discretion of the learned Registrar cannot in any way be faulted.

II   485   SUPREME COURT PRACTICE
                        Issue 0

Chapter and page numbers (there are page and paragraph numbers not yet used)

Title of book and issue number (0 = original issue)

THE LEGAL PROFESSION

Apart from the *Hong Kong Lawyer* (see ▮Journals▮) which is the vehicle of the Hong Kong Law Society, each profession — the Bar and the Law Society — publishes annual reports or statements which may be of some interest. For example, the Bar has carried out surveys of its members' views on certain issues which are published in the *Annual Statement*. Both professions now have pages on the Internet — the Bar at **<http://www.hk-barristers.org/>** are the Law Society at **<http://www.hklawsoc.org.hk>**.

Other Publications

The Law Society has published lists of its members, and recently has also produced a guide to professional ethics.

Law Society Circulars

These are hardly a major source of law. Nonetheless they may occasionally contain information of interest to non-members of the Law Society. The circulars from 1965 to 1989 have been indexed and bound. Below is a part of the Index and the beginning of a corresponding Circular. It is to be found in the volume on Counsel.

| 133/84 | 29 OCT | COUNSEL | COMPLAINTS | COMMITTEE | CO | COMMITTEE SET UP RO ADJUDICATE COMPLAINTS OVER COUNSEL FEES NOT BEING PAID |
| 023/85 | 04 FEB | COUNSEL | COSTS | CERTIFICATE | CT/CO | CERTIFICATE MUST BE OBTAINED FOR COUNSEL IN ANY HEARING BEFORE A MASTER IN CHAMBERS |

```
                THE  LAW  SOCIETY  OF  HONG  KONG
                ********************************


CIRCULAR TO MEMBERS NO. 133/84.          29th October, 1984


                     Complaints about Fees


         Because of the normally close professional relationship
    between solicitors and barristers, the obligation of solicitors
    to pay counsel's fees is often left as a matter of implication:
    for example, attending upon counsel to seek advice in conference,
    or where unexpected circumstances arise in the course of a
    case and no arrangements regarding fees have been made in
    the Brief for such eventuality.  Disputes sometimes arise as
    a result.

         The Bar Committee and the Council of the Law Society
    consider it in the interests of the profession that some
    informal machinery should be established for the resolution
    of such disputes.  Accordingly, an informal committee, composed
    of Mr. Anthony Rogers, Q.C. and Mr. Peter H. Davies has been
    appointed to deal with these matters.

         No precise terms of reference have been laid down
    for the operation of this Committee.  In broad terms, this
    Committee will informally "adjudicate" on matters referred
    to it either by the solicitors and barristers concerned or,
    indirectly, by the 2 governing bodies of the profession.
```

BIBLIOGRAPHIES

You may not be familiar with books about books such as bibliographies. These are lists of books, or books and articles, etc., usually on particular topics. They may simply be lists, or they may be annotated — telling you something about the items listed. They may even be evaluative annotations, which try to tell you what the bibliography compiler thinks of the pieces. Sometimes there may be a discussion which puts the pieces listed into a historical or intellectual context.

There are a number of legal bibliographies. For example,

- the multi-volume Szladits' *Bibliography on Foreign and Comparative Law*, up-to-date until 1990 (at the time of writing)
- Fu-shun Lin *Chinese Law Past and Present* (published in 1966 — so of somewhat historical interest)
- Mangel *Animal Rights*

There are books on human rights, on colonial law, etc. There is an obvious disadvantage to these books — they are even more out-of-date than the books or articles they record! But they can still be a useful way to approach materials on a subject strange to you. Here is an example of an entry in the *Animal Rights* book, which is an annotated bibliography:

> **88 Morris, Clarence**. ''The rights and duties of beasts and trees: A law teacher's essay for landscape architects.'' *Journal of Legal Education* 17 (1964): 185–92. Interesting, ground-breaking argument for the recognition of legal rights for animals and the natural environment, inviting comparison with C. D. Stone's [107] rationale for legal standing of natural objects. Contrasts the ancient Chinese respect for the harmony of nature (which should be only minimally disturbed by humans) with the modern Western view of nature as instrumental for human use. Argues for a presumption in favor of the natural; the burden of proof is on those who propose to disturb nature. Calls for legal action developing safeguards affirmatively creating nature's legal rights in the form of conservation laws, game laws, forest and park protection – all backed by police, inspectors and judges.

And here are some extracts from Sladits, 1989–1990 (compiled by Pechota), published Dobbs Ferry: Oceana, 1994:

Geographical Index

HONG KONG

GENERAL PART - Sources in general
812

GENERAL PART - Statutory law
857

FOREIGN AND COMPARATIVE LAW -
Surveys of foreign laws, introductory works
2060, 2075, 2076, 2092

FOREIGN AND COMPARATIVE LAW -
Laws, acts and decrees
2231, 2232

FOREIGN AND COMPARATIVE LAW -
Legal translations generally
2316

Name Index

1638 • WESCHLER, LAWRENCE

WESCHLER, LAWRENCE
11319

WESLEY-SMITH, PETER
1673, 2092, 11846

2090. Szawlowski, Richard: Reflections on 'The laws of the People's Republic of China, 1979-1986'. Int'l & Comp. L.Q. 38:197-207, 1989.
This is a review article on The laws of the People's Republic of China, vols. I & II, compiled by the Legislative Affairs Commission of the Standing Committee of the National People's Congress of the People's Republic of China (Beijing 1987).

2091. Tamanaha, Brian Z.: A proposal for the development of a system of indigenous jurisprudence in the Federated States of Micronesia. Hastings Int'l & Comp. L. Rev. 13:71-114, 1989.

2092. Wesley-Smith, Peter: The legal system. *In* R. Wacks, ed., The law in Hong Kong 1969-1989 (Hong Kong 1989), pp. 17-48.

SELF-STUDY QUESTIONS

🕐 Five minutes.

1. Where might you find examples of personal injury damages in Hong Kong?

2. What is the 'White Book'?

3. What is an 'abstract'?

4. What is an annotated bibliography?

Unit 16 Other Systems

OBJECTIVES

By the end of this Unit you will:

- be aware of a number of situations in which you might wish to consult the law of jurisdictions other than Hong Kong and the UK
- know which countries in the world are the principal common law jurisdictions
- know the names of some civil law jurisdictions, and understand what 'civil law' means
- be aware of the main sources (which you are likely to have access to) on the law of the major common law countries, and some which while not 'main' are geographically close to Hong Kong
- be able to find cases and journal articles, and in some cases legislation, from those countries.

☺ At least five hours if you find the material in your library and do the exercises.

Thus far we have been looking (except when discussing Journals) at materials from Hong Kong and England. But you may well have cause to look at the law of other systems as well.

WHY LOOK AT OTHER COUNTRIES?

Among the possible reasons (other than for sheer interest) are:

- Hong Kong legislation has copied or drawn from that of another country.

- Another country has a type of legislation which does not exist, or no longer exists, in the UK, e.g. the UK has no Bill of Rights, whereas many other countries do.

- Another country has changed the law in a way in which it is worth considering for Hong Kong.

- Another country faces similar social, political or economic conditions as Hong Kong

- As a lawyer you might have a client whose problem involves the law of another country. The most obvious one is China; and there are commercial transactions where a contract might, for example, specify that it is to be governed by the law of another country.

- Because cases from other jurisdictions are of persuasive authority for Hong Kong courts even now, and it can be argued that when the Basic Law is in force Hong Kong courts will be more inclined to look at the decisions of a wider range of courts.

- When evaluating the state of Hong Kong law it may be helpful to see how other jurisdictions have tackled the problem.

- The experience of other countries can be very useful to raise questions for research in Hong Kong. If you are to write an essay for example, and you discover a particular issue has been the subject of concern by the courts or legislature or by writers elsewhere, it can lead you to ask whether this is a topic worth investigating here.

SYSTEMS OF LAW

There are three great legal traditions in the world today: the **civil law tradition**, the **common law tradition** and the **Muslim law tradition**.

This is the sort of statement which is bound to give rise to criticism and allegations of ethnocentricity! I would justify it by saying that, of course there are other religious systems, but these tend to be limited in their geographical and other scope, such as Jewish law and Hindu law. There could also be said to be a Confucian tradition in relation to law,

> ### Comparative Law
>
> 'I do not think that the law of a single country can be an independent object of study' — Gordley in (1996) 43 *Am J Comp. Law* 555.
>
> However, students should be aware of the pitfalls of comparative law study — see Watson *Legal Transplants*, (Edinburgh: Scottish Academic Press, 1974), especially Chapter 2.

but to a considerable extent this is an **anti**-law tradition! There are also many systems of customary law, with greater or lesser vigour in modern Indonesia, Africa, India and so on. It would be difficult to describe all these as constituting one system. You will find material on all these types of law, and they should not be neglected if you want to write an essay on the subject of the nature of the law in different societies, or simply to broaden your mind by taking a fresh look at law, but access to these materials does not require the sorts of library skills with which this book is mostly concerned.

❖ To see what I mean, you might, however, try the following search in your library catalogue: the word Law combined with Customary or Adat[1] or Jewish or Hindu or Muslim or Islamic. ☯ Five minutes.

I shall not discuss Islamic law here either. You should remember, if you ever have to deal with strongly Muslim countries, that they may apply Muslim law (Sharia which actually means 'path' in Arabic), in some areas of life at least. Thus you might find Muslim family law applies. In some countries there have been the adoption of the concept of Islamic Banking intended to make banking compatible with the sharia ban on interest. (Try an OPAC search combining Islam and Bank or Banking.) Finally, there was something which might be considered a socialist legal tradition, but this is fading (try OPAC — Socialism and Law).

We cannot discuss here all the possible jurisdictions. For most purposes other common law countries are the easiest to look at since we understand the underlying principles of the legal system. For people in Hong Kong the law of other countries in the region, such as most obviously the PRC and also Taiwan, Japan, etc., are also of interest. There is some literature in English on these, and some material in Chinese on the PRC and Taiwan which is available, but beyond the competence of this author to discuss. The countries discussed in this section are those which are larger, more important in terms of their contribution to the common law, or closer to Hong Kong.

Common Law Systems

Canada, Australia and New Zealand are the countries which you might first turn to for any common law type of subject. There is now a good deal of exchange of ideas between these countries, and England. The High Court of Australia has been at various times one of the best courts in the Commonwealth.

Canada, Australia and India are worth looking at for general constitutional issues. Why not New Zealand? Because it does not have a written constitution. On the other hand, it does have a Bill of Rights (which Australia does not). The US may sometimes also be worth looking at — it has been a leader in many areas, including human rights issues (the American cases on freedom of expression are extremely interesting).

You might consider it worthwhile to look at **Singapore**. In some ways it faces problems similar to those of Hong Kong.

There are one or two other countries which might be worth looking at — one easy to overlook is Ireland. The Republic has not been part of the Commonwealth since 1948 (and

---

1 Adat is used to refer to customary law in Indonesia especially.

effectively not for longer) but is very much part of the common law world. Israel, which was ruled by Britain under a League of Nations Mandate from the end of the First World War until 1948 has a common law system to some extent. Scotland applies very similar law to the rest of the UK in some areas (remember that *Donoghue v Stevenson* was a Scottish case!) and very often has similar statutes.

Civil Law Systems

Civil law systems are those which derive ultimately from Roman law. The phrase 'civil law' is used almost as confusingly as 'common law'! It may mean, within the common law systems, **not** criminal law. It may also mean **not** common law systems, as I am using it here, and occasionally you find it used in other senses too (e.g. **not** military). The core civil law countries, as it were, are those of continental Europe (that is Europe excluding England, Wales and Ireland; Scotland has a civil law system for historical reasons into which you would not wish me to go!). By virtue of imperialism civil law spread: via Spain and Portugal to Latin America, via France to French Caribbean colonies, French African colonies (and those places which were French and became British such as Louisiana, Quebec, Mauritius and Seychelles), via the Netherlands to South Africa and Sri Lanka (and Indonesia). In modern times it has also spread, more often via Germany, to Japan and China. Eastern European countries including Russia also have essentially civil law systems.

As you should know by the time you reach this Unit, a key factor in the common law is the place of the judiciary. Originally the common law was the creation of judges and even today the judge plays a more prominent role than in the civil law systems. The doctrine of precedent does not apply in civil law systems, styles of legislative drafting and interpretation are very different. The role of writers, or jurists, is much greater in the civil law. The main source of civil law in modern times has been 'Codes' — statements of the law in a systematic form, resembling legislation in the common law, but usually much less detailed. It is common to find a Penal Code, a Code of Criminal Procedure, a Civil Code, a Commercial Code, and so on.

SINGAPORE, MALAYSIA AND BRUNEI[2]

The legal literature of Malaysia and Singapore is often combined. Singapore was part of Malaysia for several years, and previously had been part of the Straits Settlements, the rest of which are now part of Malaysia. Quite a lot of legislation is similar in the two countries. Brunei is part of the island of Borneo, but is an independent state.

2　Prepared with the helpful guidance from Judith Sihombing, for which I am most grateful.

Malaysia

Introduction

Malaysia is a federation consisting of the following constituent parts:

Nine States which were formerly Protected States. Of these the four listed on the right used to constitute the 'Federated Malay States'. This is important because certain publications, prior to Independence, covered the Federated Malay States, and it may be helpful to know which were referred to.

Perlis	Perak
Kedah	Panang
Kelantan	Selangor
Trengganu	Negri Sembilan
Johore	

Two former colonies in Peninsular Malaysia: Penang, Malacca

Two former colonies on the island of Borneo which now constitute East Malaysia: Sabah, Sarawak

Labuan, consisting of seven islands off the coast of Borneo, is an international financial centre governed as part of the Federation.

The applicable law

Malaysia has a written Constitution, with a Bill of Rights. An important implication of a federal system is that the power to make legislation is divided between the Federal Government and the States. Any legislation which a State passes which is beyond its powers under the Constitution, or which the Federal Government passes on a topic reserved for the States, will be invalid.

The country applies English Statutes of General Application which were in force in England on a certain date. In the case of Sabah that date is 1 December 1951, and in the case of Sarawak it is 12 December 1949, while in West Malaysia it is 7 April 1956. These statutes can be amended by local statute, and there are very few English statutes which have any practical relevance to Malaysia today.

(The concept of 'statutes of general application' is one which was a very common device for identifying which English law should apply in colonies of Britain. The idea is that statutes which changed the law generally, as opposed to those which were of application only to individuals, or some small class of British people, should be regarded as exported to the colony along with the rest of the common law. Among the common examples are the Fatal Accidents Acts, the Infants Relief Act, and the Libel Acts. This system no longer applies in

Hong Kong since the Application of English Law Ordinance.[3])

Some Malaysian legislation is based on Indian statutes. Most important is the Penal Code which is based on the Indian Penal Code, and the Criminal Procedure Code is also based on that of India, as are the Evidence Act and the Contracts Act. This means that Indian cases will commonly be cited for the interpretation of these pieces of legislation.

As well as the common law, Islamic Law (the Syariah) also applies in certain situations to Muslims in Malaysia, and Muslim law also influences some legislation. There are also several systems of customary law; indigenous customary law being termed 'adat'. In Sarawak Chinese customary law and Hindu law may apply to certain types of situation, such as family law.

The courts of Malaysia

The highest court is the **Court of Appeal** which, with the **Federal Court**, forms the **Supreme Court**. Appeals to the Privy Council were abolished in 1985 (indeed, appeals on criminal and constitutional matters had been abolished in 1978). The Court of Appeal was created in 1994 to provide a second tier of appeals.

Below the Supreme Court is the **High Court** which has original jurisdiction in major cases, and appellate jurisdiction over lower courts, as well as the power of judicial review.

The lower courts include **Sessions Courts** and **Magistrates Courts**. There are also **Syariah Courts** for Muslim law matters, and in Sabah and Sarawak there are **Native Courts**.

Further reading

Rutter, *The Applicable Law of Singapore and Malaysia* (Singapore: Malayan Law Journal, 1989).

Shaikha Zakaria, 'The Legal System of Malaysia' in Hooker, ed., *Malaysian Legal Essays* (Kuala Lumpur: Malayan Law Journal, 1986) 335.

Majid and Abdul Rashid, 'The Courts in Malaysia and Their Jurisdiction' (1995) 21 CLB 297.

---

3   See Wesley-Smith, *The Sources of Hong Kong Law* Chap. 8.

Singapore

Introduction

From 1826 to 1946 Singapore was part of the Straits Settlements. After liberation from the Japanese occupation it was separately administered, becoming self-governing in 1959. It became independent in 1963 as part of Malaysia, but broke away in 1965.

The applicable law

Unless amended or repealed in Singapore, English statutes of general application which were in force in England as at 27 November 1826 are in force in Singapore. As elsewhere, these will only apply if suitable for local circumstances, and they can be amended by local legislation. Current English commercial law was adopted by statute in 1879 (statutes such as the Sale of Goods Act, for example) unless replaced by Singapore legislation.

The courts

The highest court for Singapore remains the **Judicial Committee of the Privy Council**, although appeals are very restricted. The only criminal cases which may be appealed to the Judicial Committee are those where death or life imprisonment is imposed and when the appeal court was not unanimous in its decision. Civil cases will only go to the Judicial Committee if the parties agreed before the case went to the appeal court in Singapore that they would be bound (if necessary) by the decision of the Judicial Committee.

The **Supreme Court** of Singapore is, on the English and pre-1997 Hong Kong model, made up of the **Court of Appeal** and the **High Court**. Below the Supreme Court are lower courts including the **District Court**, the **Magistrates Courts** and the **Small Claims Tribunal**.

Further reading

See Rutter (above, under Malaysia)
Woon ed., *The Singapore Legal System* (Singapore: Longman, 1989)
Phang, *The Development of Singapore Law* (Singapore: Butterworths, 1990)

Brunei

Historically Brunei ruled Sabah and Sarawak, but became a British protectorate in 1888, and independent in 1984. For a number of years the judges all came from Hong Kong, but the pressure of work on the Hong Kong judges has reduced their role considerably and there are now local judges also. The final appeal court is the **Judicial Committee of the Privy Council**, though not for appeals from the **Interpretation Tribunal** set up under section 86 of the Constitution.

The Legal Literature of Malaysia, Singapore and Brunei

Below is a list of law reports, and other literature, relating to Malaysia and Singapore. It is derived from *Mallal's Digest*, which is itself briefly discussed on the next page. I have put an asterisk (*) beside those items which are found in the HKU Library, and placed a hash (#) beside those which are in the City University Library.

REPORTS AND PUBLICATIONS AND THEIR ABBREVIATIONS

	Abbreviation
BRADDELL'S LAW OF THE STRAITS SETTLEMENTS -a commentary by the Honourable Dato Sir Roland St John Braddell, KB, DPMJ, MA, 2nd ed, in 2 volumes, published in Singapore in 1931-1932	BLSS *
BRADDELL'S COMMON GAMING HOUSES -a commentary on Ordinance No 45 (Common Gaming Houses) by Dato Sir Roland St John Braddell, KB, DPMJ, MA, 2nd ed, 1932 published in Singapore	BCGH
DE MELLO'S MANUAL OF THE LAW OF EXTRADITION AND FUGITIVE OFFENDERS applicable to the Eastern Dependencies of the British Empire, by Aloysius de Mello, 2nd ed, 1933 printed at the Government Printing Office, Singapore	De Mello
FEDERATED MALAY STATES LAW REPORTS -published by authority in Kuala Lumpur. These reports were commenced in 1922 and had reached the 7th volume in the old series and are cited by the volume. The new series began in 1931 and ended with the volume for 1941 and are cited by the year	FMSLR
INNES' REGISTRATION OF TITLE -a short treatise on Registration of Title in the Federated Malay States with reports of cases decided in the Supreme Court under the Land and Mining Laws from 1907-1913, by JR Innes, printed at Kuala Lumpur, 1913	Innes
JOHORE LAW REPORTS -published by authority and edited by J Bernard Weiss, in two volumes, containing cases decided between 1915 and 1937	JLR
JOURNAL OF THE MALAYAN BRANCH ROYAL ASIATIC SOCIETY -published by the Malayan Branch, Royal Asiatic Society. Cited by the year, volume and part	JMBRAS
KYSHE'S REPORTS -cases heard and determined in Her Majesty's Supreme Court of the Straits Settlements 1808-1884, edited and reported by JW Norton Kyshe, printed at Singapore, 1885 and 1886, in 3 volumes-Volume 4 published subsequently in 1890:	
Vol I contains Civil Cases	1 Ky
Vol II contains Criminal Rulings, Admiralty, Bankruptcy, Ecclesiastical and Habeas Corpus, Cases	2 Ky (Cr, Ad Bk, Ecc and HCC)
Vol III contains Magistrates Appeals	3 Ky
Vol IV contains cases on all subjects from 1885 ~ 1890	4 Ky
MAGISTRATE'S APPEAL CASES -1884-1893 1 Vol	MAC
MALAYAN CASES -published by the Malayan Law Journal Office:	
Vol I being a collection of old and important cases which are still law, edited by Bashir A Mallal and Nazir A Mallal and published in 1939	1 MC*
Vol II being a collection of important cases hitherto unreported, edited by Bashir A Mallal and published in 1958	2 MC *
Vol III being a collection of important cases hitherto unreported, edited by Bashir A Mallal and published in 1964	3 MC *
Vol IV being a collection of important cases hitherto unreported, edited by Al-Mansor Adabi and - published in 1980	4 MC*
MALAYAN LAW REPORTS -containing reports of cases decided in the Federation of Malaya and the Colony of Singapore; published by authority at Kuala Lumpur; commenced in 1950 and ceased publication with Vol V, 1954. Cited by number of volume	MLR

MALAYAN LAW JOURNAL -a monthly Journal and Law Reporter edited by Bashir A Mallal,commencing from 1932. Published by Malayan Law Journal Sdn Bhd, Malaysia from 1992; cited by year of volume. Current publication . . . . MLJ*#

MALAYAN LAW JOURNAL 1948~49 SUPPLEMENT -containing full reports of cases noted in   [1949] MLJ under Notes of Cases and a few hitherto unreported cases. Published in 1957 . . . . [1948-49] MLJ Supp

MALAYAN LAW JOURNAL 1949 SUPPLEMENT -containing full reports of a few of the cases noted in [1949] MLJ under Notes of Cases. Published in 1951 . . . . [1949] MLJ Supp

MALAYA LAW REVIEW -formerly University of Malaya Law Review, published by the Faculty of Law, National University of Singapore . . . . Mal LR *

MALAYAN UNION LAW REPORTS -published by authority in Kuala Lumpur. These reports comprise cases decided in the Malayan Union for the years 1946 to 1947, published in two volumes . . . . MULR

QUARTERLY NOTES -cases decided in the Supreme Court of the Straits Settlements published in Singapore by authority; from 1 January 1926 to 30 September 1927; 5 parts in all cited by number of part . . . . QN

STRAITS LAW JOURNAL, printed at Singapore:
Vol I June 1888 to May 1889 . . . . 1 SLJ
Vol II June 1889 to May 1890 . . . . 2 SLJ
Vol III June 1890 to December 1890 . . . . 3 SLJ
Vol IV January 1891 to June 1891 . . . . 4 SLJ

SINGAPORE LAW REPORTS -published by authority 1946 to 1949 and 1953 to 1956. Ceased publication with the volume for 1956. Recommenced publication in 1992. Cited by year of volume. Current publication . . . . SLR *#

STRAITS LAW REPORTS -being a report of cases decided in the Supreme Court of the Straits Settlements, Penang, Singapore and Malacca by Stephen Leicester, printed at Penang, 1877 . . . . SLR Leic

STRAITS LAW REPORTS, New Series-from July 1891 to April 1892, being the reports issued in connection with Volume V of the Straits Law Journal . . . . SLR NS

STRAITS SETTLEMENTS LAW REPORTS -old series published under the direction of the court; commenced in 1893 and ended with Vol 15. Vol 9 has an appendix containing Federated Malay States Reports Vol 1 with separate pagination and index, but a common title. Cited by the volume number. New Series, published by authority began in 1926 and ended with volume for 1941-42. Cited by year of volume . . . . SSLR

STRAITS SETTLEMENTS LAW REPORTS, Supplement No 1-being cases determined in the years 1897 to 1899 by the Court of the Judicial Commissioner of the Federated Malay States; published under the direction of the Committee of the Singapore Bar with the approval of the Judicial Commissioner . . . . SSLR Supp

SUPREME COURTS REPORTS -being the Law Reports for the State of Sarawak: pre-war 1928-41and post-war 1946 to 1951; and Law Reports for the States of Sarawak, North Borneo and Brunei from 1952 to 1963. Cited by years of volume . . . . SCR

UNIVERSITY OF MALAYA LAW REVIEW -now Malaya Law Review, published by the Faculty of Law, University of Malaya . . . . UMLR *

WOOD'S ORIENTAL CASES -a selection of Oriental cases decided in the Supreme Courts of the Straits Settlements collected and arranged by RC Woods, printed at Penang 1869 (reprinted by Sweet & Maxwell Ltd, London) . . . . WOC

This list, useful as it is, is not complete with respect to journals, as opposed to law reports. You are therefore referred to the Unit on Journals for these.

Other literature

You may also find in Hong Kong, apart from a few collections of old legislation, especially from the Straits Settlements, and from Kedah, now in Malaysia (the legislation in the latter in both Malay, written in the Arabic (Jawi) script, and English, and using the Islamic calandar), the following:

Literature covering both Malaysia and Singapore

Table of Straits Settlement Laws: A very useful publication which expired at the outbreak of the Second World War. It lists the year's legislative changes and includes references to cases.

Mallal's Digest: This is mainly based upon cases reported in the *Malayan Law Journal*. It is a digest of cases, with several volumes of consolidated Index. The Fourth Edition was published in 1991 and covers up to 1988, but individual volumes are being updated and reissued. By mid-1996 all except volumes 6, 7 and 11 had been reissued. ➤ Always check how up-to-date the reissued volumes are: Volume 3 covers until the end of 1992, for example. ➤ The Consolidated Index has not been reissued, and the numbers of the cases in the Reissued Volumes are different. For the cases in those volumes, therefore, it is better to use the Index of Cases (if you already know the name), or the very detailed Contents pages in the individual volumes.

In the Consolidated Index volumes there is a Table of Cases, but no Table of Statutes.

Privy Council Cases: This publication (4 volumes + Index) was edited by Visu Sinnadurai and prints in full all the Privy Council Cases from Singapore, Malaysia and Brunei from 1875-1990. The 5th volume contains a subject index, an alphabetical index of cases, a chronological table of cases, a table of legislation considered and a table of cases considered.

For all jurisdictions the *Commonwealth Law Bulletin* may contain useful information. The Constitution of each country will be found in Blaustein ed. *Constitutions of the Countries of the World*.

Literature covering Malaysia

Current Law Journal is a law report series with a few short articles. The cases include a few from overseas. Some of the local High Court cases are in Bahasa Malaysia (the Malay language). It is published fortnightly.

Malayan Law Journal has become a weekly publication. It is also mainly a law report with a few articles. It also has tables of personal injury damage awards.

Survey of Malaysian Law: An annual publication. It consists of chapters discussing the year's development in different areas — Constitutional Law, Contract, Family Law, etc. There is also a useful bibliographic chapter.

There are at least two series of annotated statutes. *Golden's Federal Statutes* is commercial reprint of the statutes since 1969. This is a loose-leaf edition which lists after each statute the subsequent changes. Periodically new leaves are issued as amendments are made to existing statutes. Minor changes are made by hand — rather as in the *Revised Edition of the Laws of Hong Kong*. At the beginning of the final volume is a cumulative Index of Statute titles. *Annotated Statutes of Malaysia* is published by Butterworth.

Literature covering Brunei

Brunei Law Reports 1965-1986

Judgments of the Courts of Brunei Darussalam: This comes out quickly, and is intended ultimately to be replaced by the *Brunei Law Reports*.

AUSTRALIA

Introduction

As a former British colony, Australia (like the other countries discussed in this chapter) has inherited (or you might say had imposed upon it) the common law. The basic system of law is therefore similar to that of Hong Kong, in terms of the existence of the common law and equity, the legislative tradition, types of trials, role of judges, etc.

➤ An important factor to bear in mind is that Australia is a federation. As with Malaysia, India, Canada, the USA and so on, this means that there are certain matters which are within the legislative and executive competence of the federal government (based in Canberra, in the Capital Territory) and certain matters which are for the State Government. There are States: New South Wales, Queensland, Tasmania, Victoria, Western Australia, plus the Northern Territory which is not a state.

The official name for the whole of Australia is the Commonwealth of Australia, and the federal government is the Commonwealth government. ➤ This should be distinguished from the Commonwealth of Nations, i.e. the grouping of the UK and former British colonies (plus Mozambique which was never a colony, and Cameroon only part of which was).

Australia has a written Constitution, like most countries these days (the UK and New Zealand being among the few exceptions, though there are plenty of countries which have written constitutions that are 'cheerfully' ignored by the government, of course!). This Constitution has no Bill of Rights.

Australia is a monarchy, which means that the Queen is Head of State though her functions are performed by a Governor-General, who is an Australian, when the Queen herself is not in Australia.

Until recently the final court of appeal for Australia was the Judicial Committee of the Privy Council, but appeals were abolished by an Act of 1985, and the highest court is now the High Court of Australia. Each state has its own legal system, and each system is different. Appeals on federal matters (that is matters which under the Constitution are a matter for the federal government) may go from State courts to the Federal Court (and thence to the High Court), though in some circumstances appeal is direct to the High Court. On State matters appeals go from the State system to the High Court.

Why Would You Want to Look at Australian Law?

Because Australia has a common law system, it is very often useful to look at the decisions of Australian courts. In a number of instances the courts of Australia have taken a different view of the law from that in the United Kingdom. An interesting example in an area which is, or will soon be, familiar to you concerns the House of Lords case *Murphy v Brentwood* [1991] 1AC 398; the courts of Australia (and indeed those of Canada) have not followed the House of Lords all the way — for example *Bryan v Maloney* (High Court of Australia (1995) 128 ALR 163). This means that a practitioner may find Australian material useful when faced with UK precedents unfavourable to a client. How will a Hong Kong court react to an Australian decision? It is unlikely that it will treat such a decision as binding, unless it is a Privy Council decision, maybe. But a decision, especially of the High Court of Australia, will be treated with respect by other courts within the 'common law world'. Already Australian decisions are cited not infrequently in Hong Kong. Students will want to look at the decisions of Australian courts for new ways of approaching problems in the law.

It will be less usual for students to want to look at Australian **legislation**. However, in some areas it may be valuable to look at legislative approaches of other countries, and it is unduly narrow-minded to restrict one's researches to the UK only. You may find that occasionally Hong Kong legislation draws on that of Australia.

Australian Law Reports

Each state has its own series of law reports (at least one), and there are also general series which cover cases from states and from federal courts. There are series which report the cases of federal courts only, and there are series which cover particular types of cases wherever decided. The following list includes only the main series available in the Hong Kong University libraries:

Abbreviation	Full Title	Notes	# Held by
ALD	Administrative Law Decisions	Vol I (1976–78)	H
ALR	Australian Argus Law Reports	Stopped 1973	H C
ACTR	Australian Capital Territory Reports	Bound with ALR	H C
ACLC	Australian Company Law Cases	1971–	H C
ACLR	Australian Company Law Reports		H C
Aust Conv R	Australian Conveyancing Reports		C
FLC	Australian Family Law Cases	1978–	H
ALR	Australian Law Reports	High Court, State courts exercising federal jurisdiction	H C
ALJR	Australian Law Journal Reports	High Court	H C
ATC	Australian Tax Cases		H C
ATR	Australian Tax Reports		C
Aust Tort Reps	Australian Tort Reports		H C
CLR	*Commonwealth Law Reports	High Court	H C
FLR	*Federal Law Reports	Federal Court	H C
IPR	Intellectual Property Reports	Vol I (1982–84)	H
NSWLR	*New South Wales Law Reports	State cases	H C
NTR	Northern Territory Reports	NT Supreme Court	H
TLR	Tasmanian Law Reports		C
VLR	Victorian Law Reports	1875–1956	H
VR	*Victorian Reports	1957–	H C

\# This symbol indicates whether there is a holding of these reports at the University of Hong Kong Library (H) or the City University Library (C). It should not be assumed that either collection is complete.

* Authorized reports.

Australians refer to series of reports which are approved by the courts as authorized. These are the series which should be cited in preference to unauthorized ones if possible. (The expression 'authorized' is not used in England and in Hong Kong.)

Research Material on Australian Law

The two main law publishers in Australia, the Law Book Company and Butterworths, each produce a set of research tools. There are thus two encyclopaedias of Australian law, plus two series of current legal developments, each of which is updated by a regular newsletter. One can represent the two competing systems in tabular form:

Law Book Co.	**Butterworths**
The Laws of Australia	*Halsbury's Laws of Australia*
The Australian Digest	
Australian Legal Monthly Digest	*Australian Current Law*
ALMD Advance	*Fast Law*

How to Find Cases in Australian Law Reports

As with other series of reports, it may be simplest to go straight to the index volume of the series in which you think you are most likely to find the case reported. This is particularly so in a federal system (like Australia) where you can go to an index volume of the reports of the particular state. In the case of Australia there are several specialized series of law reports as you will see from the list above. If you know the case you want is a tort case, it might well be best to go straight to the *Torts Reports*.

If you are looking for cases on a particular topic, rather than for a specific case, try the *Australian Digest*. This is similar to *The Digest* in that it contains summaries of cases. However, the current (3rd) edition of the *Australian Digest* is in loose-leaf form. This edition is not yet quite complete, so for some topics you must refer to the 2nd edition; however, the 3rd edition is nearly complete and I shall therefore not deal with the 2nd edition here.

The best place to begin a search is with the volume called *Key and Research Guide*. This will tell you which edition and volume to go to. For example, for Nuisance you will be referred to Torts (whereas in the 2nd edition Nuisance was a separate topic). Under Torts you will find this:

	Vol 51.
Chapter THREE. NUISANCE [159-175]	
Pt I. WHAT CONSTITUTES [159-162]	671
Divn 1. Public Nuisance [159-160]	671
Subdivn A. *Relevant Principles* [159]	671
Subdivn B. *Particular Cases* [160]	673
Divn 2. Private Nuisance [161-162]	676
Subdivn A. *In General* [161]	676
Subdivn B. *Particular Cases* [162]	684

Release 61   II-538

This shows that you are looking for Volume 51 Chapter Three, and that Nuisance covers paragraphs 159-175. You will also see that this part of the Key was in Release 61. If you go to Volume 51 Chapter Three you will find case summaries corresponding to the headings, and very similar to those in *The Digest* in England. Updating pages are yellow and follow the main, white pages.

For recent cases try either the *Australian Legal Monthly Digest* or *Australian Current Law*. ➤ It might be wise to familiarize yourself with **one** of these and make it your primary research tool for Australian law.

To continue with the topic of Nuisance. Each month the *Australian Legal Monthly Digest* appears in two parts: the Digest which, as its name suggests, summarizes recent developments in the law, and Cumulative Tables. One of the latter is the Updater for the *Australian Digest*. In that Table you would find the following updating on Tort:

> 1996
> [8] Jun [10] Jul [13] Mar [22] Apr, May
> [28] Jan (§399) [31] Apr [32] Jul [33] Jan (§§398, 400) [37] May-Jul [38] Mar [39] Jul [42] Mar, Apr [43] Jul [44] Feb, Jul [49] Jul [50] Jul
> [51] Jun [52] Mar [53] Jun [54] Jan (§401)
> [55] Mar [56] Feb, Jun [60] Jan (§402), May
> [65] Jul [66] May, Jul [68] Jul [71] Jul
> [73] Jan (§403) [84] Feb [91] Feb [94] May
> [102] May [103] Feb [105] May [109] Feb
> [111] May [116] May [123] Feb
> [125] Jan (§404), Apr, Jul [126] Feb [137] Jul
> ➪ [162] Jan (§407) [166] Jun [232] Mar [241] Jul
> [249] Jan (§§548, 549)

Remembering that Nuisance is covered in paragraphs 159–175, you will realize that there are two new cases: one updating para. 162 in the January 1996 issue of the ALMD §407 and the other in the June issue updating para. 166. The January one is this:

This was actually published before the 3rd edition got to Nuisance, so it was published as an updating for the 2nd edition. By July, when the Updater was published, the 3rd edition covered Nuisance and so now the case updates that edition.

> ### NUISANCE
> Aust Digest, 2nd Ed, Vol 29
>
> For [21] — see now ENVIRONMENT LAW
>
> **407** [3]
> **What constitutes — Private nuisance — Particular cases — Withdrawal of support from land — Damages.** *Held*, that in so far as erosion is caused because there has been a disturbance of the natural surface and natural soil by excavation, then that is part of the damages which flow from negligence or nuisance.
> FYVIE *v* ANAND (1994) 6 BPR 13,743 *(NSW Sup Ct, Young J)*.

In *Australian Current Law* you need to choose 'Reporter' (there is another series called 'Legislation' which refers you to amendments to legislation, to new legislation and to cases on legislation — a legislation citator). In the Cumulative Index for issues 1–9, 1996, you will find this:

```
Tort see Damages
  defences
  — contractual interference
      belief in contract's enforceability  .  (Iss 3) 420
          FC 4
  general
  — cause of action
      assignment . . . . . . . . .  (Iss 4) 120 FC 16
  — contractual interference
      defences . . . . . . . . . .  (Iss 3) 420 FC 4
  — inducement of breach of contract
      certifying architect  . . . . .  (Iss 9) 65 VIC 6
  liability
  — whether incurred as owner or occupier
      injury to guest  . . . . . .  (Iss 7) 415 NSW 2
  malicious prosecution
  — findings of fact
      findings open to judge . . .  (Iss 6) 415 VIC 1
  — malicious prosecution
      delay  . . . . . . . . . . .  (Iss 6) 415 QLD 1
  — misleading conduct
      establishment of claim . . .  (Iss 6) 415 WA 1
  negligent misstatement
  — feasibility study
      gas well . . . . . . . . . .  (Iss 5) 170 FC 1
  nuisance
  — sewerage
      council liable . . . . . . .  (Iss 3) 265 NSW 3
  — work of contractor
      knowledge of owner  . . .  (Iss 5) 415 NSW 1 ⤶
```

This tells you to find Issue 5, Title 415 (which is Tort) and the first case from New South Wales:

NEW SOUTH WALES

[415 NSW 1]   **Proprietors of Strata Plan No 13391 v Abate** — *Supreme Court, NSW, Court of Appeal — Mahoney P, Handley and Cole JJA — 27 Mar 1996 CA40168/92, BC9600790, 16 pages*

Nuisance — Discharge of stormwater — Run off from neighbour's roof — Water piped into dish drain — Drain concentrated water and discharged it against sandstone wall of house — Undermined foundations of house — Whether knowledge of consequences relevant to liability — Installation of water pipes by independent contractor — Effect on liability

Held, dismissing the appeal: (i) An occupier of land is not subject to a duty to search for nuisances which may or may not exist, but that does not mean that an occupier who is not subjectively aware of the fact of the nuisance or of the conditions which can give rise to a nuisance can in no circumstances be held liable for the nuisance when it occurs. (ii) Prudence required that attention be given to where the increased flow of water would be discharged. (iii) It was foreseeable that to concentrate and discharge water in this manner would be apt to lead to the flow of water onto the neighbouring property and cause this type of damage. (iv) Instructing an independent contractor to do work which concentrated and discharged large quantities of water onto the neighbouring property was instructing the plumber to do an act, the natural consequence of which was to cause damage to the plaintiff.

Burnie Port Authority v General Jones Pty Ltd (1994) 179 CLR 520; (1994) 120 ALR 42; (1994) 68 ALJR 331; (1994) Aust Torts Reports 81-264; *Cambridge Water Co v Eastern Counties Leather Plc* [1994] 2 AC 264; [1994] 1 All ER 53; [1994] 2 WLR 53; [1994] 1 Lloyd's Rep 261, applied.

➤ Note the similarities and differences between the two systems. Both have separate Cumulative Indexes, unlike the UK *Current Law* which includes this at the end of each month's issue. Only ACL appears as two separate series, one on cases and literature and the other on legislation. Both appear monthly. ACL refers you to an issue, a title, a jurisdiction and a case number. ALMD refers you simply to a paragraph (though within the issue the material is divided into titles corresponding to the *Australian Digest*, and there is a cross reference to the *Australian Digest* volume number).

Current awareness services: Each of these two series is supplemented by an A4-size news-sheet of the most recent cases.

> *ALMD Advance* appears fortnightly. It contains unreported cases and legislation and some analysis.

> *Fast Law* also appears fortnightly. There are three version: the cream one has New South Wales, Australian Capital Territory and High Court and selected Federal Court decisions; the grey version has Victoria, South Australia and High Court and Federal Court decisions; the white version has Queensland, Western Australia, Northern Territory and High Court and Federal Court decisions. It contains summaries of cases only.

Electronic Sources for Australian Law

 You may find that you have access to one or both of the *Australian Digest* or *Australian Current Law* on CD-ROM. Here is an introduction to various other resources:

LawPac CD-ROM case law

There is a series of CD-ROMs which cover Australian case law: Queensland, New South Wales, Victoria, Unreported cases.

Guide for simple searches on LawPac

When you load the programme you will have the Main Menu in front of you. Click on the first item: Search Menu. That menu has a number of possibilities:

> Search cases — for searching the full text of the judgments
> Find case — to find a case by name
> Catchword — to find cases by their 'keywords'
> Headnote — citation to find cases in which other specified cases are cited

I used the CD-ROM of Queensland reported cases. I used 'Search cases'. I typed in Defamation. Result 0! Then I tried Libel and got quite a lot of cases. Why? Because the word used in the judgments was 'libel'; 'defamation' appears in the catchwords.

I also tried 'Murphy and Brentwood' — result 0! Apparently the Queensland courts have not cited it!

They **have** cited *Donoghue v Stevenson*. It worked if I typed 'Donoghue and Stevenson' or 'Donoghue v Stevenson'. The words need not be adjacent: I also tried 'libel and damages' to find cases in which both these words appeared.

When you have typed in your word(s) press ⏎ . If there are any 'hits' a list of cases will appear, with the first one highlighted. Above the list of cases you will see: 'Search result — Document 1-18 out of 25' (if you have 25 hits).

Press ⏎ again. The beginning of the first case will appear. If you press ⏎ again you will see the part of the case in which the word you typed first appears, to show the context in which it is used.

Press the Home key on the keyboard to go to the beginning of the case; press End to go to the end. At the bottom of the screen it tells you what to press to go the Catchwords in the case, or the headnote, or the beginning of successive individual judgments.

To go backwards press the Esc key on the keyboard, ultimately as far as the first screen, then X for eXit.

Internet for Australian cases

You will find that you can get Australian Cases on the Internet. The best route, as I write, would be through the Australasian Legal Information Institute, of which the url is:

<http://www.austlii.edu.au/>

though you can get there by 'clicking on' lists at the HKU Law Faculty or Library (see Unit 1).

You will find decisions of the High Court of Australia as well as several other courts, in full text and searchable — with a Boolean search possibility. ➤ As is often the case with Internet searching techniques, these are not as sophisticated as are available in commercially published CDs. (Cases may be added within a month of their being decided, which is much more recent than you would ever find in printed sources from Australia in Hong Kong, and probably more recent than CD databases.)

Encyclopaedias

Both *The Laws of Australia* and *Halsbury's Laws of Australia*[4] are new. Both appear in a

---

4   Warning: There is also an *Australian Commentary on Halsbury's Laws of England* which is not easy to use and is now quite out of date. Don't confuse it with the *Halsbury's Laws of Australia*!

CD-ROM format (see below) and both have looseleaf hard copy versions. Neither is complete. Volumes are being regularly published and each will be complete in the sense that every title has been published over the next few years. I have tried the CD-ROM of the *Laws of Australia*.

Laws of Australia: CD-ROM Version — A Guide to Making Simple Searches

When you have the title screen in front of you, click on the Main Menu button. The Main Menu you will then see has a list of items including Table of Contents, Table of Cases, Table of Statutes, General Index, etc.

Suppose you want to know how Australian courts have dealt with *Murphy v Brentwood* [1991] 1 AC 398. Click on Table of Cases; you will see a Table very much like the paper version. You can scroll through the list, but better to click on the icon for Query (top left of the screen — a button with a little magnifying glass!) You will then be able to type in your query. If you type in 'Murphy and Brentwood', the following will appear on the screen:

$$\left. \begin{array}{l} \text{Murphy} \quad — \ 431 \\ \\ \text{Brentwood} — 22 \end{array} \right\} \& — 11$$

Indicating that there are 11 references to both these words (probably to this case). (This little section of the screen shows very quickly indeed how many 'hits' your search has scored. You can very easily change the search, by adding additional words — with care — if there are too many hits. But rather than doing this, you might try the method mentioned below under Table of Contents.)

Click the OK button. You would then see the name of the case followed by the chapter and paragraph numbers in which it is mentioned: **5.10:** 61, 62; **27.7:**13, etc. If you click on a paragraph number you will be taken straight to the paragraph. If there is only one reference, or a very few, this is enough. If there are many, you can click on the word <u>V</u>iew on the top of the screen.

There is an icon for 'contents'. Click on this if you want to move to the Table of Contents. If you are in the Table of Contents, you can click on <u>V</u>iew and you will see the words you asked for, surrounded by one or two words of context, against the title of the chapter in which they appear. This will help you decide which reference is the most useful. In fact you can click on the cross beside the Chapter Number and Name and you will be shown the sub-divisions of the Chapter. Click again and you will see the paragraph numbers and headings. At each level you will see whether the words you were searching appear in that section of the work. If you click on the paragraph number you will go to the text of the paragraph.

You can also click on General Index. This appears on the screen just like the Index Page of a book, but there are cross references (see also xxx) in maroon colour. Tick on one of these and you will go to the other entry in the General Index. If you want to go to the text relating to a particular entry in the General Index, click on it (when a little hand appears on the screen it means you can click here).

Basically you use this CD very much like a book. You can get into the text via a number of routes: scrolling through the Index, or a Table, typing in the name of a case or some key words. If you click on Search you can also make more specific searches (like for articles or books).

If you have a number of 'hits' you may move on to the next one by clicking on ▶▶.

Electronic sources for Australian legislation

Australian legislation may not be fully available in paper format in Hong Kong libraries, but some of it, ➤ especially Commonwealth legislation, on CD or the Internet.

Diskrom Australia — Commonwealth statutes:
This is only one of a number of CD versions of Australian statutes, Commonwealth or state. You may find that the library you are using has another. This is just to show you how one works. This is a CD-ROM of the statutes of the Commonwealth of Australia and of the State of Victoria.

Guide to simple searches:
You will probably wish to one of two things: either to go straight to a particular statute if you already know it exists, or to ask for a particular word or phrase and see what the legislation has to say about it.

> **If you know the name of the statute:**
> Click on the word Browse.
> Then on 'Direct Access'.
> Then on 'Act Titles'.
>
> You may then scroll through the titles. Unless you want an Act beginning with A, the best technique is to type the first three letters of the title, e.g. if you want the Privacy Act type PRI and you will be taken to the Price Surveillance Act. You can easily scroll from there to the Privacy Act. Then click on the OK button and you will be taken to the beginning of the text of the Act.

If you do not know the name of the statute:
Click on the icon (top left) for Search expression. You will then be able to type in your word(s) or phrase. I tried Defamation or Libel or Slander. I was then told that there were:

> Defamation [33]
> Libel [9]
> Slander [7]

and 42 hits in which at least one of these words appeared.

Click on 'Results'. A box will open with the relevant legislation listed, indicating Part and Section as well. You can scroll through them, and when you see what looks relevant, click on the item which then will be highlighted. Then click on 'Go to Text' and the section will appear on the screen, with the cursor at the line on which the sought for word first appears.

Internet

The Australasian Legal Information Institute (AustLii) has a database of legislation — see p. 242 above.

Journals

Most of the Australian law schools produce their own journals. As those from the older law schools, such as the *University of New South Wales Law Journal*, the *Melbourne Law Review*, the *Adelaide Law Review* and the *University of Tasmania Law Review*, you may find journals from the various new law schools — Bond, Griffith, Wollongong, to name a few of the many. The *Australian Law Journal* is an old established journal for the profession and academic readers. There are also a number of specialist journals. All the Australian journals often carry material about the law of other jurisdictions.

It is possible to find references to articles from the *Australian Digest* and the ALMD, though the *Australian Current Law* system seems more satisfactory.

Australian Current Law: Reporter

This is a fortnightly publication which includes a Table of Books, Articles and Other Publications. The coverage is wide and includes press releases and some items from non-Australian legal literature.

The cumulative indexes (including a cumulation of the Table of Books etc.) is published as a separate booklet every six issues. In between cumulations, the Books etc. list is for the particular issue only. Every year there is a hardback cumulation, and also there are three year cumulations for 1991–93 and 1994–96, including a three-year List of Books etc.

Here is an extract from the cumulation for issues 1–19 of 1996:

Author   Title of article   Year   Volume (issue)   Abbreviation

TABLE OF BOOKS, ARTICLES AND OTHER MATERIALS   Page

Doyle The Hon CJ, 'Judicial Law Making — Is Honesty the Best Policy?' (1996) 17(2) *Adel LR* 161

Evans R, 'Family Court: more cuts likely' (1996) 31(4) *Aust Lawyer* 3

Government Continues to Appoint Women to County Court News Release Attorney-General (VIC) 16 Jan 1996

Howell M, ' "Your Time is Up" - The Imposition of Time Limits for the Presentation of Cases at Hearings' (1996) 5(3) *JJA* 170

Kirby M, 'Ex Tempore Judgments — Reasons on the Run' (1995) 25(2) *UWAL Rev* 213

Kneebone S, 'Claims against the Commonwealth and States and their Instrumentalities in Federal Jurisdictions: Section 64 of the Judiciary Act' (1996) 24(1) *FL Rev* 93

Lane PH, 'The Changing Role of the High Court' (1996) 70(3) *ALJR* 246

Liverani MR, 'Marching on Goliath — Pressure mounts for easier class actions' (1996) 34(2) *LSJ* 41

Liverani MR, 'Public Defenders: Keeping the law in order' (1996) 34(1) *LSJ* 33

'New Review for Courts — Courts Administration Authority Reviews Court Process' (1996) 18(4) *Law Soc Bull* 8

Olsson The Hon J 'Australian Institute of Judicial Administration' (1996) 70(5) *ALJ* 374

Seifman RD, 'Night Court — Dispensing Justice After Dark or Time to Turn Off the Lights?' (1996) 5(4) *JJA* 221

Streckner E & Megens P, 'The new Domestic Building Tribunal' (1996) 70(7) *LIJ* 32

Taylor P, **Ritchie's Supreme Court Procedure New South Wales** Sydney, Butterworths, 1996, ISBN No 0 409 31215 0

Weatherburn D & Lind B, 'Sentence Disparity, Judge Shopping and Trial Court Delay' (1996) 29(2) *ANZJ Crim* 147

Westling WT & Waye V, 'Promoting Fairness and Efficiency in Jury Trials' (1996) 20(3) *Crim LJ* 127

Wilkin J, 'Representative proceedings in Victoria — No change in contract cases?' (1996) 70(8) *LIJ* 36

Young Mr Justice PW, 'Court Delays' (1996) 70(8) *ALJ* 593

130 — Criminal law

Arenson KJ, 'Causation in the Criminal Law: A Search for Doctrinal Consistency' (1996) 20(4) *Crim LJ* 189

Blazey-Ayoub P, '*Doli Incapax*' (1996) 20(1) *Crim LJ* 34

Bronitt S, 'Cultural blindness — Criminal Law in Multicultural Australia' (1996) 21(2) *Alt LJ* 58

Byard R, 'Brothels, the Prostitution Control Act and planning' (1996) 70(1) *LIJ* 37

Daisley B, 'Sleepwalking defence accepted in B.C. sex assault' (1996) 15(41) *Lawyer's Weekly* 4

Davies L, 'What Grandpa Did: Delayed Disclosure in Sex Abuse Cases' (1996) 23(3) *Brief* 11

Freckelton I, 'Repressed Memory Syndrome: Counterintuitive or Counterproductive?' (1996) 20(1) *Crim LJ* 7

Gough S, 'Intoxication and Criminal Liability: The Law Commission's Proposed Reforms' (1996) Vol 112 (April) *LQR* 335

Green The Hon Sir G, 'The Concept of Uniformity in Sentencing' (1996) 70(2) *ALJ* 112

Henning T, 'Psychological Explanations in Sentencing Women in Tasmania' (1995) 28(3) *ANZJ Crim* 298

Hope J, 'A Constitutional Right to a Fair Trial? Implications for the Reform of the Australian Criminal Justice System' (1996) 24(1) *FL Rev* 173

Howie R & Johnson P, **Annotated Criminal Legislation New South Wales** Sydney, Butterworths, 1996, ISBN No 0 409 31280 0

Press release   Book

Law Reform

Australia has some very active law reform commissions. There is one at the Commonwealth level and others at state level. The Commonwealth Commission has a Web site: **http://online.anu.edu.au/alrc**

Further Reading

Morris, Cook, Creyke and Geddis. *Laying Down the Law* (4th ed. Sydney: Butterworths, 1992).

Watt. *Concise Legal Research* (2nd ed. Sydney: The Federation Press, 1995).

Dayal. *LDL Online — Laying Down the Law: Computer Assisted Legal Research* (Sydney: Butterworths, 1996).

NEW ZEALAND

New Zealand is a monarchy, like Australia and Canada. Unlike those two countries it is not a federation. Appeals still go to the Privy Council. The Court of Appeal in recent years has been an interesting and creative court. New Zealand has been a pioneer in some legal developments, most notably in its adoption of a no-fault compensation system for accident victims. It adopted a Bill of Rights a few years ago, although it does not have a written Constitution.

Law Reports

You may find the following law reports from New Zealand:

New Zealand Privy Council Cases	1840–1932
The New Zealand Jurist	1873–1874 (1 volume)
	1874–1875 (1 volume)
The New Zealand Jurist (New Series)	Until 1878 (4 volumes)
Oliver, Bell & Fitzgeralds' Reports	1878–1880 (1 volume)
New Zealand Law Reports	1883– (1 volume a year when bound) #
Criminal Reports of New Zealand	1985–86 to 1992–93 (9 volumes)
New Zealand Bill of Rights Reports	1992–
New Zealand Tax Cases	1973–1991 (13 volumes, CCH) #
New Zealand Company Law Cases	1981–83 to 1992–93 (6 volumes, CCH — as always with this publisher there is a very odd numbering system for the pages. In the final volume page 68 586 is followed by 260 201.)

📖 All these are in the HKU Library, and those marked # in the CityU Library.

Statutes

You are unlikely to find the paper version of the legislation in a university library in Hong Kong, though the CD-ROM version may be available.

Journals

The *New Zealand Law Review* is essentially a professional journal. Each law school (of which there are five) has its own journal, so you may find the *Otago Law Review*, the *Victoria University of Wellington Law Review*, the *Canterbury Law Journal*, *University of Auckand Law Journal*, the *Waikato Law Review*. There is also the *New Zealand Universities Law Review*.

The quarterly *New Zealand Law Review*, recently renamed from the *New Zealand Recent Law Review*, is mainly devoted to discussions of recent developments in the law.

Reference Material

There is the *Abridgement of New Zealand Case Law* volumes 1–18, plus the Supplement to volumes 1–17, a later supplement to volumes 1–28 (dated 1978) and the Annual Supplement for 1986 ▯ in the HKU Library. The Supreme Court Library has the encyclopedia — *Laws of New Zealand*, rather like the various series of *Halsbury's Laws of XXX* but in the form of a series of pamphlets (it started in 1992, and is not yet complete).

INDIA

India is the largest common law country. It has also been an innovator in a number of fields especially constitutional. The Supreme Court of India has been one of the most exciting courts in the world. There is a strong sense of social justice in civil society in India, and coupled with the extent of its social problems, admittedly great, it offers some very interesting legal issues and legal developments. India is a republic (it became independent as a republic, and was the first republic in the Commonwealth). It is also a Federation of 25 states and 7 territories.

Law Reports

The main series of reports is *All India Reporter*. This publishes mainly cases, but also includes a section of federal legislation, and a small section of articles. It appears monthly and is then bound at the end of each year into a number of volumes. Two of these are Supreme Court cases (the numbering is consecutive through the two volumes). In addition there are now[5] the following sections each year (bound together where the sections are not long enough to warrant separate volumes):

5　Until independence in 1947 there were volumes of cases from what are now Pakistan and Bangladesh, and from Burma — for example Lahore, Peshawar, Sind, Rangoon.

Allahabad (cases from Uttar Pradesh)	Kerala
Andhra Pradesh	Madhya Pradesh
Bombay (cases from Maharashtra)	Madras (cases from Tamil Nadu)
Calcutta (cases from Bengal)	Orissa
Delhi	Patna (cases from Bihar)
Gauhati (cases from Assam)	Punjab (including Haryana)
Gujarat	Rajasthan
Himachal Pradesh	Journal (short articles)
Jammu & Kashmir	Acts (federal not state Acts)
Karnataka	Notes of Cases

During the colonial period High Courts were set up in what were known as the Presidency Towns of Bombay, Calcutta, Madras, and these names have been retained for the sake of continuity, and maybe sense of history, although now the High Courts cover the states of which they are the capital cities.

The correct form of citation is AIR date abbreviation page (no brackets) e.g.

Maneka Gandhi v Union of India AIR 1978 SC 597

You may also find the *Supreme Court Reports* and the *Supreme Court Cases* (the latter being more up-to-date and containing some short articles — a very common pattern in Indian law reports series).

Many other series are published in India, some specialized by state and some by subject, but they are not generally available in Hong Kong.

The *All India Reporter* is becoming available in CD-ROM format.

Journals

Indian law journals tend to be somewhat sporadic. The most regular is *Journal of the Indian Law Institute*. Also good is *Parliamentary and Constitutional Studies*.

Reference Material

Although India is such a large country, there is a dearth of reference materials of the *Halsbury's Laws* or *Hong Kong Law Digest* type. The *AIR Manual* gives the names and citations, plus brief summaries of cases on legislation. ➤ Check date of publication — it may be very out of date.

There is a CD-ROM: *Supreme Court Case Finder* — of summaries only of cases reported in *Supreme Court Cases*.

CANADA

Canada, like Australia, is a Federation. The constituent parts are known as Provinces. The country was a British colony until 1867, although one province, Quebec, was originally a French colony. In consequence of this dual history, Quebec applies mainly French law, while the rest of Canada applies the common law.

For many years the Canadian Constitution was contained in the British North America Act 1867, an Act of the UK Parliament. However, in 1982 the Canadian Constitution was 'repatriated', and was re-adopted with some modifications by the Parliament of Canada.

One important feature of the 1982 Act was the introduction of the Canadian Charter of Rights and Freedoms, a set of fundamental human rights under which, among other things, legislation may be declared unconstitutional. (This should be distinguished from the earlier Bill of Rights 1960 under which legislation could not be invalidated in this way.)

Each Province has its own system of courts, which apply both provincial and federal law. Appeals in cases under both systems of law may go to the Supreme Court of Canada. There is also a Federal Court, which itself has two divisions, the Trial Division and the Federal Court of Appeal, which deals with certain matters under federal law. Appeals to the Judicial Committee of the Privy Council were abolished in 1949.

The Province of Ontario is the most important in the sense that it includes the capital, Ottawa, and also Toronto. It evidently generates the most legal developments. British Columbia, which includes Vancouver, is the next most legally active Province. There are other very large provinces with much smaller populations — Alberta, Saskatchewan and Manitoba; and there are also the small, East Coast Provinces, known as the Maritimes — Prince Edward Island, Nova Scotia, New Brunswick and Newfoundland. There are also two territories, with fewer powers than provinces — Northwest Territory and the Yukon Territory.

Canada is a monarchy, with the Queen as Head of State, represented by a Governor-General, and, at the provincial level, Lieutenant-Governors.

Why Would You Want to Look at Canadian Law?

Perhaps the main area of interest in Canadian law for Hong Kong lawyers in the last few years at least has been in connection with human rights. Since the Bill of Rights was enacted in 1991 there have been quite a lot of references to Canadian cases in Hong Kong courts, although this slackened off after an initial enthusiasm. Most of these cases have been in the field of criminal law and particularly procedure.

The law of Vancouver (British Columbia) and to a lesser extent Toronto (Ontario), is of interest to Hong Kong because of the large number of Hong Kong people who have settled there. There is also, partly because of the latter factor, a considerable amount of trade and other contact between Hong Kong and Canada. As a general matter, Canada is a substantial common law jurisdiction, with traditions closer to those of the UK in many ways than to the USA. As well as general issues of the common law and statutory interpretation being similar in Canada to Hong Kong, it is worth noting that Canadian provinces still have a Workmen's Compensation Act, stemming from the same root as the Hong Kong Employees' Compensation Ordinance, and some of the expressions used in the latter are also used in the former — such as 'arising out of' and 'in the course of employment'.

Law Reports

Below is a list of some Canadian law reports, with an indication of which University libraries hold them.

CCC	Canadian Criminal Cases		H C
CCLT	Canadian Cases on the Law of Tort	1979–84	H
CRR	Canadian Rights Reports	Vol 17 (1994) –	H C
DLR	Dominion Law Reports	Now in its 4th series	H C
OR	Ontario Reports	Now in its 3rd series	H C
PPSAC	Personal Property Security Act Cases	Series 1 + series 2	H
SCR	Supreme Court Reports	The official series, all cases reported, in English and French	H
WWR	Western Weekly Reporter	British Columbia, Alberta, Manitoba and Saskatchewan	H

H = Hong Kong University   C = City University

Research Tools

Canada has a set of publications which serve the same sorts of functions as those published in the UK and other jurisdictions. There is a publication like *Halsbury's Laws of England* — the *Canadian Encyclopedic Digest*, and one like *The Digest — The Canadian Abridgement*. ➤ Don't be confused — the *Canadian Encyclopedic Digest* is not the equivalent of *The Digest*, despite the similarity in name! There are also publications which serve the same function as a statute citator, a case citator, as the *Hong Kong Law Digest/Yearbook* etc. The situation is slightly complicated, however, by the fact that Canada is a federation. Although its population is not so great, its legal situation is somewhat complex.

Canadian Encyclopedic Digest

The *Canadian Encyclopedic Digest* (the encyclopaedia of Canadian law, for which the abbreviation is CED) is published in two versions. One covers the law of Ontario and federal law. The other covers the law of the western provinces (British Columbia, Alberta, Manitoba and Saskatchewan) and the federation. Both of these are in their third edition.[6]

---

6   📖 The HKU Library's copy is not being updated (as at the time of writing).

The 34 volumes of the CED have the topics covered on their spines. However, as with Halsbury, there is a risk that taking only this approach will lead you to miss some aspect which is dealt with under another heading. Unless your search is relatively simple, it is better to look in the *Research Guide and Key* volume which includes a general index.

Below is an extract from the section in the CED (Ontario) on Nuisance, contained in Volume 23. You could have discovered this either from looking at the spine (Narcotic Control to Oil and Gas) or from the Key. The heading of Nuisance is No. 102 in the overall scheme of the CED. The reference in the Index to the first paragraph below is 23–102 §13.

II   Principles

1. CHARACTER OF NEIGHBOURHOOD AS FACTOR

§**13**   Whether or not an occurrence is considered to be a nuisance on the basis of personal discomfort depends, in part, on the character of the neighbourhood where it takes place, including the standard activities and associated consequences thereat.[1]

> 1. *Rushmer v. Polsue & Alfieri Ltd.*, [1907] A.C. 121 (H.L.), quoting Halsbury L.C. in *Colls v. Home & Colonial Stores Ltd.*, [1904] A.C. 179 (H.L.); *Howarth v. Canadian Red Cross Society of Calgary*, [1943] 2 W.W.R. 692 (Alta. T.D.); *R. v. Capilano Timber Co.* (1949), 96 C.C.C. 141 (B.C. Mag. Ct.); *Miller v. Krawitz*, [1931] 1 W.W.R. 577 [Man.]; *J.F. Brown Co. v. Toronto (City)* (1916), 29 D.L.R. 618; affirmed 37 D.L.R. 532 (S.C.C.) [Ont.]; *Walker v. Pioneer Construction Co.* (1975), 56 D.L.R. (3d) 677 (Ont. H.C.) (even in mixed neighbourhood, noise level to be reduced at night to accommodate sleeping habits); *Bottom v. Ontario Leaf Tobacco Co.*, [1935] 2 D.L.R. 699 at 702, 703, per Macdonnell J.A. (Ont. C.A.) (living in district occupied by tobacco factories, plaintiff having to submit to discomforts incident to industrial community).

§**14**   The law does not stipulate a tolerance level that is applicable to all neighbourhoods. Each case must be decided having regard to all of its surrounding circumstances and any local standards that may exist.[2] For example, urban residents cannot expect to enjoy air that is as pure and free from odour and noise as that found in the country; yet unreasonable excess of city smoke, odour and noise may provide a right of action.[3]

> 2. *R. v. Capilano Timber Co., ante*; *Oakley v. Webb* (1916), 33 D.L.R. 35 at 37, 38 (Ont. C.A.), quoting Middleton J. in *Appleby v. Erie Tobacco Co.* (1910), 22 O.L.R. 533 (Div. Ct.), and adopted by Sutherland J. in *Beamish v. Glenn* (1916), 28 D.L.R. 702 (Ont. C.A.); *Drysdale v. Dugas* (1896), 26 S.C.R. 20 at 24 [Que.]; see also *J.F. Brown Co. v. Toronto (City)* (1916), 36 O.L.R. 189 at 211; affirmed 55 S.C.R. 153 (lavatories and urinals and conveniences of that class not necessarily nuisances; depending upon locality; intolerable nuisance in one place not necessarily nuisance in another).

> 3. *Colls v. Home & Colonial Stores Ltd., ante*; see also *Drysdale v. Dugas* (1896), 26 S.C.R. 20 [Que.]; *Lyon v. Borland* (1911), 20 O.W.R. 321 (C.A.) (where new trial ordered on appeal by defendants); *Zegroo v. Johnston* (1924), 26 O.W.N. 25 (H.C.); *Belisle v. Canadian Cottons Ltd.*, [1952] O.W.N. 114 (H.C.); but see *Godfrey v. Good Rich Refining Co.*, [1940] 2 D.L.R. 164 (Ont. C.A.) (discussion of effect of change in character of whole district from residential to industrial).

The CED is updated by supplements on yellow pages filed before the main entry in the volume. Then the main entry itself will ultimately be replaced on white paper. ➤ At the bottom of each page, whether main (white) or supplementary (yellow), is the date the page was issued. The first paragraph above was updated by a new case mentioned in the supplement:

§13 note 1

MacGregor v. Penner, [1993] 1 W.W.R. 245 (Man. Q.B.); affirmed [1994] 2 W.W.R. 251 (Man. C.A.) (sewage lagoon on hog farm not unreasonable in agricultural area).

The advantage of going to the CED is that it will alert you to the fact that there is legislation which may differ from that of UK or Hong Kong.

It is possible that what you really want is simply cases. The CED does refer you to these. As you will have noticed, the Canadian courts are obviously used to referring to English cases as well as Canadian ones.

The Canadian Abridgement

You may also go to the *Canadian Abridgement*. This appears in only one version covering the whole of Canada. There is a volume called *Key and Research Guide*, which lists the various topic headings, and suggests research strategies etc. There is a list of topics in alphabetical order. If a topic is the subject of a major entry, the contents pages of that entry will be reproduced. If the topic is grouped under a broader subject, you will be referred to that subject. Suppose you are still looking at Nuisance; in the list under Nuisance you will find:

NUDUM PACTUM – *See Contracts IV.1, IV.2.a, IV.2.e, IV.2.g, IV.3; Construction Law IX.11.a; Sale of Land VI.2.d.iii; Specific Performance III.1*

NUISANCE – *See Criminal Law VII.10; Torts IX*

➤ Note that although in the CED Nuisance as a topic is treated separately, as topic 102, in the Abridgement it is under Tort (or under Criminal Law). This is so even though the publishers of the two works are the same — Carswell. You would therefore turn to the heading Torts where you would find the following:

• TORTS •

CONTENTS R34

I. Abuse of Process
II. Conversion
III. Detinue
IV. Interference with Contractual Relations
V. Interference with Economic Relations
VI. Intimidation
VII. Invasion of Privacy
VIII. Malicious Prosecution and False Imprisonment
IX. Nuisance
X. Replevin
XI. Trespass
XII. Miscellaneous Torts

RELATED TITLES

- Tort of civil conspiracy - see CONSPIRACY

- Tort of defamation - see DEFAMATION

- Tort of negligence generally - see NEGLIGENCE

- Injury to trespasser - see NEGLIGENCE VI.2.e

- Tort of passing off - see TRADE MARKS

- Injunctions to restrain tortious conduct generally - see INJUNCTIONS

➤ Note the following: though some torts are dealt with under this heading, e.g. Nuisance as we have seen, some, e.g. Defamation and Negligence, are separate topics. This sign: R34 refers to the volume number.

After the list of cross-references to Related Titles, the detailed Contents list of the Torts topic begins, including this: ⇨

IX. NUISANCE

1. **Nuisance generally**
   a. What constituting nuisance
   b. Private nuisance
   c. Public nuisance
   d. Private and public nuisance distinguished
   e. Miscellaneous issues
2. **Factors giving rise to right of action**
   a. Character of neighbourhood
   b. Nature of property or non-natural use of land
   c. Miscellaneous factors

You will see that the point on the 'Character of the neighbourhood' dealt with in the CED extract above, is Topic IX.2.a under Torts in the Abridgement. If you turn to Volume R34 and the relevant section you will find:

4648.   (IX.2.a)
Nuisance – Factors giving rise to right of action – Character of neighbourhood. Whether noise constitutes a nuisance is a question of degree, and no arbitrary standard applicable to all localities can be instituted. Where the evidence did not disclose annoyance and disturbance which went beyond the legitimate use of the premises, which were used as a nurses' residence, or which could be regarded as excessive or unreasonable, held, although the standard in this particular district might have been higher than in other localities, nevertheless there did not exist an actionable nuisance.

Howarth v. Canadian Red Cross Society, [1943] 2 W.W.R. 692 (Alta. T.D.).

4649.   (IX.2.a)
Nuisance – Factors giving rise to right of action – Character of neighbourhood – Lavatories. Per Lennox J.: "Lavatories and urinals and conveniences of that class are not necessarily nuisances. It depends upon the locality. What is an intolerable nuisance in one place may not be a nuisance at all in another."

J.F. Brown Co. v. Toronto (City) (1916), 36 O.L.R. 189, 29 D.L.R. 618 (C.A.), affirmed (1917), 55 S.C.R. 153, 37 D.L.R. 532.

Note that each case has its own number (top left) and that the section number, here IX.2.a, appears at the top right.

Should you wish to find a case by its name rather than by reference to the heading, you should start with the *Consolidated Table of Cases*. This is in five volumes and covers the entire work.

Keeping Up-to-date

The Abridgement itself is kept up-to-date in the following fashion:

The *Table of Cases* is loose-leaf and is updated. The main volumes themselves, such as volume R34, are themselves replacements of the original volumes of the second edition (hence the R). Sometimes the original volumes must be replaced by more than one volume prefixed R, for example Volume 11 on Criminal Law has been replaced by Volumes R11A to R11D. Supplements are produced to the R volumes, themselves labelled RS. And periodically a volume may be replaced yet again, in which case it will say on its spine '1993 Reissue' or whatever date the reissue appears.

If we look at [1995] R34 Supp., that is the 1995 supplement to volume R34, we find this case:

520. (IX.2.a)
Nuisance – Factors giving rise to right of action – Character of neighbourhood – Plaintiffs establishing "urban dwelling" across from hog farm operation. Plaintiffs acquired a residential site in an agricultural area. At the time of the purchase, defendant farmer operated a hog farm across the road from plaintiffs' site. A large open sewage lagoon was located on the farm in close proximity to the road. Plaintiffs claimed that the odours emanating from the farm and the large number of flies attracted to the area by the farm constituted an unreasonable interference with their enjoyment of their property and sued farmer in nuisance. Held, the action was dismissed. The farm had always been zoned an agricultural area and was recognized as such long before plaintiffs established their "urban dwelling" in the countryside. The hog operation, albeit expanded with municipal approval, was one that pre-existed plaintiffs' residential development across the roadway. The standard of cleanliness and overall husbandry of the farm was as good if not better than the average operation in the neighbourhood. Any interference with plaintiffs' enjoyment of their property was not unreasonable.

MacGregor v. Penner (1992), [1993] 1 W.W.R. 245, 82 Man. R. (2d) 178 (Q.B.), affirmed (1993), [1994] 2 W.W.R. 251, 92 Man. R. (2d) 39, 61 W.A.C. 39 (C.A.).

You will see that this carries the same section number as the earlier Nuisance cases from the Abridgement: IX.2.a and is the same case as mentioned in the updating of the CED.

To be even more current it is necessary to turn to *Canadian Current Law*. This appears in several series:

- *Index to Canadian Legal Literature* (see p. 259)
- *Case Law Digests*
- *Canadian Current Cases*
- *Canadian Statute Citations* (see p. 258)
- *Legislation* (recent legislation, amendments, etc.)

Case Law Digests, published monthly, is the current awareness publication for the *Abridgement*. The cases are under the same heading as in the *Abridgement*, and the summary in the box above originally appeared as para. 2197 in the February 1994 issue of *Case Law Digests*. Because it is published monthly it will be more up-to-date than the *Abridgement* supplement. It has an index which cumulates every few months, so one can find the case above by looking for 'Nuisance' in the index.

Canadian Current Cases is the equivalent of the *Case Citators* in Hong Kong and UK: it is where you find out whether a case has been applied, overruled, distinguished and so on. Here is an extract. You will see a familiar case, *Anns v Merton*, applied in a case in the Federal Court of Appeal and considered in the Manitoba Queen's Bench in 1995.

> **Anns v. Merton London Borough Council**
> [1978] A.C. 728 (U.K. H.L.)
> ⎯
> Ⓐ Comeau's Sea Foods Ltd. v. Canada (Minister of Fisheries & Oceans) (February 27, 1995), Doc. A-650-92 (Fed. C.A.)
> Ⓒ Albionex (Overseas) Ltd. v. Agro Co. of Canada Ltd. (March 21, 1995), Doc. Winnipeg Centre 85-01-06148 (Man. Q.B.)

Canadian Cases on the Internet

At the time of writing, the only Canadian courts of which decisions appear in full text on the Internet are those of the Canadian Supreme Court and some courts of British Columbia — though no doubt developments will be rapid. There is a joint site for the Supreme Court with the University of Montreal for which the url is: **http://www.droit.umontreal.ca/**. Cases appear here very rapidly, and can be downloaded in WordPerfect format. The database of cases is also searchable.

For the British Columbia courts try: **http://www.courts.gov.bc.ca/**

Legislation

You are less likely to want to use Canadian legislation. You may find that some library in Hong Kong has a CD-ROM of such legislation. There is, for example, Canadian Statute Service.

Canadian Statute Service contains not only the text of Canadian ➤ federal (but not state) statutes, but is also a case citator — that is, you can see what cases have been decided on a particular provision. It goes further than a paper version of a citator would, as it includes summaries of the cases.

It is divided into two parts — the statutes and the citator, but you can shift very easily between them. Thus you can look up an expression which appears in Hong Kong legislation, such as the Bill of Rights, first looking to see what the corresponding provision was in the Canadian Charter of Rights, and then going to the citator to see what decision there have been on it.

However, if what you are interested in is not federal legislation, but is, for example, the equivalent of the Employees' Compensation Ordinance, you can look up recent cases by looking at the issues of the (paper) *Canadian Statute Citations*. A brief extract appears below:

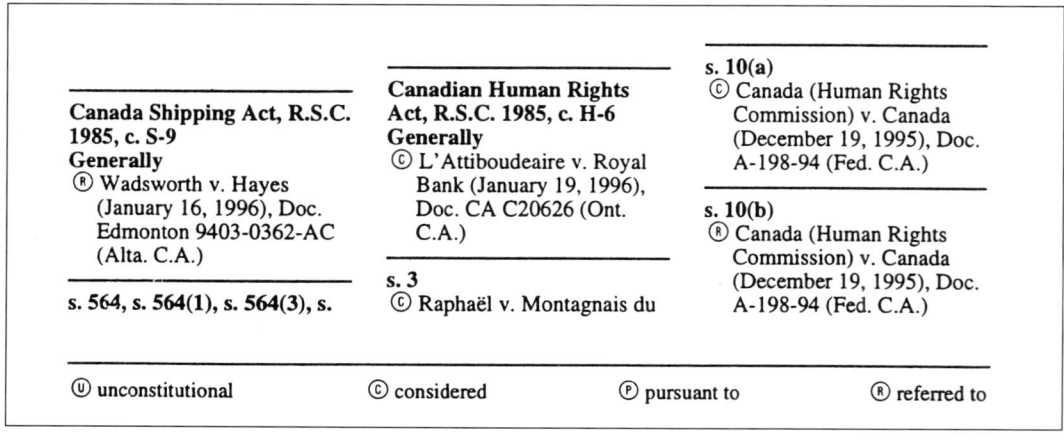

You will see that this publication, which gives unreported as well as reported decisions, is not ideally tailored to the needs of a library which does not have access to the unreported decisions! ➤ This suggests that if you are looking for cases on provincial legislation, you would do best by looking at the relevant provincial law reports.

Canadian Periodicals

Among the leading Canadian journals are:

CBR	*Canadian Bar Review*
Can Bus LJ	*Canadian Business Law Journal*
Crim LQ	*Criminal Law Quarterly*
McGill LJ	*McGill Law Journal*
Osgoode Hall LJ	*Osgoode Hall Law Journal*
Sup. Ct. L Rev	*Supreme Court Law Review*
UBCLR	*University of British Columbia Law Review*
UTLJ	*University of Toronto Law Journal*
Windsor YB Access Justice	*Windsor Yearbook of Access to Justice*

Index to Canadian Legal Literature

This is one of the parts of *Canadian Current Law*. This indexes not only journals, but also Government publications, books (including the *Canadian Encyclopedic Digest*), theses and even teaching materials. It has four indexes: Subject, Author, Table of Cases and Table of Statutes. An item which discusses a case and a piece of legislation may appear in all four! Here is part of a page from the subject index of a recent issue:

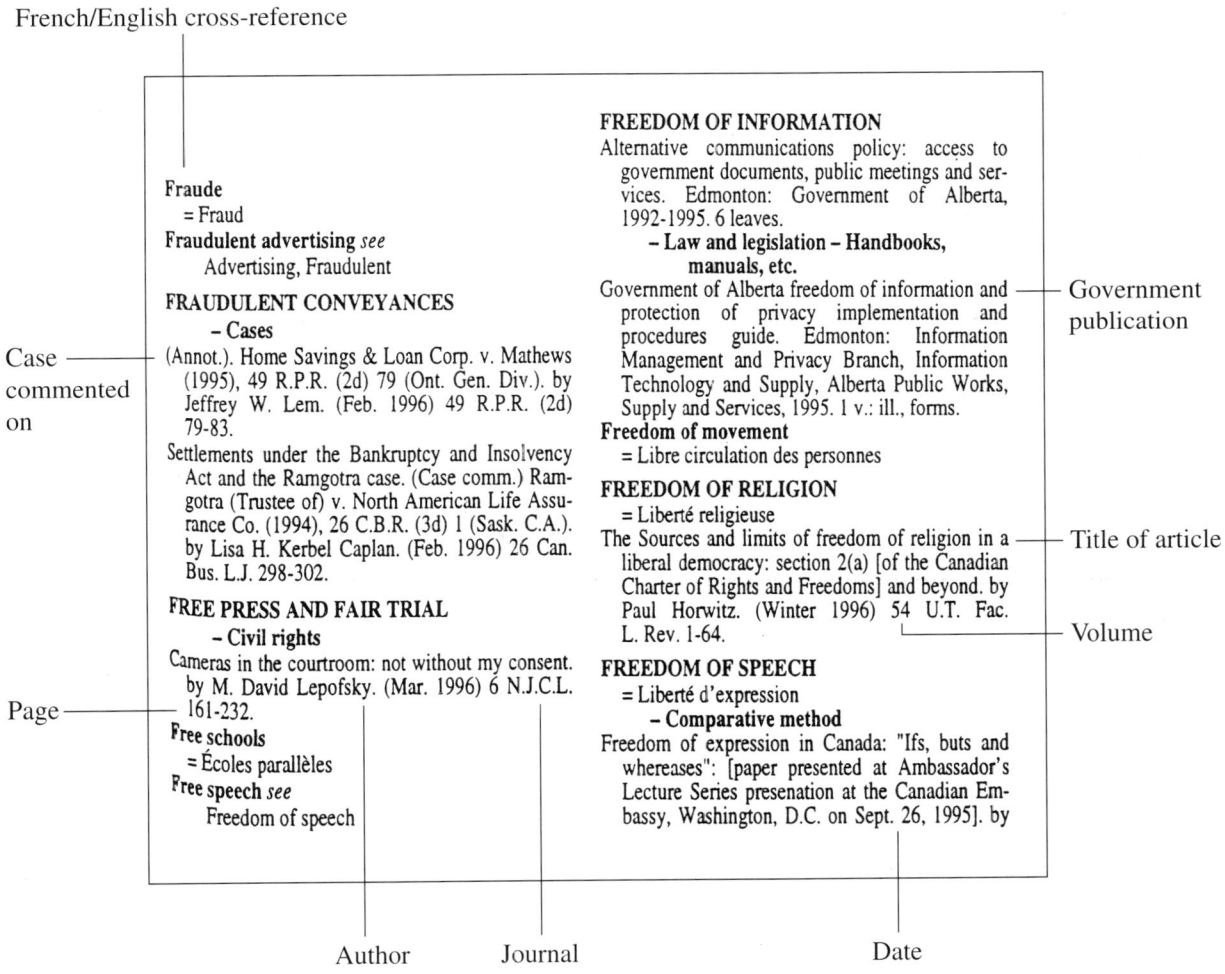

French/English cross-reference

Case commented on

Page

Fraude
= Fraud
Fraudulent advertising *see*
Advertising, Fraudulent
FRAUDULENT CONVEYANCES
– **Cases**
(Annot.). Home Savings & Loan Corp. v. Mathews (1995), 49 R.P.R. (2d) 79 (Ont. Gen. Div.). by Jeffrey W. Lem. (Feb. 1996) 49 R.P.R. (2d) 79-83.
Settlements under the Bankruptcy and Insolvency Act and the Ramgotra case. (Case comm.) Ramgotra (Trustee of) v. North American Life Assurance Co. (1994), 26 C.B.R. (3d) 1 (Sask. C.A.). by Lisa H. Kerbel Caplan. (Feb. 1996) 26 Can. Bus. L.J. 298-302.

FREE PRESS AND FAIR TRIAL
– **Civil rights**
Cameras in the courtroom: not without my consent. by M. David Lepofsky. (Mar. 1996) 6 N.J.C.L. 161-232.
Free schools
= Écoles parallèles
Free speech *see*
Freedom of speech

FREEDOM OF INFORMATION
Alternative communications policy: access to government documents, public meetings and services. Edmonton: Government of Alberta, 1992-1995. 6 leaves.
– **Law and legislation – Handbooks, manuals, etc.**
Government of Alberta freedom of information and protection of privacy implementation and procedures guide. Edmonton: Information Management and Privacy Branch, Information Technology and Supply, Alberta Public Works, Supply and Services, 1995. 1 v.: ill., forms.
Freedom of movement
= Libre circulation des personnes

FREEDOM OF RELIGION
= Liberté religieuse
The Sources and limits of freedom of religion in a liberal democracy: section 2(a) [of the Canadian Charter of Rights and Freedoms] and beyond. by Paul Horwitz. (Winter 1996) 54 U.T. Fac. L. Rev. 1-64.

FREEDOM OF SPEECH
= Liberté d'expression
– **Comparative method**
Freedom of expression in Canada: "Ifs, buts and whereases": [paper presented at Ambassador's Lecture Series presentation at the Canadian Embassy, Washington, D.C. on Sept. 26, 1995]. by

Government publication

Title of article

Volume

Author   Journal   Date

Further Reading

Banks, *Banks on Using a Law Library* (5th ed., London, Ont.: Carswell, 1991)

Castel and Latchman, *The Practical Guide to Canadian Legal Research* (Scarborough: Carswell, 1994)

THE UNITED STATES OF AMERICA[7]

Introduction

Although the Unites States of America is a common law country (except for Louisiana which has a French system), it is not very common for its decisions to be cited in most other common law countries, except in the field of constitutional law, and more specifically human rights, where the Supreme Court of the US has been very influential. With such a large country, there is a richness of case-law which can be very stimulating. In some other fields US legislative developments have been very interesting (for example, in anti-monopoly law, called anti-trust in the US), or sometimes the literature of the US is influential.

The US has a written Constitution, the first ten amendments of which constitute the Bill of Rights. It is, of course, a Republic, that is, it does not have a monarch. In fact its head of state and head of government are combined in the person of the elected President.

The USA is also a federation, composed of 50 states. Certain matters are the responsibility of the states and certain matters of the federal government. On the whole 'lawyers' law' (such as contract, tort, company law, criminal law) are the responsibility of the states. However, there are various factors which tend towards similarity in some fields of law: for example the fact that the federal government can regulate 'inter-state' trade, or the existence of Uniform Laws which states may chose to adopt). Each state has its own judicial system, and system of appeal courts, and appeals from the states may also end up in the US Supreme Court. There are certain matters which go to a separate system of courts, the federal courts, with its own system of Courts of Appeal, and with the US Supreme Court at its apex.

The existence of 51 jurisdictions (50 state and 1 federal) has an impact on the literature of the law. For example, you will not find much discussion of legislation in some literature because it is too difficult to deal with all the possible variations. However, law journal articles will sometimes discuss the law of a specific state. Although the doctrine of precedent applies in the US, it is not perhaps applied with the same force in constitutional litigation — what matters is ultimately the words of the Constitution. The Supreme Court has for longer than the House of Lords considered itself not bound by its own decision. And

---

7   See Logan, *United States Legal Research* (London: Legal Information Resources Ltd., 1990).

it is standard for lawyers, and students, to be aware of the precedents from a wide range of jurisdictions, even though they may be technically persuasive only.

One guide says, 'American lawyers have a distinct preference for fact-based law rather than rule-based law'.[8] In order to make this possible there is a form of literature in US law which does not really have an equivalent in UK or Hong Kong law: the annotation which is essentially a summary of substantial number of cases on a relatively narrow point (see *Law Reports* and *American Law Reports* below).

Law Reports

The *Supreme Court Reports, Lawyers' Edition* are available in some libraries. If you have a reference just to the Supreme Court Reports (which will appear just as 'US') you will have to find, from the spine of the volumes, which Lawyers' Edition volume the case appears in (under the big volume number for the Lawyers' Edition, you will see the corresponding number of the US reports — occasionally parts of more than one volume of the US reports will appear in the volumes of the *Lawyers' Edition*). You might, for example, see on the spine: 117

> L. Ed. 2d.
> U.S. 502 (part)
> U.S. 503 (part)

 In fact very often the *Lawyers' Edition* reference is given too. ➤ Look out for it.

There is a set of *General Index* volumes published periodically. This is a subject index (and has a table of statutory provisions cited).

If you want the citation of a case of which you have only the name you could look in the *Quick Case Table* volume.

You will also find 'Annotations' in these reports (see above). They summarize Supreme Court cases on a particular topic. They are indexed in the *General Index*.

The *Lawyers' Edition* is updated by pocket parts inserted in the backs of each volume. ➤ The *Lawyers' Edition* tends to be a couple of years out-of-date. This makes the following publication particularly valuable:

US Law Week: This prints the entire opinions in Supreme Court cases and gives summaries of other cases as well as information on pending cases.

See also ALR below.

---

8   Ibid. p. 9.

Statutes

The most commonly available source is *United States Code Annotated* (USCA). Its nearest UK equivalent is *Halsbury's Statutes of England*. Updating takes place by means of 'pocket parts' which slip into the back of each volume. Sometimes these become too big and become separate volumes. Then there are 'pamphlets' during the year which further update the information as Congress passes new laws, etc. There is an annual General Index. Here is a specimen search from the 1996 General Index topic Hong Kong:

United States policy,
  Congress.
    Consultation by President with, **22 § 5724**
    Findings and declarations, **22 § 5701**
    Sense of,
      Bilateral ties with U.S., **22 § 5711**
      Commerce between U.S. and Hong Kong, **22 § 5713**
      Cultural exchanges, **22 § 5715**
      Educational exchanges, **22 § 5715**
      International agreements, rights under, **22 § 5712**
      Multilateral organizations, participation in, **22 § 5712**
      Trade status, **22 § 5712**
      Transportation, **22 § 5714**
  Consultation, President with Congress, **22 § 5724**
  Executive order suspending application of certain provisions, **22 § 5722**
  Factors, consideration, application of provision, **22 § 5722**

This refers to Title 22, which spreads over several bound volumes, and is on Foreign Relations. Here is part of the page which includes paragraph 5722 (found in the pocket part but not in the main volume):

22 § 5721   FOREIGN RELATIONS

(b) International agreements

For all purposes, including actions in any court in the United States, the Congress approves the continuation in force on and after July 1, 1997, of all treaties and other international agreements, including multilateral conventions, entered into before such date between the United States and Hong Kong, or entered into before such date between the United States and the United Kingdom and applied to Hong Kong, unless or until terminated in accordance with law. If in carrying out this subchapter, the President determines that Hong Kong is not legally competent to carry out its obligations under any such treaty or other international agreement, or that the continuation of Hong Kong's obligations or rights under any such treaty or other international agreement is not appropriate under the circumstances, such determination shall be reported to the Congress in accordance with section 5731 of this title.

(Pub.L. 102–383, Title II, § 201, Oct. 5, 1992, 106 Stat. 1452.)

§ 5722. Presidential order

(a) Presidential determination

On or after July 1, 1997, whenever the President determines that Hong Kong is not sufficiently autonomous to justify treatment under a particular law of the United States, or any provision thereof, different from that accorded the People's Republic of China, the President may issue an Executive order suspending the application of section 5721(a) of this title to such law or provision of law.

(b) Factor for consideration

In making a determination under subsection (a) of this section with respect to the application of a law of the United States, or any provision thereof, to Hong Kong, the President should consider the terms, obligations, and expectations expressed in the Joint Declaration with respect to Hong Kong.

(c) Publication in Federal Register

Any Executive order issued under subsection (a) of this section shall be published in the Federal Register and shall specify the law or provision of law affected by the order.

(d) Termination of suspension

An Executive order issued under subsection (a) of this section may be terminated by the President with respect to a particular law or provision of law whenever the President determines that Hong Kong has regained sufficient autonomy to justify different treatment under the law or provision of law in question. Notice of any such termination shall be published in the Federal Register.

383rd Public Law of 102nd Congress. Title (Part) II of the Act, § 202, passed 5.10.92, Vol. 106 Statutes at Large p. 1453

(Pub.L. 102–383, Title II, § 202, Oct. 5, 1992, 106 Stat. 1453.)

Reference Works

AmJur — *American Jurisprudence*, an encyclopaedia of the law, a bit like *Halsbury's Laws of England*. This is also updated by means of pocket parts. Here is a specimen paragraph: 91 in volume 57A in the 2nd edition, topic Negligence.

57A Am Jur 2d   NEGLIGENCE   § 92

§ 91. Particular relationships giving rise to duty

A relation sufficient to constitute the foundation of a duty of care may be that of master and servant,[89] innkeeper and guest,[90] landlord and tenant,[91] carrier and passenger,[92] or shipper and consignee.[93] But no duty of care arises from a vendor-vendee relationship.[94]

A relationship of dependence may create a special relationship.[95] Persons who undertake to become custodians of children or others thereby place themselves in a special relationship which requires special precautions and care and they assume, among other obligations, a duty to protect those in their custody from criminal attacks by third persons.[96] In this connection, a section of the Restatement of Torts[97] provides that one who is required by law to take or who voluntarily takes the custody of another under circumstances such as to deprive the other of his normal opportunities for protection is under a similar duty to the other, while another section[98] provides that one who takes custody of another under circumstances such as to deprive the other of his normal power of self-protection, or to subject him to association with persons likely to harm him, is under a duty to exercise reasonable care so to control the conduct of third persons as to prevent them from intentionally harming the other, or from creating, by their conduct, an unreasonable risk of harm to him, if the actor (1) knows or has reason to know that he has the ability to control the conduct of the third person, and (2) knows or should know of the necessity and opportunity for exercising such control.

Schools, colleges and universities may be held liable for negligence resulting in injuries to students.[99]

§ 92. —Social relationship

A duty may arise from a social relationship.[1] However, the mere fact that defendants were the organizers of a party has been held not to create a special

---

88. J'Aire Corp. v Gregory, 24 Cal 3d 799, 157 Cal Rptr 407, 598 P2d 60.

In the law of negligence, the question of duty is simply the problem of the degree to which one's uncontrolled and undisciplined activities will be curtailed by the courts in recognition of the needs of organized society. Elbert v Saginaw, 363 Mich 463, 109 NW2d 879.

89. 53 Am Jur 2d, MASTER AND SERVANT §§ 139 et seq.

90. 40 Am Jur 2d, HOTELS, MOTELS, AND RESTAURANTS §§ 81 et seq.

91. 49 Am Jur 2d, LANDLORD AND TENANT §§ 767 et seq.

92. 14 Am Jur 2d, CARRIERS § 739.

93. Edwards v Southern R. Co., 233 Ala 65, 169 So 715, 106 ALR 1133.

94. Weggen v Elwell-Parker Elec. Co. (SD Iowa) 510 F Supp 252.

95. Baldwin v Zoradi (5th Dist) 123 Cal App 3d 275, 176 Cal Rptr 809.

96. Wallace v Der-Ohanian (5th Dist) 199 Cal

App 2d 141, 18 Cal Rptr 892, wherein the proprietor of a camp was liable in negligently failing to exercise due care in preventing the rape of an 11-year-old girl camper.

Annotation: 10 ALR3d 619 § 8.

In an action by an individual allegedly injured by a convict who had been given probation on the condition that he enter defendant's private drug and alcohol rehabilitation program and who allegedly escaped from the institution and went on a crime spree, no special relationship existed and consequently defendant owed no duty of care to plaintiff. Beauchene v Synanon Foundation, Inc. (1st Dist) 88 Cal App 3d 342, 151 Cal Rptr 796.

97. Restatement, TORTS 2d § 314A.

98. Restatement, TORTS 2d § 320.

99. 15A Am Jur 2d, COLLEGES AND UNIVERSITIES §§ 39, 40; 68 Am Jur 2d, SCHOOLS §§ 319 et seq.

1. Williams v Jackson Co. (Ala App) 359 So 2d 798, cert den (Ala) 359 So 2d 801.

147

There is a cross reference to the *American Law Reports* (ALR). This is a sort of hybrid. It does contain actual reported cases, but it is mainly a compendium of reviews of particular topics. It is now in its 5th series. Suppose you are interested in whether the management of a restaurant has a duty to help a customer who shows signs of choking. You can look up 'Restaurants' in the *Quick Index* volume, which is reissued periodically. (There is also a multi-volume set of indexes.) You would find this:

> **RESTAURANTS AND OTHER EATING PLACES**
>
> Assault or other criminal activity on or near franchise premises, tort liability of franchisor for injuries allegedly caused by, 2 ALR5th 369, 31 ALR5th 550
>
> Beverages, liability for injury or death allegedly caused by contamination or spoilage, 87 ALR4th 804
>
> Business hours, validity of municipal ordinance regulating time during which restaurant business may be conducted, 53 ALR3d 942
>
> Choking, duty of retail establishment, or its employees, to assist patron choking on food, 2 ALR5th 966

➤ Note how this index includes not only legal concepts such as 'Negligence' but factual situations like 'Restaurants'.

You see there is a reference to the second volume of the 5th series:

---

2 ALR5th 966

DUTY OF RETAIL ESTABLISHMENT, OR ITS EMPLOYEES, TO ASSIST PATRON CHOKING ON FOOD

by
Frank J. Wozniak, J.D.

Each year in the United States more than 3900 people strangle because food becomes stuck in their throats. When incidents such as this occur in restaurants or in other retail establishments, a question is raised concerning the duty of the establishment or its employees to assist the patron who is choking on food. In the recent case of Drew v LeJay's Sportsmen's Cafe, Inc. (1991, Wyo) 806 P2d 301, 2 ALR5th 1172, the court stated that although there was no duty to render first aid to a choking patron, there was a duty to exercise reasonable care and that this duty could be satisfied by the summoning of medical assistance within a reasonable time. This annotation collects and discusses the cases in which the courts have considered the duty of a retail establishment, or its employees, to assist a patron who eats food on the establishment's premises, chokes on it, and is either injured or killed.

Drew v LeJay's Sportsmen's Cafe, Inc., is fully reported at page 1172, infra.

966

The Annotation basically reviews many cases on the topic, and, as you will see, reports one fully. A pocket part adds, among other things, that in Illinois there is a statute providing that there is **no** duty to aid a choking patron!

$20,000 of additional underinsured-motorist benefits under any of three auto insurance policies providing excess insurance, based on argument that, under provision in each of excess policies, if insured sustained bodily injury while occupying vehicle which was not his, coverage under policies applied only in amount by which they exceeded primary coverage, term "primary coverage," not expressly defined by policies, referred to amount already paid to insured by insurer—$80,000—since it was clear, reading provision in context of part of policy in which it appeared in its entirety that term "primary coverage" referred to limit of liability declared in primary policy—$100,000, less amount otherwise paid by second insurer, which, in case, was $20,000—rather than amount insurer paid to insured, and term "primary coverage" was not ambiguous. Gober v State Farm Mut. Auto. Ins. Co. (1994, 2d Dist) 263 Ill App 3d 846, 201 Ill Dec 584, 636 NE2d 1016, reh den (Jul 29, 1994).

2 ALR5th 966–976

§ 3. Duty to assist—generally

Although apparently recognizing that a restaurant operator may have a duty to provide assistance to a choking patron by summoning an ambulance, the court nevertheless upheld the dismissal of the complaint as there was no evidence that anyone in the restaurant knew that the victim was choking, no allegation that the restaurant employees discovered the choking patron and refused to call or delayed in calling for medical assistance, and no allegation that but for the failure to summon an ambulance the victim would have lived. Parra v Tarasco, Inc. (1992, 1st Dist) 230 Ill App 3d 819, 172 Ill Dec 516, 595 NE2d 1186.

§ 4. —Duty to render first aid
[a] View that there is no duty to provide first aid

Also recognizing that retail establishment, or its employees, has no duty to assist patron choking on food:

Fla—City Nat. Bank v 4000 Restaurant, Inc. (1979, Fla App D4) 372 So 2d 1146.

Estate of man who died after choking on piece of food could not recover on wrongful death action against restaurant as restaurateur had no duty to rescue a customer from a danger not caused in the first instance by the restaurateur. Even if such a duty existed, restaurateur would have been protected from liability by statute, Ill. Rev. Stat. 1989, ch. 56-1/2, par 605, providing that no liability would be imposed for attempting to help, or failing to help, a choking person in a restaurant. Parra v Tarasco, Inc. (1992, 1st Dist) 230 Ill App 3d 819, 172 Ill Dec 516, 595 NE2d 1186.

Legislature has enacted statute providing that no liability exists for either attempting to help, or failing to help, choking person in restaurant. Parra v Tarasco, Inc. (1992, 1st Dist) 230 Ill App 3d 819, 172 Ill Dec 516, 595 NE2d 1186.

You will also see in the AmJur paragraph a reference to the *Restatement of Torts.*

Restatement of Law

The *Restatement of American Law* is a project designed to produce a sort of codification of the common law. It has now become a type of encyclopaedia in its own right, since it comes out in periodic new editions, and also there are commentaries which give references to cases in which the Restatement is cited. It has become very influential and is sometimes cited in courts outside the US.

Note: This is a very elementary introduction to US sources. Even those mentioned here are quite complex, and a full-scale US Law Library has many other sorts of materials which are up-dated and cross-referenced in many ways. This should at least give you some idea of how to get material you might be interested in.

US Law on the Internet

The main electronic source for US law has been On-line databases: LEXIS and Westlaw. But there are sources for US cases and legislation on the Internet, and therefore a good deal cheaper! The best way into these is perhaps via the Cornell Law School: **http://.www.law.cornell.edu**. You will find that you can click on sites for recent cases from the US Supreme Court, the New York Court of Appeals (a federal court), federal legislation and some state legislation as well as *The Journal of Online Law* and some issues of the *Cornell Law Journal*.

❖ Take one of the following subjects, which might be essay topics, and try to find relevant materials using the **paper** sources described in this Unit, for each of the following countries: Australia, Canada and USA.

- Child abuse
- Regulation of Broadcasting
- HIV/AIDS and the Law
- Copyright in electronic media

Try to find each of the following:

- a case
- a statute
- a journal article

☺ Done carefully in a way which would give you some familiarity with the sources for each country, it would probably take you up to an hour for each country.

❖ You can try this as a sort of competition with a friend.

First of all chose a country: either Australia, Canada or the USA. Then chose one of the following topics:

- Privacy
- Defamation
- Liability of an employer in negligence to employees
- Occupiers' liability

One of you should take the paper resources, and the other take the Internet (you might have to draw lots for that!).

Then see which of you can find **more quickly** the latest case on the chosen topic.

Compare notes: Did you get the same answer? If not, why not? Which of you found the search easier? What does this tell you about how easy or difficult, how up-to-date, etc. the various resources are?

Further Reading: Lewis, *Using American Law Books* (4th ed., including On-line and CD-ROM Services) (Dubuque, Iowa: Kendall Hunt, 1995).

SELF-TEST QUESTIONS

☺ Twenty minutes.

1. Name three countries (apart from Hong Kong and the UK) which might be worth looking at for innovative ideas **in the courts** about:
   (a) contract and tort
   (b) human rights
   (c) constitutional law

2. Which of the following are common law jurisdictions and which are (primarily) civil law:
   - Republic of Ireland
   - Quebec
   - India
   - New Zealand
   - Louisiana
   - Australia

3. You should by now be familar with *Halsbury's Laws of England*, *Current Law* and *The Digest*. Which of these does each of the following most resemble?
   - *The Australian Digest*
   - *Laws of Australia*
   - *Australian Current Law*
   - *Canadian Current Law*
   - *The Canadian Abridgement*
   - *The Canadian Encyclopedic Digest*
   - *American Jurisprudence*

4. What are 'pocket parts'? Which publications have them?

5. Which of the following consist mainly of case reports (full reports, not digested ones):
   - *Malayan Law Journal*
   - *All India Reporter*
   - *US Law Week*
   - *Australian Current Law*
   - *(Malaysian) Current Law Journal*
   - *Canadian Current Law*

6. The highest courts (by whatever name) of which of the following countries have their decisions on the Internet?
   - Australia
   - Canada
   - India
   - New Zealand
   - Malaysia
   - Singapore
   - USA

Unit 17 'Non-Law' Materials

OBJECTIVES

By the end of this Unit you will:

- have given some thought to the possible relevance to your studies of books which are not, or not primarily, about law
- have some appreciation of the range of journals not primarily about law which may be relevant to your studies
- be aware of some of the indexes and abstracts which help you find relevant 'non-law' material, including CD-ROM databases

☺ About an hour if you go to the library to look at some of the sorts of material discussed.

Non-law is placed in quotation marks in the heading to this Unit to convey the idea that it is not right to draw a definite line between legal and non-legal materials. In law journals you will very often find articles which relate legal issues to social reality and to theory; in journals which are not ostensibly about law you will sometimes find very similar articles. And it will be readily apparent that articles about social issues which have a legal dimension (divorce or suicide to take two examples) could well be relevant to a student studying the law on these topics, especially if writing an essay.

➤ Be warned, however, that sometimes you may find an article about law in a non-legal journal which is extremely superficial, or even wrong, about the law, because it is written by someone who has no real understanding about the law. I have sometimes found social scientists describing legal issues simply by reproducing ideas and information from other sources — by lawyers. This may be good enough for other social scientists, but **you** should go to the original source.

❖ You may remember the suggested essay topic back in Unit 11 — on Corruption. Think for a few minutes about the sorts of **non**-law materials that might be useful in order to put a discussion of the law into its full context. (Then turn to the end of this Unit where you will find a few suggestions in a box.) ☺ Five minutes.

BOOKS

It is hardly necessary to remind you of the existence of non-law **books**. You have been using these all your lives. You should bear in mind that a good deal of illumination about law can be obtained from books on history, economics, anthropology, political science, philosophy, psychology, etc. To take a couple of examples:

- History: Ming Chan, 'Labour vs Crown: Aspects of Society-State Interactions in the Hong Kong Labour Movement Before World War II', in E. Sinn ed., *Between East and West*: *Aspects of Social and Political Development in Hong Kong*.
- Literature: 'Red, Amber, Green', a short story by David T.K. Wong from *The Lost River and Other Stories* which is about the incomprehensible nature of a criminal trial.

BIBLIOGRAPHIES

You may be helped in the process of locating relevant material by bibliographies.

Below is an extract from a regional bibliography: Diana Chan and Painan Wu, *A Bibliography of Asia-Pacific Studies Volume II: China and Hong Kong* (Hong Kong Institute of Asia-Pacific Studies, 1992).

HOUSING

1. Annual departmental report, Hong Kong. Quartering Authority. Govt. Printer : Hong Kong, 0000-,
   UC UL   doc JQ676.Z6 A3.

2. Green paper : housing subsidy to tenants of public housing / Housing subsidy to tenants of public housing, Hong Kong. Committee on Housing Subsidy to Tenants of Public Housing and Hong Kong Housing Authority. {Govt. Printer : Hong Kong }, 1985,
   Cover title \ At head of title: Hong Kong Housing Authority.
   UC UL   doc HD7288.78.H65H68.

3. The home ownership scheme in Hong Kong : a study of residential changes and satisfaction, Tsang, Flora Po-ling. {Chinese University of Hong Kong : Hong Kong}, 1986,
   Thesis (M.Phil.) — Chinese University of Hong Kong.
   Cover title.
   UL UC   doc HD7288.78.H65H66.

There is a specifically Hong Kong bibliography, annotated, by Ian Scott (Oxford: Clio Press, 1990). And there are a number of other bibliographical sources, though they are mostly rather out-of-date.

Subject-specific bibliographies will also sometimes contain material on Hong Kong and, anyway, you will not want to restrict your researches to material on Hong Kong. There are so many bibliographies on so many topics that it is pointless to list them here.

HISTORICAL DOCUMENTS

It is unlikely that during your undergraduate course you will want to look in depth into Hong Kong's legal history. But for the sake of completeness, you should be aware that there are some historical records mostly from the Hong Kong Government in the Public Records Office (now housed in Tuen Mun). Most records were destroyed during the Second World War so the collection is disappointing in comparison with the public archives of many countries. See the PRO web site: **http://www.info.gov.info/fpro.htm**.

Right from 1843 there have been records kept by the British Government — Governors have to write reports home, for example, and there has been a constant correspondence between Hong Kong and London. The originals of these are kept in England. But this correspondence has been microfilmed, and copies of this format are available in Hong Kong.

The Annual Report of the Hong Kong Government to London (from 1841–1941) have recently been republished (in some cases published for the first time) as Jarman, ed., *Hong Kong Annual Administration Reports* (Archive Editions, 1996) 6 volumes.

See Birch et al., *Research Materials for Hong Kong Studies* (Hong Kong: Centre of Asian Studies, HKU, 1984).

JOURNALS

You may be less familiar with academic journals than with books. There are a tremendous number, some of which are very general, for example on 'history'. Others concentrate on sub-divisions of a particular discipline, such as a certain period of history, or the history of a certain country, or the history of certain institutions or ideas, such as the history of religion. Yet others deal with a particular aspect of social/political/economic life from a variety of perspectives — such as peace, or war, or children. Law being about life, any of these may contain some material relevant to law and the role of law in society, though probably not written by lawyers nor materials analysed in the way lawyers tend to. Hong Kong is, not unnaturally, attracting a good deal of attention in the run-up to 1997, and there are articles in a variety of 'non-law' journals which are relevant to Hong Kong law and politics.

The next page contains a sort of collage of extracts from contents pages of recent non-law journals or journals on law and other disciplines (e.g. law and economics, law and psychiatry, etc.), just to show what an interesting range of materials can be found in less traditional sources (that is, less traditional for lawyers and law students).

SOCIAL PROBLEMS

VOLUME 43 : NUMBER 1 : FEBRUARY 1996

77   Identity, Strategy, and Feminist Politics: PATRICIA GAGNÉ
     Clemency for Battered Women Who Kill

The Journal
of
Interdisciplinary History

Volume XXVII, Number 1   Summer 1996

Punishing Assault: The Transformation of   Peter King   43
Attitudes in the English Courts

SIGNS   SUMMER 1996   VOLUME 21   NUMBER 4

952   Asking about Gender in Courts

Judith Resnik

Business
Ethics
Quarterly

July 1996

Vol. 6 No. 3

International Journal of the Sociology of Law

March 1996

CONTENTS

Vol. 24, no. 1

Articles

Dunford, L. and Ridley A., "No Soul to be Damned, No Body to be Kicked": Responsibility, Blame and Corporate Punishment 1

Laster, K. and O'Malley, P., Sensitive New-age Laws: The Reassertion of Emotionality in Law.

Li, J., The Structural Strains of China's Socio-legal System: A Transition to Formal Legalism?

Sheptycki, J.W.E., Law Enforcement, Justice and Democracy in the Transnational Arena: Reflections on the War on Drugs

TABLE OF CONTENTS

WILLIAM S. LAUFER, Corporate Culpability and the Limits of Law.... 311

141
159

Utilitas
Volume 8 Number 2 July 1996

CONTENTS

Articles
The Morality and Utility of Organ Transplantation
ROBERT AUDI
On Life, Death, and Abortion   D. W. HASLETT

Asian Journal of Political Science

Volume 4 Number 1 (June 1996)

Party Politics and Elections in Transitional Hong Kong
Ian Scott

PHILOSOPHY EAST & WEST

A QUARTERLY OF COMPARATIVE PHILOSOPHY

Special Issue: Seventh East-West Philosophers' Conference

Understanding Justice in an Islamic Context: Some Points of Contrast with Western Theories   A. Smirnov

It is the difference in the ways of seeing "obvious things" that creates cultural diversity. With this in mind, the fundamental ideas behind the notion of justice in classical Islamic thought are examined, such as the nature of truth and the relation of "things" to time and space, and the meaning of the "law" that follows from these ideas. Certain features of Islamic justice (e.g., latitude in making judicial and legislative decisions) are treated as natural and even logical consequences of these fundamental ideas.

INDEXES AND ABSTRACTS

There are serial publications which themselves offer a way to find material in non-law journals, for example, *International Political Science Abstracts*. This contains short summaries of journal articles divided by broad topic, such as Governmental and administrative institutions, Political process, International relations. There is also an index which is usually the best place to begin. See extracts below:

From the Index

```
Hong Kong
    1993, public opinion, gender differences:
      1926
    democratization, and economic growth :
      2330
    elite, pro-China : 1853
    public opinion, 1993, gender differences:
      1926
    -China : 2195
    1997- : 2103
    Hong Kong elite : 1853
House of Commons see UK, House of Commons
House of Representatives, USA see USA,
    House of Representatives
Housing policy, USA, federalism, and local
    government : 1592
Human nature, psychology : 1322
Human rights : 1423
    foreign aid, USA : 2213
    foreign policy : 1439
    international protection : 2025
    international treaties, reservations :
      1981
    self-ownership : 1346
    treaties : 2061
    UN : 2029
    Special Rapporteur on Former Yugo-
      slavia : 2004
Canada
    Charter of Rights : 1648
    discourse : 1656
China : 1629
```

46 refers to the volume, and the other number is that of the paragraph.

46.2103 CHUNG Jae Ho ; LO Shiu-hing — **Beijing's relations with the Hong Kong special administrative region : an inferential framework for the post-1997 arrangement.** *Pacific Affairs* 68 (2), Summer 95 : 167-186.

This article explores the post-1997 relationships between Beijing and the Hong Kong Special Administrative Region from a central-local relations perspective. At the same time, inferences are made from the trends emerging from China's current dealing with Hong Kong during the transition period. The article posits an inferential framework adopting four areas of interaction : planning and co-ordination, fiscal arrangements, personnel management and policy implementation. It concludes that the transition and post-transition arrangements can be viewed as a gradual and incremental process of learning and mutual adaptation by both sides. Moreover, administrative decentralization in China will coexist with Beijing's penetrative capacity in exerting political control over Hong Kong. Yet, Beijing will continue to selectively allow autonomy of post-1997 Hong Kong as long as the expanded autonomy does not amount to producing a penetration crisis. [R]

46.1629 LIU Binyan — **The expansion of personal freedom in China.** *Asian Perspective* 19 (1), Spring-Summer 95 : 151-161.

At present, the actual degree of freedom enjoyed by the Chinese people cannot be judged by the regime's arbitrary attitude towards liberalization. Since 1981, Deng Xiaoping has not been willing to make political and ideological compromises. Yet, in 1986, and in 1988-1989, there was an obvious expansion of freedom in China's press, art, and popular expression that Deng and the conservative officials then in charge of the propaganda machine of the Communist Party were helpless to prevent. In a country ruled by people and inconsistenly by law, the political attitude of a departmental head or regional official is usually more determinant of the political atmosphere than the center's policies and directives, as the ruling mechanism no longer runs smoothly. [See *Abstr.* 1657]

There are many electronic indexes and abstracts in disciplines in which you might well find material relevant to law study. Examples are *Sociofile* which has abstracts of articles in the social sciences, including some on criminology and criminal justice more generally, *International Political Science Abstracts* and the *Philosophers' Index* — self explanatory! The last could well be a good source of material on legal theory. There are also publications with full text of articles, for example the massive *Business Periodicals on Disc* (BPO) some of which will have relevance to law.

SELF-STUDY QUESTIONS

☺ Ten minutes.

1. What is an abstract?

2. What are the disadvantages of using a published bibliography?

3. Why should you be wary of using writing by non-lawyers that simply discusses what the law is?

4. What are the positive reasons for using non-legal materials when writing a law essay?

5. Where are the historical public documents which are open to the Hong Kong public kept?

Some suggestion on non-legal materials that can relate to the topic 'Corruption' (refer to p. 152 of Unit 11).

Corruption: You might want to discuss culture and corruption (are certain sorts of gift-giving more acceptable in some cultures, which might involve **anthropological** writing, or even **historical**). Possibly **psychological** — why is it that people want to give gifts? The **sociology** and **politics** of corruption are obvious possible angles. How about **economics** — perhaps someone has written on the economic costs (or even benefits) of what we think of as corruption.

Unit 18 Electronic Sources

OBJECTIVES

Objectives

Substitute:

By the end of this Unit you will:

- have a clearer idea of what resources are available through the Internet, including the Hong Kong Bilingual Laws Information Service (BLIS), and on LEXIS
- know some search techniques for simple searches
- have practised finding material on BLIS

☺ You could read the material in a thoughtful way in an hour, but might need an extra 30 minutes for a search on BLIS if you have not done one before.

E arlier Units have introduced you to the electronic sources which you are most likely to want to use as a student. The purpose of this Unit is to put together information about some of the major ways of getting information electronically. All the resources discussed here can be used for more than one type of material, that is, they may be used to find more than one of the following: cases, legislation, journal articles or references, other information. Earlier you have encountered individual aspects of some of these resources, notably BLIS, and a little information about Internet resources. You have also been introduced to some of the more one-dimensional resources, that is those which contain just cases or statutes, etc.

➤ This Unit presupposes that you have read the introductory material on electronic resources contained in Unit 11. If you have not done so, I suggest you do it **now**!

The first item is BLIS. Individual exercises using this resource have been suggested in Units 6, 7 and 10. However, here is a guide which brings all the necessary information together.

AN INTRODUCTION TO BLIS (BILINGUAL LAWS INFORMATION SERVICE)

⊘ Allow at least half an hour if this is your first experience of BLIS!

• Here are a few elementary searches:

1. If you know the number of the Ordinance you want, you may simply fill in its number in the Chapter row box (click on the ○ next to Ordinances and Subsidiary Legislation if you want both) and click | View Now |

    You will probably find you see a list of Ordinances which begin *approximately* with the one you want! ➤ This works especially badly towards the end of the list. I wanted a list of all "national laws" (see p. 146) but was quite unable to produce anything by typing 1553 (the Basic Law) in the box. Even typing 1000 did not work. When I (in desperation) typed 545 the list of laws began with one over 1000! Eventually by clicking repeatedly on "Next List" I got to the national laws.

2. Click on the blue arrow pointing to the Ordinance you want. If you have clicked Ordinances and Subsidiary Legislation you will now see a list of titles of that Ordinance and its Subsidiary Legislation. Click on the blue arrow next to the one you want to see more of, and you will see a list of sections/regulations. For example, if you wanted the Marine Fish Culture Ordinance you would see these screens (only parts of screens shown) :

➤	Chapter 352 PARTITION
➤	Chapter 353 MARINE FISH CULTURE
➤	Chapter 354 WASTE DISPOSAL
➤	Chapter 355 PYRAMID SELLING PROHIBITION

    After clicking on the blue arrow next to Cap 353 you would see:

➤	Chapter 352 PARTITION

    ▼ Chapter 353 MARINE FISH CULTURE
    - ➤ CAP 353 MARINE FISH CULTURE
    - ➤ CAP 353A MARINE FISH CULTURE
    - ➤ CAP 353B FISH CULTURE ZONE (DESIGNATION)
    - ➤ Chapter 354 WASTE DISPOSAL

Note: this arrow ▼ indicates that this item has been expanded, and should be clicked to remove the items below it and leave just the general heading of Cap 353.

And after clicking on the blue arrow next to 353A you would see:

▼ CAP 353 MARINE FISH CULTURE
   ▼ CAP 353A MARINE FISH CULTURE
   Cap 353A Empowering section   30/06/1997
   Cap 353A reg 1 Citation   30/06/1997
   Cap 353A reg 2 Demarcation of fish culture zone boundaries   30/06/1997
   Cap 353A reg 3 Applications for licences and permits   30/06/1997
   Cap 353A reg 4 Period of licences and permits and renewal thereof   30/06/1997
   Cap 353A reg 5 Mooring and anchoring of rafts   30/06/1997
   Cap 353A reg 6 Structures on rafts   30/06/1997
   Cap 353A reg 7 Marking and lighting of rafts and impoundments   30/06/1997
   Cap 353A reg 8 Inspection of rafts and impoundments   30/06/1997
   Cap 353A reg 9 (Repealed)

Note: all the dates given are 30 June 1997 (i.e. law in force immediately prior to the Handover) unless they have been later amended or introduced.

After clicking on reg 6 you would see something like this:

| Previous section of enactment | Next section of enactment | Switch language | Back to list of law |

Section of Enactment

| Chapter: | 353A | Title: | MARINE FISH: | Gazette Number |
| Regulation : | 6 | Heading : | Structures on rafts | Version Date: | 30/06/1997 |

(1) Except with the written permission of the Director, no licensee or permittee shall erect, or permit to be erected, any structure on a raft.

(2) The Director shall specify in the permission granted for the purposes of paragraph (1) the dimensions of the structure permitted and any conditions subject to which the permission is granted.

If you need to go beyond the last regulation, it seems you need to click on "Next Section" — there is no button for "next 25 sections" or something of the sort. However, see more advanced searches below.

3. If you want to search for a phrase in enactments, decide first whether you want Ordinances, subsidiary legislation or both — and ➤ don't forget to click on "View Now". Then you may click (see boxes at top of screen) on Simple Search or Advanced Search. I tried Simple, using "Waste" asking for synonyms, and asking for 25 hits. This was the result:

´M ¤ UCᵃᵒµ²ᵃG: waste

25¥÷¤ å¥ó²Å/X·j´M±ø¥ó

	Version Date
Cap 354 s 33 Regulations	30/06/1997
Cap 354 s 20B Permit required for the export of waste from Hong Kong	30/06/1997
Cap 354A reg 2 Interpretation	30/06/1997
Cap 354 s 20I Interpretation and application	30/06/1997
Cap 354 sched 6	30/06/1997
Cap 354 s 20A Permit required for the import of waste into Hong Kong	30/06/1997
Cap 354 sched 7	30/06/1997
Cap 354C s 2 Interpretation	30/06/1997
Cap 354 s 2 Interpretation	30/06/1997
Cap 132BJ bylaw 18 Duty of owner of waste chute	30/06/1997
Cap 354J s 2 Interpretation	30/06/1997
Cap 132BK bylaw 18 Duty of owner of waste chute	30/06/1997

Note: the hieroglyphics at the top represent Chinese characters.

A simple search can be a boolean one, not just one word like my example.

How about an advanced search? You have several possibilities:

Search for section(s) or enactment(s) this is obviously a better method for finding the text of a specific section in a specific enactment if you know what you are looking for.

Search for word(s) permits boolean searches (and, or, near, in same sentence, in same paragraph) case sensitive or not.

Search for word(s) in definition(s) a good way to find out whether a particular term has been defined in another Ordinance — the first time Hong Kong has had words and phrases *statutorily* defined! Note: it finds not only words actually defined, but all words used in definitions.

Search for internal cross reference: references within a statute ➤ but this does not seem to work well (perhaps it searches for any instance of the number you enter — so if you ask for section 5 it finds other sections that refer to Cap. 5!)

Search for external reference references in one statute to another. However, it does not seem to include references to foreign statutes. ➤ The same problem occurs here as with the internal cross-reference. If you search for Cap. 1, for example, you will find all sorts of sections referring to various section 1s or sub-section 1s!

Version Dates

BLIS's base date is 30 June 1997. Any new legislation since that date of course cannot have a version dated 30 June 1997! However, if any piece of legislation has been or is amended since that date, BLIS preserves both the old and the new versions. So if you have a client who committed a crime you can check what the law was on that date.

To make use of this facility you must be careful to click on the Current and Past versions button and then "View Now".

Then you must use an "Advanced Search", specifically "Search for Law as at a specified date." It is also possible to search for all version of a law between two dates: "Search for Law between a range of dates"

➤ When making an Advanced Search you may ask for various maximum "hits". The smallest number is 10 and the largest 4999. Of course the more hits you ask for the longer it takes to list the results. But if you do not ask for more than there turn out to be, you cannot know how many hits there are. I redid the "waste" search asking for 4999 hits. There turned out to be 415. If I had asked for any number fewer than 415 how would I have known how many there were? There is no indication of total hits; I assume the program stops when it has found the number you asked for regardless of the total possible hits. Moral is — ask for a lot.

Printing

If you are using an ordinary browser you can print or download sections of the Ordinances. The formatting will be untidy, and it is much more satisfactory to use the Lotus Notes software.

➤ There are fuller and helpful notes on the various types of search, as well as on using Lotus Notes at the home page of BLIS itself.

LAW ON THE WEB

To tell you anything about looking for law on the Internet is like trying to hit a moving target. New sites are constantly being created, and other disappear or cease to be kept up-to-date. These notes just pull together a few pieces of information, as things are as I write.

Getting Started

1. I suggest that you start through the 'home page' of one of the Law Faculties in the Hong Kong, or the home page of the Library. Check out the various possibilities (the City U and HKU Law Faculties and their libraries). Identify which of them seems to have the most useful list of other Internet law resources. In the box below insert the url of this Website.

Institution	url

2. Whichever the page you decide to make your starting point you can click on hypertext links to move to other Web sites. Some of those will be pages elsewhere in the world which themselves link to many other sites.

What Will You Find on the Web?

Broadly you might divide the suppliers of information on the Web into the following categories:

*   government bodies
*   academic institutions
*   those for whom this is a business venture — including solicitors' firms
*   individuals
*   others: non-governmental organizations, professional associations, etc.

The sorts of information which you may find are so varied that they are impossible to catalogue fully (and this is even without going outside law-related sites to those where you will find recipes, travel information, pictures and so on). However, you might be interested in the following, mainly:

*   cases
*   legislation
*   electronic journals
*   teaching materials (you can see for example the materials which are used at other law schools for some of the courses you are doing)

Searching the Net

There are a number of methods of finding what exists on the Net. You will find it is possible to get to these from your University home page. For example there are Yahoo.com, Infoseek and Alta Vista. New ones keep appearing. These will search the Internet for types of information. ➤ If you just put in 'law' you will come up with thousands! Be more specific. Yahoo also has a classified list of Internet sites worldwide. Two major law-specific sites are Law Crawler (**<http://lawcrawler.findlaw.com>**) and Internet Legal Resource Guide (**<http://www.ilrg.com>**).

Moving Around

You move from one document to another by clicking on the highlighted word(s) or symbol (known as a hypertext link).

It is sometimes quicker to go direct to the site you want by typing in the url in the space at the top of the screen (the url will begin http:// and very often http://www which will already be on the screen as it is part of the home page you start on, so you need only type in the rest.

Many resources on the Net are now searchable; you may be able to type in a word or words that you would like to look for. How complex the search facilities are varies, but they are getting more sophisticated all the time and you can sometimes do **BOOLEAN SEARCHES**.

Keeping What You Find

It is possible to print the documents you find or save them to disk. You may find your library does not allow you to do the former — perhaps because some of the documents are so enormous you will be there for a long time using up the paper! You can download onto a disk.

How Useful Is the Internet?

The potential of this form of communication is enormous. However, the legal resources available so far are somewhat limited. The Australian material could be useful, but on the whole as an undergraduate student you are likely to find what you want within the

A Few Terms

The Internet: a world-wide network of computer networks.

World Wide Web: 'documents' on computers all over the world, linked through the Internet in such a way that you can move from one to another simply by clicking on a highlighted word or symbol. The documents themselves may be words, or video, or sound, or combinations.

Netscape: one of the programmes which enables you to read the documents on the Web. There are several others, all of which work on similar principles, such as Microsoft Internet Explorer. They are known as 'browsers'.

url: uniform resource locator — the 'address' which every Website has.

confines of your library. This is not to discourage you, but you should be warned that surfing the Net can be very time-consuming and often out of proportion to the benefits you will gain. However, some students have found useful materials especially for essays for which they need to do their own research.

Further reading: there are now some books about law on the Internet and you should perhaps check whether your library has them if you are serious about wanting to use the Net.

LEXIS

LEXIS is an On-line database for which the information is stored in a computer in Dayton, Ohio. It is a commercial database and is expensive. On the whole undergraduate students will rarely want to use it, and with other forms of electronic database becoming available it is likely to be less used outside the USA. However, it may be a selling point with solicitors that you have some familiarity with it when you are looking for a job! US law students, who have the benefit of free access (catch them young!) are apparently reluctant to use anything else! The fact is that it remains a very effective research tool, even for non-US material. Cases are put into the database very quickly, weeks before they are reported, and some UK cases that are there are never reported.

Hong Kong Cases is available on LEXIS, but this is more likely to be of use to those outside Hong Kong.

The main use of LEXIS is for US materials, especially cases, though it does have full text of many law journals too. (WestLaw, another US On-line service, has more journals in full text.)

Since LEXIS is so expensive, you will only be able to use it, if at all, under instruction. You should then receive some fuller information than is given here, though what is here would enable you to carry out a simple search.

The Steps for an Elementary LEXIS Search, and a Few More Sophisticated Ideas

1. You sign in with an ID (when working as a lawyer you will also have to identify the client for whom you are doing the search).

2. You will then see a screen full of the names of 'Libraries', for example ENGGEN (short for English General) which includes English cases, legislation and a very few journals.

3. Type in the name of the library you want.

4. You will then see a list of files within the library, e.g. Cases.

5. Type in the name of the file you want.

6. You will then be invited to type in your search.

    - You can do a Boolean Search (one word **and** another, or one word **or** another).
    - You can ask for one word near another, e.g. construction w/10 safety — 'construction' within 10 words of the word 'safety'.
    - You can specify a time period e.g.:
      Date Is 7/8/96 **or**
      Date Is 1995   **or**
      Date aft April 1 1994 **and** Date bef Nov 1 1995

7. You will then be told how many documents corresponding to your search have been found.

8. You may chose to see:
    - a list of the documents with their citations **or**
    - the complete documents **or**
    - the words you have asked for surrounded by a few words of context so you can judge if this is a document you are interested in

    To achieve this you must specify which you want. There may be a template on the computer indicating which function key to press. Or you can type .ci or .fu or .kw (which stand for cite, full and kwik (quick!) respectively.

9. If there are too many documents you may modify your search by adding some other requirement. Press the key indicated or type .mo.

10. There is a good deal to be said for using cite (.ci) if you think the documents will be available to you in print form in your library. You can just note the citations and save money by going to the printed version.

11. You can move from document to document by pressing the appropriate key or typing .nd. Pressing return (↵) will take you from page to page.

12. If you know the citation of a case, for example, you can go straight there by using the LEXSEE service. While any screen is visible you can type in LEXSEE 159 F.2d 169, for examples. This is the citation of *United States v Carroll Towing Co.*, a case referred to in some English tort books. The result is very quick ➤ and cheaper than going to the right Library and File and asking for Carroll and Towing. ➤ This only works for US cases.

13. There is a similar service for US statutes called LEXSTAT.

14. You can use LEXIS as a citator. You can use LEXCITE to find all cases which cite a case, and journal articles about it. Again this is available for US materials.

15. You should train yourself to be an efficient (and therefore less expensive) searcher. Always know just what you are looking for. Check with the paper information so you know which Library and File you will need. You can use the short cut technique, which means that from the library screen you can type something like:

enggen;cases;contributor! w/5 negligen! and dr*nk! and drive!;.ci

which would mean: English General library, cases file, and the search is contributory or contributorily within five words of negligent or negligently or negligence, and drink or drinker or drunk or drunken, and drive or driver or driven, and that you then want to see the results in CITE format — a list of citations.

Actually this would probably produce a very large number of results, but you see the idea.

Further Reading

There is a good deal of information in Holborn *Butterworths Legal Research Guide*; US oriented but very thorough is McKnight *The Lexis Companion: A Concise Guide to Effective Searching* (Reading, Mass.: Addison-Wesley, 1995).

Dayal, S. *LDL Online — Laying Down the Law: Computer Assisted Legal Research* (Sydney: Butterworths, 1996).

Unit 19 How to Cite, Quote and Present Your Material

OBJECTIVES

By the end of this Unit you will:

* know the correct way to refer to all the various types of legal material which you have learned to use and find in the earlier Units
* understand why this is important
* have given some thought to the habits and practices which you need to develop in order to be able to ensure you can cite correctly without frustration
* be able to present a piece of writing such as an essay in a way which looks professional

☺ Only about 30 minutes to read, but you will need to refer to this Unit when writing essays etc.

You have collected your material for an essay or a moot brief, and you sit down to write it. How do you refer to the material in a neat and clear way so that your reader will know where to find it? The art of referring is called 'citing'. In the United States a great deal of effort goes into learning how to do this correctly. You can find in a library here what is known as the Blue Book, which is the bible (it is almost as thick as the Bible!) on how to cite. In the Hong Kong/English system things are less complex, and rather less rigid. However, this Unit will suggest what might be described as 'best practice' — use it and you will never be accused of giving too little information!

Why does it matter? I would suggest a number of reasons:

* It is professionally correct practice. This may sound like observing a ritual for the sake of it! But when you are young in any profession you are likely to be judged by your seniors to some extent on first impression. And something that will be noticed very soon is incorrect ways of citing things. Why irritate someone whom you should be seeking to impress? If you should be writing for certain academic purposes (such as a thesis for a postgraduate degree or an article for publication) you may find that you fail (your thesis

must be resubmitted or your article will not be published) unless you have done this type of thing properly.

- It is a courtesy to your reader to make it clear where you have obtained your material so that the reader can also find it.

- It is actually something in your favour when you are, for example, writing an essay, to be able to show the range of sources you have used.

- To fail to give proper credit to the other authors whose work you have read and made use of is a form of dishonesty and at worst is plagiarism.

Plagiarism

Plagiarism is the practice of using or copying someone else's ideas or work and pretending that you thought of it or created it.' — *BBC English Dictionary*.

So it is plagiarism to take another person's **words** without acknowledgement. It is also plagiarism to take someone else's **ideas** without acknowledgement.

Why does it matter? (After all, you may feel that someone else's words or ideas are better than your own!)

- If you are using someone else's words it is very likely that you are not really thinking thoroughly about their ideas. You only really learn by thinking.

- In the context of education where you write to be evaluated, it is very difficult for the evaluator to know how much you understand when you do not use your own words. The reader who realizes that you are not using your own words may be tempted to assume that you are using another person's words to conceal your own lack of understanding. In other words, plagiarizing may actually be underselling yourself!

- It is dishonest. You may not mean to mislead, but the truth is that you do so. You are putting forward as your own, ideas or words which are not your own. How would you feel if someone copied your essay and did not bother to do their own work? It is no different if you copy from a textbook, or an article in a journal, or anywhere.

(continued)

- The function of education is not just to get a degree! You are being educated for the rest of your life. In life, and work, you are expected to have your own ideas, and to recognize and acknowledge when you are using other people's ideas.

Why do people plagiarize?

Students interviewed in a study in Singapore* suggested that the temptation to plagiarize might arise because of:

- inadequate understanding of what they are reading

- poor time management

- poor note-taking

(* 'Where is my citation? Embarrassingly, I have lost the original!' Keep your notes safely!)

To this one might add some other suggestions:

- Not reading enough material: If you have only read one view on a particular topic it may be difficult to see other approaches, and you may be more tempted to use that one person's views. Also, reading different views is more likely to stimulate your own ideas. Anyway, at the undergraduate level one is not necessarily expected to have many ideas of one's own! One of the things you are learning is to make intelligent use of other people's ideas. If you have read only one person's work, it is tempting to conceal that fact by not giving due acknowledgement. If one has read quite a lot of material there is a certain pride in citing them so that one's readers know how diligent one has been!

- Lack of confidence in one's own command of the language: Even if you understand what you are reading you may feel that you don't know how to say it in any other way. The better your English the less of a problem this will be. Again, if you read more material on the same subject you will find other ways of talking about the same subject matter, and develop your own way of doing so.

(continued)

Some suggestions

1. Plan your time carefully so that you do not end up with too little time.

2. Think about your project so that you can find enough material to avoid the temptation to plagiarize.

3. Take notes in a way which involves **thinking** about what you are reading. Do not simply copy out great chunks of what you read (if you do you may be tempted to copy them out again into your essay!) Also, this temptation will be there if you simply photocopy. It is better to take notes than to photocopy (but that is a counsel of perfection!)

4. If you do take notes, make sure you take down the correct reference so that you can acknowledge properly, or you may again be tempted not to give credit because you can't remember where the material comes from!

5. When you write, do so without someone else's words in front of you. Make a plan of your answer in note form and write from that. If you have the eloquent words of someone else in front of you, it is often very difficult to have the courage to use your own ordinary words.

6. Be punctilious in putting quotation marks around exactly quoted words and phrases in your essays.

7. Be punctilious in giving citations for the sources of your quotations and of your ideas.

FOOTNOTE REFERENCE

In legal writing the form is usually to put a number and then the footnote at the bottom of the page or the end of the chapter or book, etc.

Books:
Wesley-Smith, Peter, *An Introduction to the Hong Kong Legal System* (Hong Kong: Oxford University Press, 1987).

Chapters in edited books:
Chen, Albert H.Y., 'Justice After 1997' in Traver, H. and Vagg, J., *Crime and Justice in Hong Kong* (Hong Kong: Oxford University Press, 1991) 172.

Article:
Jayawickrama, Nihal, 'Human Rights in the Draft Basic Law — A Critique' (1988) 18 HKLJ 370.

In a student essay there is no objection to the use of the form more often used in social science writing (see the extract from Duff et al. *Juries: A Hong Kong Perspective* below).

> In a more recent British study, Baldwin and McConville (1979) found a slightly higher proportion of jury verdicts were questioned by other courtroom participants. They could not categorize a significant proportion of those cases where the professionals disagreed with the verdict of the jury as being the result of the jury's application of different values to the case. In fact, they could identify no common factor to explain these cases (see Baldwin and McConville, 1979, Chapter 4). Significantly, they also found that there were a substantial number of convictions by the jury with which the legal professionals disagreed. In several cases, this was thought to be the result of racial prejudice by the jury but, more commonly, the explanation was thought to lie in the failure of the jury to understand the proceedings satisfactorily (see Baldwin and McConville, 1979, Chapter 5).

This refers to the bibliography at the end of the book, in which entries appear thus:

Baldwin J. and M. McConville, *Jury Trials* Oxford: OUP, 1979.

➤ Note: this requires that there be one list of references at the end in **rigidly alphabetical order**. It is suitable only for giving references and not for additional material contained in footnotes.

Referring to Pages

It is not necessary in footnotes and other sorts of references to give the end numbers of articles.

➤ You should give the page on which an article or a chapter in a book starts. And you should also give the precise page on which a quotation, or an idea referred to, is to be found. You may put 'p' for 'page' before the number; it is also acceptable when identifying the page simply to put start page of an article chapter or case, followed by the number of the quotation. To take the two of the items given as examples above:

Italics or <u>Underlining</u>?

The tradition is to underline names of books and names of cases in manuscript or typescript. You will have noticed that in books both of these are usually printed in *italics*. The convention is that underlining indicates to the printer that italics should be used. Now that even most students have access to word processors which can produce italics, there is no reason why you should not do this. It does not matter but, as always, be consistent.

Books:

Wesley-Smith, Peter, *An Introduction to the Hong Kong Legal System* (Hong Kong: Oxford University Press, 1987), p. 100. This refers your reader to p. 100 in the book.

Chapters in edited books:

Chen, Albert H.Y., 'Justice After 1997' in Traver, H. and Vagg, J., *Crime and Justice in Hong Kong* (Hong Kong: Oxford University Press, 1991) at p. 180. This indicates that p. 180 is not the beginning of the chapter by Chen, but the precise place within that chapter to which you are making reference.

Article:

Jayawickrama, Nihal, 'Human Rights in the Draft Basic Law: A Critique' (1988) 18 HKLJ 370, 375. This indicates that the article begins on p. 370, but you are particularly referring your reader to p. 375.

References within references:

In most circumstances you should read and cite original sources. Sometimes, however, the truth is that you are using a reference to material which you have found in another person's writing. Correct practice requires that you acknowledge this, rather than give the impression that you have found for yourself, and read, material which you have only read about in someone else's work. Indeed, even if you have gone to the original, it may still be appropriate to indicate that the passage you are relying on was identified by the 'intermediate author'. The correct form would be to give the fullest information you have about original item, and then say 'as quoted in' (or 'as cited in' if the intermediate author does not use the original author's actual words) and then give the full information about the intermediate source. For example:

> Julius Stone described the per incuriam doctrine as 'confusingly amorphous'.[1]
>
> ---
>
> 1   *Precedent and Law: Dynamics of Common Law Growth* (Sydney: Butterworths, 1985) 72, quoted in Wesley-Smith, *The Sources of Hong Kong Law* (Hong Kong: Hong Kong University Press, 1994) 62n.

Referring to Cases

You should observe the conventions used in the particular jurisdiction from which a case comes. In Hong Kong and England you should be sure to use the correct bracket (see Unit 6). In the US the system is slightly different — the date comes in round brackets at the end. ➤ If in doubt you will usually find at the beginning of a volume of law reports something which tells you the correct way to cite cases in it.

Unreported judgments: I recommend that you give **all** the following pieces of information for Hong Kong unreported judgments:

- name
- reference number
- date of judgment

If you took it off INFOLAW you might include that fact in brackets. I have not seen this done, but it would seem to be a helpful convention to develop.

Cases off LEXIS: It would be helpful, if the cases are unreported, to include: LEXIS, Library name, file name, e.g. LEXIS Enggen Cases. If they are Hong Kong cases, I would still recommend the use of the other information suggested above.

Legislation

In Hong Kong you should give the Cap number (in the Laws of Hong Kong for statutes which have been reprinted, and Cap ?? of ???? if it is still in the Gazette). In the UK this is unnecessary — give the date for modern legislation.

For subsidiary legislation: in Hong Kong give the Legal Notice number (LN 38 of 1996) and in the UK the SI number (SI 12/1996).

Official Publications

In Hong Kong official publications do not have a numbering system. ➤ So be careful to give the full information so far as you have it, including the Department which produced it and the date.

In the UK many publications have Command numbers. Be sure to include these; sometimes this number is used as an indexing tool. There may be other numbering systems, for example HC ??? which means a House of Common Paper.

For Law Reform Commission Papers (Law Commission in UK) give the number of the report (the number of the topic in Hong Kong) or of the working paper, as well as the title and the year of publication.

Legislative Proceedings

In Hong Kong refer to these as 'Proceedings of the Legislative Council' with date and page. In UK give the column number, and refer to them as HC or HL Official Proceedings (House of Commons or House of Lords).

6   *Peter Wesley-Smith*

Article 8 of the Basic Law provides that the 'laws previously in force in Hong Kong', including the common law, 'shall be maintained' in the SAR. The common law previously in force is the common law of England[5] as ultimately determined by the House of Lords. Thus the Basic Law appears to sanction the continuing binding effect of House of Lords decisions in Hong Kong. And since the law previously in force includes the rule of precedent that Privy Council decisions, whatever their provenance, must be followed in the territory, the Basic Law appears to sanction the continued binding effect of Privy Council decisions as well.

To appreciate the reasoning process followed here it is necessary to examine several doctrines of law or theory upon which the courts have relied.

Curial hierarchy and stare decisis

Fundamental to the doctrine of binding precedent is the rule that a court is bound by decisions of a court above it in the hierarchy. Unless a higher court's decision on a material issue is distinguishable, or has been abrogated by statute, or has been subsequently overruled or not followed by itself or a yet higher court, it may not be departed from. This of course depends on the existence of a clear hierarchy of courts and a retrieval system by which previous decisions can be known. The Judicial Committee of the Privy Council is at the apex of the structure of the Hong Kong court system, being the final appellate court for Hong Kong litigants, and its decisions are usually reported and thus available. When hearing an appeal from Hong Kong it is a Hong Kong court[6] and its decisions in that capacity bind all other courts in the Hong Kong curial hierarchy.

This rule has never been doubted[7] and was the principal reason why the High Court of Australia declined to continue to be bound by Privy Council decisions once appeals to the Privy Council from that court were abolished: 'The law of precedent depends upon the the existence of a hierarchy of courts and now there is no longer a hierarchy. Therefore the strict law on precedent cannot be applied. Therefore strictly the decisions of the Privy Council are no longer binding on this Court.'[8] Whether it is considered a rule of law, or bears some other label such as a

---

[5]   Interpretation and General Clauses Ordinance (cap 1. LHK 1989 ed), s 3.

[6]   See Kenneth Roberts-Wray, *Commonwealth and Colonial Law* (London: Stevens, 1966), 457 (citing *Woolworths [NZ] v Wynne* [1952] NZLR 496, 523, *Hull v M'Kenna's Journal* [1926] IR 402, 403–4, and *British Coal Corporation v R* [1935] AC 500, 521–2) and Bartholomew in (1952) 1 ICLQ 392, 394–5. In *Hull* the Privy Council sat as 'an Imperial Court which represents the Empire, and not any particular part of it', but this 'metaphysical' notion was discarded in *Ibralebbe v R* [1964] AC 900 (see A R Blackshield, *The Abolition of Privy Council Appeals: Judicial Responsibility and the 'Law for Australia'* [Adelaide: Adelaide Law Review Association. 1978], 51–2).

[7]   See, for example, *Favelle Mort Ltd v Murray* (1975–6) 133 CLR 580, 591: 'The ultimate foundation of precedent which thus binds a court is that a court or tribunal higher in the hierarchy of the same juristic system, and thus able to reverse the lower court's judgment, has laid down that principle as part of the relevant law.'

[8]   *Viro v R* (1976–8) 141 CLR 88, 151; see also 93, 129, 130, 132, 174.

Abbreviations

Most series of law reports have their own abbreviations. If the one you cite is well known then you should use the abbreviation. But if it is not there are two approaches: one is to use the abbreviation and then have a list of abbreviations attached to your essay or article etc. (if you have a lot of unusual ones this might be a good idea). But for just one or two unusual ones, your reader might simply overlook your short list. Why not just spell out the full name of any unusual law report or journal? This may not be entirely orthodox, but it is helpful and seems to me to be common sense.

On p. 292 is a page from Peter Wesley-Smith, 'The Common Law of England in the Special Administrative Region' in Wacks, ed., *Hong Kong, China and 1997: Essays in Legal Theory* (Hong Kong: HKU Press, 1993) 5, 10, which shows what good footnotes should look like, and includes most of the types of material mentioned above.

For Records from the Internet

> ### Style Sheet
>
> (Endorsed by the Alliance for Computers & Writing)
> WWW Sites (World Wide Web)
>
> Janice R. Walker (jwalker@chuma.cas.usf.edu)
> Department of English
> University of South Florida
>
> To cite files available for viewing or downloading via the World Wide Web, give the author's name (if known), the full title of the work in quotation marks, the title of the complete work if applicable in italics, the full http address, and the date of visit.
>
> Burka, Lauren P. 'A Hypertext History of Multi-User Dimensions'. *MUD History —* http://www.ccs.neu.edu/home/lpb/ mud-history.html (5 Dec. 1994).

For the legal context you might want to cite an article from an electronic journal, for example: Paliwala, Abdul, 'From Academic Tombstones to Living Bazaars: The Changing Shape of Law Reviews' 1 JILT 1966 — **http://ltc.warwick.ac.uk/elj/jilt/issue1/abdul/**.

Similarly if you want to cite an unreported case from a database on the Internet, for example: *Wynn v NSW Insurance Ministerial Corporation* F.C. 95/051 which was the first case listed on the Australasian Legal Information Institute's database for the High Court of

Australia when I was preparing this Unit. I would suggest that you give the title and reference number as above, plus the information — 'High Court of Australia: 21 December 1995', plus '**AustLii http://www.austlii.edu.au**' rather than the full address of the particular list.

Further Reading: French, *How to Cite Legal Authorities* (London: Blackstone, 1996).

QUOTING

You know you must not quote without putting the quotation in inverted commas. It is possible to present a quotation in a different way: by indenting it (that is by having the margins beside the quotation wider so it stands out clearly). It is good to do this if the quotation is rather long (say more than about four lines of text). You sometimes see such an indented quotation in inverted commas and sometimes not. There is no reason why I should impose my preference on you!

What I do urge on you is not to quote too much. As a guideline I would suggest you should only quote someone else's actual words if:

* the statement is particularly authoritative (such as the *ratio decidendi* of a case),
* it makes the point so neatly and clearly that, despite your best efforts (which you should make), you cannot think of any other way of making the point, **or**
* the statement is so elegant or amusing or beautiful that you really want to share it with your reader.

SELF-TEST QUESTIONS

☺ Five minutes.

1. Do you remember when you should use round brackets and when square ones?

2. Is it plagiarism to copy the essay of your classmate with her permission?

3. How should you cite a quotation from publication (or case) A which you actually found in publication B?

Appendix I   Law Libraries in Hong Kong

M any law firms have good libraries of their own. These notes relate only to what might be described as 'public' law libraries, in the sense that they are publicly funded.

- The City University of Hong Kong
- The University of Hong Kong
- The Supreme Court
- The Legal Department

The first two are open to the members of the University, to approved visitors and to members of other tertiary institutions in Hong Kong by the use of the appropriate card obtained from one's 'home' institution.

The Supreme Court Library is open to the judiciary (though judges also have small libraries in their own chambers) and to the legal profession, and access by members of the public has recently become easier.

The Legal Department Library is intended for the use of lawyers in the Department but is also open to others by agreement with the librarian.

Students are unlikely to have need of these latter two libraries and undergraduate students especially are likely to find everything they want in their home institution library, unless they are preparing for an esoteric topic for a moot, maybe!

FINDING OUT ABOUT HOLDINGS

The two University Libraries (and other tertiary institutions in Hong Kong, including the Chinese University of Hong Kong, the Polytechnic University of Hong Kong and the University of Science and Technology, all of which have some courses or research involving law) are linked electronically and one can peruse their library catalogues through computers in the libraries of any of the other institutions.

For serial publications, one can consult the *Union List of Hong Kong Serials*, which includes law reports as well as journals. This is inevitably not quite up-to-date, but is a good place to start. It lists journals alphabetically, and then indicates by abbreviations which libraries have holdings. All the libraries mentioned here are included.

Below are a few notes about each library indicating features that might be useful. Inevitably the holdings of the various libraries are the same in terms of their core collections, especially of Hong Kong and UK materials. Equally inevitably each library has some special features. A few of these are pointed out.

CITY UNIVERSITY

Organization: The Law Library occupies part of the Main University Library, though a separate suite.

Holdings: You will find some series of law reports here which are not in the other libraries. Also the holdings of journals will be different. A couple of special strengths of this library are:
• English legal history
• US journals on environmental law

Electronic material: World Wide Web stations in a main part of the library; CD-ROMs include Legal Journals Index, Index to Foreign Legal Periodicals, etc. LEXIS terminal in law library.

Classification: Library of Congress

UNIVERSITY OF HONG KONG

Organization: The Law Library is separate from the Main University Library and housed in the same building as the Law Faculty. There is also a sizeable collection of law books, and a few law-related periodicals in the Main Library, especially in the areas of constitutional law and construction law.

Holdings: Areas of special strength include:
• Human Rights (including law reports)
• Aviation Law

Electronic sources: World Wide Web access available from Law and Main Libraries; most of the CDs mentioned in this book; LEXIS and Westlaw to be available shortly (already available to library staff).

Classification:
*   Law Library: Moys
*   Main Library: Dewey Decimal

Classification Systems

In a small library it is possible to keep the books in alphabetical order of author, and that is the way you will usually find a fiction collection shelved. But it is usual in large libraries to keep the books on similar topics together. This has the advantage that having found one book on a topic, you are likely to find other books on the same topic close by. It helps the process of finding things by happy accident — a very important research technique (known by the delightful name of 'serendipity')! Each book will have a unique number or combination of letters and numbers which enables you to identify the right one.

There are three common classification systems used for law books, and all of them are found in Hong Kong! Many university libraries use what is called the Library of Congress system — used by the Library of the US Congress. This is the one found at City U. Different disciplines have different letters: all law books, identification numbers begin with K. The University of Hong Kong Law Library uses the **Moys system**. This was designed by a University Librarian in the UK before the Library of Congress had got to the letter K. It is designed to accommodate more easily books from a range of jurisdictions. It is actually quite different from the City U **Library of Congress system** though all law books' call numbers still begin with K. The University of Hong Kong Main Library classification system is not the Library of Congress one but the **Dewey decimal system**, so law books there have different identification marks from in the Law Library. The Dewey system used only numbers, except for the initial of the author's name. Law comes in the range 340-349. Thus we find that a book on the law of contract in Hong Kong by Carole Pedley Chiu is at KT5376 C559 in the HKU Law Library and at 346.202 C55 in the Main Library (in each case the C refers to the initial letter of the author's surname). In the City U Library the same book's call number is KYQ1370.C47.

SUPREME COURT

Holdings: The emphasis is naturally on works for the practice of law; thus it has fewer monographs than the university libraries. The main area of strength is:
*   law reports, including series from the UK not available elsewhere (many nominate reports), and also from other jurisdictions.

Electronic sources: A few CD-ROMs

Classification: Law reports and other primary materials by jurisdiction. The main oddity of this library is that the books and monographs (ie not law reports, journals, legislation) are organized alphabetically by order of author. Indeed, by the first three letters of the author's name only! And occasionally there is a book which is organized by title and not by name of author.

LEGAL DEPARTMENT

This is the smallest library among those discussed here. However, it does have holdings of some materials which might be difficult to find elsewhere, such as:

- UK Hansard in paper format
- Irish Reports
- law reports from a number of African countries (though not very up-to-date — strongest in the 1960s)

Classification: Library of Congress

Appendix II A Dictionary

Words in **CAPITAL LETTERS** like this are themselves are also entries in this Dictionary.

Act Used in the United Kingdom and a number of other countries but **not** in Hong Kong to refer to a piece of legislation made by the principal **LEGISLATURE** of the country, or sometimes of a State or Province.

Amend To change an existing piece of legislation.

Amendment Change in an existing piece of legislation.

Apply Used when referring to a **CASE**, which uses a rule laid down in a **STATUTE** or a previous case. It means the court followed the rule.

Assent The approval of the Head of State or equivalent required to complete the **ENACTMENT** process of a piece of legislation (the Governor, or Chief Executive, in Hong Kong, the Queen in England, the President in the US, etc.).

Authority has many meanings. The most specifically legal one is effectively the same as **PRECEDENT**.

Bill A draft piece of legislation in the form in which it is presented to the **LEGISLATURE**.

Binding precedent An earlier decision which a later court is obliged to follow — unless it can be **DISTINGUISHED**.

Boolean Search Used for searches of electronic resources including on-line library catalogues, LEXIS etc. The sort of search where one can ask for one word **and** another, one word **or** another, one word **but not** another. The technique may vary from one resource to another and is not available for all electronic resources.

Call number Used to refer to the individual combination of letters and numbers used in a classification system in a Library to indicate where the book is to be shelved.

Catchwords The words in a reported case, coming just after the title and dates of hearing which summarize in short words and phrases what the case was about, but before the statement of facts in the **HEADNOTE**. May be used as the basis for indexing the case.

Case Used in several senses (see Unit 4) — it may mean the dispute between parties which goes to court, and the record of the decision, as issued in written form by the court or as published in a **LAW REPORT**.

Casenote A shorter article in a law journal which discusses one (or occasionally more than one) recent **CASE**, usually putting it into context, and explaining its significance; may also be critical of the decision.

Citation The full reference to a source, especially used for the reference to a reported **CASE**.

Civil action This refers to a case which is not **CRIMINAL**. In other words, it means a situation in which an individual or body is taking another individual or body to court, not to seek punishment, but in order to get compensation or to get a situation put right; simplest examples would be an action for breach of contract or for a tort.

Coram Latin for 'before' or 'in front of' — used in law reports to indicate which judges were on the court.

Criminal charge The criminal law is that branch of the law which is concerned with the punishment of activities which the state (either through its **LEGISLATURE** or through its courts) has decided should be prohibited. In the Hong Kong system the formal accusation is known as a 'charge'.

Decree Used in some countries to refer to legislation made by undemocratic procedures; military regimes sometimes rule 'by Decree'; not used in Hong Kong.

Delegated Legislation Legislation made under the authority of a **STATUTE**.

Dewey Decimal System of classifying books in a library which uses figures — main classification before a decimal point and further figures after indicating sub-categories.

Distinguish Means that a court has decided not to follow the **PRECEDENT** laid down in a previous case, but not by saying the previous **CASE** was wrongly decided: the court shows how the earlier case is different from the one before it and therefore need not be followed.

Doctrine of Precedent A distinguishing feature of the common law — that courts will follow decisions in earlier cases which are similar. The earlier case or **PRECEDENT** may be **BINDING** on the later court, or it may be **PERSUASIVE**, in which case it does not have to be followed. It is another way of saying that the courts make law.

Enact To make a piece of legislation — used in the passing of **STATUTES** rather than of **SUBSIDIARY LEGISLATION**.

Enactment Synonym for **STATUTE**.

Force (to come into) To be given legal effect; a **STATUTE** will have this effect in Hong Kong when it is published in the **GAZETTE** — unless the statute itself provides for its being brought into force later.

Gazette In Hong Kong — the *Hong Kong Government Gazette* in which all official and some other notices must be published; supplements include Bills, Statutes and Legal Notices.

Hansard The official record of proceedings of the Legislative Council in Hong Kong (or of the UK Parliament). Originally the name of a printer of the UK Proceedings. The Official Title of Hansard in Hong Kong is *Proceedings of the Legislative Council*.

Headnote In a published law report: the section at the beginning which summarizes what the case was about and what it decided.

Keywords see **CATCHWORDS**.

Law In Hong Kong has no official meaning; used to mean the entire body of legal rules, or the abstract concept 'law'. In some countries it is used to refer to certain types of legislation — e.g. in Nigeria, during civilian Governments, is used to refer to statutes of the States rather than the National Government.

Law Report Published version of cases, usually in the form of a series of books. May appear frequently and then be bound at year's end into volumes.

Legal Notice Used in Hong Kong to refer to **DELEGATED LEGISLATION** as published in the **GAZETTE**.

Legislation From the Latin words 'law' and 'to propose'; actually means law-making output of those with the power to lay down the law. In modern usage also refers to judge-made law, in which case 'judicial legislation' (the entire phrase) will be used.

Legislator Member of the Legislative Council in Hong Kong (or **LEGISLATURE** elsewhere); used generally of such people, not only when they are legislating.

Legislature The constitutional body with the power to make law — Legco in Hong Kong.

Library of Congress (US Congress) — used to refer to system of book classification created in that Library, where each area of thought has a number (Law being K). Each title has a unique combination of letters and numbers to indicate its place on the shelves.

Moys, Elizabeth — Law Librarian who invented a classification system for law books, to fit into the **LIBRARY OF CONGRESS** overall system.

Obiter Latin: short for *obiter dictum* — a remark made by a judge which is not required for the decision.

Order in Council Made by the Monarch either in exercise of the Royal Prerogative or under the authority of a **STATUTE**.

Ordinance In Hong Kong used to refer to enactments of the Legislative Council. Word used by the UK to refer to legislation of colonial legislatures. Preserved in some countries for limited purposes, e.g. in India the President or State Governor has the power to make Ordinances of temporary effect when it is not practicable to hold a sitting of the legislature.

Overrule Used when one court decides that an earlier decision was wrong although relevant to the case in front of it. Can only be done by a court which is not **BOUND BY** the earlier decision, and is appropriate when the earlier case was decided in the same system and is now replaced by the new case. One would not say that the Hong Kong Court of Appeal overruled a decision of the Supreme Court of India because the Hong Kong case is not binding in Indian courts.

Per According to (or literally 'through') a court or a judge. Used most often in **LAW REPORTS**. It may refer to a statement made on behalf of the court, or by one judge; usually not used to refer to a statement which is part of the **RATIO DECIDENDI** of the decision. In the case of the remark of the court one would find the report says '*per curiam*' — through the court; if one judge it would say '*per* Yang CJ', etc.

Per incuriam Some courts are **BOUND BY** their own decisions. In such a situation, one of the few exceptions is if the earlier case was 'per incuriam', meaning in ignorance of a binding case or statute.

Persuasive authority Means that a case is not **BINDING** on the current court. This phrase can be used as a 'concrete' noun (referring to the earlier case) or more abstractly to refer to the quality of having authority, but not being binding. One could say that all decisions in the common law world are of persuasive authority; in reality the expression is often used either when a court wishes **not** to follow the earlier case, and wishes to emphasize that it is not bound to do so, or when the court wishes to follow an unusual case (from another country perhaps) and wishes to bolster the importance of the case by referring to its quality as of persuasive authority. Persuasiveness may vary according to the court, the judge or even the closeness of the earlier situation to the present one.

Precedent Used to refer to a case the legal reasoning of which is used as argument in a later case. See **DOCTRINE OF PRECEDENT**.

Primary materials or sources Used to refer to **LEGISLATION** and **CASES** in a library — the raw material of law study, rather than secondary material which is **about** the primary material.

Ratio decidendi Latin. Used to refer to the core element of the legal reasoning in a case which is essential for the decision of the case. Complex concept: see Unit 4 and books cited there.

Reading Presentation of a **BILL** to the **LEGISLATURE**; this happens three times for each Bill. It must be voted through on each occasion before it goes to the Governor for **ASSENT**.

Regulation Species of **DELEGATED LEGISLATION**.

Repeal Opposite of **ENACTMENT** — legislation is removed from the **STATUTE BOOK**; unmade, as it were.

Reverse Used if an appellate court decides that the lower court in the case before it was wrong. Not to be confused with **OVERRULE**, which refers to deciding that some quite different case was wrongly decided. Reversal may be on the basis of a wrong decision of fact or of law.

Rules Use of certain types of **DELEGATED LEGISLATION** — especially rules of court procedure made by the Chief Justice, for example.

Statute A piece of enacted law; in Hong Kong an **ORDINANCE**, in the UK an **ACT** of Parliament.

Statute Book Usually used in a slightly abstract sense to mean the entire body of legislation.

Statutory Instrument Use in the UK to refer to published **DELEGATED LEGISLATION**. Some delegated legislation is not so published.

Subsidiary Legislation See **DELEGATED LEGISLATION**.

Appendix III Abbreviations

Y ou will very soon see that it is not normal for references to cases to appear in a form which spells out the title of the report in full. The same is true of references to articles in law journals. They are usually abbreviated to a set of initials or shortened forms of the titles. Here is a list of some of the most important. You will find fuller lists in:

- Raistrick *Index to Legal Citations and Abbreviations*
- some of the legal dictionaries, notably: Osbornes *Concise Legal Dictionary*, Curzon *Concise Dictionary of Law*
- French *How to Cite Legal Authorities* (UK emphasis)

A.C.	Appeal Cases
A.J.C.L.	American Journal of Comparative Law
A.J.I.L.	American Journal of International Law
A.L.J.	Australian Law Journal
A.L.R.	American **or** Australian Law Reports
All E.R.	All England Law Reports
A.P.L.R.	Asia Pacific Law Review
B.C.C.	British Company Law Cases
B.C.L.C.	Butterworths Company Law Cases
B.J .Crim	British Journal of Criminology
B.J.I.B.& F.L.	Butterworths Journal of International Banking and Financial Law
B.L.R.	Building Law Reports
B.T.R.	British Tax Review
B.Y.I.L.	British Yearbook of International Law
Ch	Chancery Division
C.L.J.	Cambridge Law Journal
C.L.P.	Current Legal Problems
C.L.R.	Commonwealth Law Reports (Australia)
C.M.L.R.	Common Market Law Reports
C.M.L.Rev.	Common Market Law Review
Crim.L.R.	Criminal Law Review
D.L.R.	Dominion Law Reports
E.H.R.R.	European Human Rights Reports
E.R.	English Reports

F.L.R.	Federal Law Reports (Australia)
F.S.R.	Fleet Street Reports
Fam.	Family Division
H.K.C	Hong Kong Cases
H.K.C.L.R.	Hong Kong Criminal Law Reports
H.K.D.C.L.R.	Hong Kong District Court Law Reports
H.K.L.D.	Hong Kong Law Digest
H.K.L.J.	Hong Kong Law Journal
H.K.L.R.	Hong Kong Law Reports
H.K.L.Y.	Hong Kong Law Digest Yearbook
H.K.P.L.R.	Hong Kong Public Law Reports
I.C.J.	International Court of Justice. Reports of Judgments ...
I.C.L.Q.	International and Comparative Law Quarterly
I.C.R.	Industrial Cases Reports
I.L.M.	International Legal Materials
I.R.L.R.	Industrial Relations Law Reports
J.B.L.	Journal of Business Law
J.W.T.	Journal of World Trade
K.B.	King's Bench
L.C.P.	Law and Contemporary Problems
L.ED.	U.S. Supreme Court (Lawyers' Edition)
L.J.	Law Journal
L.M.C.L.Q.	Lloyd's Maritime and Commercial Law Quarterly
L.Q.R.	Law Quarterly Review
L.S.Gaz.	Law Society's Gazette (England)
L.T.	Law Times
Mal L.R.	Malay Law Review
M.L.J.	Malayan Law Journal
M.L.R.	Modern Law Review
O.J.L.S.	Oxford Journal of Legal Studies
P.	Probate
P.L.	Public Law
Q.B.	Queen's Bench
S.C.R.	Supreme Court Reports (several countries use the same abbreviation)
S.J.	Solicitors' Journal
S.T.C	Simon's Tax Cases
T.L.R.	Times Law Reports
W.L.R.	Weekly Law Reports
W.W.R.	Western Weekly Reports

Appendix IV Case Reference Numbers in Hong Kong

E very case started in the courts has a reference number. The number is prefaced by letters which indicate the court and the type of proceeding. Sometimes you will see the letters for the court omitted (you may see just A for action instead of HCA or PI for personal injury instead of HCPI, for example). Recent circulars from the judiciary have tidied up the system and clarified the situation.[1]

Each magistracy has its own two letter abbreviation: ES (Eastern) FL (Fanling) KT (Kwun Tong) NK (North Kowloon) SK (South Kowloon) SP (San Po Kong) TM (Tuen Mun) TW (Tsuen Wan) and WS (Western).

Many of these you will never see, at least while a student. Criminal cases at first instance are virtually never reported and decisions are not circulated (in the case of jury trial the decision is not reasoned, in the sense that no reasons are given by the jury).

The court letters are followed by a letter or letters indicating the type of proceeding — except in the case of the Labour Tribunal.

Here is a list of the full set of letters for the most important types of cases, plus a few that are interesting or new or which illustrate how the system works. Since you will still see older cases I have given the old and the new prefixes.

---

1   I am grateful to Professor Michael Wilkinson for providing this information.

Type of Case and Court	Old Prefix	New Prefix
Civil Appeal in CFA		FACV
Criminal Appeal in CFA		FACC
Miscellaneous Proceedings in CFA - Civil (used for applications for leave to appeal)		FAMV
Miscellaneous Proceedings in CFA - Criminal		FAMC
Civil Appeal in CA	Civ App	CACV
Criminal Appeal in CA	Cri App	CACC
Application for Review of Sentence in CA (under s. 81A of the Criminal Procedure Ordinance)	AR	CAAR
Secretary for Justice's Reference		CASJ
Reservation of Question of Law		CAQL
Attorney-General's Reference	AG's Reference	CACG
Civil Action in CFI	HCA	HCA
Administrative Law Proceedings	HCAL	HCAL
Admiralty Action	HCAJ	HCAJ
Commercial Action	HCCL	HCCL
Companies Winding Up	HCCWU	HCCW
Matrimonial Causes in CFI	HCDJ	HCMC
Miscellaneous Proceedings in CFI	HCMP	HCMP

Type of Case and Court	Old Prefix	New Prefix
Personal Injuries Actions in CFI	HCPI	HCPI
Criminal Case in CFI	HCCC	HCCC
Magistracy Appeal in CFI	HCMA	HCMA
Small Claims Tribunal Appeal in CFI	SCTA	HCSA
Probate Action in CFI	HCAP	HCAP
Civil Action in District Court	DCCJ	DCCJ
Employee Compensation Claim in DC	DCEC	DCEC
Criminal Case in DC	DCCC	DCCC
Matrimonial Cause in Family Court	FCDJ	FCMC
Application for possession under Part I of Landlord and Tenant (Consolidation) Ordinance	H, K HE or KE	LDPA
Application under Building Management Ordinance	BM	LDBM
Obscene Articles Tribunal Classification (Comics book)	OAT/CB	OACC